Internet Explorer Construction Kit FOR DUMMIES®

Internet Explorer Construction Kit For Dummies®

Cheat Sheet

Browser Editor Command Groups

As you use the Browser Construction Kit's editor, you'll constantly switch from one command group to the next. Here's a short roadmap to the commands and their locations.

Address Bar:

- Go Button
- Favorite 1
- Favorite 2
- Favorite 3
- Favorite 4

Browser:

- Top
- Left
- Width
- Height
- Border
- Start Site

Functions:

- Log File
- Alarm
- Lock
- Approved List
- Spy
- Popular Sites

Menu Bar:

- File
- Edit
- View
- Favorites
- Tools
- Help

Status Bar:

- Icon
- Clock
- Timer
- Date
- Current URL

Toolbar:

- Home
- Back
- Forward
- Stop
- Refresh
- Search
- Favorites

Window:

- Color
- Icon
- Style
- Buttons
- Border
- Skin
- Title

Internet Explorer Construction Kit For Dummies®

Cheat Sheet

Graphical Theme-Element Sizes

You can create your own custom images for use with the Browser Construction Kit. Following is a list of the images you can use, as well as their sizes.

- **Borders:** 784 x 32 pixels
- **Skin:** 784 x 559 pixels
- **Buttons:** 32 x 32 pixels
- **Icons:** 16 x 16 pixels
- **Address bar:** 784 x 24 pixels
- **Toolbar:** 784 x 42 pixels
- **Status bar:** 784 x 24 pixels

Special Browser Functions

The Browser Construction Kit can build browsers that incorporate special features not found in conventional browsers. Following is a quick overview of these features:

- **Log file:** A list of all Web sites visited
- **Alarm:** An audible or popup alarm that signals the end of the time period used with the countdown timer
- **Lock:** Prevents the custom browser from further browsing
- **Approved list:** A list of Web sites to which browsing is limited
- **Spy:** Screen captures taken once a minute
- **Popular sites:** A list of the most visited sites

Item 7491-4.
For more information about Wiley Publishing, call 1-800-762-2974.

Internet Explorer Construction Kit FOR DUMMIES®

by Clayton Walnum

WILEY

Wiley Publishing, Inc.

Internet Explorer Construction Kit For Dummies®

Published by
Wiley Publishing, Inc.
111 River Street
Hoboken, NJ 07030-5774
www.wiley.com

Published by Wiley Publishing, Inc., Indianapolis, Indiana

Published simultaneously in Canada

For general information on our other products and services, please contact our Customer Care Department within the U.S. at 800-762-2974, outside the U.S. at 317-572-3993, or fax 317-572-4002.

For technical support, please visit www.wiley.com/techsupport.

Wiley also publishes its books in a variety of electronic formats. Some content that appears in print may not be available in electronic books.

Library of Congress Control Number: 2004107916

ISBN: 0-7645-7491-4

Manufactured in the United States of America

10 9 8 7 6 5 4 3 2 1

1B/SR/RQ/QU/IN

About the Author

Award-winning author **Clayton Walnum** has been writing about computers since the early '80s. During that time, he's published nearly 60 books and hundreds of articles and reviews. He's also published fiction, humor, and interviews. Clay has a degree in Computer Science and is the former editor of two nationally distributed Atari computer magazines, *ANALOG* and *ST-Log*.

Dedication

To Lynn.

Author's Acknowledgments

I'd like to thank the many people who helped make this book the best it could be, including, but not limited to, Greg Croy for signing me up and being an all-around great guy, Kelly Ewing for her skilled editing and for keeping things rolling and organized, Clint Lahnen for his awesome browser themes, Nancee Reeves for her layout supervision, and Lee Musick for checking the facts.

Publisher's Acknowledgments

We're proud of this book; please send us your comments through our online registration form located at www.dummies.com/register/.

Some of the people who helped bring this book to market include the following:

Acquisitions, Editorial, and Media Development

Project Editor: Kelly Ewing

Acquisitions Editor: Greg Croy

Technical Editor: Lee Musick

Editorial Manager: Carol Sheehan

Permissions Editor: Laura Moss

Media Development Specialist: Travis Silvers

Media Development Manager: Laura VanWinkle

Media Development Supervisor: Richard Graves

Editorial Assistant: Amanda Foxworth

Cartoons: Rich Tennant (www.the5thwave.com)

Composition

Project Coordinator: Nancee Reeves

Layout and Graphics: Andrea Dahl, Lauren Goddard, Denny Hager, Joyce Haughey, Melanee Prendergast, Heather Ryan

Proofreaders: David Faust, John Greenough, TECHBOOKS Production Services

Indexer: TECHBOOKS Production Services

Publishing and Editorial for Technology Dummies

Richard Swadley, Vice President and Executive Group Publisher

Andy Cummings, Vice President and Publisher

Mary Bednarek, Executive Acquisitions Director

Mary C. Corder, Editorial Director

Publishing for Consumer Dummies

Diane Graves Steele, Vice President and Publisher

Joyce Pepple, Acquisitions Director

Composition Services

Gerry Fahey, Vice President of Production Services

Debbie Stailey, Director of Composition Services

Contents at a Glance

Table of Contents

Introduction

I think it's safe to say that practically every personal computer on the planet has some sort of Internet browser installed on it. The Internet has become — in a very real sense — an extension of our own machines, often so perfectly integrated with our computer's operating system that we sometimes can't tell the difference.

With Internet browsers taking such a huge place in the computing world, it seemed to me that it'd be cool to have a little fun with them, to come up with a way to put together a browser in the same way that you might glue together a model. The idea was to provide a set of components and settings and then let the user decide what he wanted to use.

And so was born the Browser Construction Kit, the software that accompanies this book.

About This Book

Using the Browser Construction Kit, you can create dozens (hundreds?) of different browser configurations, from browsers that look much like any other Windows application to some way out designs, with custom graphics, buttons, menus, and so on.

Some of this book is the software manual for the Browser Construction Kit, whereas other parts of the book provide hands-on projects for building many types of Web browsers. Such browser designs include a safe browser for children, a specialized browser for small businesses, and even an April Fool's browser that's sure to drive your April 1 victims batty.

Conventions Used in This Book

Whenever you see ⇨, it means you choose multiple commands from the command menu. For example, if you see File⇨Save, you first choose the File command and then, from the drop-down list that appears, you choose the Save command.

What You're Not to Read

Some elements of this book provide information that you need not bother with. What's the point of having this stuff clogging up the works? Well, you just might want to read this extra information, especially if you're interested in learning something over and above the basic instructions for using the software.

Foolish Assumptions

The Browser Construction Kit requires no programming, so don't get the idea that you need to be a computer scientist to get the thing to work. Designing a new Web browser is easy! It would be nice if you know something about the Internet — from a user's point of view — and have some experience with Microsoft Internet Explorer. But, regardless of your experience level, within a short while, you'll be cranking out browser designs like a pro. What do you need to get going? The following list is a good start:

- A Windows computer
- An Internet connection
- A user's knowledge of Web browsers
- The desire to create interesting browser designs of your own

Although you have no need of programming skills to use the Browser Construction Kit, the complete Visual Basic .NET source code is included on this book's CD. If you know how to program with VB .NET, you can look over the source code to see how the program works. You can even load it into your copy of VB .NET and make whatever modifications you like.

How This Book Is Organized

This book has six parts, but you don't have to read the parts in any special order. If, for example, you want to build a browser or two right away, feel free to jump ahead to Part V, where you'll find step-by-step instructions for building eight unique browser designs. If you want to know more about the Browser Construction Kit's many commands, Part II gives you what you need. Get the idea? To help you on your way, here's a brief roadmap of the book.

Part I: Making Your Own Internet Explorer

If you want to get a quick introduction to the Browser Construction Kit and the things you can do with it, Part I is the place to start. Along the way, you also discover good reasons for creating browsers (as if you need any), as well as discover what parts of a browser are easily customizable.

Part II: Customizing the Look of the Browser

This part goes through the Browser Construction Kit in detail, showing you how to use its many controls and commands, as well as how all the parts fit together to create a unique browser design.

Part III: Creating Browser Graphics

Many components of your custom browser can display images that you create yourself with a paint program. These images include backgrounds for the window, border images, button images, and much more. In this part of the book, you discover how to make the images you need for your browser — and all without having to go to art school for four years!

Part IV: Controlling the Behavior of the Browser

This is the second part of the book that deals in detail with the workings of the Browser Construction Kit. Here, you find out about alarms, locks, passwords, timers, automatic screen captures, log files, and more.

Part V: Designing Customized Web Browser Projects

The Browser Construction Kit is all about creating browsers, of course, and this part is where you put together browser designs that I've created for you, to demonstrate the many ways you can use the Browser Construction Kit. In this part, step-by-step procedures lead you through the construction of eight different browsers.

Part VI: The Part of Tens

For people who want to really expand their custom-browser-creation horizons, this part of the book offers ten themed browser projects, as well as ten tools and resources for learning more about programming Internet Explorer — if you choose to take it that far.

Icons Used in This Book

Throughout this book, little pictures, known as *icons,* appear in the margin. These icons give you a quick visual aid to the following categories:

Whenever you see this icon, you'll find information on how to do something more efficiently.

This icon marks information that you need to know in order to get the most out of the software.

This icon provides technical background information that you may or may not find interesting. You don't need to read the material if you don't want to.

Be careful! When you see this icon, pay special attention because it notes places where you could run into trouble.

This book is accompanied by a CD, and whenever you see this icon, you're getting a heads up that you should have your CD ready to use.

Where to Go from Here

You can use this book in a couple of ways. Like any book, you can start at the beginning and read your way to the end. That's probably the best way to learn about the Browser Construction Kit software and the things you can do with the custom browsers you build. You can, however, skip around in the book, if you like, just reading the sections that provide the information you need at any given moment. Because of this nonlinear approach, after you know how to use the software, this book makes a great reference.

The Browser Construction Kit represents a whole lot of hours of programming, so I expect you to get the most out of it. But more than anything, I expect you to have fun!

Part I

Making Your Own Internet Explorer

"I'm not saying I believe in anything. All I know is since it's been there our browser is running 50% faster."

In this part . . .

Why on earth would you want to build your own version of Internet Explorer? I can think of a number of reasons, and in this part of the book, I share those reasons with you. You also find out a little about the parts of a browser you can customize. In addition, you get your first look at the Browser Construction Kit, exploring the features you can use, the custom graphics you can incorporate, and the agreement you must make with Microsoft (not as scary as it sounds).

Chapter 1

Exploring the Benefits of Browser Customization

In This Chapter

- Simplifying a browser application
- Targeting a special purpose or user
- Installing the Browser Construction Kit

You've probably used your favorite Web browser for a long time. Your browser is a trusted friend that accompanies you on your many treks through the complex world of the World Wide Web. You can't help but feel warm and fuzzy when you load your browser. (Geez, maybe we all should get out more.) After all, it provides the gateway to many cool adventures, from looking up the latest gossip on your favorite celebrity to more mundane tasks like research. Why on earth change something that works so well?

I can come up with plenty of reasons! Of course, not all of these reasons apply to you. Reasons for creating a custom Web browser are as varied as the people using them. You may just want to make the browser easier to use, or you may need a browser customized for a special purpose. Whatever your reasons, this book and its accompanying software are just the ticket. This chapter explains why you may want to build a customized Web browser.

Application Simplification

I bet that you have no clue what most of your Web browser's buttons and commands do. If you're like most people, you use a few buttons and commands all the time, and the rest sit there, waiting for you to figure them out — a task you and I both know you never get to. So why bother with that extra clutter on the screen, when you're not using it anyway?

Application simplification is the process of stripping out parts of a program that you don't need and may never use. Getting rid of that overhead makes your browser easier to use for a number of reasons:

- Fewer commands makes a browser less intimidating.
- Fewer commands also means that you work faster because you don't have dozens of commands to search through.
- Fewer controls leaves more screen room for the main display area.
- Fewer controls and commands may help the browser load faster.

Application simplification is automatic with the Browser Construction Kit. You start with only an empty window, as shown in Figure 1-1, and then add only the program elements you want. In this way, nothing extra clutters the browser's window or menus.

You may think that the browser customization process is difficult, but the first time you create your own browser, you'll be amazed at how easy the Browser Construction Kit is to use.

Figure 1-1: The stripped-down browser window as it appears in the Browser Construction Kit's editor.

Special-Purpose Browsers

Most Web browsers target the general user. Because so many different types of people use browsers, the browser makers try to please everyone. This attempt yields browsers overloaded with features, most of which the average user never needs. Moreover, such browsers lack special features that a few people may want. A *special-purpose browser* — the kind you can create with the Browser Construction Kit — boasts features not found in a conventional browser. A special-purpose browser, for example, can include features that prevent children from accessing unsuitable Web sites.

For more information on special browser features, refer to Part IV. In that part, you can read about timers, site-approval lists, locks, and other cool features.

Want an example? What if you want a kids' browser that disables surfing to unsavory Web sites? Or how about a browser that accesses a set of favorite sites with a button click (see Figure 1-2)? Maybe you have a small store, and you want a browser that accesses your catalog, but cannot go elsewhere on the Web. (Hey, you don't want your customers checking out the competition's Web site, do you?) Reasons for creating special-purpose Web browsers are more numerous than dust bunnies under my bed — and that's a lot of reasons!

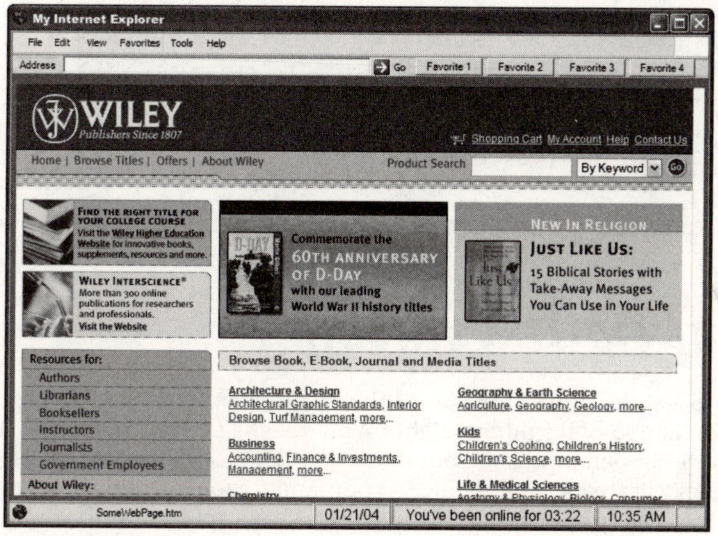

Figure 1-2: A Web browser with buttons that enable you quickly to select a favorite Web site.

Specific-Audience Browsers

A fine line divides special-purpose browsers from those targeting a specific audience. For example, a browser designed for children has both a special purpose and a specific audience, right? Yep. In fact, special-purpose and specific-audience browsers often have much in common. The difference is that, when I talk about special-purpose browsers, I'm referring to browser functionality. On the other hand, when I talk about *specific-audience browsers,* I'm referring to the way a browser looks. Specifically, I mean the types of graphics you use for buttons and other areas of the browser's window.

That special-audience browser for your hardware store looks better if it's designed with images related to hardware. As another example, suppose that you're crazy about gardening. (Hey, weirder things have happened.) Wouldn't it be cool to have a Web browser covered with garden-type images (see Figure 1-3)? I'd rather have bikini models, of course, but that's just me.

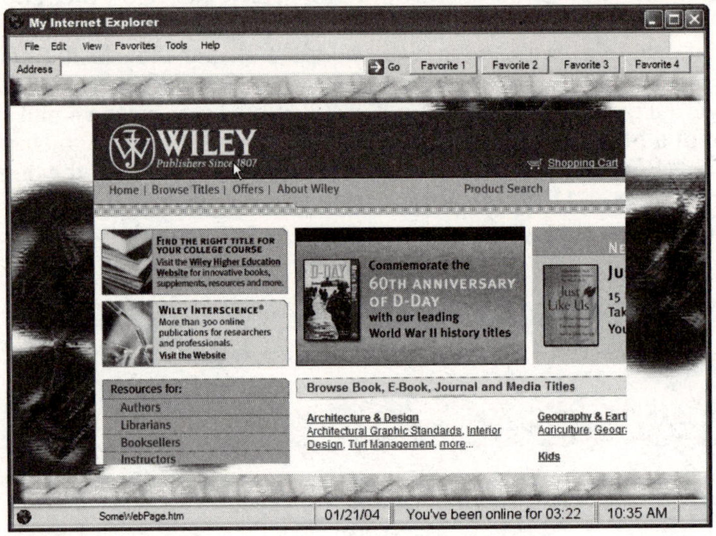

Figure 1-3: A Web browser for the garden enthusiast.

The Joy of Do-It-Yourself

Don't forget the most important thing about customizing a Web browser: It's fun! You like to build things, right? Who doesn't? (Okay, my crazy Uncle Satch would rather paint crickets, but that's another story.) Unlike that jigsaw puzzle of a black cat that's been sitting in your family room for the past three weeks, a custom Web browser is actually useful. That puzzle . . . well, you're just going to break it up and throw it back into the box.

To make a Web browser project even more stimulating and exciting, load up your favorite paint program (or use the one on this book's CD) and create custom images for your browser projects. Such images include borders, backgrounds, status bars, and even buttons, as shown in Figure 1-4. If your browser project was any more fun, it would be illegal!

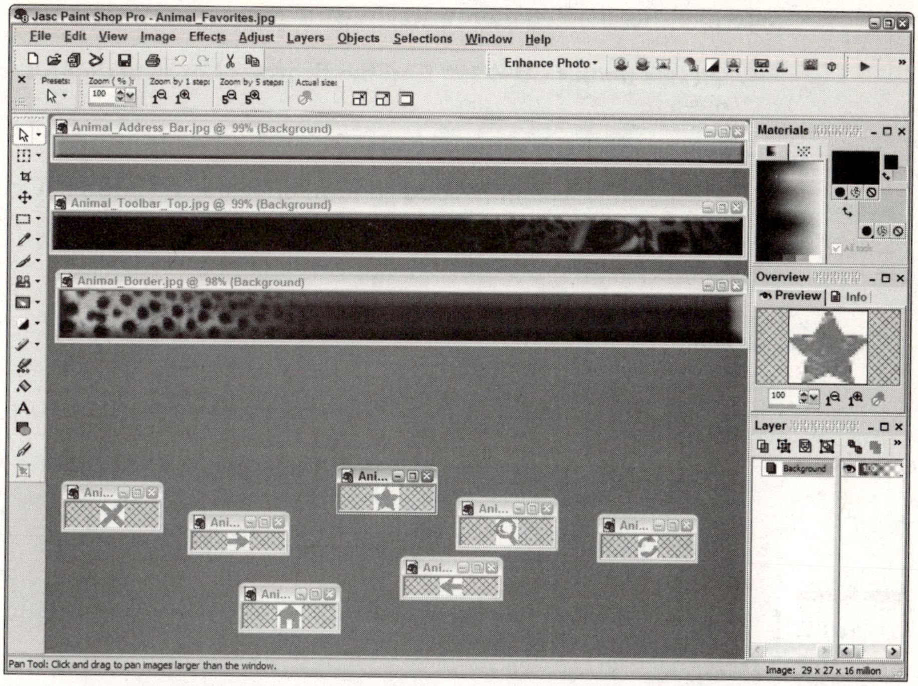

Figure 1-4: Designing button graphics with Paint Shop Pro.

Don't go hog wild creating browser graphics just yet. You need to understand the types of images the Browser Construction Kit expects. Each type of image, for example, must be the correct size. Failure to follow the rules can lead to some very weird looking browsers! Check out Part III for more information.

Browser Construction Kit Installation

Before you can design your own Web browsers, you need to install the Browser Construction Kit, located on this book's CD-ROM. The Browser Construction Kit is a software package comprising a browser editor and a browser compiler. You design your browser using the WYSIWYG (what you see is what you get) editor and then run the browser with the browser compiler. You don't need to be a programmer to use the Browser Construction Kit, but if you're interested in that kind of thing, I wrote the software using Visual Basic .NET. All the software's source code is also on the CD.

Here's how to install the Browser Construction Kit:

1. **On this book's CD-ROM, find the Browser Construction Kit folder and open it.**
2. **Double-click the setup.exe file.**

   The installer's Setup Wizard window appears, as shown in Figure 1-5.

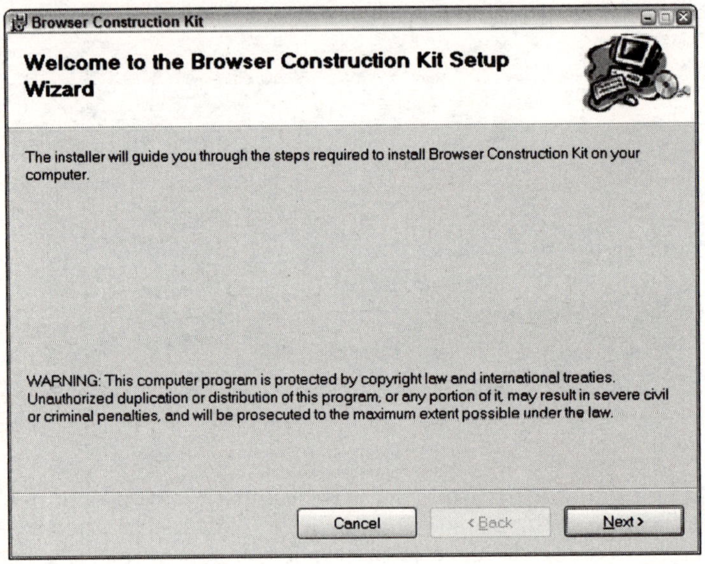

Figure 1-5: The installer's Setup Wizard window.

3. **Click the Next button to continue with the installation.**

   The Select Installation Folder window appears (see Figure 1-6).
4. **Select the folder into which you want the Browser Construction Kit installed.**

   Normally, you just leave the default folder selected.
5. **Select either the Everyone or Just Me button, depending on whether you want to install the program for every user on your system or just for you.**
6. **Click Next.**

   The Confirm Installation window appears, as shown in Figure 1-7.
7. **Click Next to start the installation.**

   The installer's window shows the installation's progress as it goes, as shown in Figure 1-8.

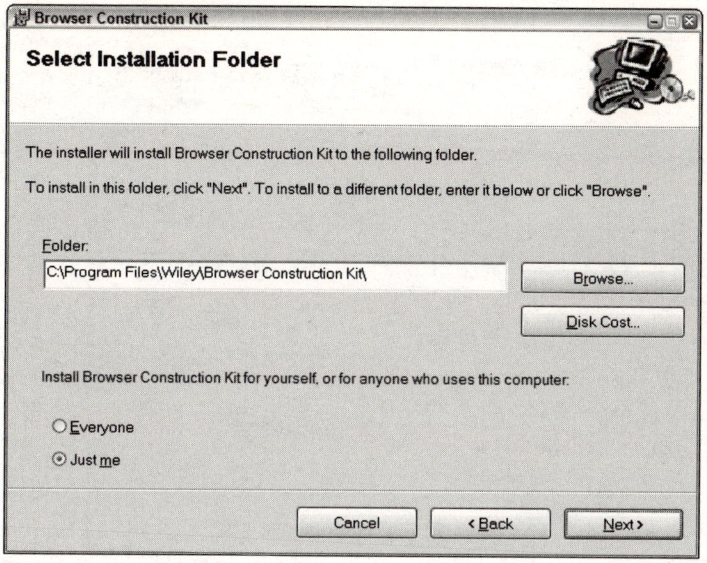

Figure 1-6: The Select Installation Folder window.

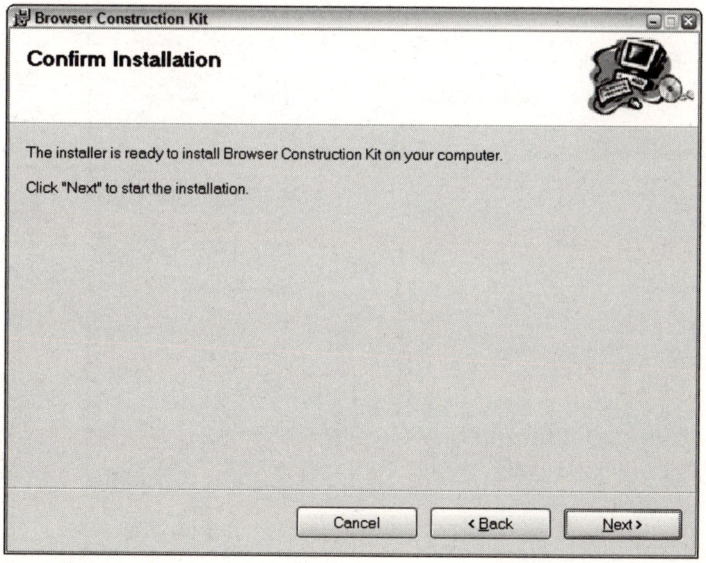

Figure 1-7: The Confirm Installation dialog box.

When the installation finishes, the Installation Compete window appears, as shown in Figure 1-9.

8. Click Close to exit.

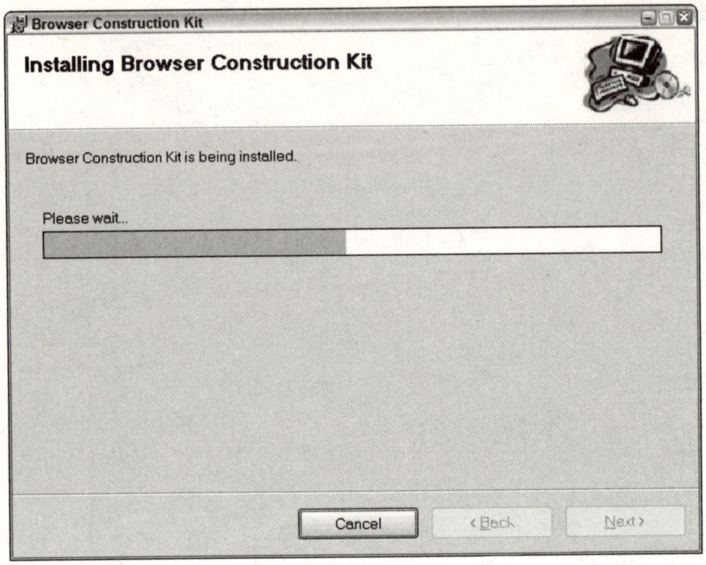

Figure 1-8: The installation in progress.

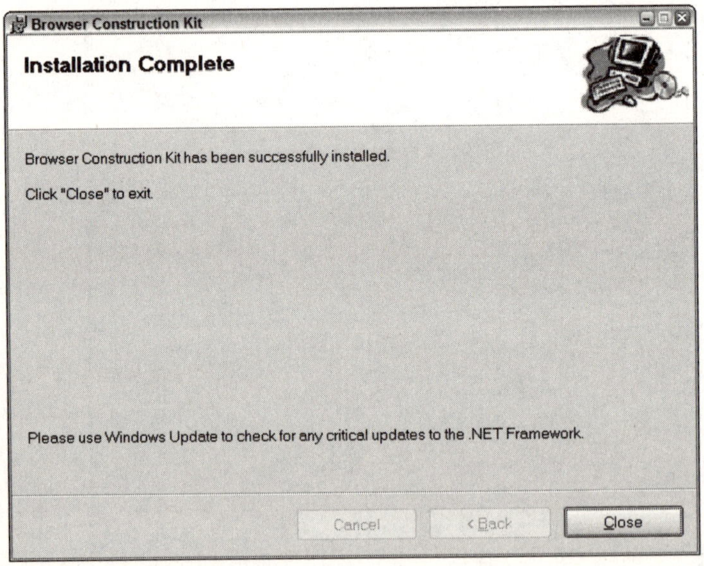

Figure 1-9: The Installation Complete window.

TIP

After installation, an icon for the Browser Construction Kit appears on your desktop. The application also appears on your Start menu. You run the program by double-clicking the icon on your desktop or by single-clicking the application on your Start menu.

Browser Construction Kit Removal

I just know that you'll love the Browser Construction Kit so much that you'll never want to remove it from your system. But, just in case, the application features a handy removal method that you can access from your Control Panel. Here's how:

1. **Go to your Start menu and choose Control Panel from the pop-up menu that appears, as shown in Figure 1-10.**

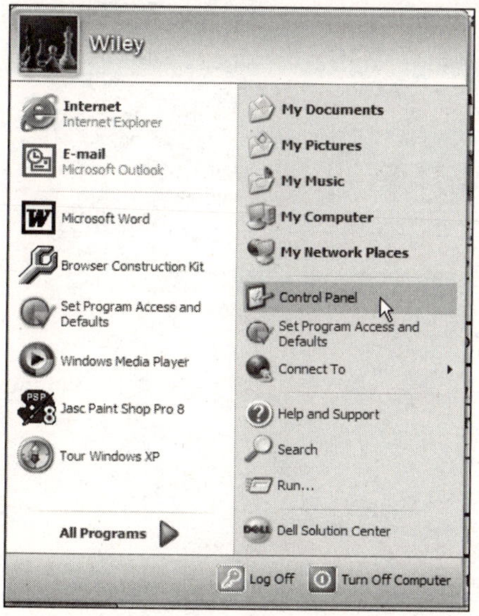

Figure 1-10: Opening the Control Panel.

2. **In the Control Panel, click Add Or Remove Programs, as shown in Figure 1-11.**
3. **In the Currently Installed Programs list, click the Browser Construction Kit.**

   The Change and Remove buttons appear.
4. **Click the Remove button (see Figure 1-12) and answer Yes when asked whether you're sure that you want to remove the program.**

   Windows removes the Browser Construction Kit from your system.

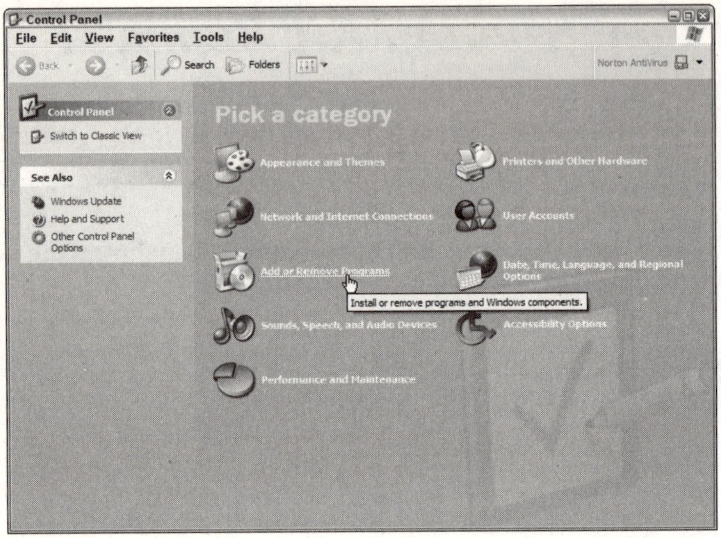

Figure 1-11: Opening the Add or Remove Programs window.

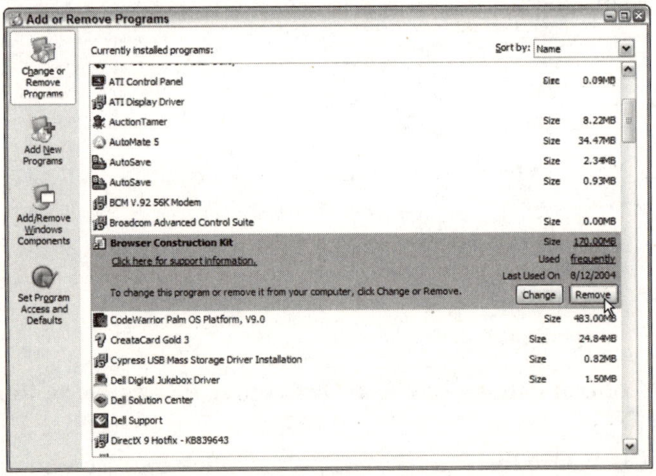

Figure 1-12: Choosing to remove the application.

After Windows has removed the application from your computer, the program files, as well as the program's entries on your Start menu and your desktop will be gone. However, any files you created with the Browser Construction Kit — that is, files that didn't exist at the time of the installation — will still be on your computer. You can remove such files manually.

Chapter 2

Figuring Out What's Customizable

In This Chapter

- Understanding the Windows user interface
- Exploring window styles
- Customizing toolbars, status bars, and menu bars

The full Internet Explorer and the browser you create with the Browser Construction Kit are very different beasts. Although these beasts share the same heart (lub-dub, lub-dub), their external features can be very different indeed. This is because, like everything else in the universe, building your own Web browser is a give-and-take situation. Specifically, your custom browser cannot have all the features of the full Internet Explorer. But what do you give up, and what do you gain? I'm glad you asked, because the answer is what this chapter is about.

The Kit Versus the Full Internet Explorer

Writing an application the size and complexity of Internet Explorer requires dozens of programmers and years of development time — not to mention the gallons of caffeine-laden pop and the bushels of nacho chips consumed. Internet Explorer is up to Version 6, and Microsoft's programmers are still working on improving it. If you think that one guy (me) sitting behind a laptop computer can compete with that kind of programming muscle . . . well, I've got some swampland in Florida you may be interested in.

Luckily, Microsoft makes the heart of Internet Explorer available to programmers so that they can quickly add Internet features to their own applications. The Internet Explorer component comes in the form of a control that the programmer adds to his program. Once the control is in place, the application sends commands to the control to make it do cool stuff, like browse to a Web site, move back through the sites in the history list, or entertain young children with reruns of Sesame Street. Okay, I'm lying about that last one.

Anyway, the point is that, when I put together the Browser Construction Kit, I didn't have to worry about the gory details of rendering HTML files into Web pages or even how to browse from one Web site to another. The Internet Explorer control takes care of everything. I did, however, have to create a user interface for the control that enables the user (that's you) to send commands to the Internet Explorer control. The cool part is that you decide which user interface elements you want to use.

HTML is the language used to create Web pages. If you've ever seen HTML, you have to admit that it's downright amazing that all that nonsense could ever create something as attractive as a Web page. For example, look at Figure 2-1. There you see a Web browser displaying the home page of my Web site. Figure 2-2, on the other hand, shows what the Web page's HTML looks like. Yikes!

The browser that the Browser Construction Kit creates lacks some features of the full Internet Explorer. (You never use those features, anyway.) That guy (me again) sitting behind the laptop computer can only do so much. That guy (yep, me again) did, however, include a lot of extra features that the regular Internet Explorer doesn't have. The point isn't to reproduce Internet Explorer, but instead to create something new and different. So, although you give up a few features, you get cool new ones like alarms, timers, kid-safety functions, and so on.

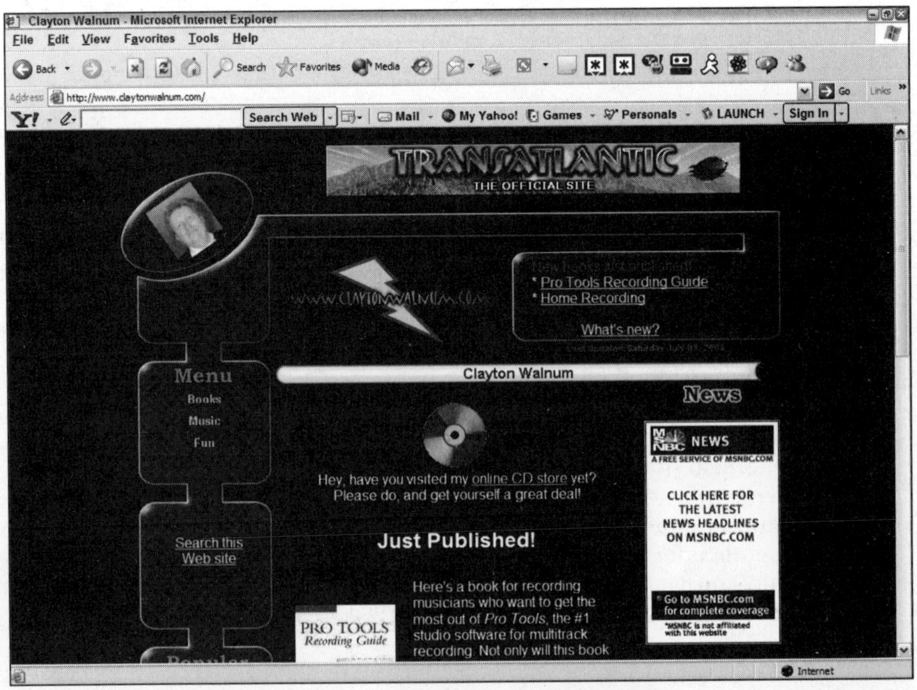

Figure 2-1: A browser showing a Web site.

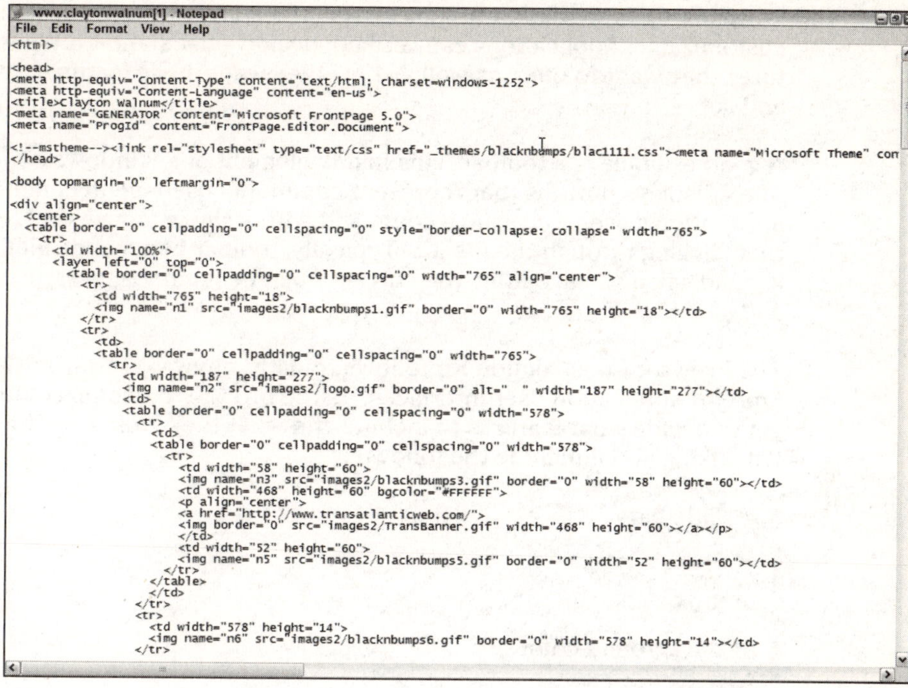


```
<html>

<head>
<meta http-equiv="Content-Type" content="text/html; charset=windows-1252">
<meta http-equiv="Content-Language" content="en-us">
<title>Clayton Walnum</title>
<meta name="GENERATOR" content="Microsoft FrontPage 5.0">
<meta name="ProgId" content="FrontPage.Editor.Document">

<!--mstheme--><link rel="stylesheet" type="text/css" href="_themes/blacknbumps/blac1111.css"><meta name="Microsoft Theme" con
</head>

<body topmargin="0" leftmargin="0">

<div align="center">
  <center>
  <table border="0" cellpadding="0" cellspacing="0" style="border-collapse: collapse" width="765">
    <tr>
      <td width="100%">
      <layer left="0" top="0">
        <table border="0" cellpadding="0" cellspacing="0" width="765" align="center">
          <tr>
            <td width="765" height="18">
            <img name="n1" src="images2/blacknbumps1.gif" border="0" width="765" height="18"></td>
          </tr>
          <tr>
            <td>
            <table border="0" cellpadding="0" cellspacing="0" width="765">
              <tr>
                <td width="187" height="277">
                <img name="n2" src="images2/logo.gif" border="0" alt="  " width="187" height="277"></td>
                <td>
                <table border="0" cellpadding="0" cellspacing="0" width="578">
                  <tr>
                    <td>
                    <table border="0" cellpadding="0" cellspacing="0" width="578">
                      <tr>
                        <td width="58" height="60">
                        <img name="n3" src="images2/blacknbumps3.gif" border="0" width="58" height="60"></td>
                        <td width="468" height="60" bgcolor="#FFFFFF">
                        <p align="center">
                        <a href="http://www.transatlanticweb.com/">
                        <img border="0" src="images2/TransBanner.gif" width="468" height="60"></a></p>
                        </td>
                        <td width="52" height="60">
                        <img name="n5" src="images2/blacknbumps5.gif" border="0" width="52" height="60"></td>
                      </tr>
                    </table>
                    </td>
                  </tr>
                  <tr>
                    <td width="578" height="14">
                    <img name="n6" src="images2/blacknbumps6.gif" border="0" width="578" height="14"></td>
                  </tr>
```

Figure 2-2: The HTML code that creates the Web site in Figure 2-1.

To get an overview of the Browser Construction Kit's many features, refer to Chapter 3.

TIP

When you're browsing the Internet, you may be overcome by the urge to look at some HTML (yeah, right). Here's how: Go to Internet Explorer's View menu and choose the Source command. *Presto!* Notepad runs and loads up the page's HTML. If you're ever interested in learning HTML, take a peek at this source code to see what other HTML folks are doing on their Web pages.

Window Elements

Almost every Windows application — Internet Explorer included — shares a set of features. This sharing isn't one program stealing good ideas from another. Nope, the features I'm talking about are written up by Microsoft in a document for programmers. This document details the way Windows applications' user interfaces should be programmed.

For example, most Windows applications sport a File menu, right? If you use Windows applications at all, you know that the File menu holds commands like New, Open, Save, Save As, Print, and Exit. Thanks to this menu consistency, you don't learn a new set of basic commands for every new Windows application.

Consistency, however, doesn't mean that the standard window elements aren't customizable. Applications can, and do, decide what standard Windows features they want to offer, as well as how they want those features to look and act.

A good example is a toolbar. This handy element of a Windows application often displays buttons that represent commonly used menu commands. The application's user can issue a command with a single mouse click, rather than digging through the menus. Typically, toolbar commands include loading and saving files, editing the current document, choosing style commands, and so on.

The Browser Construction Kit follows (mostly, anyway) the Windows guidelines for application user interfaces. As the browser customizer, however, you get to decide what features to include and what they look like. The features I'm talking about include the following:

- Title bar
- Icon
- Style
- Background color
- Buttons
- Client area

The title bar and icon

In a Windows application, the title bar is the horizontal area at the top of the window. The title bar usually displays, among other things, the following items:

- Application icon
- Application name
- Window control buttons

Figure 2-3 points out these features of a window. With the Browser Construction Kit, you can customize these window features as you like. You can choose an icon to display in the title bar. You can also name the application, as well as specify the control buttons (minimize and maximize) that appear in the title bar.

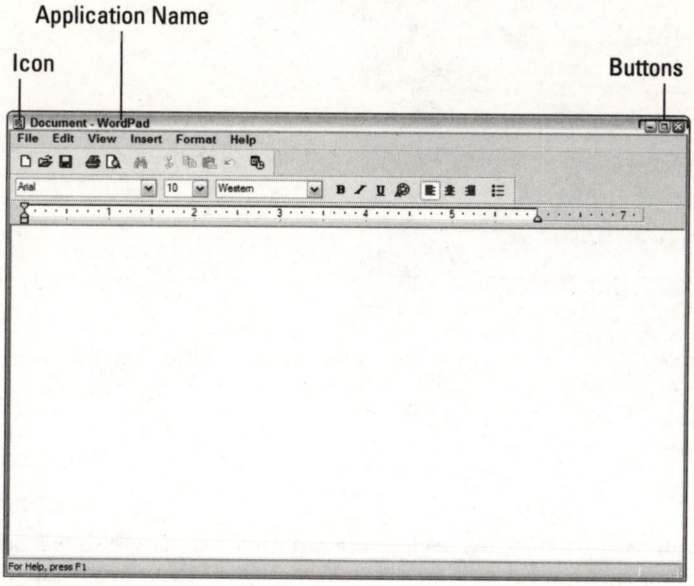

Figure 2-3: Main elements of a window's title bar.

The window style and color

Not every window looks alike. You may have noticed, for example, that an application's main window looks very different from a dialog box (which is also a type of window). You may even have seen windows that are nothing more than rectangles on the screen (Figure 2-4). In fact, in its simplest form, that's exactly what a window is: a rectangle in which an application draws its display.

A window's style determines how the window looks and acts. Microsoft built these window styles into Windows, but the Browser Construction Kit lets you choose the style for your browser. Here are the styles supported by the my kit:

- **Normal:** A standard window.
- **Normal Unsizable:** A standard window that cannot be resized.
- **Toolbox:** A window with a small title bar and only a close button (no minimize or maximize buttons).
- **Toolbox Unsizable:** Same as a toolbox window, except the user cannot resize the window.
- **No Controls:** A simple rectangular window with no controls.

To find out more about these window styles, refer to Chapter 4.

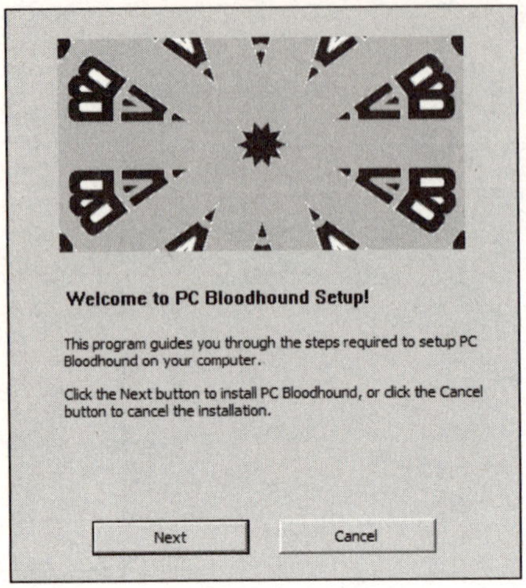

Figure 2-4: A simple rectangular window.

Besides choosing a window style, you can also set the window's *background color,* which is the color that fills the main part of the window, usually called the client area. The *client area* is where an application displays its data. In the case of a Web browser, the client area displays the current Web page.

The buttons and client area

Most windows have three buttons, one for closing the window and two for controlling the size of the window. These buttons live in the upper-right corner of the window. Not every window has the same buttons, however. In fact, some windows have no buttons at all. Here's what the three buttons do:

- **Minimize button:** When clicked, this button reduces the window to an icon on the taskbar.
- **Maximize/Restore button:** The first time you click this button, it increases the window to the full size of the screen. The button then changes to a Restore button, which, when clicked, returns the window to its original size.
- **Close button:** This button — the one with the X — closes the window. Clicking this button is the same as choosing the File menu's Exit command.

The Browser Construction Kit enables you to decide which of these buttons to include in your browser's window. These choices, though, depend on the window style you choose. A toolbox-style window, for example, can never have Minimize and Maximize buttons.

The Browser Construction Kit enables you to include one, both, or neither of the Minimize and Maximize buttons. In this way, you can control the way the user manipulates your custom browser window.

The Browser Construction Kit places the browser pane in the window's client area. The client area provides space for two extra items as well: graphical borders and backgrounds. You can use your favorite paint program to create these borders and backgrounds and then add them to your custom browser. The thematic possibilities are endless. Please refer to Part III for more information on creating browser graphics.

The Browser Pane

The *browser pane* is the graphical representation of the Internet Explorer control. This component of the browser does most of the work of browsing the Internet. Normally, this pane consumes the entire client area of the window, but the Browser Construction Kit lets you place the browser pane anywhere you want in the client area. You can also set it to any size you want. Figure 2-5 shows the browser editor with a small browser pane in the right side of the window's client area.

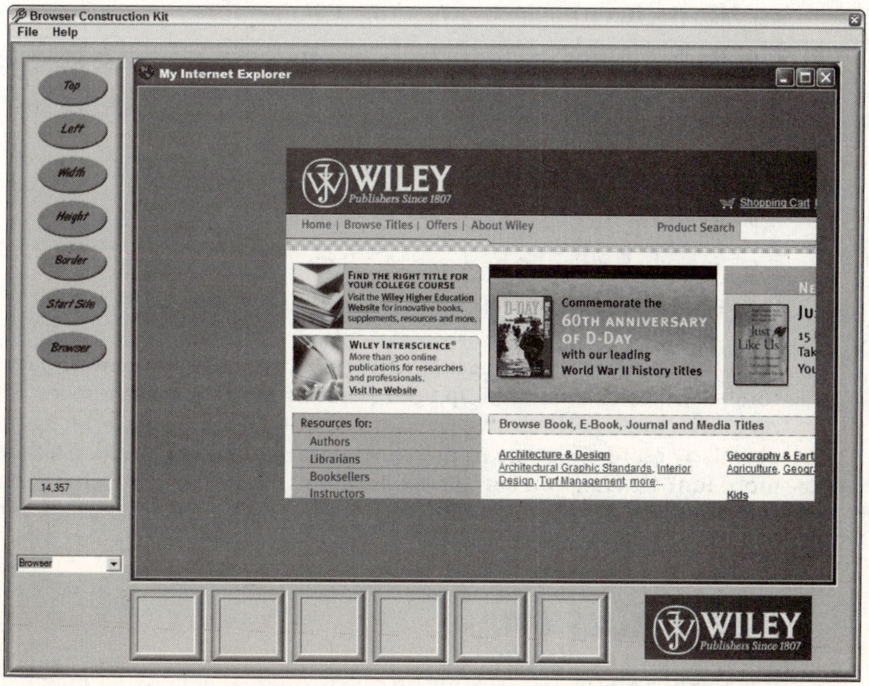

Figure 2-5: You can place the browser pane anywhere in the window's client area.

REMEMBER

When you're online with your custom browser, the browser pane displays the current Web page. This fact means that, although you can choose any size and position you want for the browser pane, practical considerations restrict your choices.

Toolbars, Status Bars, and Menus

Most full-featured Windows applications have a toolbar, a status bar, and a menu bar. Your custom browser is no different. Well, maybe it is, depending upon how you design it. Although you can add a toolbar, status bar, and menu bar to your browser, you don't have to. Congress hasn't passed that law yet, although I understand that they're close to requiring all Web browsers to feature a large presidential-campaign donation button.

The toolbar

If you add a toolbar to your browser, you can also add one or more standard browser buttons. You use these buttons all the time. Really, you do. Here's a list of those buttons:

- **Home:** Returns the browser to the home page.
- **Back:** Returns the browser to the previously viewed page.
- **Forward:** Returns the browser to the page viewed before clicking the Back button.
- **Stop:** Stops loading the current page.
- **Refresh:** Reloads the previous page.
- **Search:** Sends the browser to a Web search engine.
- **Favorites:** Displays links to favorite Web sites.

With the Browser Construction Kit, you can assign your own images to the toolbar buttons. Just load up your paint program, create images of the correct size, and use the browser editor to add the images to the buttons. You can also create an image to use for the toolbar background. Could this be more fun? I mean, you can have a toolbar that looks like a sheet of metal or one the color of spicy mustard, although I don't recommend the latter.

The status bar

If you add a status bar to your browser, you can specify an image for its background. Moreover, you can choose from among four special displays, three of which aren't available in the regular Internet Explorer. These displays are as follows:

- **Icon:** A small image that appears at the far left of the status bar.
- **Clock:** Displays the current time.
- **Timer:** Displays the amount of time online or a countdown timer.
- **Date:** Displays the current date.

The menu bar

Almost every Windows application has a menu bar, which is where the application's commands hang out. Your custom browser can have a menu bar, too. Or not. The choice is yours. If you choose to have a menu bar, you then decide which menus to include, although the content of the menus depends on the features you include in your browser. In any case, the Browser Construction Kit supplies the appropriate command entries for the menus you choose to include. These menus are supported by the Browser Construction Kit:

- **File**
- **Edit**
- **View**
- **Favorites**
- **Tools**
- **Help**

Notes for Visual Basic Programmers

ON THE CD

If you're not a programmer, skip this section. If you are a programmer, you may be interested to know that the Browser Construction Kit is programmed using Visual Basic .NET. You may be even more interested to know that the complete source code is on this book's CD-ROM. This fact means, of course, that not only can you explore the program to see how it works, but you can also add your own features.

WARNING!

Although you're free to modify the Browser Construction Kit for your own use, you cannot distribute the program, which is copyrighted by Wiley, the publisher of this book. The Browser Construction Kit is licensed only to the owner of this book.

Chapter 3

Meeting the Browser Construction Kit

In This Chapter

- Understanding Internet Explorer licensing
- Looking over the browser editor
- Exploring browser features
- Discovering custom browser functions

In Chapters 1 and 2, you find out why you'd want to design a custom Web browser, as well as discover the types of browser elements you can fiddle with. In this chapter, you examine the Browser Construction Kit and get a handle on the power it gives you to design the perfect Internet browser — perfect, that is, with respect to the use you have in mind. You don't actually design a Web browser in this chapter (dang it!), but you can see the many commands that you can use with the Browser Construction Kit.

Microsoft Licensing

Although Microsoft gives away Internet Explorer with every copy of Windows, and even though programmers can take advantage of Internet Explorer's power in their own applications, Microsoft still retains full rights to the software.

As an Internet user, you don't need to know anything special about Microsoft's licensing requirements, but if you plan to create Web browsers for distribution, you need to have a license from Microsoft. Don't start moaning about paying Mr. Gates even more cash. Believe it or not, the license you need is, just like the browser itself, free. Microsoft just wants to know who's using its software. The company also wants assurances that you will use its software according to the agreement that accompanies your license.

How do you get your license? No, you don't have to travel to Redmond, Washington, and meet with Bill. All you need to do is load up your Web browser and go to Microsoft online at `www.microsoft.com/windows/ieak/license/existing/default.asp`. When the Web page appears, click the Licensing And Registration link in the text and complete the form that appears.

Of course, if you're just designing browsers for your own use or to share with family members, you don't need a license. All you need is the Web Browser Construction Kit and the information in this book.

Don't distribute a custom Web browser based on Internet Explorer (which is the type of browser the Browser Construction Kit creates) without getting the proper license from Microsoft. Doing so is a violation of Microsoft's copyrights. Because the Browser Construction Kit is included on this book's CD-ROM, this publisher had to acquire the license, too.

The Browser Editor

You can use the Browser Construction Kit to design a custom browser in two ways:

- By using the Kit's included editor (the easy way)
- By writing browser script files by hand (the hard way)

Most of the time, you're going to want to use the editor because it's a whole lot easier than memorizing the commands that can be in a browser's script file. If you like monkeying around with technical things, though, you can dig into the script that the editor creates for you or even build your own from scratch. For most of this book, I assume that you're always going to use the editor. (I talk about scripts in Chapter 20.)

Starting the editor

To start the editor, just double-click the Browser Construction Kit icon on your desktop. (If you haven't installed the Browser Construction Kit, see Chapter 1.) You can also find the icon on your Start menu (where it requires only a single click). In Windows XP, for example, just open the Start menu and go to All Programs/Browser Construction Kit (or whatever folder you chose when you installed the software from the CD).

When you start the Browser Construction Kit, the editor appears (see Figure 3-1).

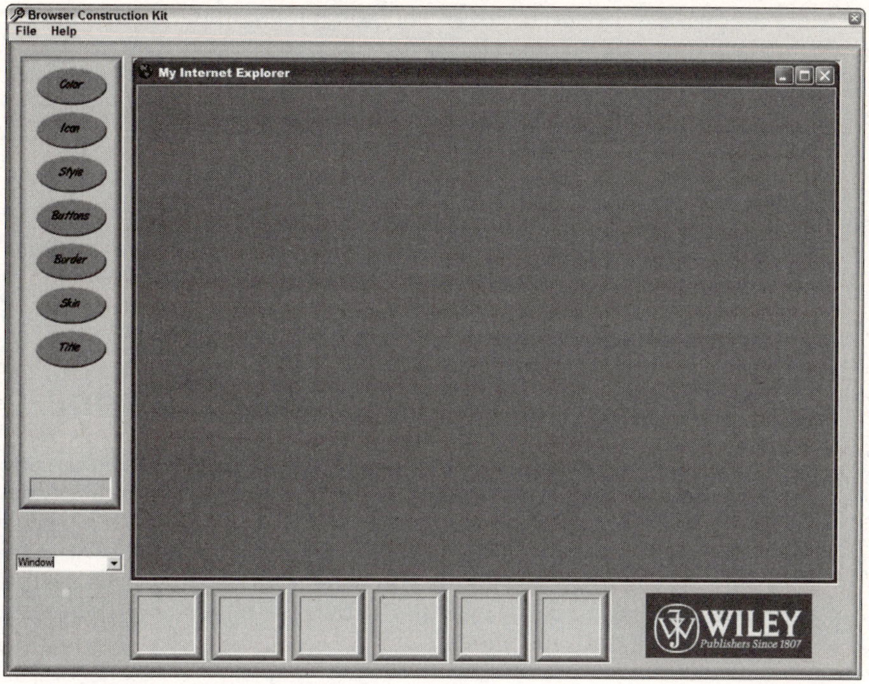

Figure 3-1: The browser editor appears on your screen when you start the Browser Construction Kit.

Introducing the toolbox

Down the left side of the editor's window is the *toolbox,* which contains the components of a Web browser and commands that you need to assemble your custom browser. The editor arranges these components and commands into the following seven categories:

- **Address bar:** Commands and components that build your browser's address bar.
- **Browser:** Commands and components of a Web browser that affect the pane in which you browse the Internet.
- **Functions:** Custom functions — such as the timer, alarm, and site-approval list — that you can add to your browser.
- **Menu bar:** Commands and components that determine the types of menus you want in your menu bar.
- **Status bar:** Commands and components that build your browser's status bar.

- **Toolbar:** Commands and components that build your browser's toolbar.
- **Window:** Commands and components that affect the browser's main window.

Only one set of commands and components can appear in the toolbox at one time. You choose the set you want from the drop-down list at the bottom of the toolbox. For example, in Figure 3-1, the toolbox contains the commands for the main window, whereas in Figure 3-2, the toolbox is set to show commands for the custom browser functions. Notice how, in each case, the drop-down list below the toolbox shows the current command category.

Exploring the browser display pane

As you build your custom Web browser, the changes you make appear in the *browser display pane,* which is the large area to the right of the toolbox. Before you start building your browser, this pane displays a basic window. As you add and customize browser components, they appear in the window. This way, you can see, even as you work, exactly what your custom browser looks like. Figure 3-3, for example, shows the editor after the user has made the following customizations:

- Changed the browser window's style to an unsizable toolbox
- Changed the browser title to My Browser
- Added a menu bar
- Added border graphics
- Added and positioned a browser pane

Exploring the custom function pane

The final part of the editor is the *custom function pane,* which is where the browser functions you add from the Functions category appear. These special functions include the following:

- A log file
- An alarm
- A locking mechanism
- A site-approval list
- A screen-capture "spy"
- Popular sites buttons

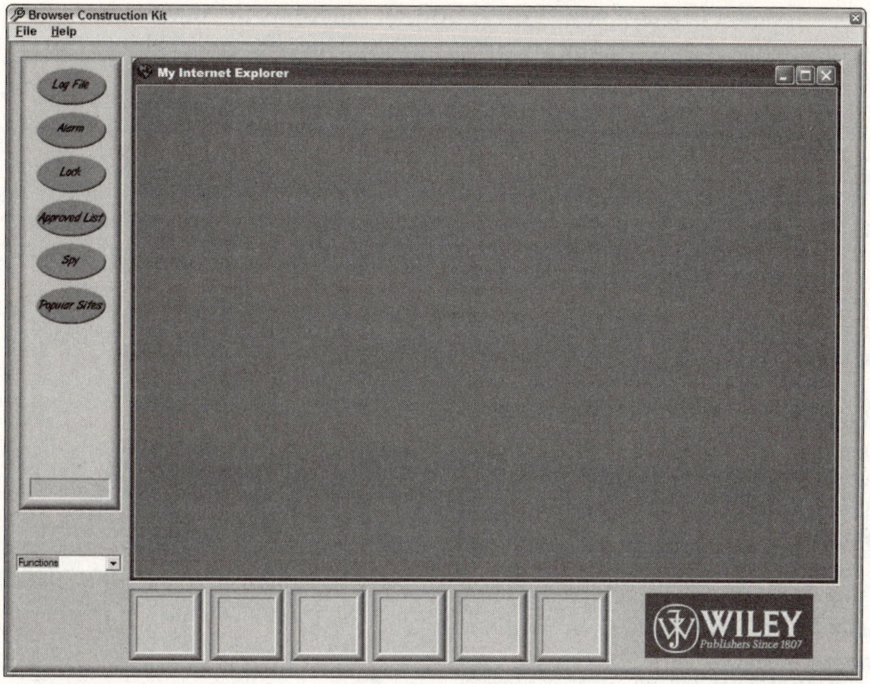

Figure 3-2: The browser editor displays the custom browser functions in the toolbox.

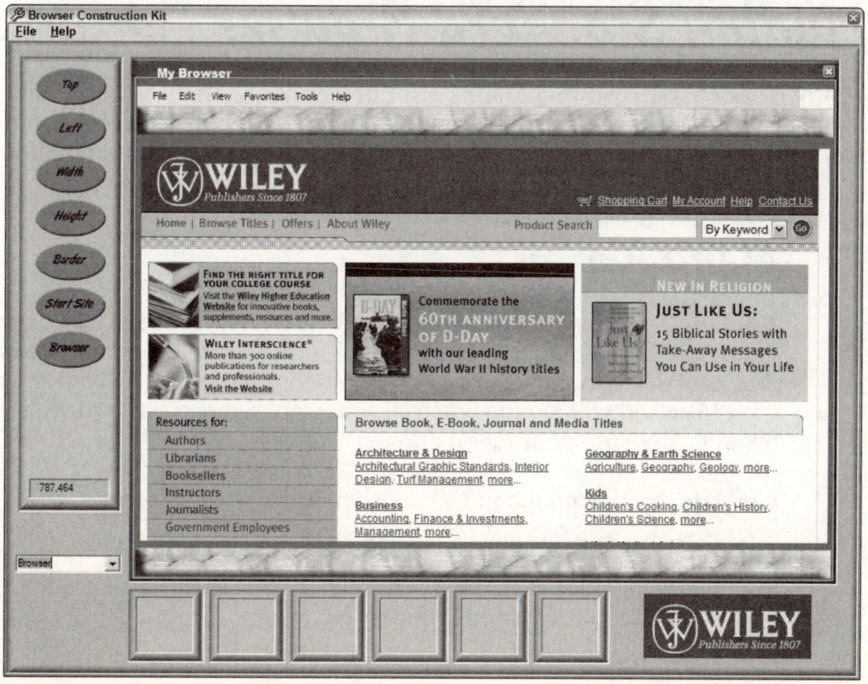

Figure 3-3: As you build your browser, the browser display panel displays the results.

When you add one of these special functions to your browser, the function's icon appears in the custom function pane. Figure 3-4 shows the editor after the user has added all the custom functions.

The custom functions whose icons appear in the custom function pane don't, for the most part, affect the way your browser window looks. For example, when you add a menu bar to your browser, you can see it at the top of the window. However, the alarm function doesn't add anything to the browser window, so it appears in the custom function pane instead, just so you know you've selected it.

Figure 3-4: The custom function pane shows the functions you've added to your browser.

Including Standard Browser Features

Your custom browser shares a set of features with the standard Internet Explorer. These features (assuming that you decide to add them to your browser) include a menu bar, a toolbar, a status bar, and an address bar.

Menu bar

Your custom browser's *menu bar* can contain many of the same commands found in the full-featured Internet Explorer, as well as access to commands that control custom features, such as locks, alarms, and log files. As you build your browser, you decide whether you want a menu bar and what menus will be on it. Here are your menu choices:

- **File:** Holds commands such as Open, Close, and Save.
- **Edit:** Contains commands such as Cut, Copy, and Paste.
- **View:** Includes commands to hide or view various browser components, such as the toolbar and status bar.
- **Favorites:** Holds commands to access favorite Web sites.

- **Tools:** Lists commands to access custom tools and functions that you may have added to your browser.
- **Help:** Contains commands to access the Windows Help system, as well as to view the browser's About dialog box.

Toolbar

The *toolbar* holds the buttons you need to navigate the Web. Anyone familiar with Web browsers has already used these buttons a zillion times. If the following buttons don't ring a bell, you may be reading the wrong book! Here's a list of buttons you can add to your toolbar:

- **Home:** Displays the browser's current home page.
- **Back:** Moves back one page in the browser history.
- **Forward:** Moves forward one page in the browser history.
- **Stop:** Stops the current page from continuing to load.
- **Refresh:** Redisplays the current page from scratch.
- **Search:** Directs the browser to a Web search engine.
- **Favorites:** Displays a list of favorite Web sites.

Status bar

Most Windows applications these days feature *status bars* in a horizontal area, usually at the bottom of the window, where the application displays status information and other messages the user may need to see. Although the status bar is a standard feature of a Web browser, including Internet Explorer, your custom browser can display information that you don't see in the full Internet Explorer. This information includes the following:

- **Icon:** Your own custom-designed icon.
- **Clock:** A digital clock showing the current time.
- **Timer:** A display showing the amount of time online or a countdown timer.
- **Date:** The current date.

Address bar

The *address bar* is just a small box where you can type URLs (Web addresses) that you want the browser to visit. Almost every Web browser has an address bar. You, however, can choose not to have one, if it suits your needs. You may, for example, want to build a Web browser that never leaves a specific Web site. In that case, you wouldn't need an address bar.

Although components like menu bars and toolbars are standard features of the full Internet Explorer, your custom components may use these standard features in different ways. For example, you can specify how your custom toolbar looks, which is something that you can't do with Internet Explorer.

Understanding Custom Browser Features

In this section, I cover the cool stuff that Internet Explorer doesn't have. These neat features coincide with the custom functions you can add to your browser, as well as a couple of the extra components that you can add to your browser window.

Passwords and the locking mechanism

A *password authentication system* protects many custom functions. If, for example, you've created a browser for your kids to use, you don't want them to accidentally (or deliberately — they are kids, you know) change any of the settings you've carefully set up. To change such function settings, the user must enter a password.

Timers

The *timer function* simply tracks how long an online session has been active. You can use the timer to keep an eye on how long you've been working on a specific online project, for example. You can also use the timer — as a count-down timer — to lock out the browser after a specific amount of time. If you want your kids (or your parents!) to be online only one hour a day, the timer, once you've set it up, can handle this need automatically, shutting off the browser after a given amount of time has elapsed.

Clock

If you don't know what a clock does, you're way over your head with this book! Just kidding. I know you know what a clock does, and the one you can add to your browser's status bar isn't much different. All it does is display the current time in digital format.

Alarms

Your custom Web browser can use alarms in various ways. The timer uses alarms that tell the user when his Web browsing time is up. This alarm can be just a pop-up window or an actual audible signal. This alarm is the signal for the browser's user to beg the browser's administrator (that's you) for more time.

Site-approval list

The Web overflows with great places to explore. Unfortunately, it also overflows with nasty places. To complicate matters further, what's nasty to one person may be perfectly okay to another. Freedom of speech dictates that these nasty places can exist, but it doesn't force you to allow your custom Web browser to display such places. That's where the site-approval list comes in.

The site-approval list is nothing more than a list of URLs to which your Web browser is allowed to connect. The list ensures that the user can never go somewhere on the Web that doesn't meet with your approval. Lots of programs have tried various ways of filtering Web content to keep unwanted sites from being viewed, but the only way to be 99 percent sure is to use a site-approval list. (That missing 1 percent covers me, just in case. . . .)

Web browsing log

The *Web browsing log* keeps a list of all the URLs visited by the browser. You may want to use the Web browsing log with older kids who need greater Web browsing freedom than a site-approval list allows, but who must also agree to the types of sites they'll visit. The browsing log gives you a quick and easy way to check that those who use your custom Web browser follow your rules.

Screen-capture "spy"

Still another safety feature is the *screen-capture function,* which takes pictures of the screen at the intervals that you specify. This feature comes in handy when used in conjunction with the Web browsing log. Web site URLs don't always have descriptive names. That dirty-joke place called Too Naughty For Kids may have the URL `www.tnfk.com`. That URL doesn't tell you anything about where your Web browser's users have gone (unless, of course, you go to the Web site yourself and check it out). The screen-capture function lets you see what the Web site looks like, without having to go there yourself.

TIP

The screen-capture function takes a lot of screen shots over the course of a Web browsing session. For that reason, try to review the images at least once a day. Otherwise, you'll be overwhelmed by the number of screen shots you need to examine.

Custom Web browser graphics

In this chapter's "Including Standard Browser Features" section, I explain the Web browser's toolbar, which contains the standard buttons browsers use to navigate the Web. I also explain the status bar and address bar. Your custom browser can go one step beyond the standard Internet Explorer by enabling you to add your own graphics to the toolbar, status bar, and address bar. These graphics include not only the bars themselves, but also the images used with each of the toolbar buttons. Cool!

To create graphics, though, you need to know how to use a paint program. This book helps you there, too. In Part III, you discover how to use your free-trial version of the famous Paint Shop Pro, included on this book's CD. You learn to use this powerful software to create graphics for use with your custom browser. Such graphics include not only the aforementioned toolbar and status bar stuff, but also *skins* (background images) and borders.

Part II

Customizing the Look of the Browser

"He found a dog site over an hour ago and has been in a staring contest ever since."

In this part . . .

Each custom browser is an assembly of components, including a menu bar, a toolbar, a status bar, border and background graphics, and more. In Part II, you find out how to add these components to your browser projects, as well as how to customize them to your taste and needs. At first, creating a new custom browser may seem like a lot of work, but by the time you explore the information in this part, you'll be banging out new browsers like a pro.

Chapter 4

Designing the Browser Window

In This Chapter

- Exploring the Window command category
- Choosing window styles
- Adding or removing window buttons
- Placing graphics in your window

Every custom browser starts with a window. Although Windows dictates to some extent what a window looks like, an application's programmer can choose to include or exclude certain features. The programmer can also decide what many of the features look like. In the case of the Browser Construction Kit, you get to be the programmer (sort of) and decide the type of window you want to use with your browser. In this chapter, you examine the many ways you can make your browser's window special.

The Window Command Category

The Window toolbox contains every command I discuss in this chapter. You display the Window toolbox by choosing the Window command category from the toolbox's drop-down list. To get started, run the Browser Construction Kit. When the editor's main window appears, choose the Window category in the lower-left corner of the window, as shown in Figure 4-1.

When you have the Window category selected, the Window commands appear on the buttons in the toolbox, also shown in Figure 4-1. To select a command, click the appropriate button. The following list describes the commands found in the Window command category:

REMEMBER

- **Color:** Specifies the color of the window's client area.

  The *client area* is the rectangle where the window displays data. As such, the client area is the largest part of the window.

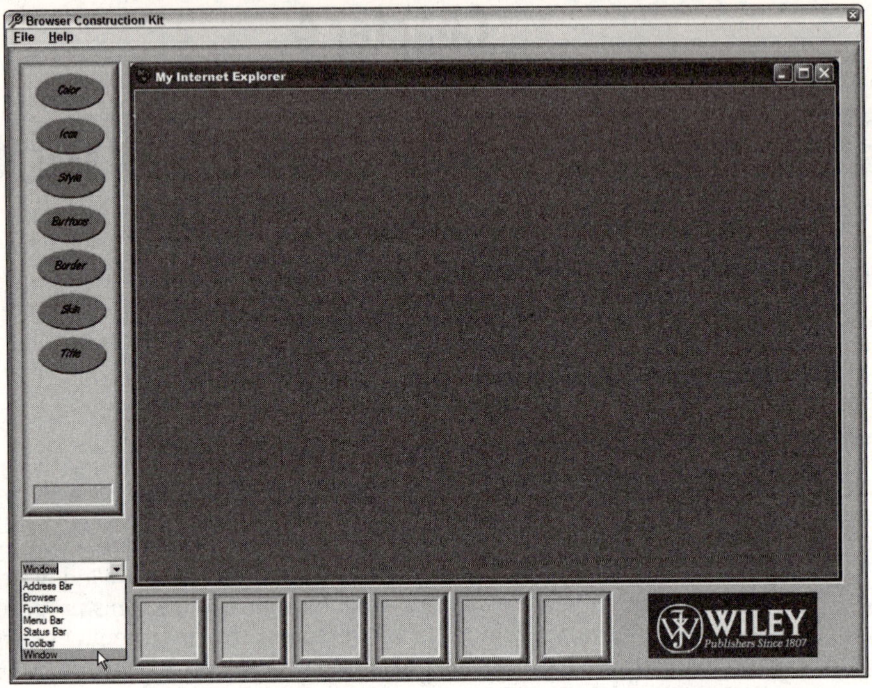

Figure 4-1: Choosing the Window category of commands.

- **Icon:** Specifies the icon that appears in the window's upper-left corner.
- **Style:** Specifies the type of window to use, such as a normal window or a toolbar window.
- **Buttons:** Specifies the buttons for the title bar.
- **Border:** Specifies a border image to appear at the top and bottom of the window's client area.
- **Skin:** Specifies an image to use as a background in the window's client area.
- **Title:** Specifies the title that appears in the window's title bar.

What you do after clicking the button you want depends on the command you choose. The rest of this chapter shows you how to apply these commands to the design of your custom browser's window.

The Window Color

You can set the background color of the window's client area to any color you want. To do so, click the Color button in the Window toolbox. When you do, the Color dialog box appears, as shown in Figure 4-2.

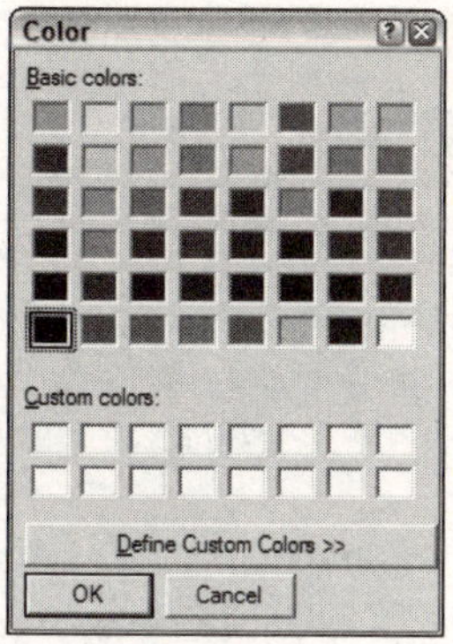

Figure 4-2: The Color dialog box.

In the Color dialog box, click the color you want and then click OK. The window's background color immediately changes in the editor's display.

If the colors in the Color dialog box don't suit you, you can define your own. Simply click the Define Custom Colors button to expand the Color dialog box, shown in Figure 4-3. Pick the hue you want from the large color box and then select the shade from the narrow box to the right. When you have your color, click the Add To Custom Colors button, and the color appears in the Custom Colors boxes. Click the color you want and then click OK.

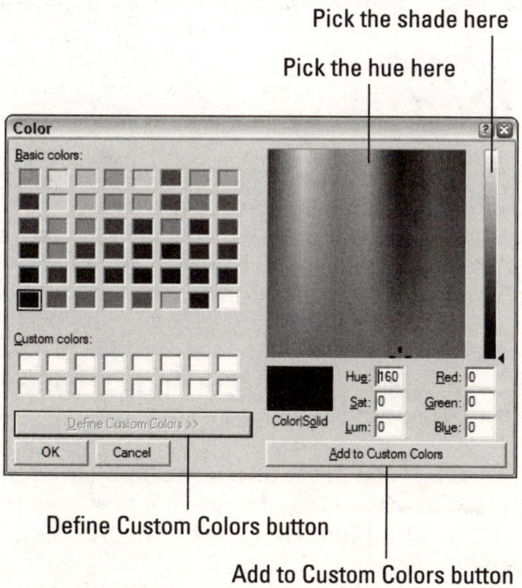

Figure 4-3: The expanded Color dialog box.

Getting an exact color

If you want a very specific color, you can type color values directly into the Hue, Sat, and Lum boxes, or into the Red, Green, and Blue boxes. Hue stands for . . . well, hue; Sat stands for saturation; and Lum stands for luminescence. The Red, Green, and Blue values, on the other hand, are the amount of red, green, and blue to mix to form the final color. These values can range from 0 to 255, with 0 being darkest and 255 being brightest. The value 0,0,0 is black, and the value 255,255,255 is white, with all other colors falling somewhere in between.

For example, the RGB value 255,0,0 is pure red, whereas 0,255,0 is pure green and 0,0,255 is pure blue. Reduce the value of a pure color, and you get a darker shade of the same color. Thus, 128,0,0 is dark red. If all three red, green, and blue color elements have the same value — 128,128,128 or 64,64,64 are a couple of possibilities — then you get a shade of gray.

As you add more of one color element over another, the resultant color becomes more like the color with the higher value. The RGB value 128,128,128 is medium gray, but 256,128,128 adds a healthy dose of red, and you end up with a shade of pink.

As you can see, you can mix the colors just as you would jars of paint, although the results are nothing like what you get with paint. The color value 256,256,0 combines red and green (but no blue), which, due to the peculiarities of RGB color values, gives you yellow. The color value 255,0,255, on the other hand, gives you a purplish-pink. When all else fails, experiment with the RGB colors by typing in different values and seeing what you get.

The Application Icon

An application's icon appears on the left end of the title bar. To add an icon to your window, click the Icon button in the toolbox. When you do, the Select Window Icon dialog box appears (see Figure 4-4). This dialog box is a standard Windows dialog box. Find your icon file as you would in any Windows program and then click the Open button. The Browser Construction Kit adds the icon to your window.

To remove an icon from the browser window, click the Icon button again. The Browser Construction Kit then removes the icon.

Window icons must be a special type of file and must be created by a special editor. If a graphics file has a file extension of `.ico`, it's probably the type of file you want. No doubt you can find tons of icons on the Internet. You can probably even do a search of your own hard drive and find plenty of them. If you want to make your own icons, refer to Chapter 16. This book's CD features a number of browser themes, each of which includes a custom icon. Feel free to use these icons in your own projects as well.

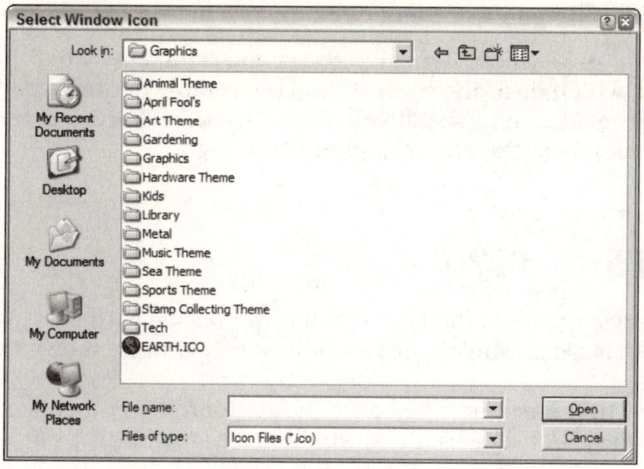

Figure 4-4: The Select Window Icon dialog box.

Not every window style can display an icon. If a window style displays no icon, adding one with the Icon command has no effect.

The Window Style

A window's style determines what the title bar and window border look like. The style can also affect the buttons that appear in the title bar. If, for example, you choose to have a Normal window style, the title bar can (if you want) display all three window-control buttons: Minimize, Maximize, and Close. If, however, you choose a Toolbox-style window, only the Close button can be on the title bar.

To select a window style:

1. **Click the Style button in the toolbox.**

   When you do, the Window Styles dialog box appears, as seen in Figure 4-5.

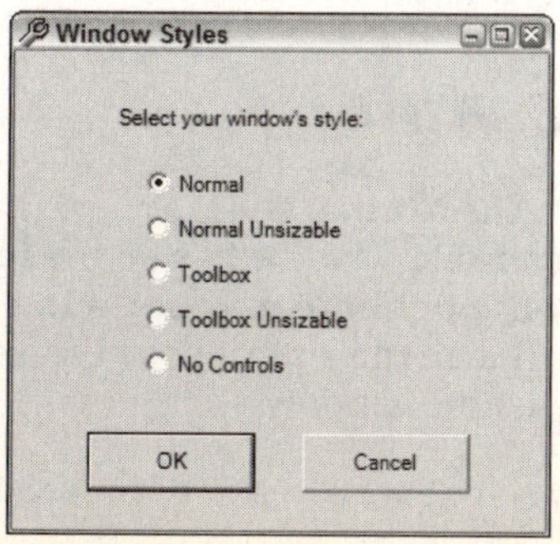

Figure 4-5: The Window Styles dialog box.

2. **Select the style you want and click the OK button.**

   If you're unsure which of the five styles you want, check out the following sections, which describe each style. The window in the display changes to show the selected style. If you click the Cancel button in the Window Styles dialog box, the editor applies no changes.

The Normal style

The Normal style contains the type of window you see with most Windows applications. A Normal window has the following features, shown in Figure 4-6:

- **Standard title bar:** The title bar is the standard height, unlike some other styles, such as a toolbox, which has a smaller title bar.
- **Icon:** This icon appears at the left end of the title bar.
- **Window title:** This title is the text you select for the window's name. The title appears to the right of the icon in the title bar.
- **Minimize button:** This button is the first one on the right side of the title bar. It reduces the window to an icon on the taskbar.
- **Maximize button:** The second button on the right side of the title bar, it enlarges the window to fill the full screen. When the window is set to full screen, the Maximize button becomes the Restore button, which returns the window to its previous size.
- **Close button:** The third button on the right side of the title bar, this button closes the application, having the same effect as choosing Exit from the menu bar.
- **Thick border:** The border is the edge of the window. A normal window has a thick border that the user can drag to resize the window.

TIP

Although some window styles display the Minimize, Maximize, and Close buttons, you're not stuck with them. You can, for example, have a Normal window with only a Close button. See this chapter's "Minimize, Maximize, and Close Buttons" section for more information.

The Normal Unsizable style

The Normal Unsizable style is similar to the Normal style, except that the user cannot resize the window. A Normal Unsizable window has all the features of a Normal window, except it has a slightly thinner border. You use this window style when you don't want the user to change the size of your browser's window. Figure 4-7 shows a Normal Unsizable window.

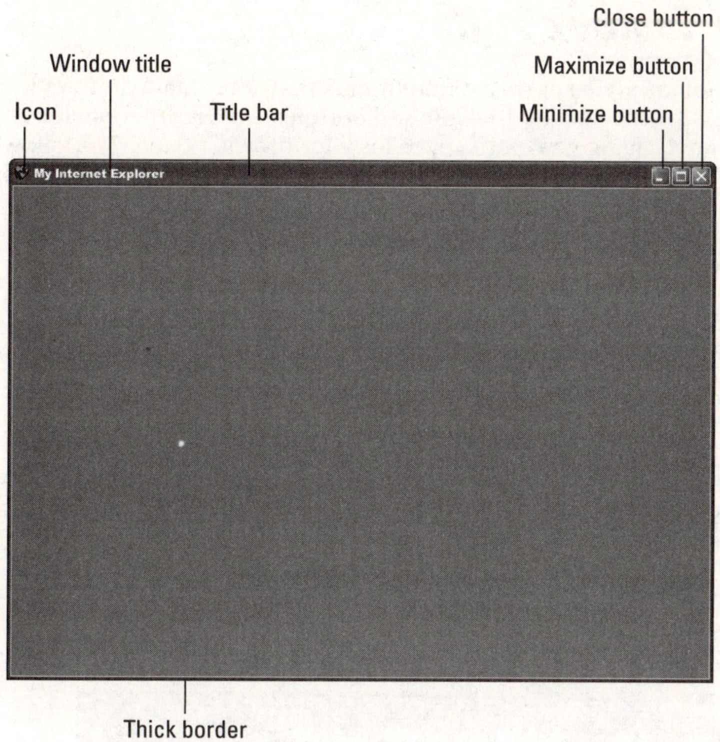

Figure 4-6: The Normal window style.

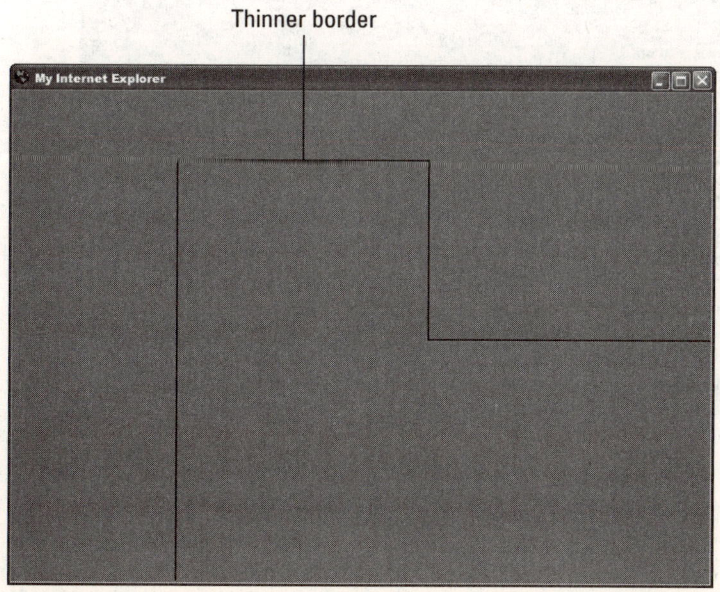

Figure 4-7: The Normal Unsizable window style.

The Toolbox style

The Toolbox style sports a different look than a normal Windows window (see Figure 4-8). The smaller title bar and buttons leave more room for the window's client area, giving you extra space for your browser pane. The following list describes the differences between the Normal and Toolbox windows:

- **Small title bar:** The height of the title bar is less than with a Normal window.
- **No icon:** The Toolbox style window displays no icon.
- **Minimize button:** Doesn't appear.
- **Maximize button:** Doesn't appear.
- **Close button:** Smaller than in a Normal style window.
- **Thin border:** A Toolbox window has a thinner border than the one on a Normal window, but the user can still resize the window.

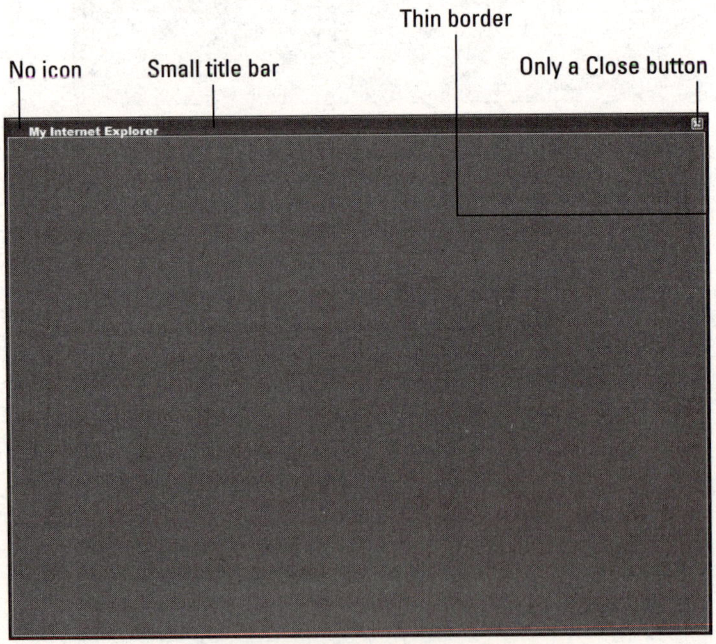

Figure 4-8: The Toolbox window style.

The Toolbox Unsizable style

The Toolbox Unsizable style window looks a lot like a regular Toolbox window, except that the border is slightly thinner, and the user can't resize the window.

This style is great for those times when you want the extra room provided by a Toolbox window, but don't want the user to change the window's dimensions. A Toolbox Unsizable window has the following features, shown in Figure 4-9:

- **Small title bar:** The height of the title bar is less than with a Normal window.
- **No icon:** The Toolbox style window displays no icon.
- **Window title:** This title is the text you select for the window's name. The title appears on the left of the title bar.
- **Minimize button:** Doesn't appear.
- **Maximize button:** Doesn't appear.
- **Close button:** Smaller than in a Normal style window.
- **Thin border:** A Toolbox Unsizable window has a slightly thinner border than the one on a Toolbox window, and the user can't resize the window.

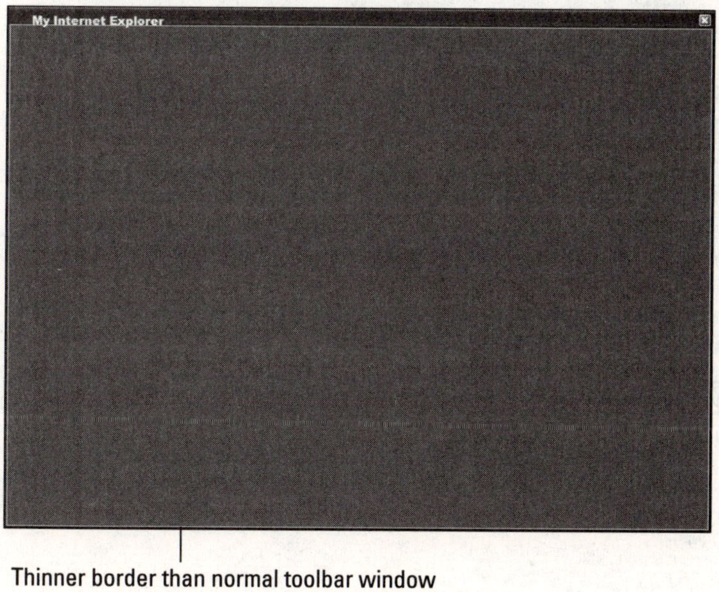

Figure 4-9: The Toolbox Unsizable window style.

The No Controls style

The No Controls style window is nothing more than a blank rectangle. The window displays no controls of any kind (unless, of course, you add things like a toolbar or status bar). A No Controls style window doesn't have any features, and the user can't resize the window (see Figure 4-10). I wouldn't recommend using this window style much, because the user has no way to manipulate the window, except to close it. Still, for special purposes, this window style can be handy, if for no other reason than it provides the biggest area for your browser pane.

Figure 4-10: The No Controls window style.

Minimize, Maximize, and Close Buttons

Although some window styles can display the Minimize, Maximize, and Close buttons, they don't have to. Specifically, you can use the toolbox's Buttons button to select the buttons that you want in your window's title bar. To do so, click the Buttons button. The Window Buttons dialog box appears, as shown in Figure 4-11.

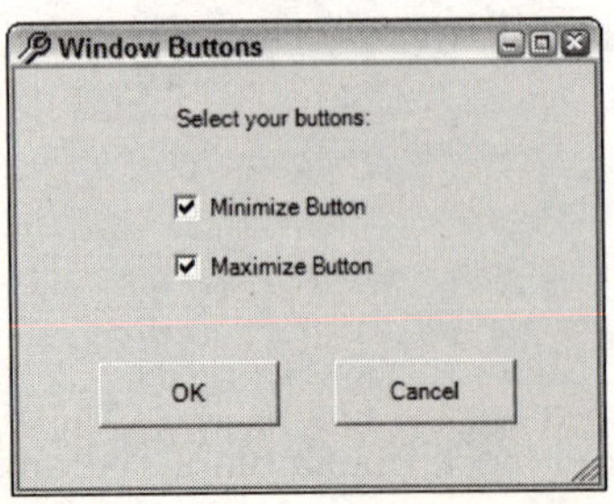

Figure 4-11: The Window Buttons dialog box.

As you can see, only the Minimize and Maximize buttons appear in the Window Buttons dialog box. These buttons are the only ones you can change. (That means if a window style normally contains the Close button, you have to live with it.) To add a button to the window, select its checkbox. To remove it, clear its checkbox. Figure 4-12, for example, shows a window with just the Maximize and Close buttons. (The Minimize button is grayed out, which means that it's disabled.)

REMEMBER

You can't add or remove buttons from a window style that doesn't include the buttons in the first place. For example, if you've chosen a Toolbox style window, changes you make with the Buttons button have no effect.

Figure 4-12: A window with only Maximize and Close buttons.

The Window Borders

If you want to spruce up your browser window, borders may be just the ticket. *Borders* are narrow images that you can place above and below the browser pane. You can use borders to give your browser a graphical theme, as shown in Figure 4-13.

To add a border, click the Border button in the Window toolbox. When you do, the Select Border Image dialog box appears (see Figure 4-14). This dialog box works just like any standard Windows dialog box. Simply find your border file as you would in any Windows program and then click the Open button. The Browser Construction Kit adds the border to your window.

To remove a border from the browser window, click the Border button again. The Browser Construction Kit then removes the border.

Figure 4-13: Borders can help give your browser a graphical theme.

Border images can be one of several file types: .bmp, .gif, or .jpg. Most paint programs can generate these types of files. Even though the Browser Construction Kit automatically resizes an image to fit the border areas of the window, to get the best results, your border images should have a size of 784 x 54 pixels. Refer to Chapter 11 for more information.

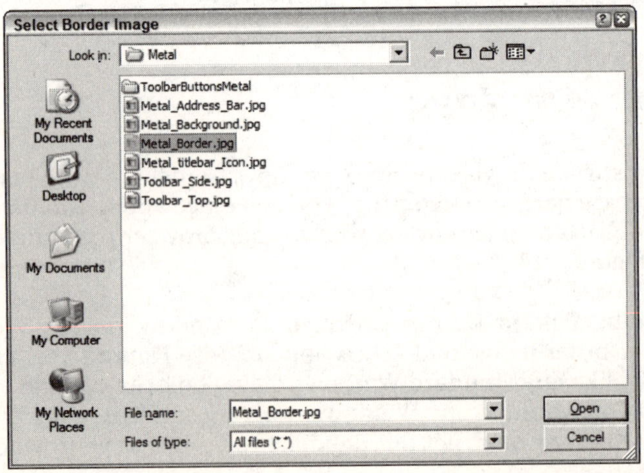

Figure 4-14: The Select Border Image dialog box.

The Window Skin

Borders are one way to add thematic graphics to your browser window (see the previous section). Another way is with a window skin. In the case of the Browser Construction Kit, a *skin* is a large image that fills the client area of the window, as shown in Figure 4-15.

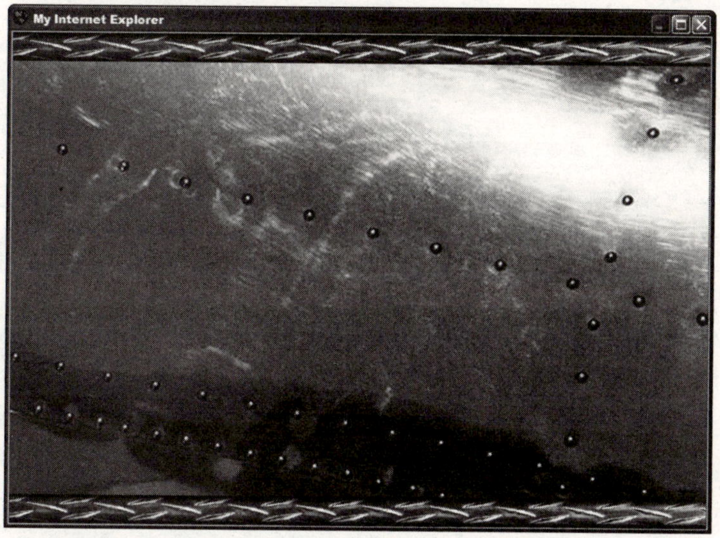

Figure 4-15: A skin adds an image to your window's background.

To add a skin, click the Skin button in the Window toolbox. When you do, the Select Skin Image dialog box appears (see Figure 4-16). Choose your skin file from the list and then click the Open button. The Browser Construction Kit adds the skin to your window.

To remove a skin from the browser window, click the Skin button again. The Browser Construction Kit then removes the skin.

Skin images can be one of several file types: .bmp, .gif, or .jpg. Most paint programs generate these types of files. Even though the Browser Construction Kit automatically resizes an image to fit the client area of the window, to get the best results, your skin images should have a size of 784 x 559 pixels. You can refer to Chapter 12 for more information.

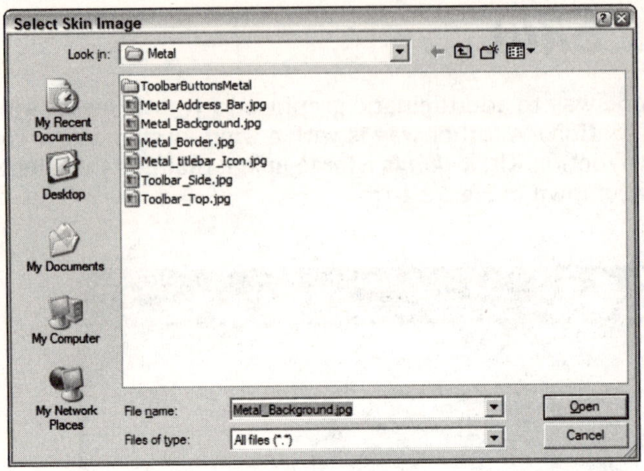

Figure 4-16: The Select Skin Image dialog box.

The Window Title

You can name your custom browser anything you like. Here's how:

1. **Click the Title button.**

   The Window Title dialog box appears.

2. **Type your browser's name into the text box.**
3. **Click OK.**

   The Browser Construction Kit places your browser's name in the window's title bar.

You can't remove the window title, because your browser needs a name. When you start a new custom browser project, the Browser Construction Kit supplies the default name of My Internet Explorer. Obviously, you can stick with the default name if you want, but your own name is better. (By your own name, I don't, of course, mean Fred, Kate, or Sam, but you knew that, right?)

Chapter 5

Adding the Browser Pane

In This Chapter

- Exploring the Browser command category
- Adding a browser pane
- Setting the browser pane's size and position
- Setting the default Web site

Just about every component you add to your custom browser supports the application's main feature, its browser pane. The browser pane is where you view the Web pages to which you connect. All the other controls in the browser manipulate the browser pane in some way, or at least perform related activities. In this chapter, you find out everything you need to know about the browser pane.

The Browser Command Category

To manipulate your browser's browser pane, you first must select the Browser command category in the Browser Construction Kit's editor, as shown in Figure 5-1. When you do, you see the following commands:

- **Top:** Specifies the location of the browser pane's top edge.
- **Left:** Specifies the location of the browser pane's left edge.
- **Width:** Specifies the browser pane's width.
- **Height:** Specifies the browser pane's height.
- **Border:** Specifies the type of border to appear around the browser pane.
- **Start Site:** Specifies the Web page the browser first displays.
- **Browser:** Adds the browser pane to the window.

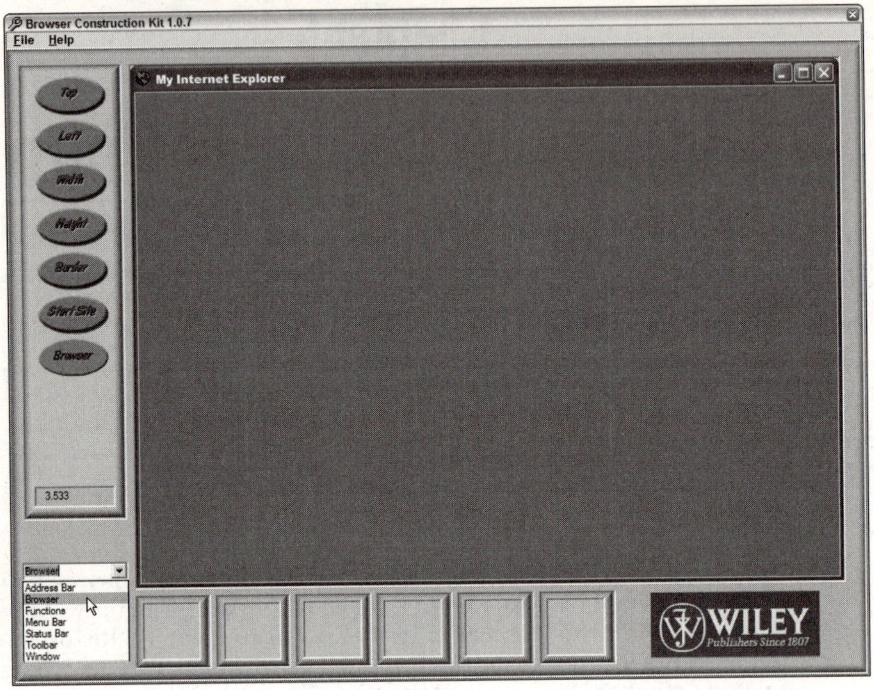

Figure 5-1: Selecting the Browser category of commands.

Besides the command buttons, the Browser toolbox displays the current mouse coordinates. You can use these coordinates to help find the correct values for the browser pane's location and size.

When you first switch to the Browser commands, only the Browser button is enabled. This is because your copy of the Browser Construction Kit is broken. Just kidding! The other buttons are disabled because, until you add a browser pane to your window, the other commands have no effect.

To add the browser pane to your window, click the Browser button. The Browser Construction Kit then adds the browser pane to the window, as shown in Figure 5-2. With the new browser pane nestled comfortably in your window, the Browser Construction Kit enables the other Browser command buttons. Seems like magic, doesn't it?

The Wiley Web site shown in the browser pane is only an image, rather than a real Web site. Don't bother trying to browse yet! After you set up your complete browser window, you create the finished custom browser, which, of course, can browse the Internet for real.

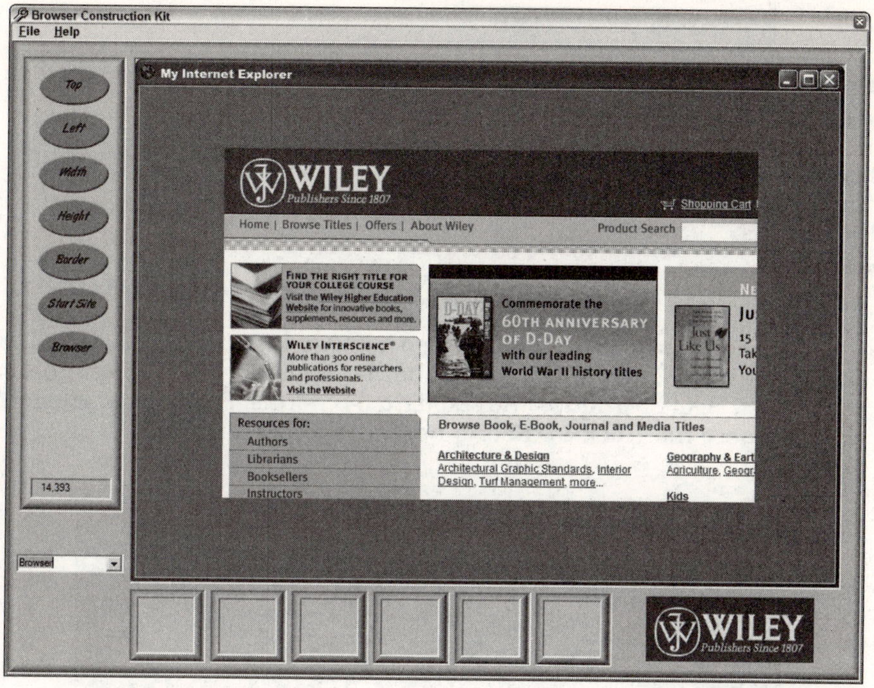

Figure 5-2: A custom browser project with the browser pane installed.

Pane Border Style

You can build a snappier looking browser pane by adding a border. Because the border takes up extra room around the browser pane, however, you should add the border before you attempt to position and size the browser pane. Of course, if you're not adding a browser-pane border, you don't need to read this section.

The Browser Construction Kit provides four different borders for your browser pane. To choose one of these borders, click the Border button. When you do, the Browser Border dialog box appears, as shown in Figure 5-3.

The normal border is a simple, rectangular box that surrounds the browser pane, as shown in Figure 5-4. Although the normal border is just a few lines, it really draws attention to the browser pane. If you want something a little subtler, go for the thin frame, which is just a narrower version of the normal border. Even this narrow rectangle can make your browser pane pop.

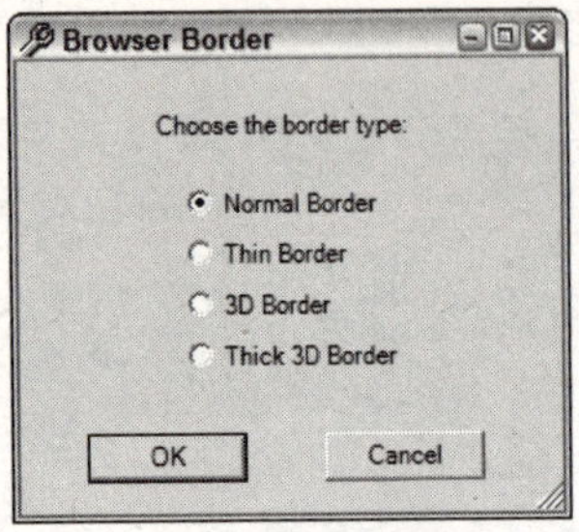

Figure 5-3: The Browser Border dialog box.

If subtle isn't your thing, you can add two types of 3-D borders. To add a standard 3-D border, select the 3-D Border option in the Browser Border dialog box. Figure 5-5 shows the standard 3-D border. For an even greater 3-D effect, choose the Thick 3-D Border option. Awesome!

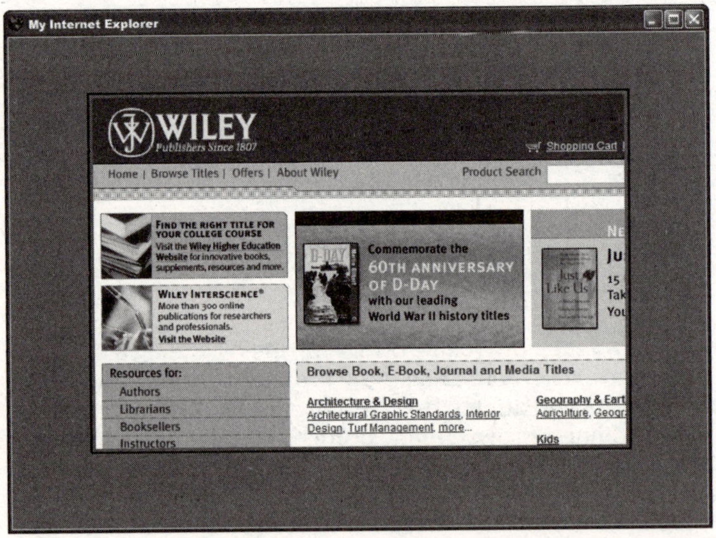

Figure 5-4: The normal browser border.

TIP

When you add a border to your browser pane, clicking the Border button a second time removes the border.

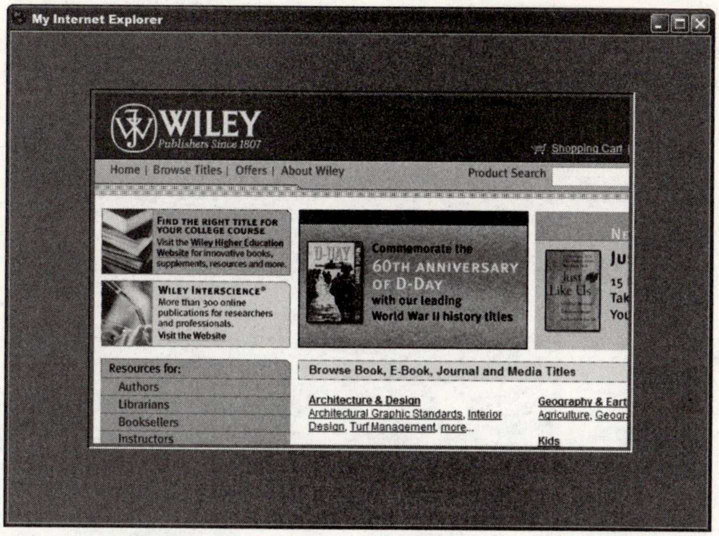

Figure 5-5: The standard 3-D border.

Pane Position

After adding the browser pane to your window, you'll almost certainly want to reposition and size it. You position the browser pane by specifying the location of its top and left edges. To do so, first place the mouse pointer at the location at which you want to position the browser. If you look at the bottom of the editor's toolbox, you can see the mouse's current location. The first value is the left position, and the second is the top.

Click the Top button, and the Browser Top dialog box appears (see Figure 5-6). Type the top value into the text box and click OK. The browser pane moves up or down to your selected location.

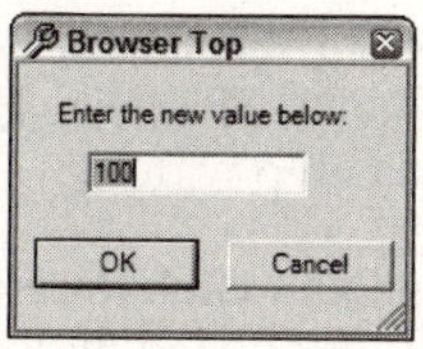

Figure 5-6: The Browser Top dialog box.

Now do the same thing for the browser's left edge. Click the Left button, enter the value for the left edge, and click OK. The browser pane moves left or right to the selected location. Figure 5-7 shows the browser pane positioned in the window's upper-left corner.

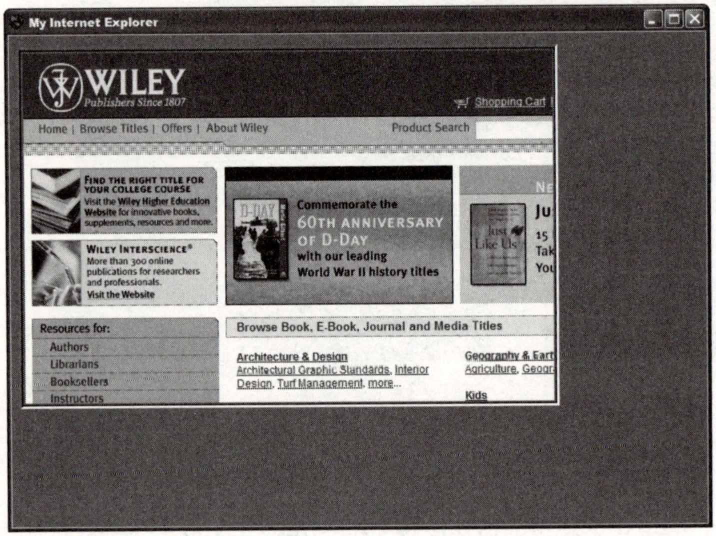

Figure 5-7: The positioned browser pane.

Pane Size

You have complete control over the width and height of the browser pane. Well, you can't make it bigger than the window, but you know what I mean. To change the width and height, guess which buttons you click? If you guessed the Width and Height buttons, you win the cigar. If you guessed your TV's power button, return this book immediately and buy *Buttons For Dummies* instead.

To set your browser pane's width, click the Width button. The Browser Width dialog box appears. Type the width value and click OK. The Browser Construction Kit sets the browser pane to your selected width.

Set your browser pane's height in the same way, except click the Height button. The Browser Height dialog box appears. Type the height value and click OK. The Browser Construction Kit sets the browser pane to your selected height. Figure 5-8 shows the browser pane after being positioned and sized.

REMEMBER

If you add a border to your browser pane, you need to allow extra room around the pane when you position and size it.

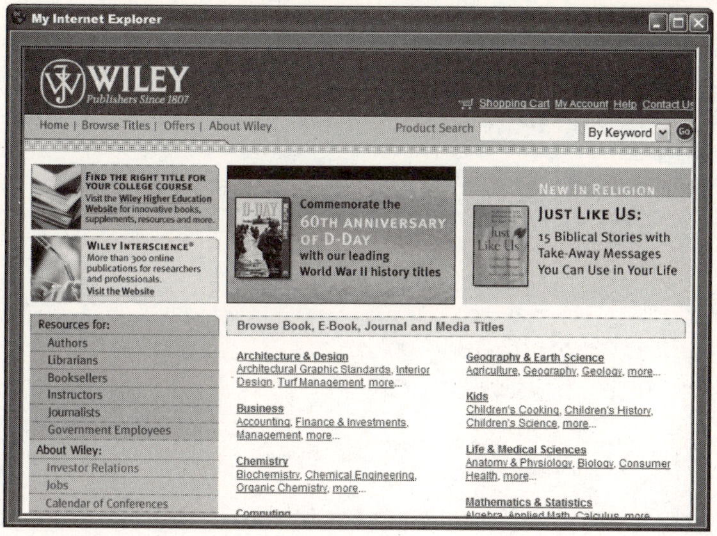

Figure 5-8: The sized and positioned browser pane.

Starting a Web Page

When you load up a browser, its window must display something. What the browser displays is the default Web page, or what some people like to call the home page. (Because the term "home page" is more commonly used to describe the first page of a Web site, I don't like to use it for the browser's start-up page; doing so makes the term a little confusing.) The Browser Construction Kit calls this default page the Start Site.

When you add the browser pane to your browser window, the start site is set to `www.wiley.com`, the home page for this book's publisher. You can, however, choose any Web site you want. To do so, click the Start Site button. When you do, the Start Site dialog box appears, as shown in Figure 5-9. Enter the Web site address you want and then click OK. That's all there is to it. When you run your Web browser, it'll automatically browse to the site you entered.

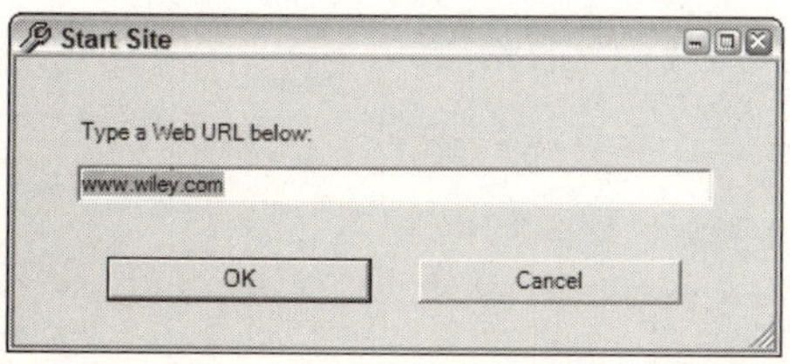

Figure 5-9: The Start Site dialog box.

Chapter 6

Assembling the Toolbar

In This Chapter

- Exploring the Toolbar command category
- Adding navigation buttons
- Specifying a favorite search Web site
- Entering a favorites list

Although a toolbar takes up valuable real estate in your browser's window, it provides a convenient way for the user to select frequently used commands. Whereas choosing a command from a menu takes two or three mouse clicks, a single click is all it takes to select a toolbar command button.

Your custom browser can have a toolbar, but, more importantly, you can customize this toolbar to exactly fit your needs. This customization includes choosing a toolbar image, as well as deciding which command buttons to display on your toolbar. In this chapter, you find out how to add a toolbar to your browser's window.

The Toolbar Command Category

To manipulate your browser's toolbar, first select the Toolbar command category in the Browser Construction Kit's editor, as shown in Figure 6-1. When you do, you see the following commands:

- **Home:** Adds the Home button to the toolbar. The Home button returns the browser pane to its default Web page.
- **Back:** Adds the Back button to the toolbar. The Back button returns the browser pane to the previously viewed Web page.
- **Forward:** Adds the Forward button to the toolbar. The Forward button returns the browser pane to the Web page viewed before clicking the Back button.

- **Stop:** Adds the Stop button to the toolbar. The Stop button cancels the loading of the current Web page.
- **Refresh:** Adds the Refresh button to the toolbar. The Refresh button reloads the current Web page into the browser pane.
- **Search:** Adds the Search button to the toolbar. The Search button causes the browser pane to display the chosen search site.
- **Favorites:** Adds the Favorites button to the toolbar. The Favorites button displays a list of favorite Web sites.
- **Toolbar:** Adds a toolbar to the window.

When you first switch to the Toolbar commands, only the Toolbar button is enabled. The other buttons are disabled because, until you add a toolbar to your window, the other commands have no effect. You can't — at least, not in this universe — add a toolbar button to a nonexistent toolbar!

To add a toolbar to your window:

1. **Click the Toolbar button.**

   The Toolbar dialog box, shown in Figure 6-2, appears.

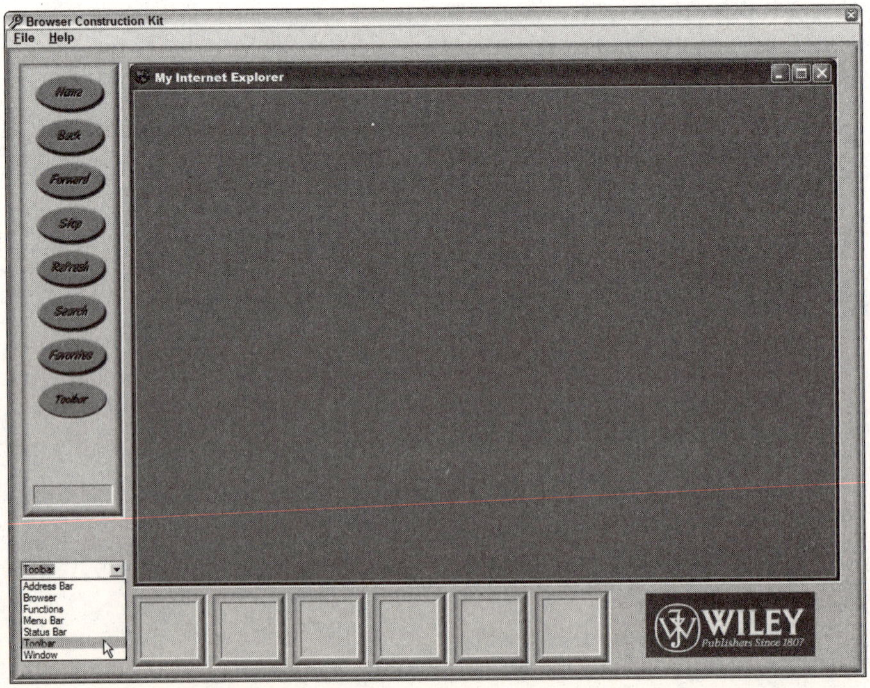

Figure 6-1: Selecting the Toolbar category of commands.

2. **Choose the toolbar's location.**

   For tips on choosing a location, see the section "Toolbar Position," later in this chapter.

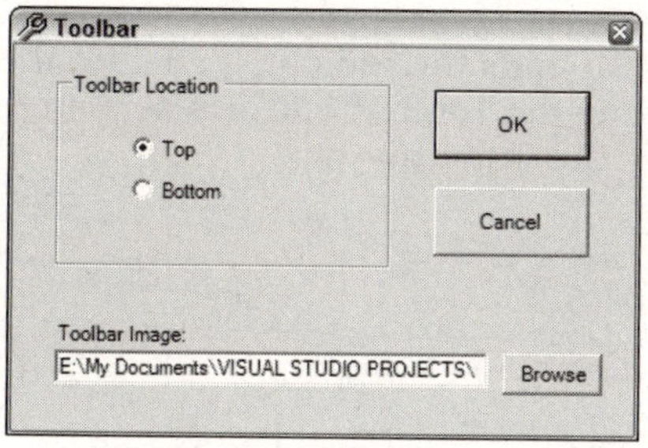

Figure 6-2: The Toolbar dialog box.

3. **Choose the image that the Browser Construction Kit uses for the toolbar's background.**

   The upcoming section "Toolbar Image" provides tips on choosing an image.

4. **Click OK.**

   The selected toolbar appears in the window. Figure 6-3 shows a custom browser window with a toolbar at the top of the screen.

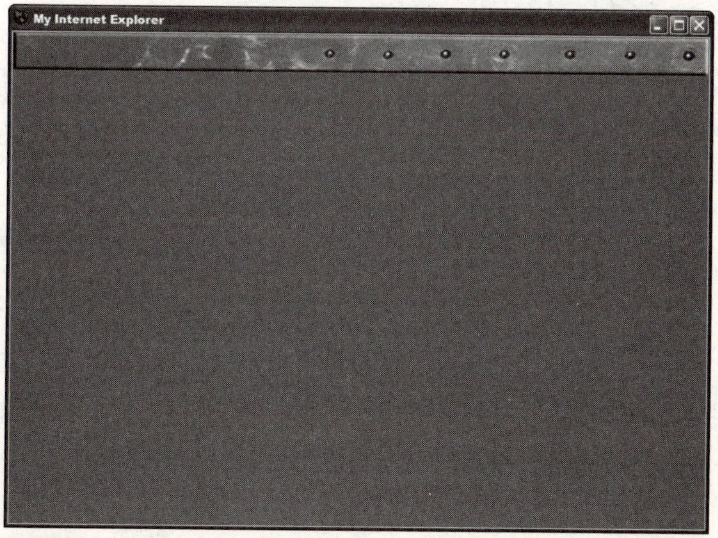

Figure 6-3: A custom browser window with a toolbar installed.

Your new toolbar displays no buttons. You must add the buttons you need using the commands in the Toolbar toolbox. (Don't confuse the buttons at the bottom of the Browser Construction Kit's window with toolbar buttons. That's the area where special function icons appear. See Part IV for more information.)

When the Browser Construction Kit adds the toolbar, it enables the other Toolbar command buttons. Clicking the Toolbar button a second time removes the toolbar and disables the other buttons.

Toolbar Position

You can place your toolbar in one of two locations: top or bottom. Select the position in the Toolbar dialog box, which appears when you click the Toolbar button in the toolbox.

The most common place for a toolbar is the top of the window, as shown in Figure 6-3. Although you can place your toolbar on the bottom of the window, I've never seen a Windows application with the toolbar in that location. Still, it's your browser. Do what you want!

Toolbar Image

When completely assembled, the toolbar is a rectangular image that holds a set of command buttons. But you knew that already, right? The Browser Construction Kit enables you to provide your own image for the toolbar's background. You can choose .bmp, .jpg, or .gif images. The image's size should be 784 x 42 pixels. (Please refer to Chapter 15 for more information on creating buttons.)

You can choose any size image you want for your toolbar, and the Browser Construction Kit automatically resizes it to fit. Resizing an image, though, often leads to a lot of image distortion. Still, this image distortion can create unusual patterns that can look cool. Feel free to experiment.

To select your toolbar image, follow these steps:

1. **Click the Toolbar button in the toolbox.**

   The Toolbar dialog box appears.

2. **Click the Browse button to bring up the Load Toolbar Image dialog box.**

3. **Select your image and click Open.**

   The image's path and filename appear in the Toolbar Image box of the Toolbar dialog box.

4. **Click the dialog box's OK button.**

   The Browser Construction Kit loads the toolbar image and adds the toolbar to your window.

Button Types

Your toolbar doesn't do much unless you add buttons to it. That's what the other commands in the Toolbar toolbox do. Also, just as with the toolbar background, you can supply your own images for the buttons. The buttons you can add to the toolbar represent the commands that most Web browsers support. In the following sections, you find out how to add these buttons to your toolbar.

Back, Forward, Stop, Refresh, and Home buttons

The Back, Forward, Stop, Refresh, and Home buttons all control the browser's Web navigation. You probably know what all these buttons do. If not, refer to the section "The Toolbar Command Category," earlier in this chapter.

To add a button to your browser's toolbar, follow these steps:

1. **Click the button's command in the toolbox.**
2. **When you do, the Load Button Image dialog box appears, as shown in Figure 6-4.**
3. **Use the file browser to locate the image file you want to use.**

   You can double-click the image to select it or single-click the image.

4. **With the image selected, click the Open button.**

   The Browser Construction Kit loads the image and displays the new button on the toolbar, as shown in Figure 6-5.

After adding a button to your toolbar, clicking the button's command in the toolbox a second time removes the button from the toolbar.

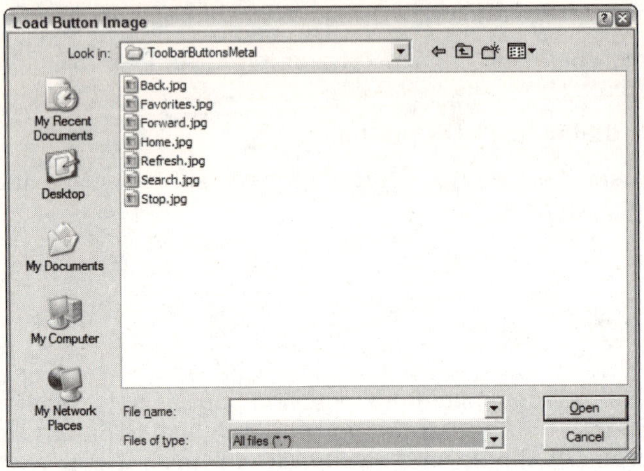

Figure 6-4: The Load Button Image dialog box.

The button images you use should be in the .bmp, .jpg, or .gif format and be 32 x 32 pixels in size. For more information about creating your button images, refer to Chapter 15.

Figure 6-5: The toolbar with a Home button added.

REMEMBER

As with many of the graphical images you use with your custom Web browser, you can choose any size image you want for your buttons. If the size is other than 32 x 32 pixels, the Browser Construction Kit resizes the image to fit. Remember, though, that resizing often leads to distorted images. The greater the difference from the recommended size, the greater the distortion.

The Search button

Adding a Search button is a little different from adding some other buttons. You specify the button's image just as you do with the other buttons, but after loading the image, you must also specify the Web address of the search site with which you want the button associated.

To add the Search button to your browser's toolbar, follow these steps:

1. **Click the Search button command in the toolbox.**

   When you do, the Load Button Image dialog box appears.

2. **Use the file browser to locate the image file you want to use.**

   You can double-click the image to select it or single-click the image.

3. **With the image selected, click the Open button.**

   The Browser Construction Kit loads the image. After loading the image, the Browser Construction Kit displays the Search Site dialog box, shown in Figure 6-6.

4. **Enter your favorite search Web site's URL into the text box and click OK.**

   The Browser Construction Kit displays the new Search button on your toolbar. If you click the Cancel button, the Search button still appears on the toolbar, but it's not associated with a Web site.

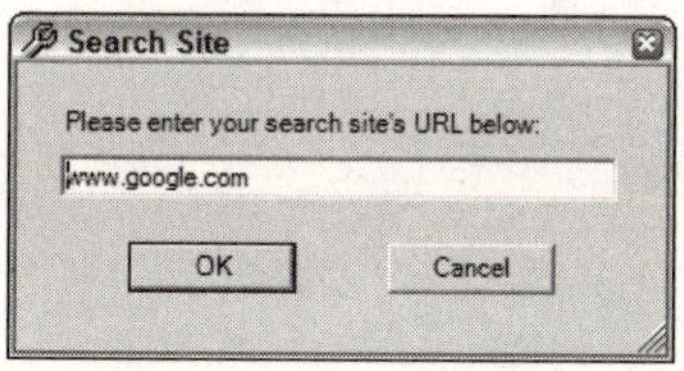

Figure 6-6: The Search Site dialog box.

The Favorites button

When you complete your custom browser, the Favorites button brings up a list of frequently visited Web sites. You add these Web sites to the list either at the time you add the Favorites button to your toolbar or when you run the finished browser.

To add the Favorites button and favorites to your browser's toolbar:

1. **Click the Favorites button command in the toolbox.**

   When you do, the Load Button Image dialog box appears.

2. **Use the file browser to locate the image file you want to use.**

   You can double-click the image to select it or single-click the image.

3. **With the image selected, click the Open button.**

   The Browser Construction Kit loads the image. After loading the image, the Browser Construction Kit displays the Favorites dialog box, shown in Figure 6-7.

4. **If you don't want to add favorite sites at this time, click the Cancel button; to add a new favorite site, type its URL into the Enter URL text box.**

5. **Click the Add button.**

   The site's address appears in the list.

   To delete an entry from the favorites list, select the entry and click the Delete button. The Delete All button removes all entries from the list. Use it with care! (Actually, you get a warning whenever you click the button.)

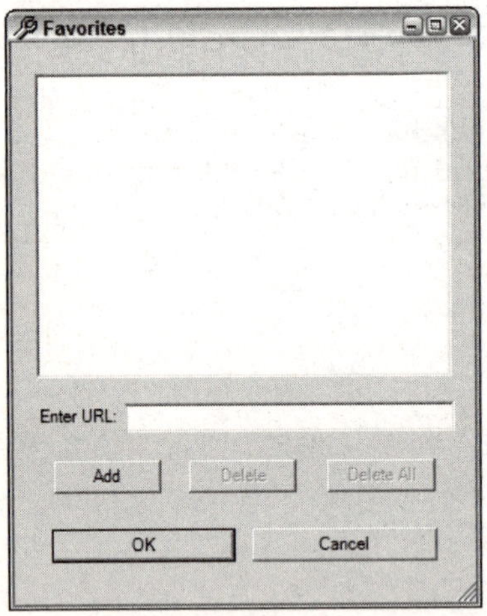

Figure 6-7: The Favorites dialog box.

6. **Repeat Steps 4 and 5 until you're finished entering favorite Web sites; then click OK.**

   The Browser Construction Kit adds the Favorites button to the toolbar.

Chapter 7

Designing the Menu Bar

In This Chapter

- Exploring the Menu Bar command category
- Placing a menu bar
- Adding menus

Windows applications frequently offer two ways to select commands. The first is clicking buttons on a toolbar, an object that you can read about in the previous chapter. The second way of giving commands is to yell at the screen. Well, not really. Actually, the second and most common way to give commands to an application is with the menu bar. (For the record, my computer completely ignores all my screaming and yelling. This is how I know that you can't give commands to a computer that way.)

Choosing commands from the menu bar, as compared with a toolbar, takes an extra mouse click or two (not that those extra clicks cramp up your mouse hand or anything). But the menu bar has the advantage of holding tons more commands than a toolbar because menus remain hidden until you activate them, and so take up very little screen space. A toolbar, on the other hand, stays on the screen. Why all this talk of menu bars? Because, in this chapter, you find out how to add a menu bar to your custom browser.

The Menu Bar Command Category

As with all the commands used with the Browser Construction Kit, the menu bar commands are organized into their own category. To manipulate your browser's menu bar, first select the Menu Bar command category in the Browser Construction Kit's editor, as shown in Figure 7-1. When you do, you see the following commands:

- **File:** Adds the File menu to the menu bar. The File menu contains commands like New Window, Open, Properties, and Close.
- **Edit:** Adds the Edit menu to the menu bar. The Edit menu contains commands like Cut, Copy, Paste, and Find.

- **View:** Adds the View menu to the menu bar. The View menu contains commands that turn components like toolbars and status bars on and off.
- **Favorites:** Adds the Favorites menu to the menu bar. The Favorites menu displays a list of favorite Web sites.
- **Tools:** Adds the Tools menu to the menu bar. The Tools menu contains commands that manipulate the custom functions like locks, passwords, and alarms.
- **Help:** Adds the Help menu to the menu bar. The Help menu contains the About command, which displays information about who created the browser.
- **Menu Bar:** Adds a menu bar to the window.

When you first switch to the Menu Bar commands, only the Menu Bar button is enabled. The other buttons are disabled because, until you add a menu bar to your window, the other commands have no effect.

To add a menu bar to your window, click the Menu Bar button. The Browser Construction Kit adds the menu bar to the top of your browser's window. (Another click removes the menu bar from the window.) Figure 7-2 shows a custom browser window with a menu bar in place. This menu bar has a complete set of menus.

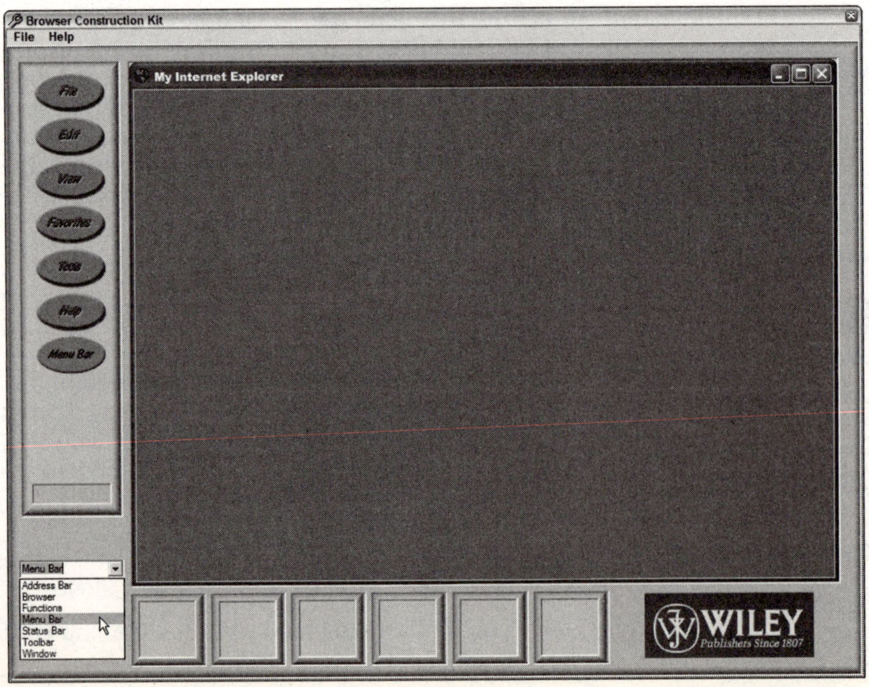

Figure 7-1: Selecting the Menu Bar category of commands.

For the most part, your custom browser's menu bar and toolbar contain a different set of commands, so, chances are, you'll want to add both to your browser's window. But, depending upon the commands that you want available in your final browser, you can choose to include either the menu bar or toolbar — or even neither one.

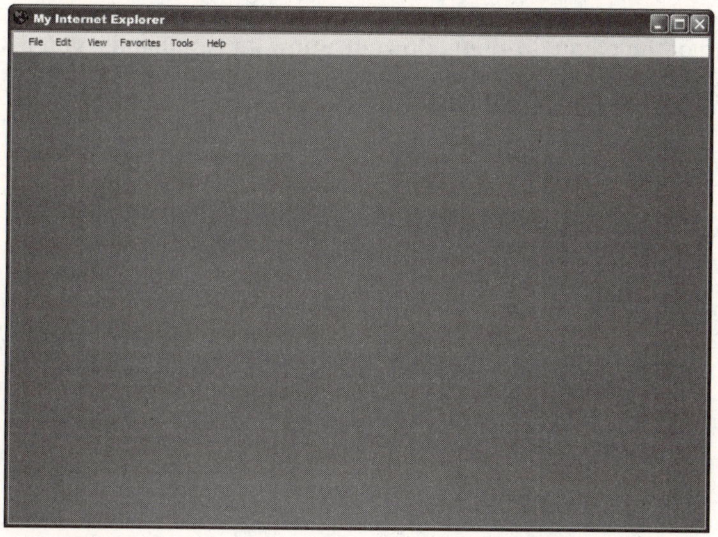

Figure 7-2: A custom browser window with a menu bar installed.

The Menus

To add a menu to your menu bar, click the appropriate command in the Menu Bar toolbox. To add the File menu, for example, click the File command. When you do, a dialog box appears, as shown in Figure 7-3. In this dialog box, you select the commands that you want included in your menu and then click OK. The Browser Construction Kit adds the menu to your menu bar. If you click the Cancel button, the menu doesn't appear in your menu bar.

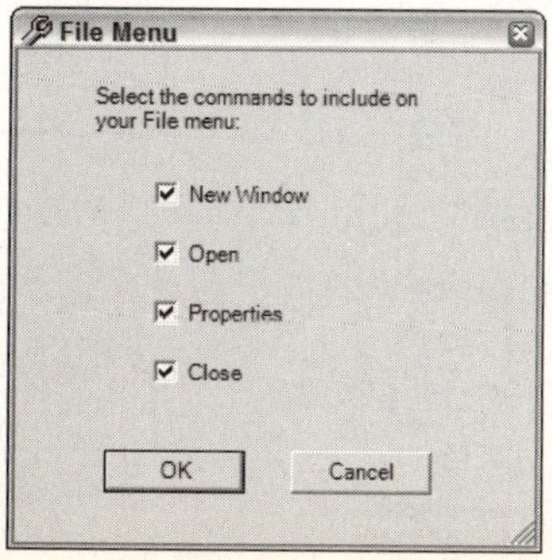

Figure 7-3: The File Menu dialog box.

After you add a menu, another click of the menu's command button removes the menu from the menu bar. If you want to select new commands for the menu or just review the commands you selected, click the menu in the browser's menu bar. The menu's dialog box, where you can make any changes you like, appears.

You may have noticed that the menu bar you add to your browser in the editor doesn't work like a normal menu bar does. When you click a menu, instead of the menu dropping down to show its commands, you get a dialog box instead. Rest assured, however, that the menus in your finished browser function as normal Windows menus.

Chapter 8

Pulling Together the Status Bar

In This Chapter

- Exploring the Status Bar command category
- Adding a status bar
- Specifying a status bar icon
- Adding dates and times
- Implementing a timer

As you work with a Windows application, information about the program appears in various places in the window. These places include not only the window's client area, which displays the application's current document, but also dialog and message boxes. Another area that can show important information about an application is the *status bar,* a small rectangular area usually located at the bottom of the window.

The type of information displayed in a status bar depends on the application. In the case of your custom browser, the status bar can display several informational areas, including time, date, icon, and so on. In this chapter, you find out how to add a status bar to your custom browser's windows.

The Status Bar Command Category

As with all the Browser Construction Kit commands, the status bar commands are organized into their own category. To manipulate your browser's status bar, first select the Status Bar command category in the Browser Construction Kit's editor, as shown in Figure 8-1. When you do, you see the following buttons:

- **Icon:** Adds an icon to the status bar.
- **Clock:** Displays the current time in the status bar.
- **Timer:** Adds a timer to the status bar. This timer keeps track of the amount of time spent online.

- **Date:** Displays the current date in the status bar.
- **Current URL:** Shows the name of the HTML document currently displayed in the browser pane.
- **Status Bar:** Adds a status bar to the window.

When you first switch to the Status Bar commands, only the Status Bar button is enabled. The other buttons are disabled because, until you add a status bar to your window, the other commands have no effect. Makes sense, right?

To add a status bar to your window, follow these steps:

1. **Click the Status Bar button.**

   The Status Bar dialog box, shown in Figure 8-2, appears.

2. **Choose the status bar's location and the image that the Browser Construction Kit uses for the status bar's background.**

   For more information on the status bar's location, please refer to the following section, "Status Bar Position."

3. **Click OK to add the selected status bar to the window.**

   Figure 8-3 shows a custom browser window with a status bar — including all its displays — in place.

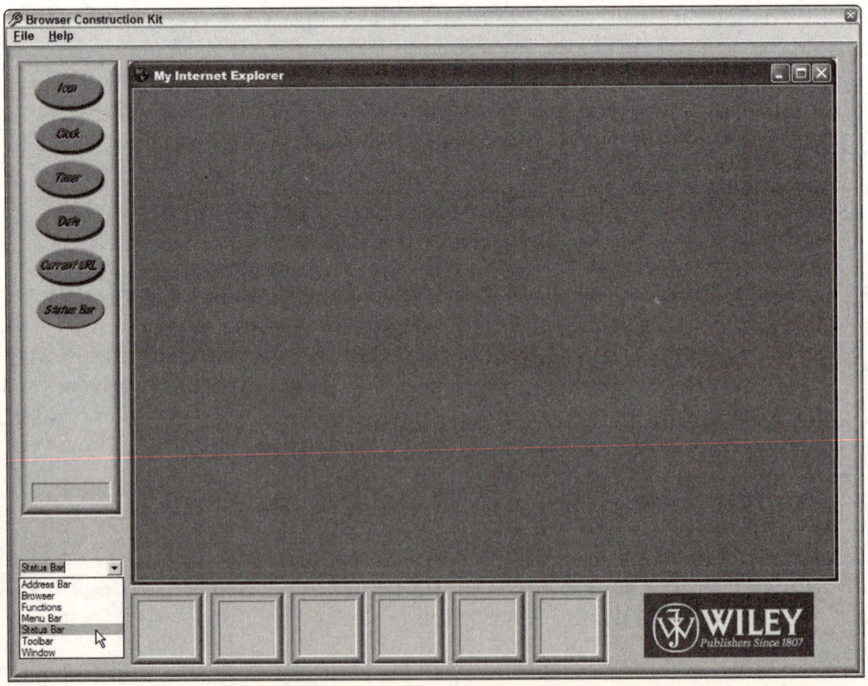

Figure 8-1: Selecting the Status Bar category of commands.

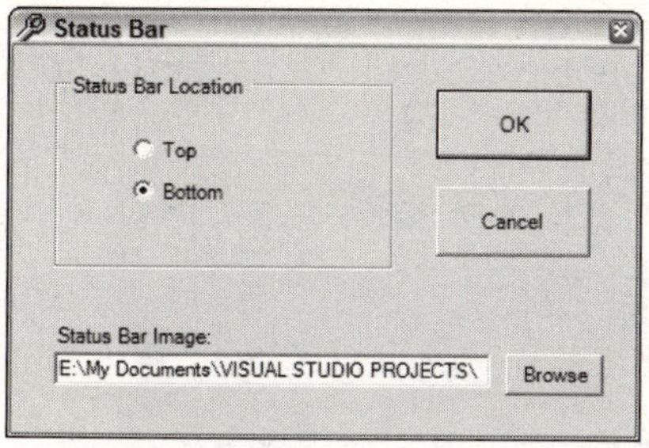

Figure 8-2: The Status Bar dialog box.

Once you add your status bar to the window, the Browser Construction Kit enables the other buttons in the Status Bar toolbox. Until then, you can't select the other commands.

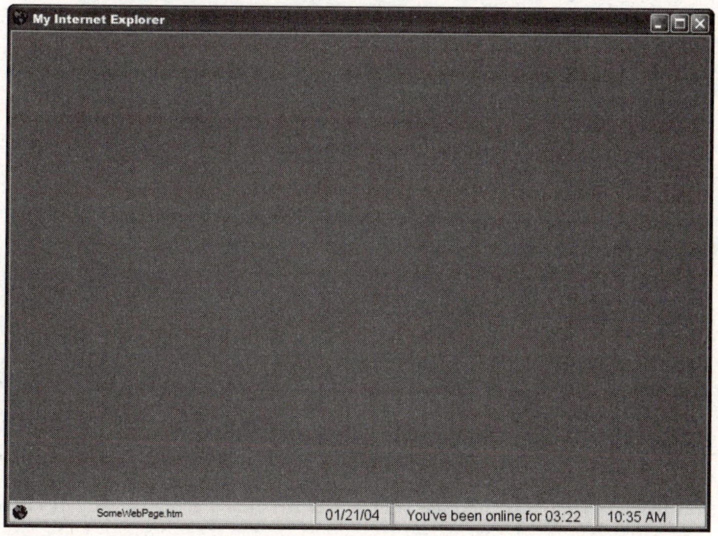

Figure 8-3: A custom browser window with a status bar installed.

Status Bar Position

You can place your status bar in one of two locations: top or bottom. Select the position in the Status Bar dialog box, which appears when you click the Status Bar button in the toolbox.

The most common place for a status bar is the bottom of the window (refer to Figure 8-3). You can, however, create more unusual browser by placing your status bar at the top of the window.

TIP

Although you can place your status bar at the top of the window, I wouldn't suggest it (see Figure 8-4). Most people expect to find it at the bottom.

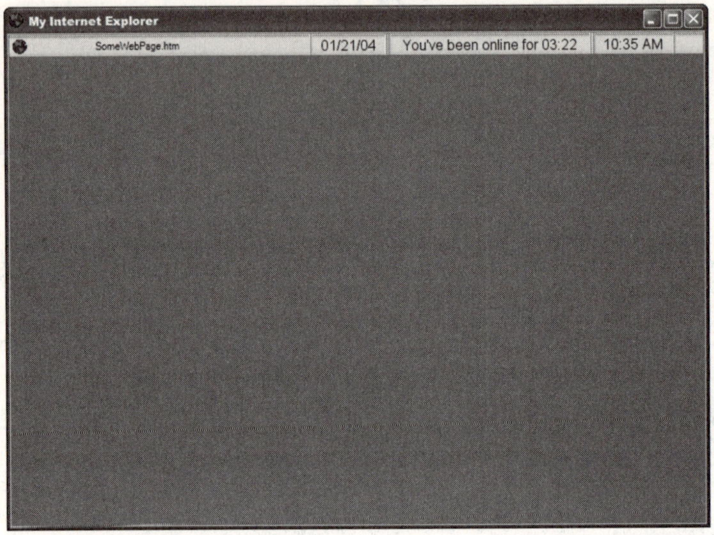

Figure 8-4: The status bar in a somewhat unusual location — the top of the window.

Status Bar Image

When completely assembled, the status bar is a rectangular image that holds a set of displays. You can provide your own image for the status bar's background, choosing from .bmp, .jpg, or .gif images. The image's size is 784 x 42 pixels. For more information about creating your own status bar image, refer to Chapter 14.

TIP

You can choose any size image you want for your status bar, and the Browser Construction Kit will automatically resize it to fit. Resizing an image, though, often leads to image distortion.

To select your status bar image, follow these steps:

1. **Click the Status Bar button in the toolbox.**

   The Status Bar dialog box appears.

2. **Click the Browse button to bring up the Load Status Bar Image dialog box (see Figure 8-5).**

3. **Select your image and click Open.**

   The image's path and filename appear in the Status Bar Image box of the Status Bar dialog box.

4. **Click the dialog box's OK button.**

   The Browser Construction Kit loads the status bar image and adds the status bar to your window.

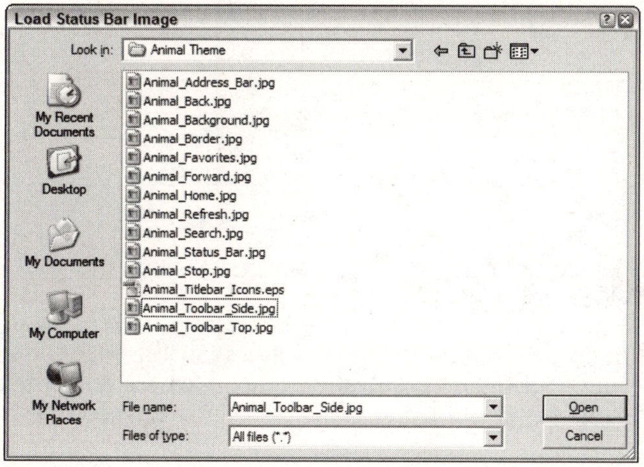

Figure 8-5: The Load Status Bar Image dialog box.

The Status Bar Icon

You can add a small icon to the far left of your status bar. This icon has no functional purpose, but can help you brand your browser (such as with a company logo) or just add an extra image to the browser's graphical theme. Heck, you don't even need a reason. Sometimes an icon just looks cool.

To add an icon to your status bar, perform these steps:

1. **Click the Icon button in the toolbox.**

   The Load Status Bar Icon dialog box, shown in Figure 8-6, appears.

2. **Navigate to the icon you want to use, select it, and click the Open button.**

   The Browser Construction Kit loads the icon into the status bar. Clicking the Icon button a second time removes the icon.

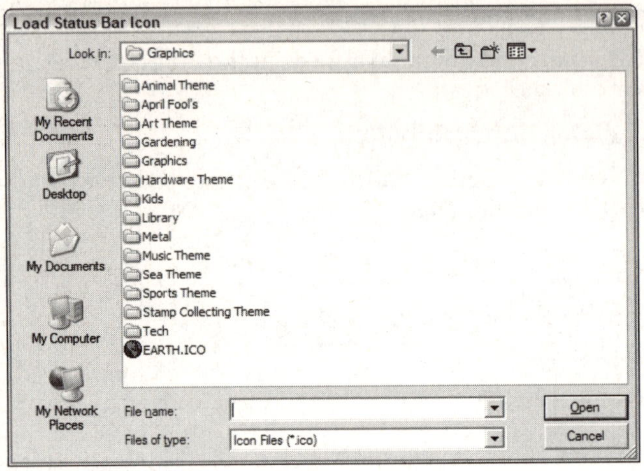

Figure 8-6: The Load Status Bar Icon dialog box.

The Status Bar Clock

The current time can be a handy thing to have available when you're spending time browsing your favorite Web sites. I mean, where does the time go? Seems like you just get started, and suddenly you've missed that haircut appointment.

To help avoid hair-care disasters, add a clock to your browser's status bar. Just click the Clock button in the toolbox, and the Browser Construction Kit adds the clock to the status bar. Clicking the button a second time removes the clock display from the status bar.

REMEMBER

The clock display that appears in your status bar doesn't actually work. What good is that, you ask? Well, when you compile your browser into the real thing, then the clock works fine. In the editor, though, the clock's image is not there to show the time, but only to let you know that you've added the clock to the status bar.

The Status Bar Timer

Similar to a clock, a timer can help you keep track of your online time. Also, if the browser has been set to run only a limited amount of time each day, the timer reports the amount of time used. Specifically, you can set whether the timer shows the time online for the current Internet session or the time remaining before the browser shuts down.

To add a timer to your browser's status bar, click the Timer button in the toolbox. The Browser Construction Kit then displays the Timer Type dialog box (see Figure 8-7), in which you specify one of three types of timer:

- **Session timer:** Shows the amount of time spent online for each Internet session. That is, every time you run the browser, the timer is reset to 0.
- **Daily timer:** Shows the amount of time spent online for the day. This type of timer is not reset to 0 each time you run the browser, but is instead reset the first time the browser is run each day.
- **Countdown timer:** Shows the amount of time remaining before the browser shuts down for the day.

Select the type of timer you want in the dialog box. If you select the countdown timer, you should also type, into the box below the Countdown Timer option, the maximum number of minutes per day allowed online. Click OK, and the Browser Construction Kit adds the timer to your status bar.

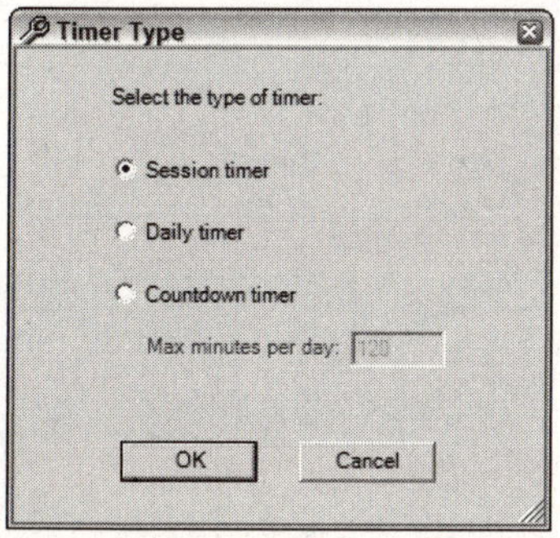

Figure 8-7: The Timer Type dialog box.

TIP: If you want to change the timer settings, click the timer's display in the status bar. When you do, the Timer Type dialog box appears, in which you can make whatever changes you require.

The Status Bar Date

If you spend a *really* long time online, you may not be sure even what day it is. Okay, that probably doesn't happen to anyone except me, but it's always handy to have the date in front of you when you're working on your computer. In case you haven't guessed, you can add a date display to your custom browser's status bar.

To add the date, click the Date button in the toolbox. With little fanfare, the Browser Construction Kit adds a date panel to your status bar. Clicking the button again removes the date from the status bar.

The Current URL

For some strange reason, some people like to see the name of the document that they're currently viewing in the browser pane. Why anyone should care about such minor details is beyond me, but being the reasonable guy I am, I went ahead and added a Current URL display to the status bar's list of cool panels.

To add the current URL display, click the Current URL button in the toolbox. The Browser Construction Kit adds a URL panel to your status bar. As you probably already know (but just in case, I'll tell you anyway), clicking the button again removes the URL display from the status bar.

Chapter 9

Customizing the Address Bar

In This Chapter

- Exploring the Address Bar command category
- Adding an address bar
- Adding a Go button
- Specifying favorite URLs

The address bar is one of the most important elements of your browser window because the address bar is where the browser's user types the URLs to which he wants to connect. Not having an address bar in your browser is a lot like not having a steering wheel in your car. Of course, as is typical with the Browser Construction Kit, you can choose whether you want an address bar. Some custom browsers may not need one. For example, if you're creating a browser that's limited to viewing a single Web site, an address bar is as pointless as a monkey in an aquarium. In this chapter, you find out all about a custom browser's address bar element.

The Address Bar Command Category

As with all the Browser Construction Kit commands, the Kit organizes the address bar commands into their own category, which is, logically enough, named Address Bar. To manipulate your browser's address bar, first select the Address Bar command category in the Browser Construction Kit's editor, as shown in Figure 9-1. When you do, you see the following buttons in the toolbox:

- **Go Button:** Adds a Go button to the address bar. Clicking this button causes the browser to connect with the URL currently entered into the address bar's text box.
- **Favorite 1:** Adds a button that enables the user to quick-select the URL that you've assigned to the button.

- **Favorite 2:** Adds a button that enables the user to quick-select the URL that you've assigned to the button.
- **Favorite 3:** Adds a button that enables the user to quick-select the URL that you've assigned to the button.
- **Favorite 4:** Adds a button that enables the user to quick-select the URL that you've assigned to the button.
- **Address Bar:** Adds an address bar to the window.

When you first switch to the Address Bar commands, only the Address Bar button is enabled. The other buttons are disabled because, until you add an address bar to your window, the other commands have no effect. Go ahead and try clicking them. See. I told you they don't work yet.

To add an address bar to your window, click the Address Bar button. The Address Bar dialog box, seen in Figure 9-2, appears. In this dialog box, you choose the address bar's location and the image that the Browser Construction Kit uses for the address bar's background. Click the OK button to add the selected address bar to the window. Figure 9-3 shows a custom browser window with an address bar — including all its parts — in place.

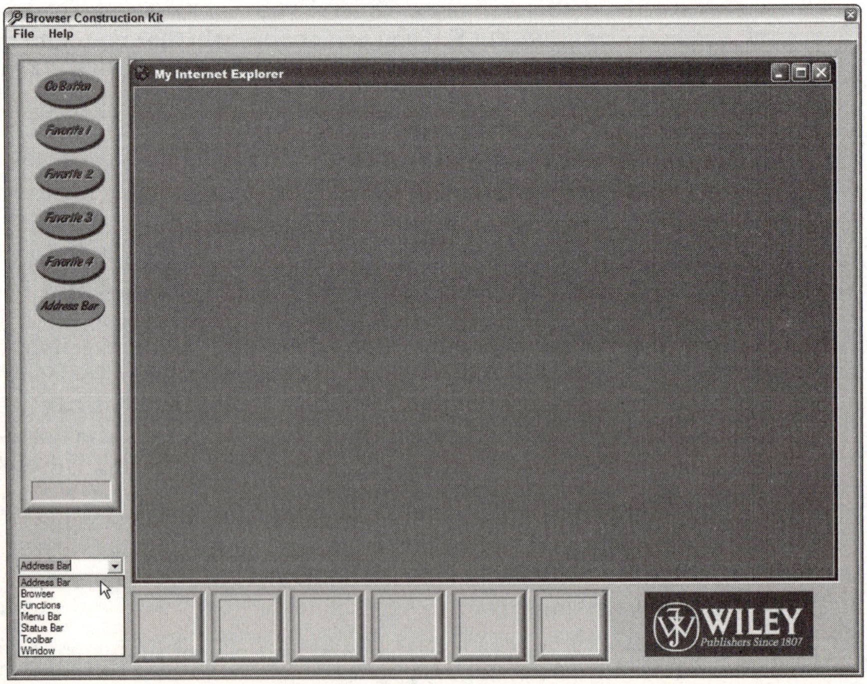

Figure 9-1: Selecting the Address Bar category of commands.

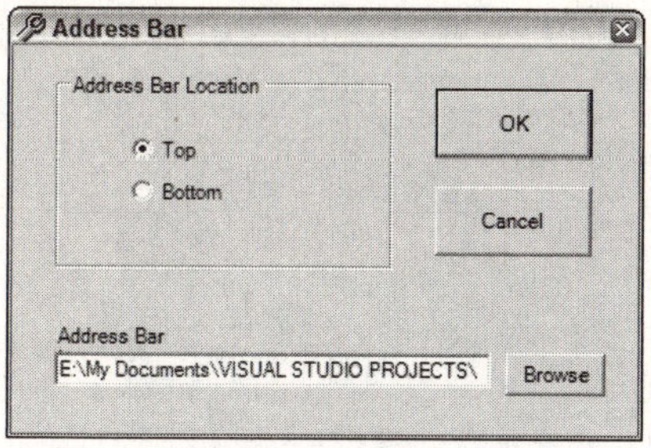

Figure 9-2: The Address Bar dialog box.

Once you add your address bar to the window, the Browser Construction Kit enables the other buttons in the Address Bar toolbox. Until then, the other commands cannot be selected.

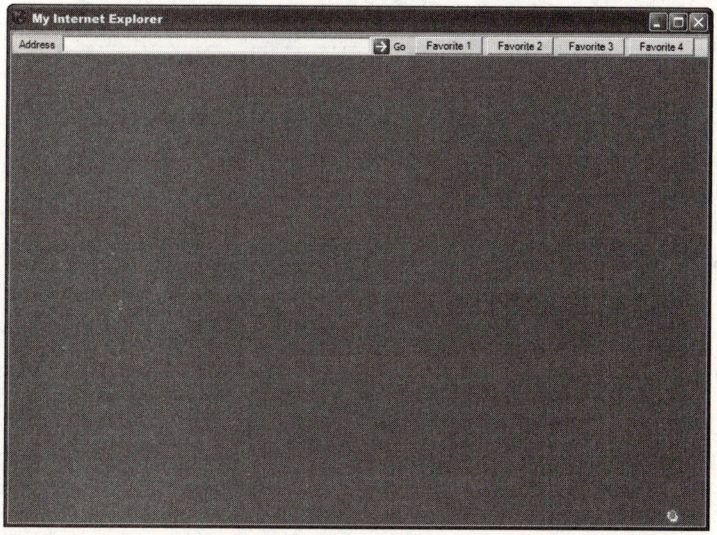

Figure 9-3: A custom browser window with an address bar installed.

Address Bar Position

You can place your address bar in one of two locations: top or bottom. (If your copy of the Browser Construction Kit allows any other positions, you've traveled to the Twilight Zone. Contact me immediately for an interdimensional return ticket.) Select the position in the Address Bar dialog box, which appears when you click the Address Bar button in the toolbox.

The most common place for an address bar is at the top of the window, as shown in Figure 9-3. You can, however, create a more unusual browser by placing your address bar at the bottom of the window (see Figure 9-4).

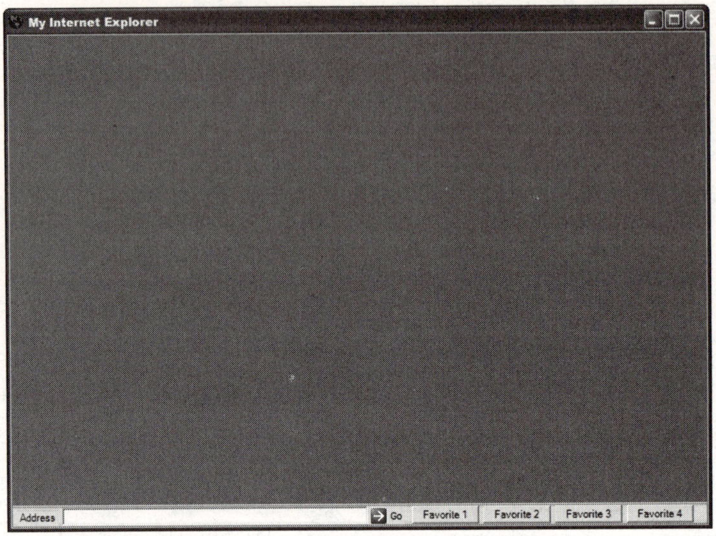

Figure 9-4: The address bar in an uncommon location — the bottom of the window.

TIP: Although you can place your address bar at the bottom of the window, that placement may disorient your users, who expect it at the top. Too bad for them, you say? I agree completely.

Address Bar Image

When completely assembled, the address bar is a rectangular image that holds several other parts, including a text box for entering URLs and some special buttons you read about later in this chapter in the "The Go Button" and "The Favorites Buttons" sections. You can provide your own image for the address bar's background, choosing from .bmp, .jpg, or .gif images. The image's size is 784 x 42 pixels. For more information about creating your own address bar image, refer to Chapter 14, which, although it's about status bars, also applies to address bars.

TIP: You can choose any size image you want for your address bar, and the Browser Construction Kit automatically resizes it to fit. Resizing an image, though, often leads to image distortion, something you may want to avoid — or not.

To select your address bar image, follow these steps:

1. **Click the Address Bar button in the toolbox.**

   The Address Bar dialog box appears.

2. **Click the Browse button to bring up the Load Address Bar Image dialog box (see Figure 9-5).**

3. **Select your image and click the Open button.**

   The image's path and filename appear in the Address Bar Image box of the Address Bar dialog box.

4. **Click the dialog box's OK button.**

   The Browser Construction Kit loads the address bar image and adds the address bar to your window.

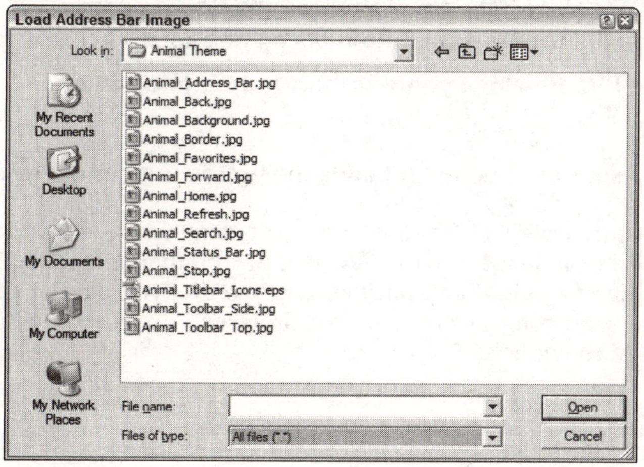

Figure 9-5: The Load Address Bar Image dialog box.

The Go Button

A typical Web browser enables you to browse to the address bar's currently selected URL in two ways:

- Entering the URL into the address bar and pressing Enter
- Entering the URL into the address bar and clicking the Go button

When you add an address bar to your custom browser's window, the text box into which you enter an URL comes with it. The Go button, however, does not. You can choose to add the button or leave it out. To add the button, click the Go Button command in the Address Bar toolbox. With no further ado, the Browser Construction Kit adds the Go button to your address bar.

After you add the Go button, you can remove the Go button by clicking the Go Button command a second time.

The Favorites Buttons

Do you ever find yourself typing the same Internet addresses over and over? What a pain, eh? You'll be happy to know that you can add up to four favorites buttons to your address bar. These buttons enable you to get to a favorite Web site with a single mouse click, a pretty cool feature if I do say so myself.

To add a favorites button, follow these steps:

1. **Click one of the favorites buttons (they're called Favorite 1, Favorite 2, Favorite 3, and Favorite 4) in the Address Bar toolbox.**

   When you do, the Favorite Button dialog box appears (see Figure 9-6).

2. **Type the URL to which you want this button to connect.**
3. **Click OK.**

   The Browser Construction Kit adds the button to your address bar.

TIP: You don't have to assign a URL to a favorites button when you add it to the address bar. You can just leave the Favorite Button dialog box blank and click OK. This idea may sound dumb until you realize that you can set the button's URL later, after you compile your custom browser. You can also change a button's URL in the editor.

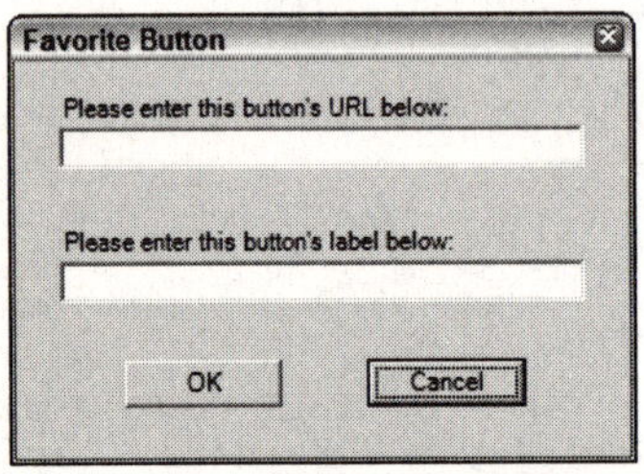

Figure 9-6: Setting a favorite button's associated URL.

When you add a favorites button, clicking the Favorites command again removes the button from the address bar. If you need to change the button's setting, just click the button in the address bar, and the Favorite Button dialog box appears, into which you can type a new URL.

Part III

Creating Browser Graphics

"Guess who found a Kiss merchandise site on the Web while you were gone?"

In this part . . .

Much of what makes a custom browser unique is the graphical elements you choose to use. Components such as a browser's border, background, and toolbar display graphics that you can create with a paint program. In Part III, you discover how to create these graphical elements, using Paint Shop Pro, one of the best paint programs out there. The best news is that a trial version of Paint Shop Pro is included on this book's CD so that you can dive right into the creation of custom browser graphics.

Chapter 10

Introducing Paint Shop Pro

In This Chapter

- Finding Paint Shop Pro
- Installing Paint Shop Pro
- Running Paint Shop Pro for the first time

One of the most important elements of your custom browser is the graphics. Although this book's CD-ROM includes many themes that you can use for your custom-browser projects, sooner or later, you're going to want to create your own. From a mechanical point of view, this task is fairly easy, but, of course, the end result depends on your artistic skill and the skill with which you use your graphical software tools. I can't help you with the former, but I can get you started with the latter. In this chapter, I introduce you to Paint Shop Pro, a program you can use to create custom graphics for your Web browsers.

Installing Paint Shop Pro

This book's CD-ROM includes a free trial version of Paint Shop Pro 8.1. Hurray! Before can use Paint Shop Pro, though, it must be installed onto your system. Nothing is ever simple, eh? Perform the following steps to get Paint Shop Pro up and running:

ON THE CD

1. **Find and double-click the psp810entr.exe file in the Paint Shop Pro folder of this book's CD-ROM.**

   The Paint Shop Pro 8 InstallShield Wizard appears on your screen (see Figure 10-1).

2. **Click Next.**

   The program extracts the setup files. The Welcome dialog box, shown in Figure 10-2, appears.

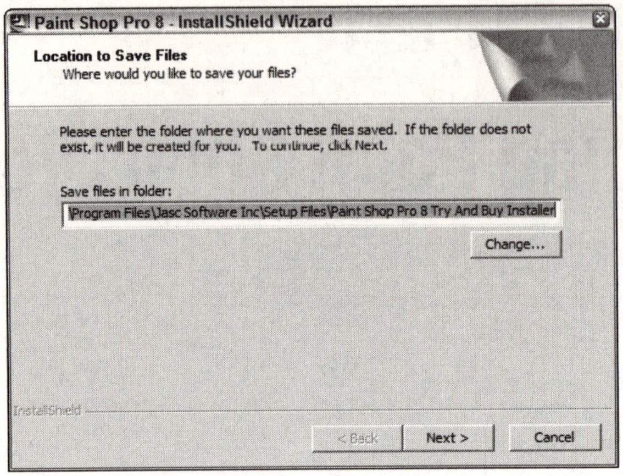

Figure 10-1: The Paint Shop Pro InstallShield Wizard.

3. **Click Next.**

   The software's license agreement appears on your screen (see Figure 10-3).

4. **Select the "I accept" option and then click Next.**

   The Customer Information dialog box appears (see Figure 10-4).

Figure 10-2: The Welcome dialog box.

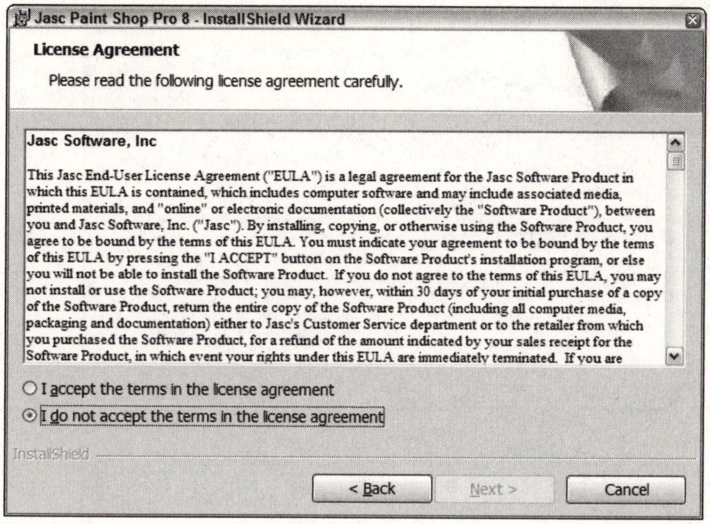

Figure 10-3: Paint Shop Pro's license agreement.

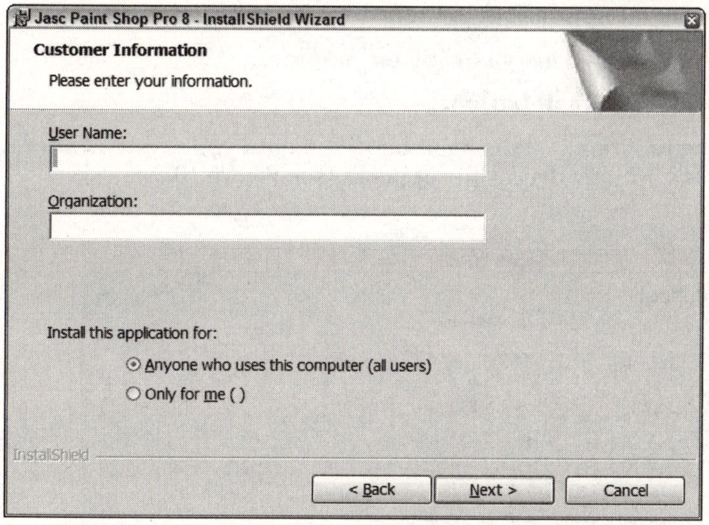

Figure 10-4: Paint Shop Pro's Customer Information form.

5. **Type your name in the User Name box and click Next.**

   You can also choose whether to install the software for just yourself or for everyone using the computer.

   The Custom Setup dialog box, shown in Figure 10-5, appears.

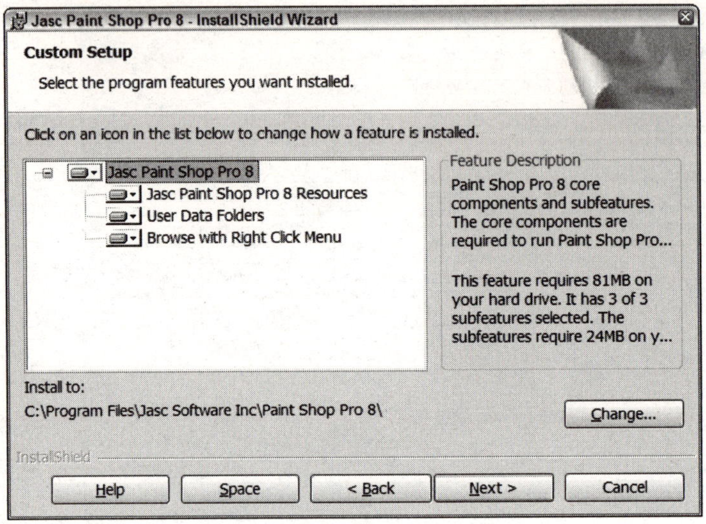

Figure 10-5: The Custom Setup dialog box.

6. **Leave all options set to their defaults and click Next.**

   The Ready To Install dialog box appears.

7. **Click the Install button.**

   The program installs Paint Shop Pro onto your system, after which the User Options dialog box appears (see Figure 10-6).

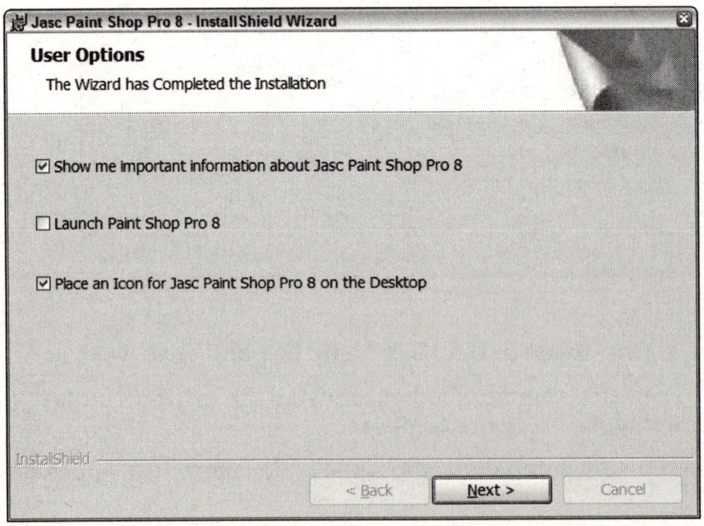

Figure 10-6: The User Options dialog box.

8. **Leave the options set to their defaults and click Next.**

   The Jasc Software Electronic Registration dialog box appears, as seen in Figure 10-7.

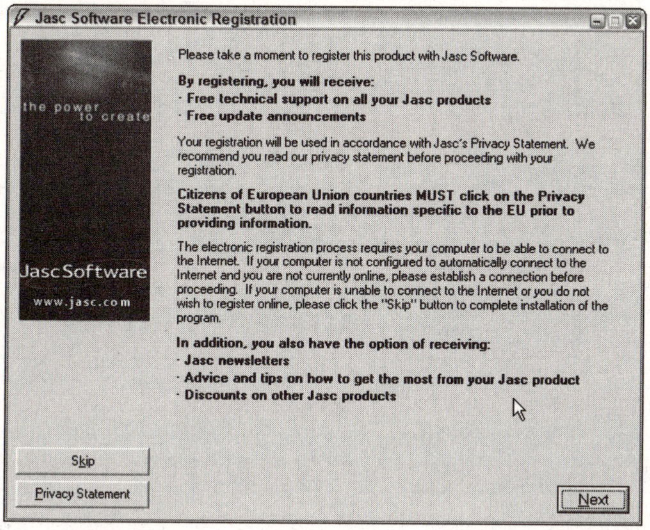

Figure 10-7: The Electronic Registration dialog box.

9. **Click Next.**

   The registration form appears, as shown in Figure 10-8.

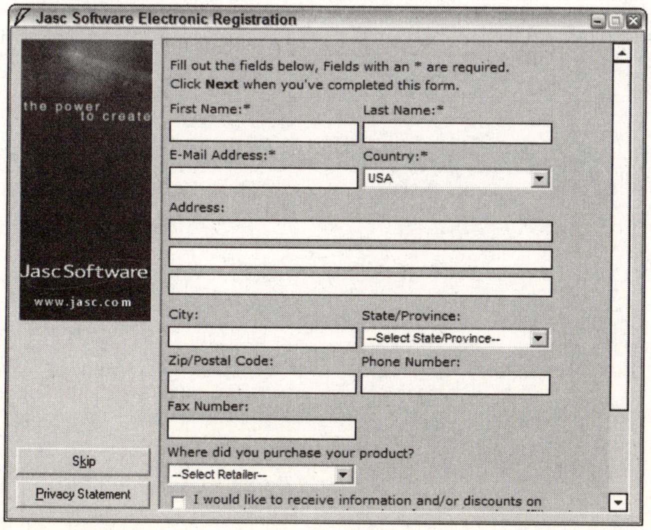

Figure 10-8: Paint Shop Pro's registration form.

10. **Type the required information and then click Next.**

    The registration confirmation screen appears, as shown in Figure 10-9.

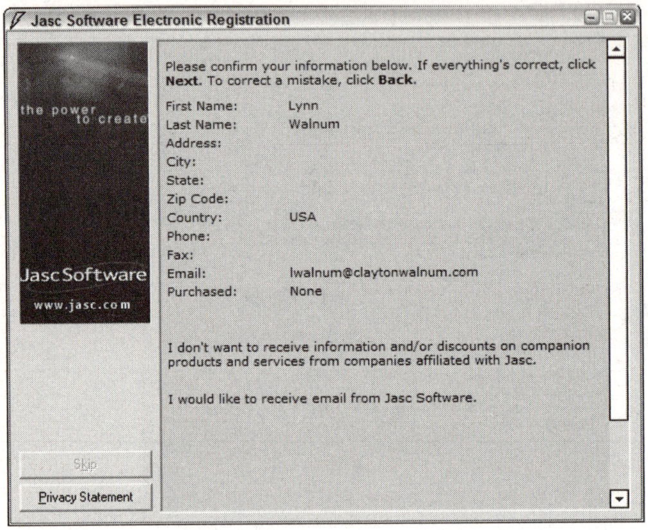

Figure 10-9: The registration confirmation screen.

11. **Scroll down to the bottom of the information and click Next.**

    The thank-you box appears, as shown in Figure 10-10.

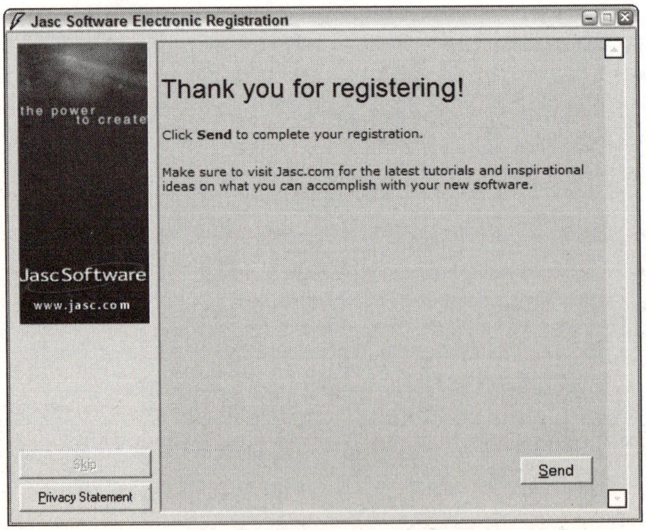

Figure 10-10: The registration thank-you box.

12. **Make sure that you're connected to the Internet and then click Send.**

    The program sends your registration information to Jasc Software, after which the InstallShield Wizard Complete screen appears.

13. **Click Finish to finalize the installation.**

Running Paint Shop Pro

When you installed Paint Shop Pro, an icon for the program should have appeared on your desktop. You can run Paint Shop Pro by double-clicking this icon. You can also run Paint Shop Pro by choosing it from your Start menu. Choose Start⇨Programs⇨Jasc Software⇨Jasc Paint Shop Pro 8.

When Paint Shop Pro appears on-screen, click the Start button in the *splash window,* which shows you information about a program while the program is loading. Then close the File Format Associations dialog box and the Learning Center dialog box by clicking the X in each window's upper-right corner. You then have a screen that looks like Figure 10-11.

Even after dismissing it from the screen, you can access the Learning Center at any time from the Paint Shop Pro Help menu. You can access the file associations by choosing File⇨Preferences.

The large gray area in the center of the window is where you work on your images. To create a new image, choose File⇨New. The New Image dialog box appears, in which you can set the basic attributes for the new image. The new image appears as a window in the gray area of Paint Shop Pro's screen. You can have several image windows open at once. You can even cut and paste between the different windows.

To work on images, you need graphical tools. If you look on the left side of Paint Shop Pro's screen, you see the toolbox, from which you can access the tools. Starting from the top of the toolbox, the tools are as follows:

- **Pan tool:** Drags image view into new positions, as well as provides access to zooming and sizing functions.
- **Deform tool:** Twists, turns, and warps an image.
- **Crop tool:** Crops images (cuts out a portion of an image, throwing away everything else).
- **Move tool:** Moves elements of an image. Also provides access to zooming and sizing functions.
- **Selection tool:** Selects rectangular or irregular shaped areas of an image.
- **Dropper:** Selects colors or replaces one color with another.

- **Paint Brush tool:** Draws on an image, as a paintbrush, an airbrush, or a warp brush (smears colors).
- **Clone Brush tool:** Creates a paint brush from a portion of an image. Also provides access to the Scratch Remover tool.
- **Dodge Brush tool:** Applies special brush effects such as burn, smudge, soften, sharpen, and emboss.
- **Lighten/Darken Brush tool:** Applies color effects such as lighten, darken, saturation change, and hue change.
- **Eraser tool:** Erases foreground or background image data.
- **Picture Tube tool:** Stamps graphical images into the image window.
- **Flood Fill tool:** Fills areas of an image with color, patterns, and gradients.
- **Text tool:** Adds lines of text to an image.
- **Preset Shape tool:** Draws predefined shapes, such a circles, rectangles, stars, arrows, hexagons, and so on.
- **Pen tool:** Draws various types of lines.
- **Object Selection tool:** Selects vector graphic objects.

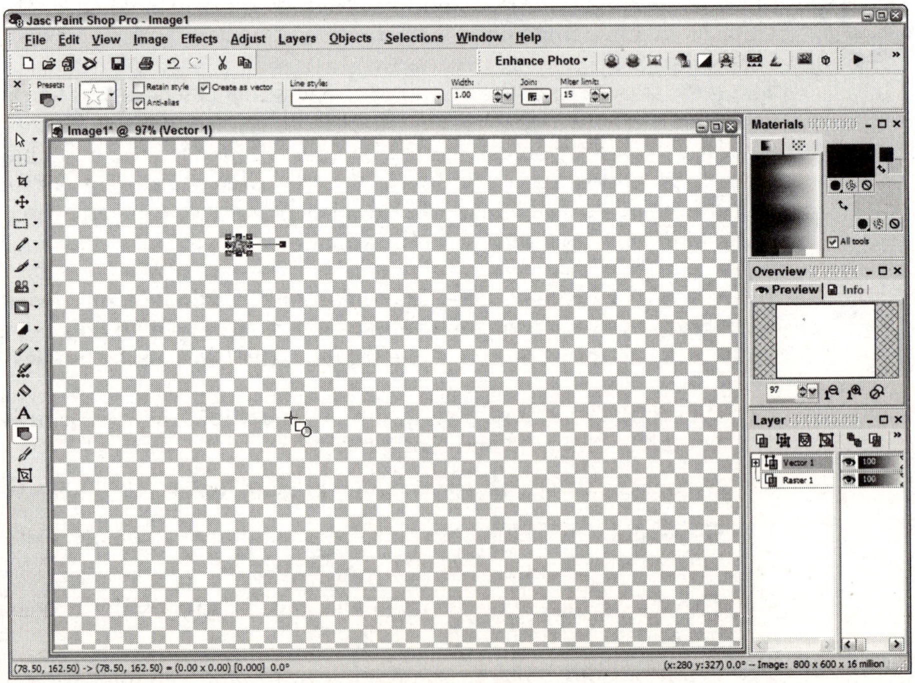

Figure 10-11: Paint Shop Pro's main screen.

The commands in the toolbars across the top of the window change depending on the tool you select. On the right side of the screen, you can view and change some attributes of the image on which you're working, as well as see a thumbnail view of your image and choose between the different layers of which the image is comprised.

In Paint Shop Pro, a *layer* is a graphical element that you can superimpose over another element. You can think of layers as transparencies that, when stacked together, create the final image. Using layers enables you to manipulate one part of an image without affecting another, even if the layers have graphical elements that overlap.

The tools and commands discussed in this chapter are only the tip of the iceberg. As you work with Paint Shop Pro, you'll discover a wealth of techniques for creating the perfect images for your custom browser. For more information on these techniques, please refer to the remaining chapters in this part of the book.

Chapter 11

Jazzing Up Your Browser with Borders

In This Chapter

- Creating a blank border image
- Filling an image with color
- Changing a rectangle to 3-D
- Adding details to the border image

Not every custom Web browser you build needs fancy border graphics, but when you decide to use borders, you want them to be attractive. You may think that you need to be an artist to create attractive graphical elements for your browsers, but that's not necessarily the case. Paint Shop Pro is readily suited for the task and can provide artistic help. In this chapter, you find out how to create borders, as well as discover a few handy graphical tips.

Understanding Border Requirements

Creating a custom border is a fairly easy task, but it does require several steps. A little artistic know-how doesn't hurt either, but Paint Shop Pro's powerful functions — once you know how to use them — can help even the most fumble-fingered artist turn out a decent border. (If you can use a little help with Paint Shop Pro, refer to Chapter 10.) If you don't believe me, you're in for a big surprise as you work through this chapter's border project.

REMEMBER

The most important things to know when creating graphics for a custom browser are the size and color depth measurements you need. The following list summarizes these attributes for a border:

- Width of 784 pixels
- Height of 32 pixels
- Resolution of 200 pixels per centimeter
- Color depth of 16 million colors (24-bit color)

WARNING! If you create your browser border with a different size or resolution, you may see some distortion when you load it into your browser. That's because the browser automatically resizes the graphics to fit inside it. The color depth is most important when working with Paint Shop Pro. After finishing your graphic, you can save it with a different color depth.

Starting a New Border

To create a border, you must start with a blank image of the correct resolution. Here's how:

1. **Choose File⇨New.**

   The New Image dialog box appears, as shown in Figure 11-1.

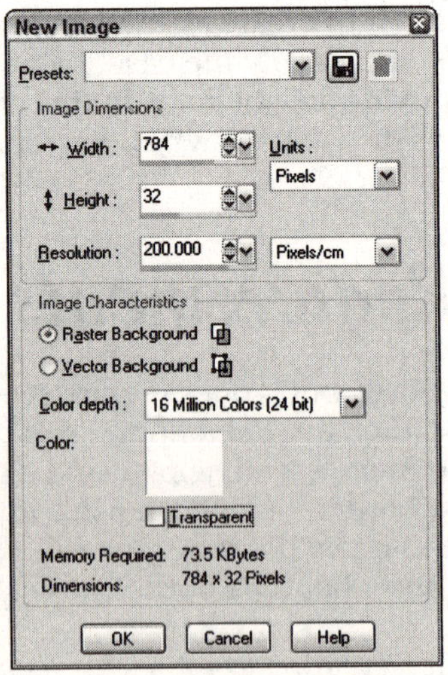

Figure 11-1: The New Image dialog box.

2. **From the Units box, select Pixels.**

   This option may be already set to this value.

3. **Using the scroll arrows, change the width to 784.**

4. **Change the height to 32.**
5. **Set the resolution to 200 Pixels/cm.**

   This option is probably already set to this value.
6. **In the Image Characteristics area, select the Raster Background option.**
7. **In the Color Depth drop-down list, choose 16 Million Colors.**

   Again, this option is probably already set to this value.
8. **Make sure that the Color box is set to white.**

   To set the color, if necessary, click the box and then choose the color from the dialog box that appears.
9. **Make sure that the Transparent checkbox is not selected.**
10. **Click OK.**

    Paint Shop Pro creates a blank image for your new border, as shown in Figure 11-2.
11. **Save this image under a name like BlankBorder.**

    You can then use this file as a template for starting new borders. Just load the template, choose File⇨Save As, and save the template under a new name.

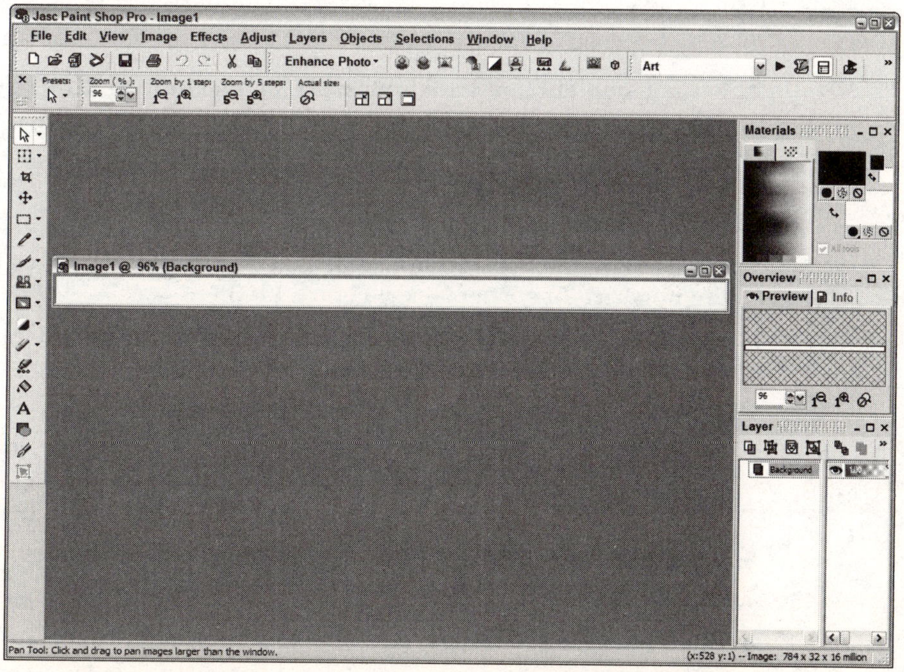

Figure 11-2: The new image's window in Paint Shop Pro's work area.

Eleven steps may seem like a lot just to get a blank image up on the screen, but once you get used to the settings, it takes only a couple of seconds to create a new image.

Filling the Background

After you have a new blank image to work with (see the preceding section), you're ready to really dig into Paint Shop Pro. For this first border, you create a simple 3-D bar. But first you need a rectangle filled with a background color. Follow these steps to get the job done:

1. **In the toolbox on the left of the window, select the Flood Fill tool.**

   It's the one that looks like a tipped paint bucket.

   The Flood Fill tool's settings appear in the toolbar (see Figure 11-3).

Figure 11-3: The Flood Fill tool's attributes.

2. **In the Flood Fill tool's attributes, set Match Mode to RGB Value.**
3. **Set Tolerance to 0.**
4. **Set Blend Mode to Normal.**
5. **Set Opacity to 100.**
6. **Click inside the Foreground color box (the first of the black boxes in the upper-right corner — see Figure 11-4).**

   The Material dialog box appears, as shown in Figure 11-5. If it isn't already selected, click the Color tab.

7. **Click the light gray square in the color selections.**

   The R, G, and B values should all change to 192. If not, you clicked the wrong color. Try again. You'll use this color as the background color for this particular border. You can use any color you like for other borders.

8. **Click OK.**

   The selected color in the Foreground color box changes to light gray.

9. **Place the tool over the image and click again.**

   Paint Shop Pro fills the image with light gray.

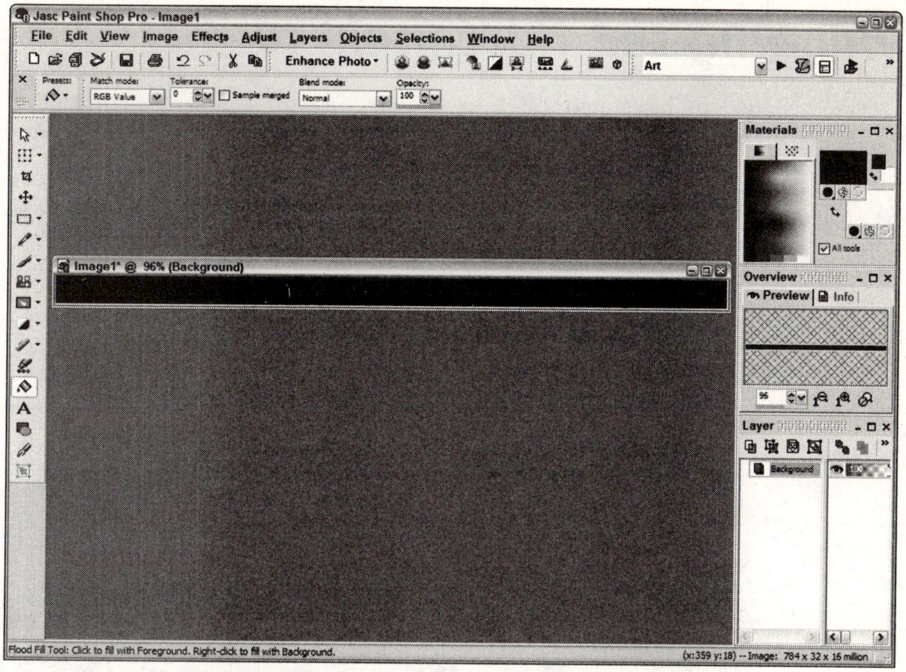

Figure 11-4: The Foreground color box.

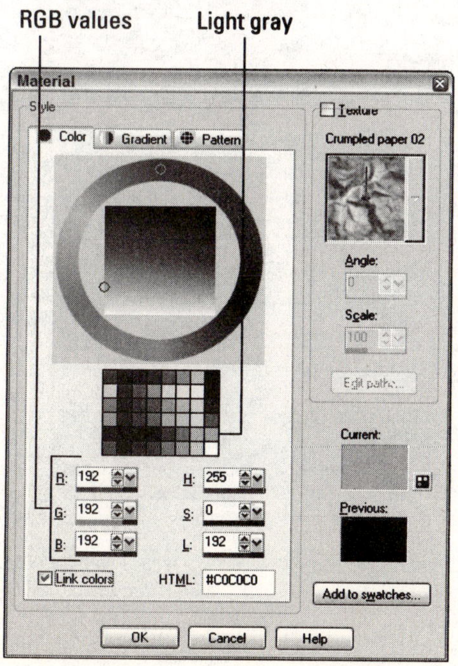

Figure 11-5: The Material dialog box.

Changing the Rectangle to 3-D

After you have a simple border, you can turn it into a 3-D border with just a little more work. Paint Shop Pro helps those people who have little or no artistic talent create pretty cool stuff.

1. **In the Effects menu, place your mouse cursor over the 3D Effects command.**

   The 3D Effects menu appears (see Figure 11-6).

2. **Choose Buttonize.**

   The Buttonize dialog box appears (see Figure 11-7).

3. **Change the Height setting to 5.**
4. **Change the Width setting to 5.**
5. **Select the Transparent edge.**

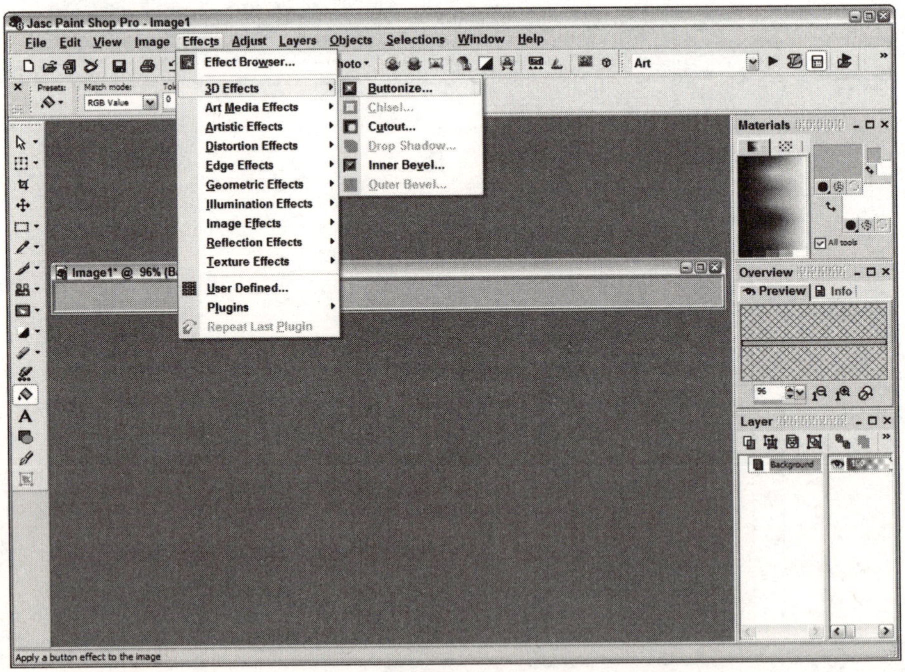

Figure 11-6: The 3D Effects submenu.

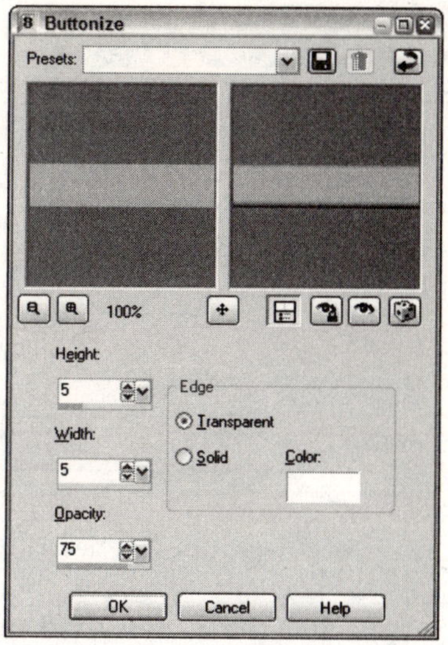

Figure 11-7: The Buttonize effect settings.

6. **Change the Opacity setting to 75.**

   As you change the settings, the pane to the right, in the dialog box, previews the result of the settings on the image.

7. **Click OK.**

   Paint Shop Pro applies the effect, giving you the border shown in Figure 11-8. Awesome!

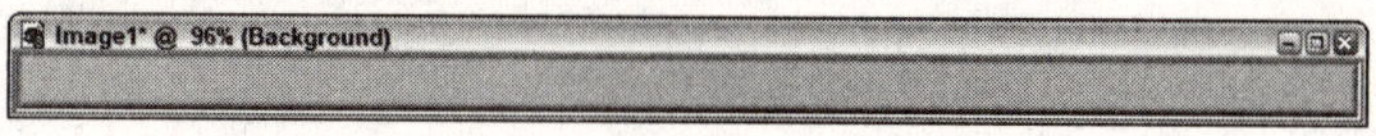

Figure 11-8: The buttonized border.

Painting a 3-D Rivet

Your simple 3-D border already looks good, but you can make it look even better by adding a couple of details. In this section, you add two rivets to the 3-D rectangle so that it looks as if it's been attached to the screen. Of course, to pull off this embellishment, you need to be an accomplished artist. Well, not really. Anyone who can click an on-screen button can add the rivets. These steps show you how to add two rivets:

1. **Create a new blank image with a size of 24 x 24 pixels. Also, in the Image Characteristics box, select the Transparent option.**

   The new image appears in Paint Shop Pro's work area.

2. **Click the Pan tool (the top tool in the toolbox, the one that looks like an arrow mouse cursor).**

   The tool's settings appear in the toolbar near the top of the window (see Figure 11-9).

Figure 11-9: The Pan tool settings.

3. **In the box labeled Zoom By 5 Steps, click the 5+ selection twice.**

   Paint Shop Pro magnifies the new 24 x 24 image to ten times its original size (see Figure 11-10).

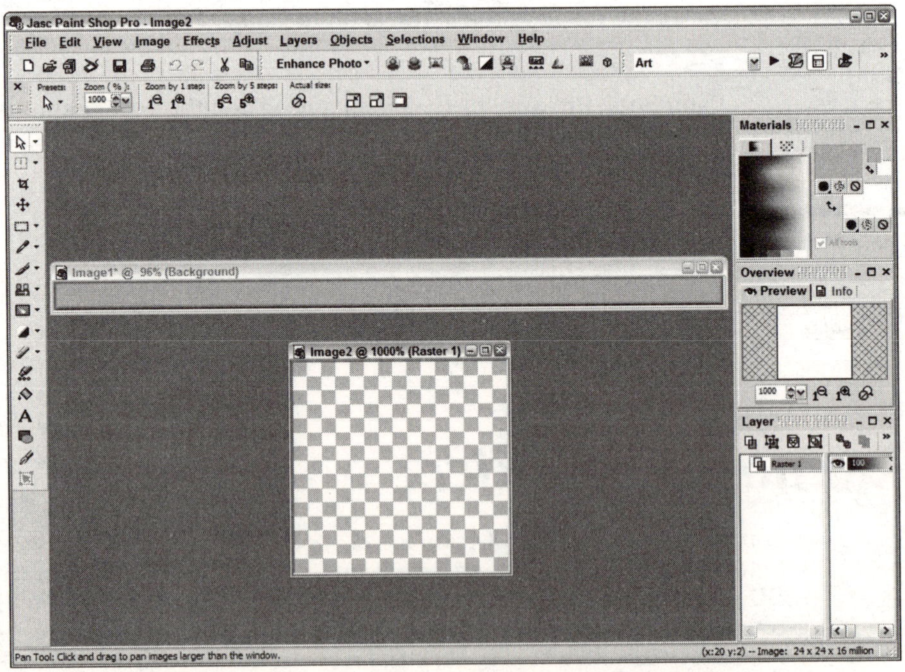

Figure 11-10: The magnified image.

4. **Click the Preset Shape tool in the toolbox.**

   The Preset Shape tool is the third tool from the bottom, the one that looks like an oval on top of a rectangle.

   The tool's settings appear in the toolbar, as shown in Figure 11-11.

Figure 11-11: The Preset Shape tool settings.

5. **In the drop-down list to the left of the toolbar, make sure that Ellipse is selected.**
6. **Deselect the Retain Style option and deselect the Create As Vector option.**
7. **In the upper-right corner of Paint Shop Pro's window, make sure both boxes in the Material pane (where you previously set the gray color) are set to the same light gray color.**

   You'll probably have to change the second one from white to gray. (If you're not sure how to change colors, refer to the previous section.) The first box controls the color of the shape's outline, and the second box controls the color of the fill.
8. **Place the mouse cursor in the 24 x 24 image's upper-left corner and, while holding down the left mouse button, drag the cursor to the lower-right corner, releasing the button when you're done.**

   A light-gray, filled circle appears in the image's window, as shown in Figure 11-12. (Ignore the gray checkerboard in the background. That's just the pattern Paint Shop Pro uses to display a transparent background.)

Figure 11-12: The filled circle.

9. **Choose Effects⇨3D Effects⇨Inner Bevel.**

   The Inner Bevel dialog box, shown in Figure 11-13, appears.

10. **Set the Width box to 4.**
11. **Set Smoothness to 0.**
12. **Set Depth to 15.**
13. **Set Ambience to -25.**
14. **Set Shininess to 0.**
15. **Set Angle to 315.**
16. **Set Intensity to 50.**
17. **Set Elevation to 30.**

    Note that the preview pane to the right shows the result of the settings on your image.

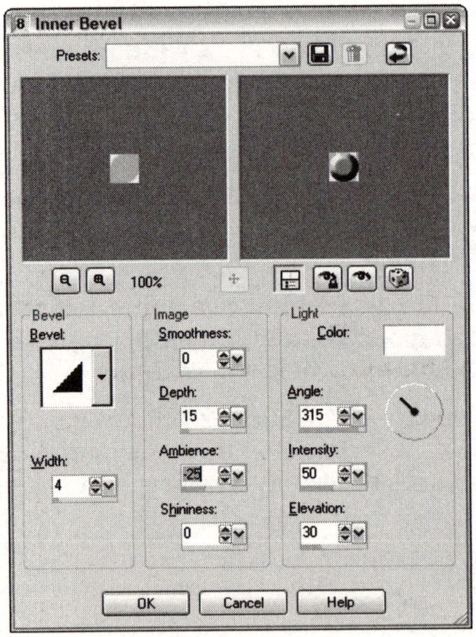

Figure 11-13: The Inner Bevel dialog box.

18. **Click OK.**

    Paint Shop Pro applies your settings, changing your simple circle into a rivet (see Figure 11-14).

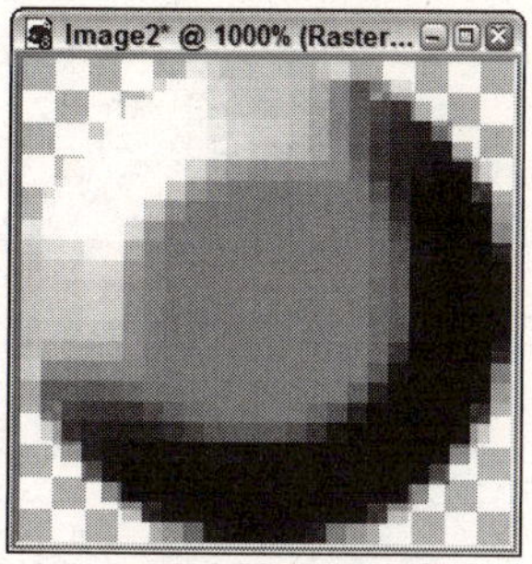

Figure 11-14: Your new rivet graphic.

Adding the Rivet to the Border

If you have two images, a 3-D rectangle and a rivet graphic, you're ready to combine everything into a single browser border. Just follow these steps:

1. **Select the entire rivet image.**

   To do so, choose Selections⇨Select All or press Ctrl+A on your keyboard. An animated outline appears around the rivet to indicate that it's been selected.

2. **Choose Edit⇨Copy (or just press Ctrl+C) to copy your image to the Clipboard.**

3. **Click the 784 x 32 rectangle title bar to select that window.**

4. **Paste the copied rivet graphic into the 3-D rectangle's window.**

   To perform this paste, either choose Edit⇨Paste⇨Paste As New Selection or press Ctrl+E. The rivet image appears under the mouse pointer. (If it doesn't, be sure that your mouse pointer is over the 3-D rectangle.)

5. **Use your mouse to position the rivet near the left end of the rectangle and click the left mouse button to paste it there.**

   Paint Shop Pro drops the image in the selected location.

6. **Paste another copy of the rivet into the window.**

7. **Position this rivet at the other end of the border graphic.**

8. **Deselect the rivet image.**

   To deselect a selection, choose Selections⇨Select None or press Ctrl+D.

   Paint Shop Pro deselects the second rivet image in the border. Figure 11-15 shows the completed border image.

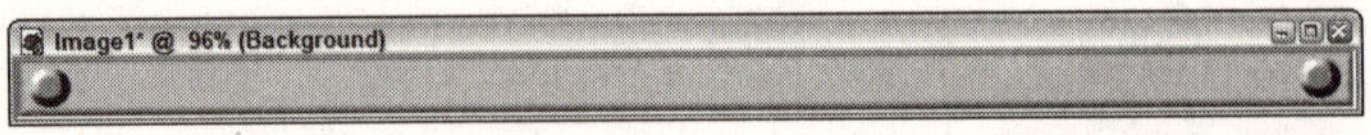

Figure 11-15: The finished border.

Saving the Border

Once your image is complete, you need to save it to your hard drive. Here's how:

1. **Choose File⇨Save As.**

   The Save As dialog box appears, as shown in Figure 11-16.

2. **In the Save In drop-down list, browse to the folder where you want to save your new border.**

3. **In the File Name box, type the name you want for the border (like maybe RivetBorder).**

Figure 11-16: The Save As dialog box.

4. **In the Save As Type box, select CompuServe Graphics Interchange (*.gif), as shown in Figure 11-17, and then click Save.**

   Paint Shop Pro saves the image to your hard drive. (If you're asked whether it's okay to reduce the colors to 256, answer Yes.)

TIP

To better organize your graphics, create a special folder for your browser images.

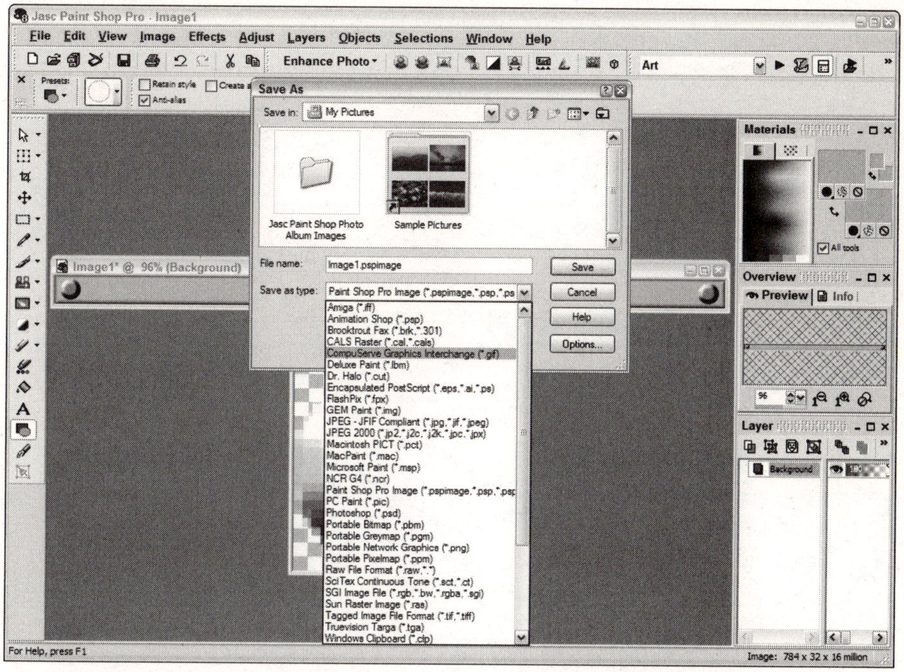

Figure 11-17: Save your image in the CompuServe Graphics Interchange (*.gif) file format.

Chapter 12

Painting Skins

In This Chapter

- Creating a blank skin image
- Filling an image with textures
- Adding patterns to an image
- Blending colors into an image

If you've created any custom browsers with the Browser Construction Kit, you already know that such a browser can have a graphical background that I refer to as a skin. Paint Shop Pro (and most other full-featured paint programs) supports all the techniques you need to create such backgrounds. In this chapter, you find out how to use Paint Shop Pro to create browser skins.

Understanding Skin Requirements

Just as with every other graphical element that you can use with your custom browsers, a skin must be of a certain size and resolution. Moreover, starting with a 24-bit image (one that can display 16 million colors) ensures that the image is compatible with any graphical processing you want to perform. That being said, here are the specific requirements for a browser background, or *skin* as I call it:

- Width of 784 pixels
- Height of 559 pixels
- Resolution of 200 pixels per centimeter
- Color depth of 16 million colors (24-bit color)

WARNING!

If you create your browser skin with a different size or resolution, you may see some distortion when you load it into your browser. This distortion results because the browser automatically resizes the graphics to fit. The 24-bit color depth is mainly for use with Paint Shop Pro, so you can use the most options when creating your image. When saving the final image, you can use any color depth you want.

Starting a Skin

The previous section covers the size and resolution requirements for creating a custom browser skin. The following steps lead you through the creation of such an image:

1. **Choose File⇨New.**

   The New Image dialog box appears, as shown in Figure 12-1.

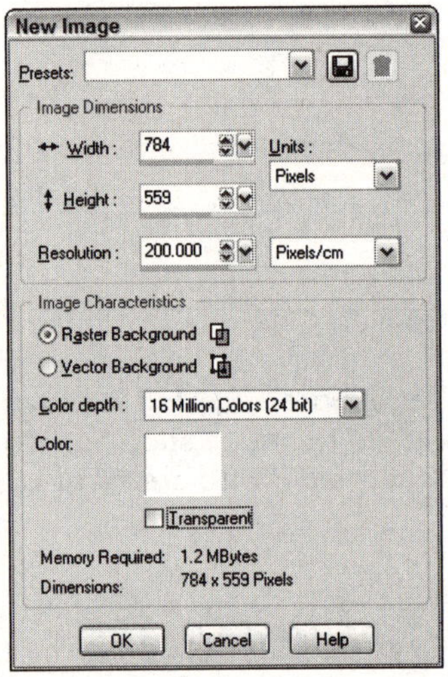

Figure 12-1: The New Image dialog box with the appropriate settings for a browser skin.

2. **Using the drop-down list, set the Units box to Pixels.**
3. **Change the width to 784.**
4. **Change the height to 559.**
5. **Set the resolution to 200 Pixels/cm.**

   This option is probably already set to this value.

6. **Make sure that the Raster Background option is selected.**
7. **Set the Color Depth box to 16 Million Colors.**

   Again, this option is probably already set to this value.

8. **Make sure that the Color box is set to white and the Transparent option isn't selected.**
9. **Click OK.**

   Paint Shop Pro creates a blank image for your new background, as shown in Figure 12-2.

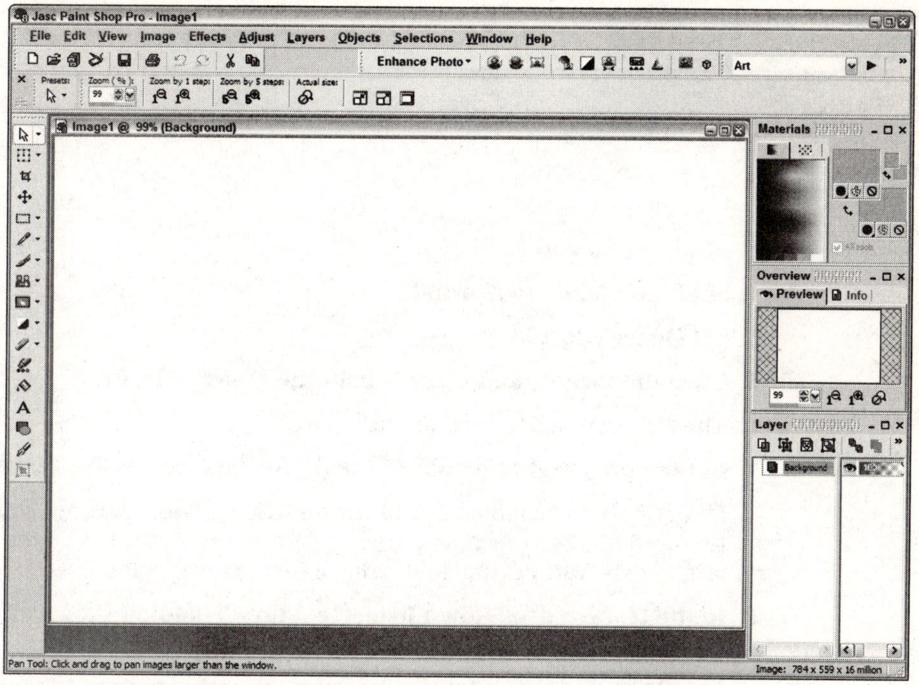

Figure 12-2: The new skin image's window in Paint Shop Pro's work area.

10. **Save your work.**

    If you've never saved the image before, the Save As dialog box appears, in which you must give your image a filename and select the image-format type. I suggest the .jpg image type.

Filling a Background with a Texture

A plain white background isn't too exciting for a browser skin. (Talk about stating the obvious!) Paint Shop Pro can help you make the background more stimulating in a number of ways. One of the easiest fixes is to add a textured fill to the image. Follow these steps to get the job done:

1. **In the toolbox on the left of the window, select the Flood Fill tool.**

   This tool looks like a tipped paint bucket. The Flood Fill tool's settings appear in the toolbar, as shown in Figure 12-3.

2. **In the Flood Fill tool's attributes, make sure that Match Mode is set to RGB Value.**

Figure 12-3: The Flood Fill tool's attributes.

3. **Set Tolerance to 0.**
4. **Set Blend Mode to Normal.**
5. **Set Opacity to 100.**
6. **Click the foreground color box in the Materials pane.**

   The Material dialog box appears.
7. **In the upper-right portion of the dialog box, select the Texture option.**

   Paint Shop Pro enables the Texture settings. With textures, you can add textured fills to your images, which are often better suited for filling large areas, rather than just using a blah, single color.
8. **In the texture drop-down list, select the Crumpled Paper 02 texture, as shown in Figure 12-4.**

   The Crumpled Paper texture adds an attractive pattern to your background.
9. **On the Color tab, select the color you want to use for the fill.**

   The Current box, to the right of the colors, shows the selected color with the texture applied.
10. **Click OK to finalize your settings and to close the dialog box.**

    Your texture and color appear in the foreground color box.
11. **Place the Flood Fill tool over the blank image and click.**

    Paint Shop Pro fills the image with the color and texture you selected, as shown in Figure 12-5.
12. **Save your work.**

    If you've never saved the image before, the Save As dialog box appears, in which you must give your image a filename and select the image-format type. I suggest the .jpg image type.

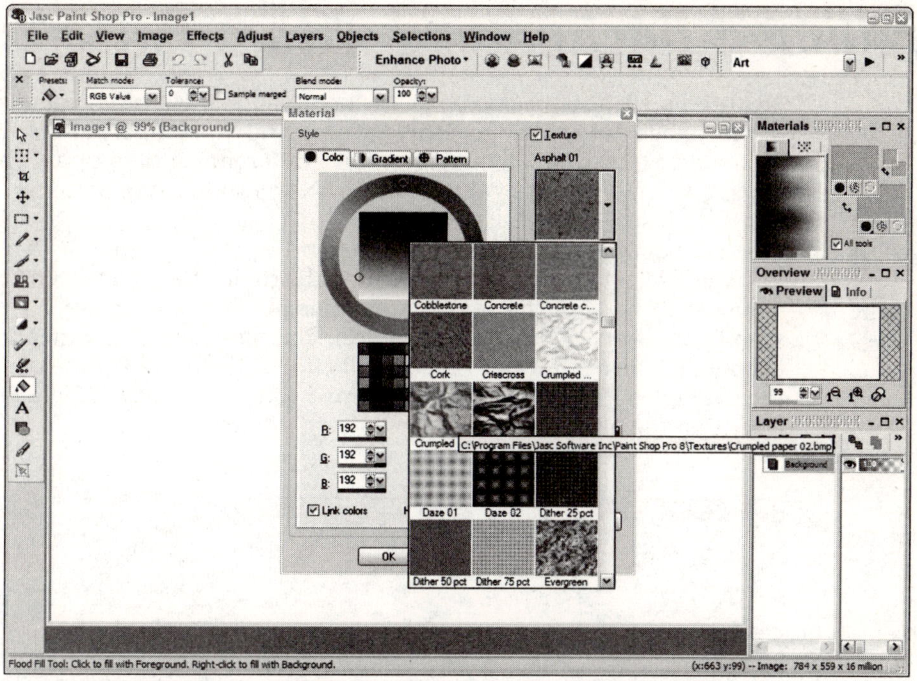

Figure 12-4: Choose your texture.

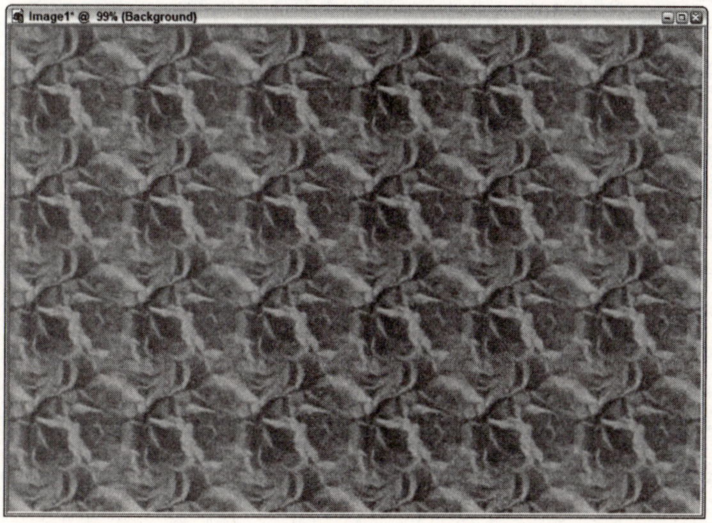

Figure 12-5: The new image filled with the selected texture.

Filling a Background with a Pattern

Textured backgrounds can be just what you need, but often you may want to use an image not available in the texture choices. Using a pattern fill is similar to using a texture fill, but gives you a different set of options. The following steps demonstrate how to create a background using patterns.

REMEMBER

The main difference between a texture and a pattern is that, with a pattern, you can't select a color. Instead, your pattern fills the image using the same colors that the pattern uses. As such, this fill technique is much like filling your image with a photograph. You can combine a pattern with a texture to accomplish an even wider range of fill effects. Figure 12-6, for example, shows the Crumpled Paper 02 texture combined with the Diamond Plate Flat pattern. Note that the fill still takes on the pattern's colors.

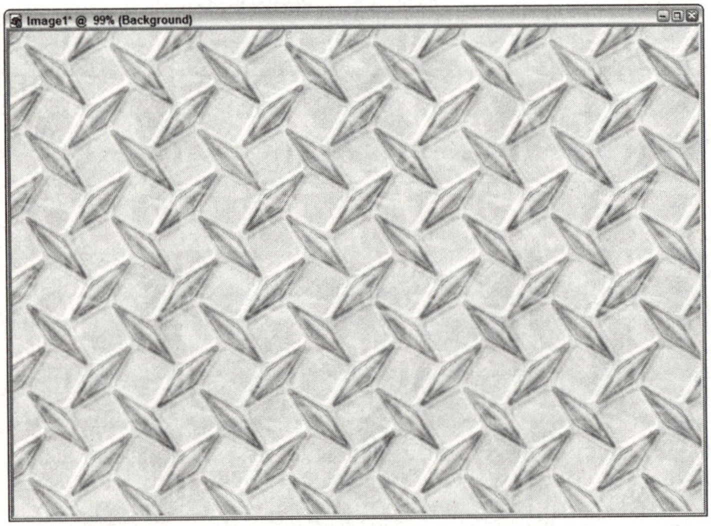

Figure 12-6: Combining textures and patterns.

1. **Create a new 784 x 559 image.**

   If you've forgotten how to do so, see "Starting a Skin," earlier in this chapter.

2. **Select the Flood Fill tool.**

   The Flood Fill tool's settings appear in the toolbar.

3. **In the Flood Fill tool's attributes, make sure that Match Mode is set to RGB Value.**

4. **Set Tolerance to 0.**
5. **Set Blend Mode to Normal.**
6. **Set Opacity to 100.**
7. **Click the foreground color box in the Materials pane.**

   The Material dialog box, shown in Figure 12-7, appears.

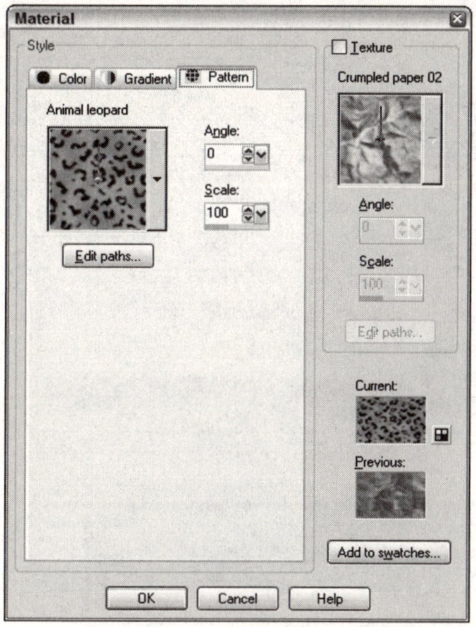

Figure 12-7: The Material dialog box.

8. **If the Texture option is still selected, turn it off.**
9. **Click the Pattern tab to select the page containing the pattern attributes.**

   The Pattern page appears in the dialog box, as shown in Figure 12-8.
10. **In the Pattern drop-down list, select the Diamond Plate Flat pattern.**
11. **Click OK to finalize your settings and to close the dialog box.**

    Your pattern appears in the foreground color box.
12. **Place the Flood Fill tool over the blank image and click.**

    Paint Shop Pro fills the image with the pattern you selected, as shown in Figure 12-9.

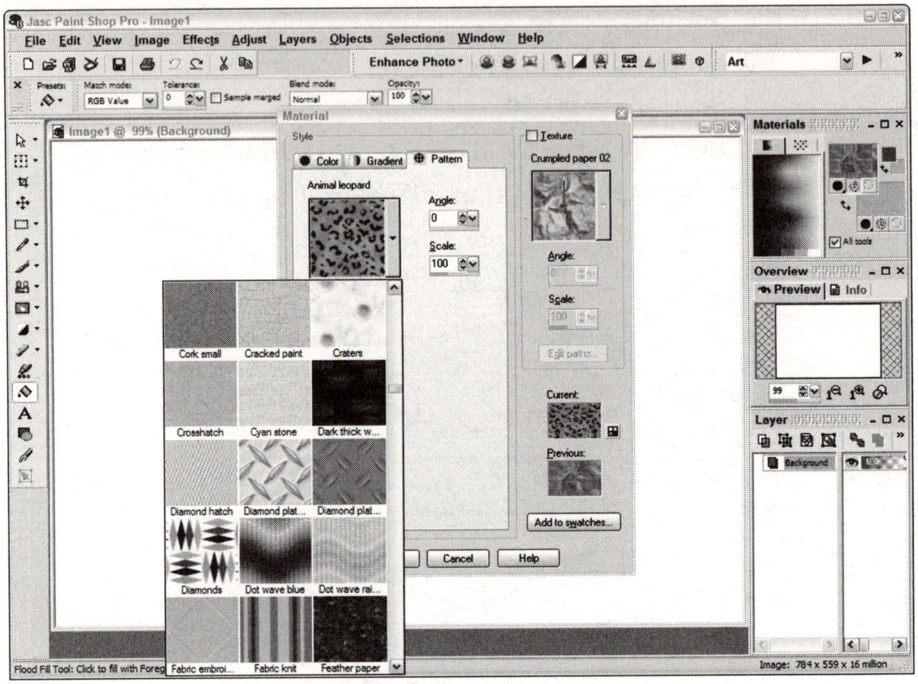

Figure 12-8: The Pattern page of the Material dialog box.

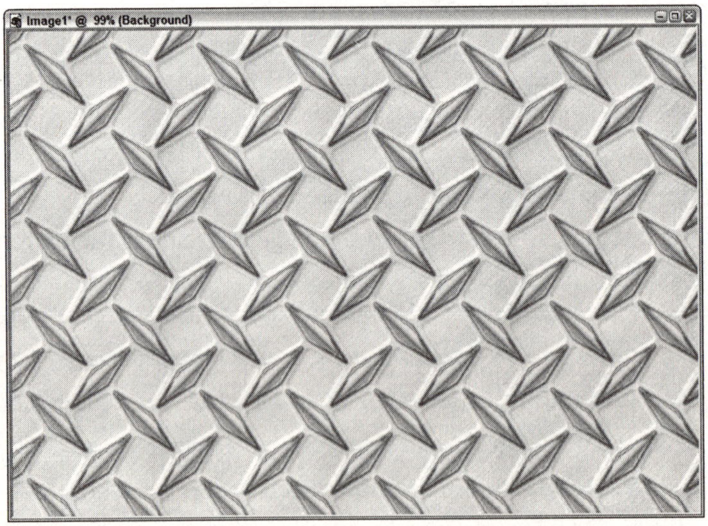

Figure 12-9: The new image filled with the selected pattern.

13. **Save your work.**

    If you've never saved the image before, the Save As dialog box appears, in which you must give your image a filename and select the image-format type. I suggest the .jpg image type.

Filling a Background with a Gradient

A *gradient* is one or more colors that blend in different shades across the surface of an image. While this description may be hard to visualize, the first time you paint with a gradient, you'll know exactly what I mean. If not, you'll be required to turn in your Custom Browser Builder's license — just kidding! As you may have guessed, painting with a gradient is exactly what you do in this section. Just follow these steps:

1. **Create a new 784 x 559 image.**

   Refer the section "Starting a Skin," earlier in this chapter, if you're not sure how.

2. **Select the Flood Fill tool.**

   The Flood Fill tool's settings appear in the toolbar.

3. **In the Flood Fill tool's attributes, make sure that Match Mode is set to RGB Value.**
4. **Set Tolerance to 0.**
5. **Set Blend Mode to Normal.**
6. **Set Opacity to 100.**
7. **Click the foreground color box in the Materials pane.**

   The Material dialog box appears.

8. **If the Texture option is selected, turn it off.**
9. **Click the Gradient tab to select the page containing gradient attributes.**

   The Gradient page appears in the dialog box, as shown in Figure 12-10.

10. **In the gradient drop-down list, select the Chrome Reflect gradient option, as shown in Figure 12-11.**
11. **Click OK.**

    Your selected gradient appears in the foreground color box.

12. **Place the Flood Fill tool over the blank image and click.**

    Paint Shop Pro fills the image with the gradient you selected (see Figure 12-12).

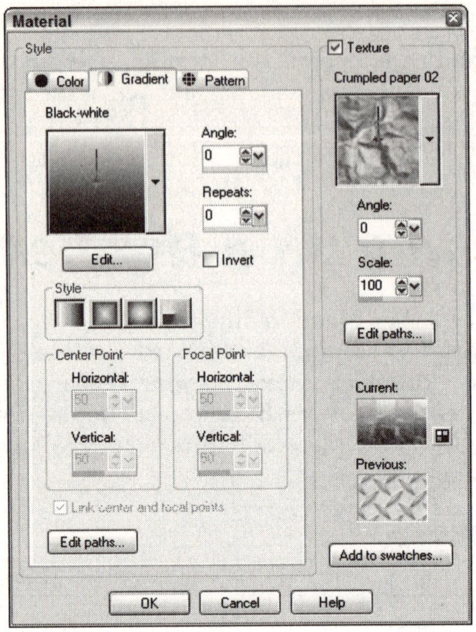

Figure 12-10: The Gradient page of the Material dialog box.

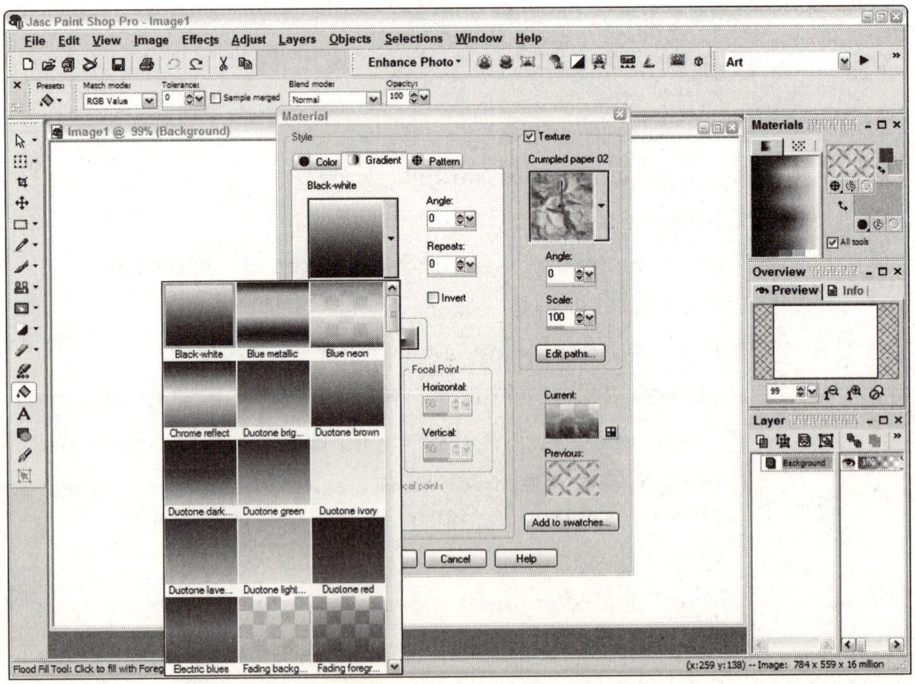

Figure 12-11: Your gradient options.

Figure 12-12: The new image filled with the selected pattern.

13. **Save your work.**

    If you've never saved the image before, the Save As dialog box, shown in Figure 12-13, appears, in which you must give your image a filename and select the image-format type. I suggest the .jpg image type.

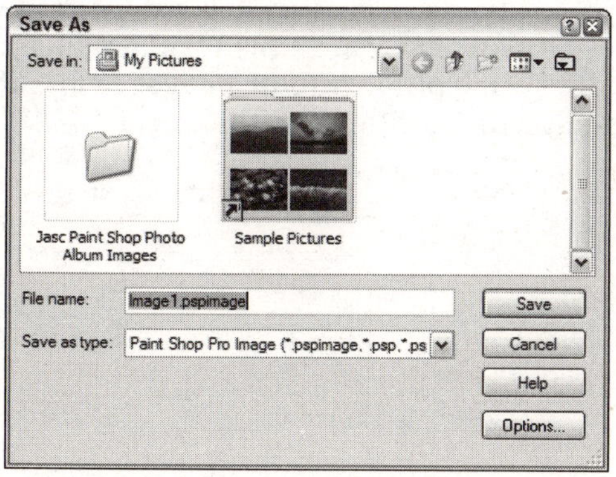

Figure 12-13: The Save As dialog box.

You can combine gradients with textures to get some very cool backgrounds. Figure 12-14 shows what you get when you combine the Chrome Reflect gradient with the Crumpled Paper 02 texture. Yowza!

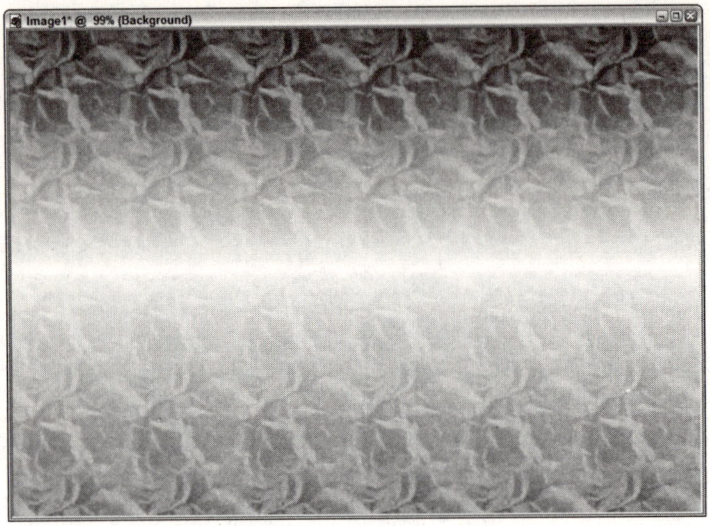

Figure 12-14: Combining a gradient with a texture.

You may remember that, when you create a new image with Paint Shop Pro, you choose 24-bit color, which allows you over 16 million different colors. This color depth is important because many of Paint Shop Pro's special graphical functions require 24-bit color. The good new is that, once you've created your image, you can save it with any color depth you want. Paint Shop Pro does the conversion for you, and, although you may see degradation in the resultant image, the conversion usually goes pretty well. If it doesn't, resave the file in a different format. (In other words, check the resultant image before you close the original!) Avoid saving photographic images in less than 24-bit color, because you'll definitely see the difference then.

Chapter 13

Creating Toolbars

In This Chapter

- Creating a toolbar image
- Filling the toolbar with color
- Adding images to the toolbar
- Changing the rectangle to 3-D

A toolbar is a handy place to put frequently used commands where the user can select them with a single button click. A toolbar sure beats hunting through the application's menus for a command! A custom browser created with the Browser Construction Kit provides room for all the basic browsing commands your Internet surfer will need to get around the huge domain of the World Wide Web. In this chapter, you find out how to create the background image for a toolbar. For information on creating toolbar buttons, refer to Chapter 15.

Understanding Toolbar Requirements

Like every other image you work with when creating a custom browser theme, the image you use for your toolbar must, for the best results, have a specific set of attributes. These attributes include not only the toolbar's size, but also the number of colors and the image's resolution. These attributes are complicated by the fact that you can have either a horizontal or vertical toolbar. Each has its own requirements. The following list summarizes these attributes for a horizontal toolbar image:

- Width of 784 pixels
- Height of 42 pixels
- Resolution of 200 pixels per centimeter
- Color depth of 16 million colors (24-bit color)

Here are the requirements for a vertical toolbar image:

- Width of 42 pixels
- Height of 562 pixels
- Resolution of 200 pixels per centimeter
- Color depth of 16 million colors (24-bit color)

WARNING! If you create your browser's toolbar image with a different size or resolution, you may see some distortion when you load it into your browser because the browser automatically resizes the image to fit the window. If you allow the user to resize your custom browser's window, however, some distortion is inevitable, because the browser will resize its images to fit the new window's size. The color depth is mostly important for use with Paint Shop Pro. You can save the final file in any color depth that looks good for your image.

Starting a New Toolbar

To create a toolbar, you must start with a blank image of the correct resolution. Those of you who have read Chapters 10 through 12 are probably already experts at this process. Give yourselves a pat on the back and feel free to smirk at people who don't know how to use Paint Shop Pro. For those of you who are new to creating blank images with Paint Shop Pro (you know, the smirkees), or for those who need a refresher course, here's how to get the job done for a toolbar image:

1. **Choose File⇨New.**

   The New Image dialog box appears.

2. **Make sure the Units box is set to Pixels.**
3. **Change Width to 784.**
4. **Change Height to 42.**
5. **Set Resolution to 200 Pixels/cm.**

   The option is probably already set to this value.

6. **Make sure that the Raster Background option is selected.**

7. **Set the Color Depth box to 16 Million Colors.**

   Again, this option is probably already set to this value.

8. **Make sure that the Color box is set to white and the Transparent option is not selected.**

   Figure 13-1 shows these settings.

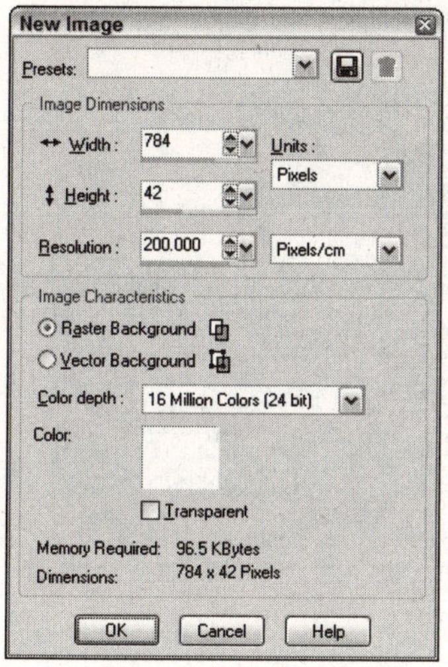

Figure 13-1: The New Image dialog box set for a blank toolbar image.

The Transparent option is for creating images that seem to be nonrectangular. Although the resultant image really is rectangular, the transparent part of the image allows the colors underneath the image to show through. Because a toolbar is a rectangular item, you have no need for transparency.

9. **Click OK.**

   Paint Shop Pro creates a blank image for your new toolbar, as shown in Figure 13-2.

10. **Save your work.**

    If you've never saved the image before, the Save As dialog box appears, in which you must give your image a filename and select the image-format type. I suggest the .jpg image type.

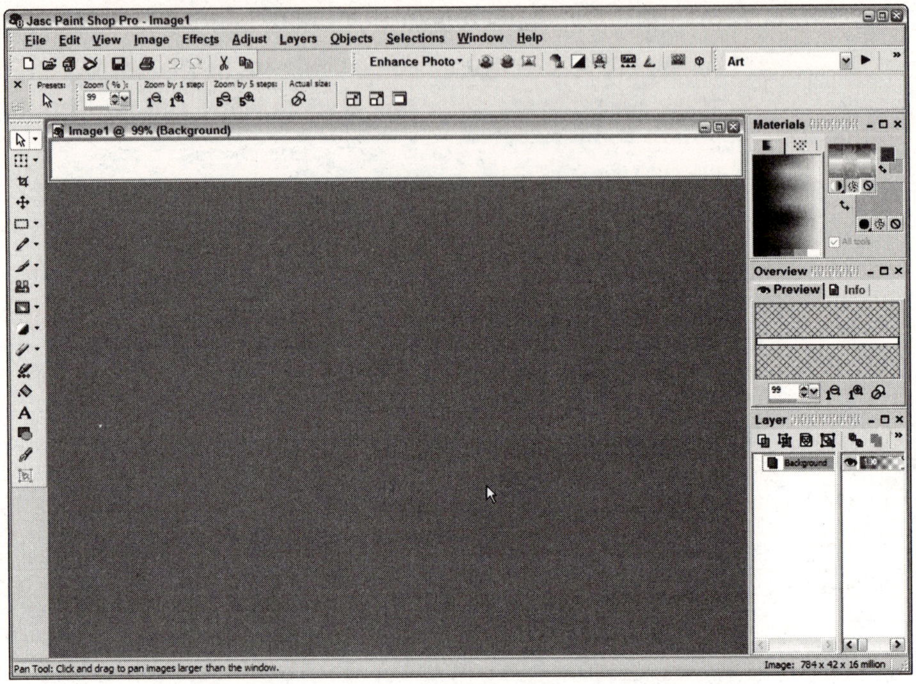

Figure 13-2: The new toolbar image's window in Paint Shop Pro's work area.

Filling the Toolbar's Background

After you have a new blank image to work with, you can start making it look more interesting. For this first toolbar, you create a 3-D image. The first step is to fill your blank rectangle with the background color you want. (Actually, the image isn't blank — it's already filled with white — but that's not going to change the process of filling the image with your selected color.) Follow these steps to fill your toolbar's image:

1. **In the toolbox on the left of the window, select the Flood Fill tool.**

   That's the thirteenth tool down, the one that looks like a tipped paint bucket.

   The Flood Fill tool's settings appear in the toolbar (see Figure 13-3).

Figure 13-3: The Flood Fill tool's attributes.

2. **In the Flood Fill tool's attributes, make sure that Match Mode is set to RGB Value.**
3. **Set Tolerance to 0.**
4. **Set Blend Mode to Normal.**
5. **Set Opacity to 100.**
6. **Click inside the foreground color box in the Materials pane (see Figure 13-4).**

   The Material dialog box appears (see Figure 13-5).

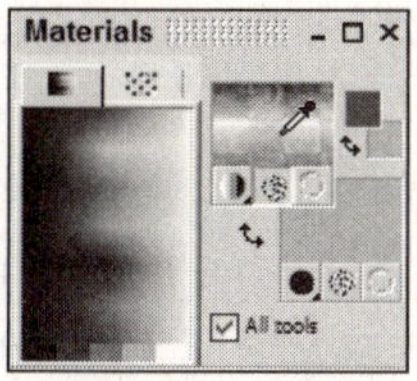

Figure 13-4: Clicking the foreground color box.

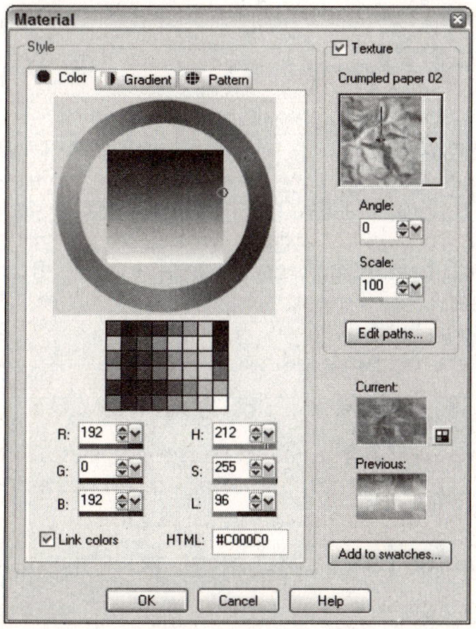

Figure 13-5: The Material dialog box.

7. **Click the Color tab and then click the light gray square in the color selections. Also make sure that the Texture option is not selected.**

   The R, G, and B values should all change to 192. If they didn't, you clicked the wrong color. Try again.

8. **Click OK.**

   The selected color changes to light gray.

9. **Place the tool over the image and click again.**

   Paint Shop Pro fills the image with light gray (see Figure 13-6).

Figure 13-6: The newly filled toolbar image.

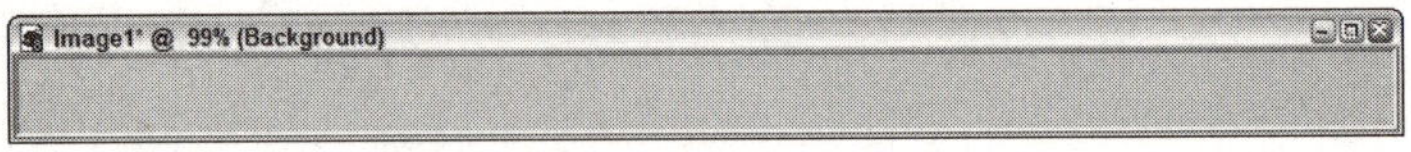

10. **Save your work.**

    If you've never saved the image before, the Save As dialog box appears, in which you must give your image a filename and select the image-format type. I suggest the .jpg image type.

Adding a Sunburst Effect

You can spend an entire day experimenting with the different effects Paint Shop Pro puts at your disposal. I don't know how much spare time you have to fool around with Paint Shop Pro, but I've got a lot of work to do, so, rather than experimenting, I'm going to suggest a very cool effect for your toolbar. The sunburst effect adds a bright light source, with rays and reflections. Perform the following steps to see what I mean:

1. **Make sure your image's window is selected.**

   You can select them image window by clicking its title bar.

   This step ensures that you apply the effect to the correct image — just in case you happen to have more than one image open in Paint Shop Pro's work area.

2. **Choose Effects⇨Illumination Effects⇨Sunburst, as shown in Figure 13-7.**

   The Sunburst dialog box appears.

3. **In the Light Spot options, set Brightness to 80, Horizontal to 70, and Vertical to 20.**

   These options determine the brightness of the light source (the higher the setting, the brighter the light), as well as the light's horizontal and vertical position.

4. **In the Rays options, set Density to 30 and Brightness to 50.**

   These options determine how many rays you get and how bright the rays are.

5. **In the Circle options, set Brightness to 100.**

   These options determine how the reflective circles of the effect look. The higher this setting, the more obvious the reflective circles are.

   Figure 13-8 shows the Sunburst dialog box with its correct settings.

6. **Click OK.**

   Paint Shop Pro applies the Sunburst effect to your toolbar image, as shown in Figure 13-9.

7. **Save your work.**

   If you've never saved the image before, the Save As dialog box appears, in which you must give your image a filename and select the image-format type. I suggest the .jpg image type.

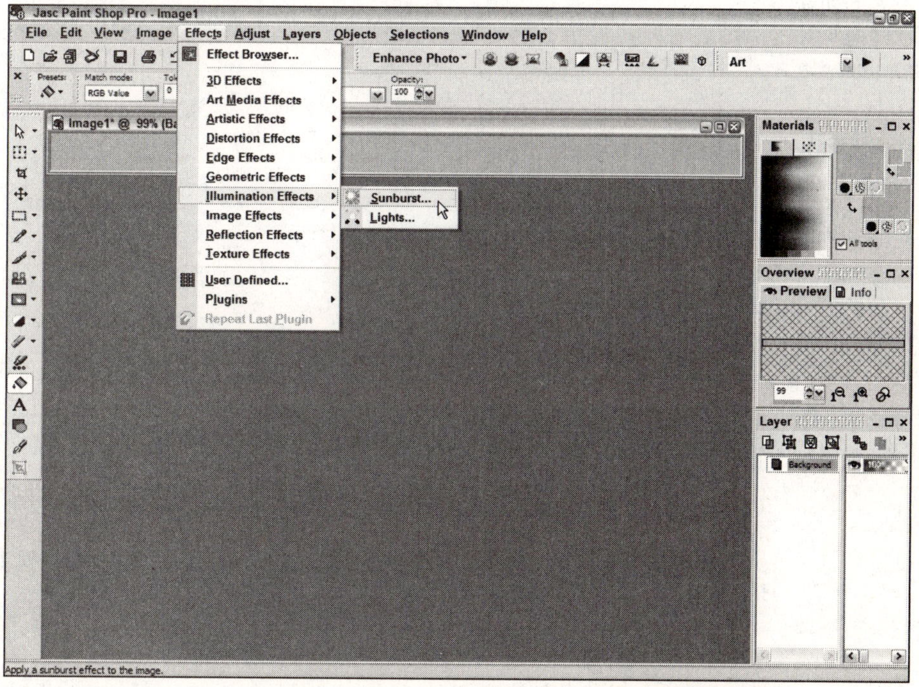

Figure 13-7: Choose these commands to cause the next dialog box to appear.

Feel free to experiment with other Paint Shop Pro effects. If you don't like what you get, you can just select the Undo command to remove the effect. You can access Undo from the Edit menu or by pressing Ctrl+Z on your keyboard.

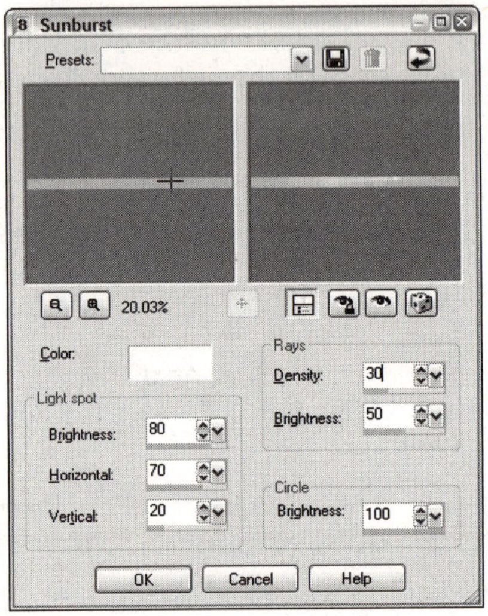

Figure 13-8: The Sunburst dialog box.

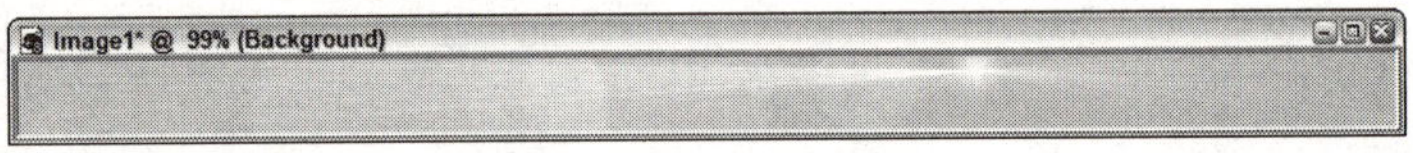

Figure 13-9: The toolbar with the Sunburst effect.

Adding a Graphic to the Toolbar

You can make a lot more changes to make your toolbar more interesting. Paint Shop Pro provides something called the Picture Tube tool that enables you to stamp detailed graphical images onto your toolbar. Sounds like fun, eh? Here's how:

1. **Make sure that your image's window is selected.**
2. **Choose Layers⇨New Raster Layer, as shown in Figure 13-10.**

   The New Raster Layer dialog box appears.

3. **In the New Raster Layer dialog box, change the Name box to Gold Star.**

   This name can be anything you want, as it just identifies the layer.

4. **Set Blend Mode to Normal.**

   The blend mode determines how layers affect each other.

5. **Set Opacity to 25.**

   Opacity determines how transparent a layer is.

6. **Set Link Set to 0.**

   Link Set determines which layers are locked together and move as a single unit.

7. **Select the Layer Is Visible setting.**

   Figure 13-11 shows the New Raster Layer dialog box with its correct settings.

8. **Click OK.**

   Paint Shop Pro adds a new layer on top of your toolbar's background layer. This extra layer enables you to manipulate any new graphics you add to the toolbar, without changing the sunburst effect underneath.

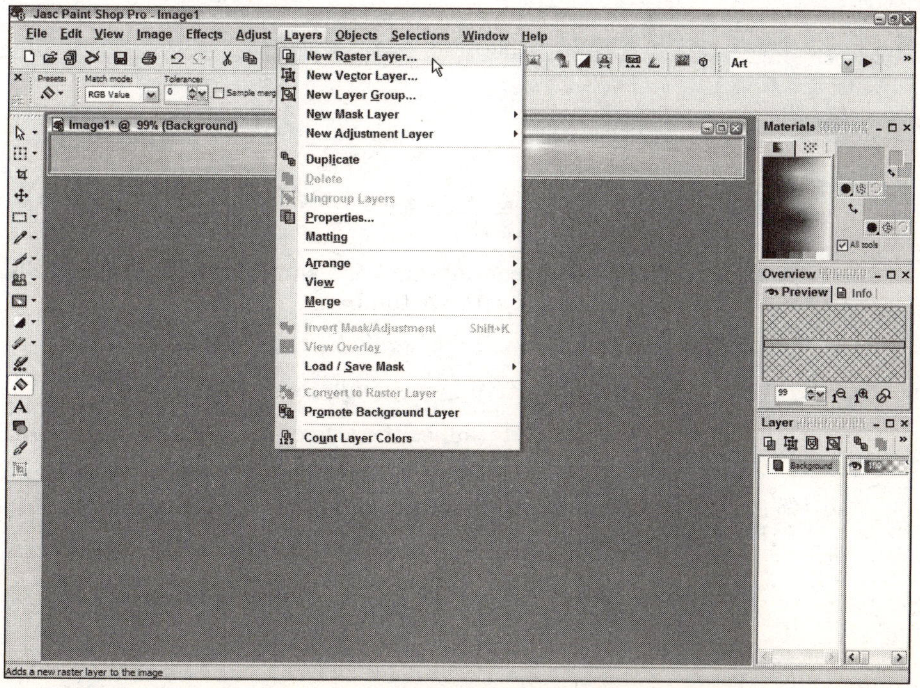

Figure 13-10: The New Raster Layer command.

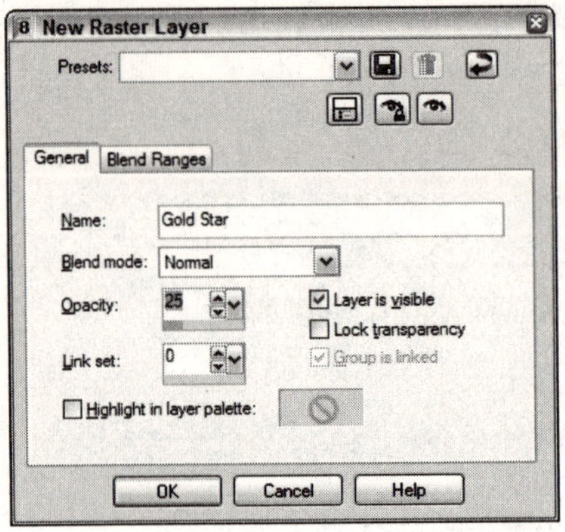

Figure 13-11: The New Raster Layer dialog box.

9. **Select the Picture Tube tool, which is the twelfth tool from the top in the toolbox, right above the Flood Fill tool.**

   The Picture Tube tool's settings appear in Paint Shop Pro's toolbar, as shown in Figure 13-12.

Figure 13-12: The Picture Tube tool's settings.

10. **In the tool's settings, select the Gold Star Garland picture tube, as shown in Figure 13-13.**

    To display the selections, click the small arrow next to the displayed shape in the tool's settings toolbar.

    The selected picture appears in the tool's settings.

11. **Also in the tool's settings, change the Scale value to 72.**

    The Scale value determines the size of the resultant graphic. The setting of 72 makes the graphic 72 percent of its original size.

12. **In the Layer pane, click the Gold Star layer to ensure that it's the selected layer (see Figure 13-14).**

    Paint Shop Pro selects the Gold Star layer for manipulation.

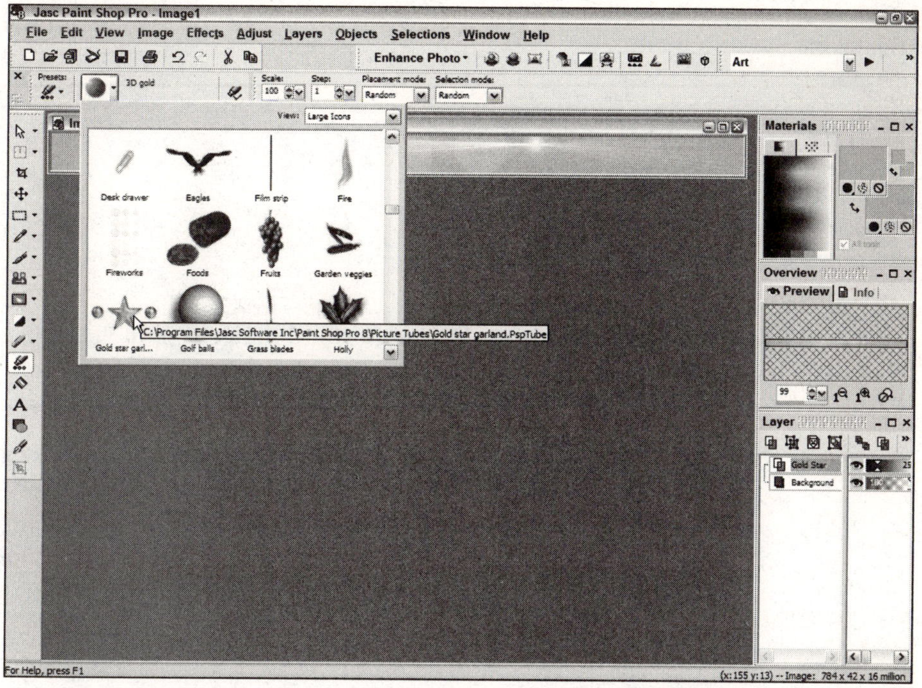

Figure 13-13: Selecting the Gold Star Garland picture tube.

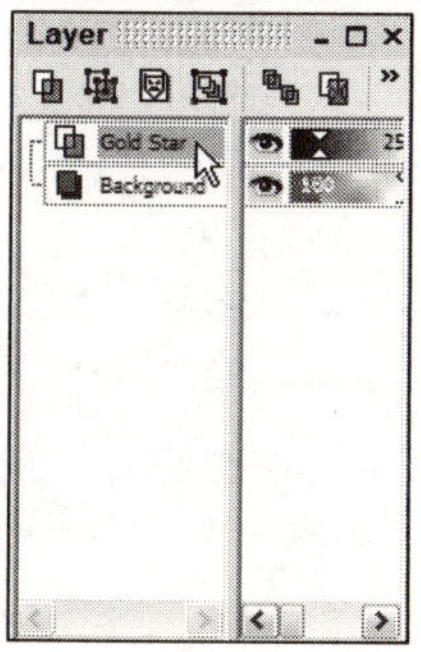

Figure 13-14: Selecting the Gold Star layer.

13. **Place your mouse cursor over the left end of the toolbar and click; if a globe appears, press Ctrl+Z to remove it and then click again.**

    A golden star with two smaller globes appears in the toolbar, as shown in Figure 13-15. Notice that the layer's transparency value of 25 allows the sunburst effect to show through. The higher this transparency value, the less of the background shows through.

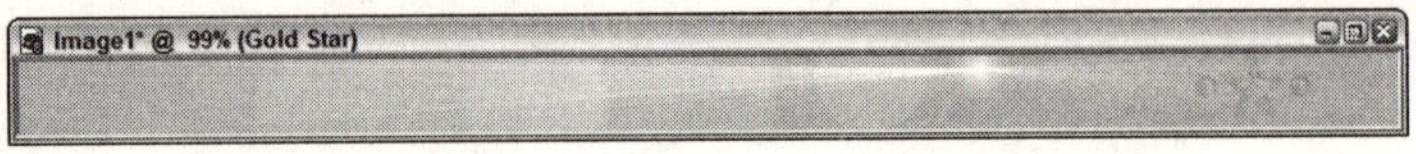

Figure 13-15: The toolbar with the Gold Star Garland picture tube applied.

14. **Add several more Gold Star Garland images (as in Step 10) to the toolbar.**
15. **Select the Move tool, which is the fourth tool down from the top.**
16. **Place the Move tool over your toolbar, on top of one of the gold stars, hold down the left mouse button, and drag the Gold Star layer to whatever position looks best.**

    Now you see the power of layers! Figure 13-16 shows your toolbar as it looks now.

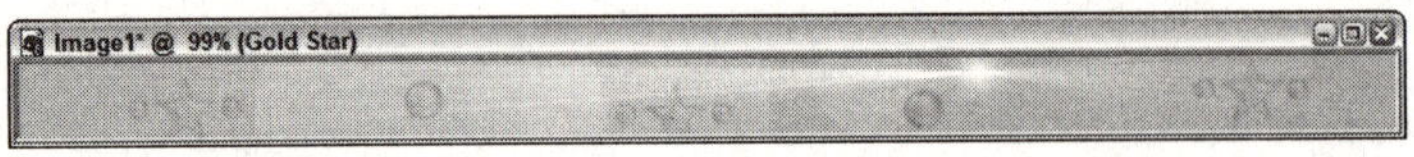

Figure 13-16: The toolbar with its finished gold stars.

17. **Save your work.**

    If you've never saved the image before, the Save As dialog box appears, in which you must give your image a filename and select the image-format type. I suggest the .jpg image type.

REMEMBER: You can add as many layers as you need in order to provide perfect control over the elements that make up your images.

Adding a 3-D Effect

You can add a 3-D effect to your toolbar in several ways. One is using Paint Shop Pro's Buttonize effect (see Chapter 11 for more information on this effect), but for your toolbar, you'll use a more subtle 3-D effect: drop shadows. To see how drop shadows work, perform the following steps:

1. **Select the Gold Star layer, if it isn't selected already.**
2. **Choose Effects⇨3D Effects⇨Drop Shadow.**

   The Drop Shadow dialog box appears (see Figure 13-17).

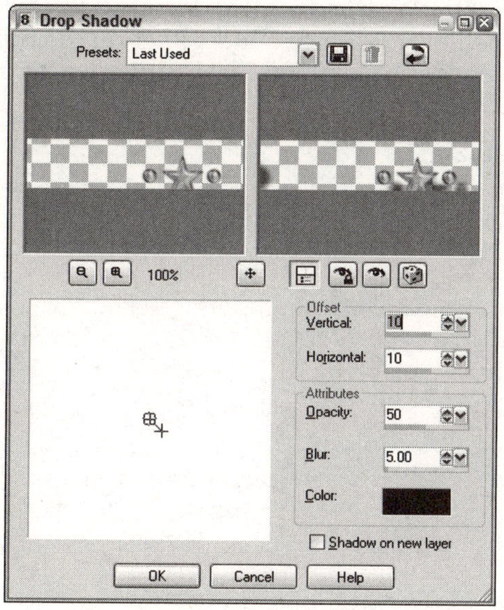

Figure 13-17: The Drop Shadow dialog box.

3. **In the Offset options, set Vertical to 8 and Horizontal to 8.**

   These options control the position of the shadows. The higher the values, the more the shadow moves away from the source graphic.
4. **In the Attributes options, set Opacity to 50, Blur to 5, and Color to black.**

   Opacity controls the shadows' transparency, whereas Blur controls the definition of the shadows' edges and Color controls the shadows' color.
5. **Click OK.**

   Paint Shop Pro adds shadows to the Gold Star layer, as shown in Figure 13-18.

Figure 13-18: The Gold Star layer with its drop shadows.

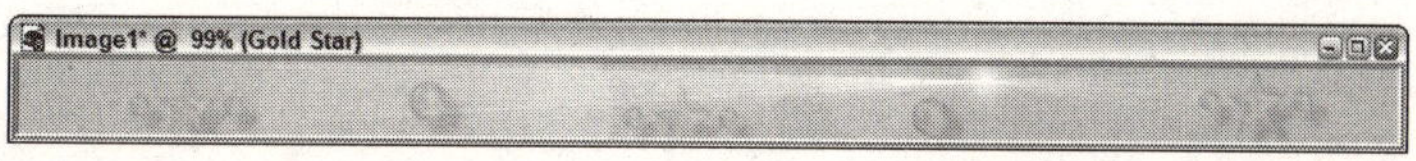

6. **Save your work.**

   If you've never saved the image before, the Save As dialog box appears, in which you must give your image a filename and select the image-format type. I suggest the .jpg image type.

REMEMBER

If you want to make the Gold Star layer more vivid, increase the transparency setting. You can do this in the Layer pane. See that slider on the right side of the Layer pane? Drag the one for the Gold Star layer to change its transparency, as shown in Figure 13-19.

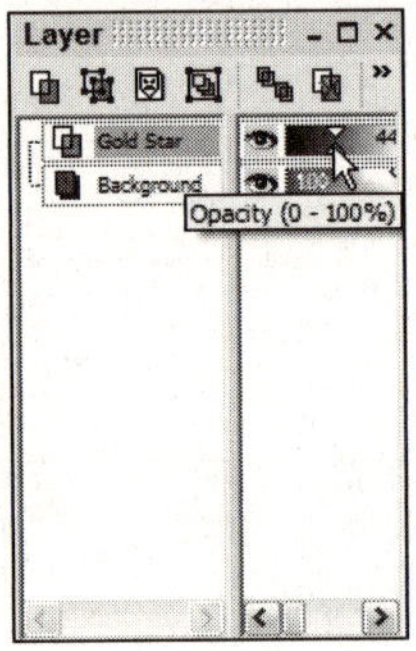

Figure 13-19: Changing the Gold Star layer's transparency setting.

Chapter 14

Painting Status Bars

In This Chapter

- Creating a status bar image
- Filling the status bar with color
- Changing the status bar to 3-D

Most Windows applications have a status bar, where the application can display messages and status information. Your custom browser can have a status bar, too. In fact, you can create your own images to use with the status bar. In this chapter, you discover how to do just that.

Understanding Status Bar Requirements

The Browser Construction Kit expects the graphical components you use to fit a set of attributes, including a specific size and number of colors. Your status bar is no different. For the best results, create your status bar with these attributes:

- Width of 784 pixels
- Height of 24 pixels
- Resolution of 200 pixels per centimeter
- Color depth of 16 million colors (24-bit color)

WARNING!

If you create your browser's status bar image with a different size or resolution, you may see some distortion when you load it into your browser because the browser automatically resizes the image to fit the window. If you allow the user to resize your custom browser's window, however, some distortion is inevitable, because the browser will resize its images to fit the new window's size. The color depth is of utmost importance to Paint Shop Pro, because you can do more with a 24-bit image than one of a lower color depth. However, when you save your final image, you can use whatever color depth best suits your purposes.

Starting a New Status Bar

The first step toward creating your status bar is to create a blank image of the correct resolution. (This is, in fact, the first step toward creating any original image with Paint Shop Pro.) Here's how to get started with a new status bar:

1. **Choose File⇨New.**

   The New Image dialog box appears.

2. **Make sure the Units box is set to Pixels.**
3. **Change Width to 784.**
4. **Change Height to 24.**
5. **Set Resolution to 200 Pixels/cm.**

   This option is probably already set to this value.

6. **Make sure that the Raster Background option is selected.**

   This option creates a *raster image,* which is an image composed of columns and rows of dots called *pixels.* A raster image is very different from a *vector image,* which is composed of movable and sizable graphical objects.

7. **Set the Color Depth box to 16 Million Colors.**

   Again, this option is probably already set to this value.

8. **Make sure that the Color box is set to white and the Transparent option is not selected.**

   Figure 14-1 shows these settings.

9. **Click OK.**

   Paint Shop Pro creates a blank image for your new status bar, as shown in Figure 14-2.

10. **Save your work.**

    To save your work, choose File⇨Save. If you haven't previously given this image a filename, the Save As dialog box appears. In this dialog box, give the image a filename and select the type of image format you want to use. I suggest that you save your browser graphics in the .jpg format.

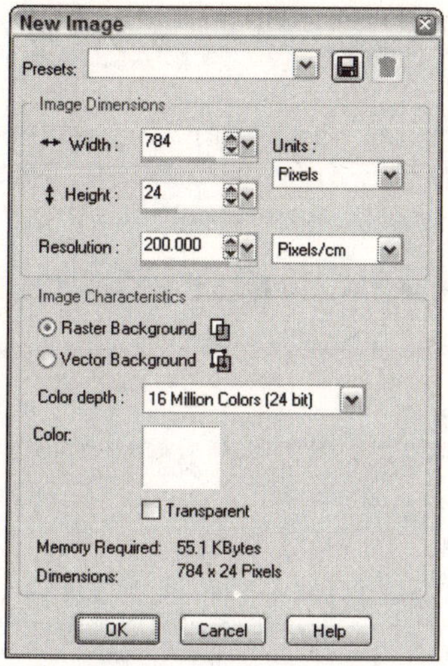

Figure 14-1: The New Image dialog box set for a blank status bar image.

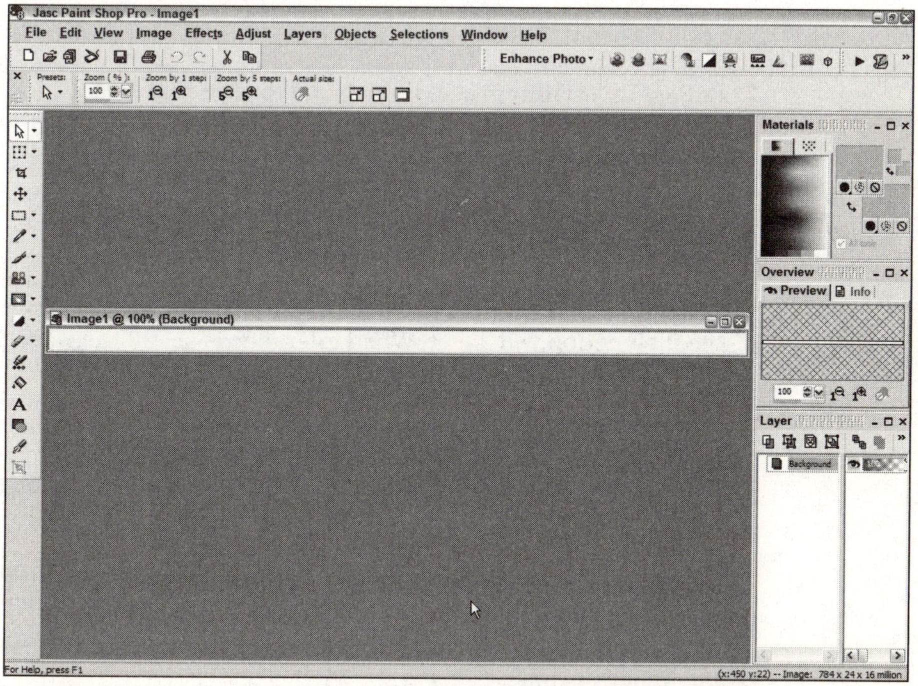

Figure 14-2: The new status bar image's window in Paint Shop Pro's work area.

Filling the Status Bar's Background

Got a new image to work with? If not, you need to jump back to the previous section and create one. When you have your new blank image, it's time to fill it with some color. Follow these steps to fill your status bar's image:

1. **In the toolbox on the left of the window, select the Flood Fill tool.**

   That's the thirteenth tool down, the one that looks like a tipped paint bucket.

   The Flood Fill tool's settings appear in the status bar (see Figure 14-3).

Figure 14-3: The Flood Fill tool's attributes.

2. **In the Flood Fill tool's attributes, make sure that Match Mode is set to RGB Value.**

   This setting tells Paint Shop Pro to fill areas based on the RGB values of colors, rather than some other color attribute like luminance.

3. **Set Tolerance to 0.**

   A tolerance of 0 limits the fill function to filling only areas of a single color. The higher you set tolerance, the greater the number of similar colors the fill function will affect. When tolerance is set all the way up, the fill function fills the entire image, regardless of the colors used in the image.

4. **Set Blend Mode to Normal.**

   The blend mode determines the way the fill function combines colors. The normal blend mode causes the fill color to replace all affected colors.

5. **Set Opacity to 100.**

   Opacity determines the transparency of the fill. A value of 100 specifies an opaque fill, whereas lower values make the fill more transparent.

6. **In Paint Shop Pro's window, click inside the foreground color box in the Materials pane (see Figure 14-4).**

   (The Materials pane is in Paint Shop Pro's upper-right corner.) The Material dialog box appears.

7. **Select the Color tab.**
8. **Click the light gray square in the color selections.**

   The R, G, and B values should all change to 192, as shown in Figure 14-5. If they didn't, you clicked the wrong color. Try again.

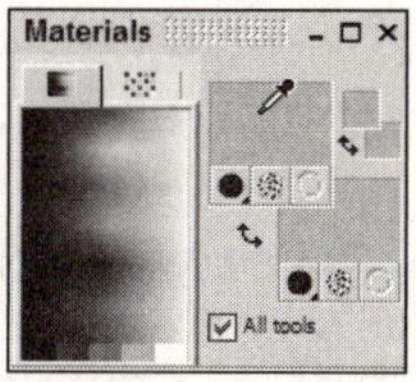

Figure 14-4: Clicking the foreground color box.

9. **Make sure that the Texture option isn't selected.**

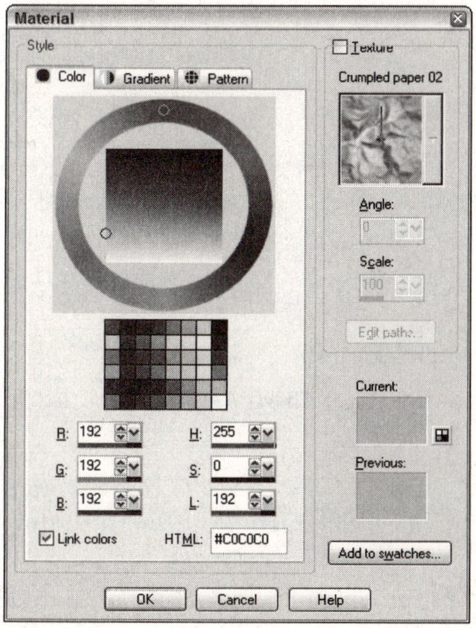

Figure 14-5: The Material dialog box.

10. **Click OK.**

    The selected foreground color in the Materials pane changes to light gray.

11. **Place the tool over the image and click again.**

    Paint Shop Pro fills the image with light gray.

12. **Save your work.**

    To save your work, choose File⇨Save. If you haven't previously given this image a filename, the Save As dialog box appears. In this dialog box, give the image a filename and select the type of image format you want to use. I suggest that you save your browser graphics in the .jpg format.

Adding the 3-D Effect

Paint Shop Pro provides many effects for changing a 2-D image to 3-D, but with your status bar, you're going to discover some tricks to draw 3-D detail from scratch. Perform the following steps to see how to add 3-D ridges to your status bar:

1. **Click the Pen tool, which is the second tool from the bottom in Paint Shop Pro's toolbox.**

   The Pen settings appear in the toolbar (see Figure 14-6).

Figure 14-6: The Pen tool's settings.

2. **Turn off the Create As Vector option.**
3. **In the Line Style box, use the drop-down list to select the Solid option, as shown in Figure 14-7.**
4. **Set Width to 1.0.**

   This setting results in thin lines. The higher the width setting, the thicker the lines.
5. **Turn off the Anti-alias option, located to the right of the Width setting.**

   Anti-aliasing combines colors in such a way as to help hide the stair-step effect you often get with computer graphics, especially on curved lines. You don't need this effect for this project.
6. **Click the foreground color box in the Materials pane.**

   The Material dialog box appears.

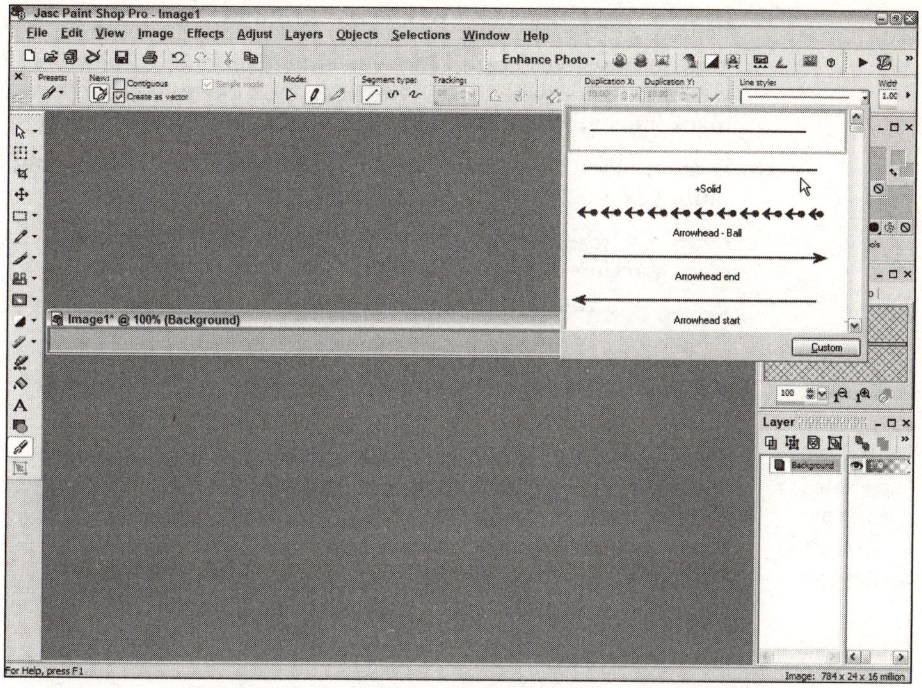

Figure 14-7: Selecting the line style.

7. **Select the white color and make sure that the Texture option is off.**

   Normally, you don't want to use textures, which add various kinds of patterns to images, as you're drawing.

8. **Place your mouse cursor in the upper-left corner of the status bar, at the location (x:0 y:0).**

   This is the location at which you'll begin drawing a line. You can see these coordinates in Paint Shop Pro's status bar.

9. **Hold down your left mouse button and drag the cursor to the upper-right corner of the status bar image, drawing a straight line between the two points.**

   In Paint Shop Pro's status bar, you should see 90.0 degrees to the right of the line's coordinates.

10. **Release the mouse button.**

    Paint Shop Pro draws a white line where you indicated.

11. **Change the foreground color to black.**

12. **Draw a black line right below the white line, starting at point (x:0 y:1).**

    This setting gives you a black line one pixel below the white line. When you're done drawing, the white lines look like reflective edges, and the black lines look like shadowed edges.

13. **Draw a black line at the bottom of the status bar image, starting at point (x:0 y:23).**

14. **Draw a white line right above the black line you drew in the previous step, starting at point (x:0 y:22).**

    Figure 14-8 shows your completed status bar image.

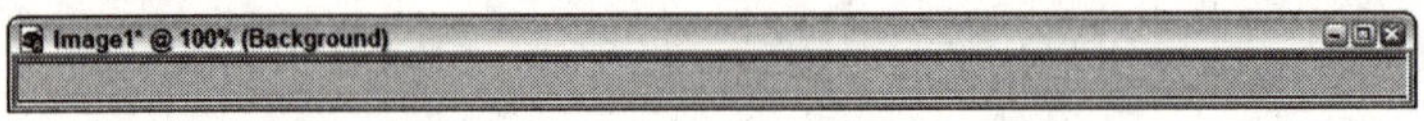

Figure 14-8: The completed status bar image.

15. **Save your work.**

    To save your work, choose File⇨Save. If you haven't previously given this image a filename, the Save As dialog box appears. In this dialog box, give the image a filename and select the type of image format you want to use. I suggest that you save your browser graphics in the .jpg format.

The white and black lines make your status bar's edges look 3-D because the colors simulate reflection and shadow.

Chapter 15

Manufacturing Buttons

In This Chapter

- Creating a button image
- Filling the button with color
- Changing the button to 3-D
- Adding a button image

While Chapter 13 tells you how to paint the background image for your custom browser's toolbar, it doesn't describe how to make buttons for your toolbar. Your custom browser's toolbar can have buttons for the complete set of navigation controls, including Home, Back, Forward, Stop, Refresh, Search, and Favorites. In this chapter, you use Paint Shop Pro to create new buttons for your browser's toolbar.

Understanding Button Requirements

Buttons may be small, but you need to take as much care in their creation as you would with larger images, such as toolbars. And, just as with toolbars or other images, you first need to start your button with a new blank image of the correct size and color depth. Here are the attributes for a button:

- Width of 32 pixels
- Height of 32 pixels
- Resolution of 200 pixels per centimeter
- Color depth of 16 million colors (24-bit color)

WARNING!

If you create your browser's button image with a different size or resolution, you may see some distortion when you load it into your browser. This is because the browser automatically resizes the image to fit the buttons in your toolbar.

Starting a New Button

A new button starts with a blank image, which has the attributes described in the previous section. Here's a step-by-step guide to creating a button:

1. **Choose File⇨New.**

   The New Image dialog box, shown in Figure 15-1, appears.

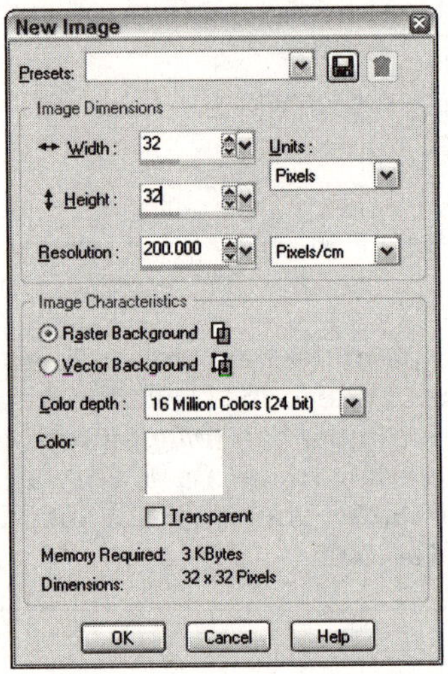

Figure 15-1: The New Image dialog box set for a blank button image.

2. **Using the drop-down list, set the Units box to Pixels.**
3. **Change Width to 32.**
4. **Change Height to 32.**
5. **Set Resolution to 200 Pixels/cm.**

   This option is probably already set to this value.

6. **Make sure that the Raster Background option is selected.**

   You want the raster background, rather than the vector background, because you won't be using vector graphics (independently manipulated graphic objects) when you create browser graphics.

7. **Set the Color Depth box to 16 Million Colors.**

   Again, this option is probably already set to this value.

8. **Make sure that the Color box is set to white and the Transparent option is not selected.**

The Transparent option specifies an image with no background color. You want a background color of white, so you want transparency off.

9. **Click OK.**

   Paint Shop Pro creates a blank image for your new button.

10. **Save your work.**

    Choose File⇨Save to save your work. If the Save As dialog box appears, give the image a filename and select the type of image format you want to use. I suggest that you save your browser graphics in the .jpg format.

Zooming In on the Button

If you followed the steps in the preceding section, your new button ended up pretty small. A small image like this one can be hard to work with. Luckily, Paint Shop Pro enables you to magnify the image so that you can better see what you're doing with it. To make your new button easier to see and work with, perform these steps:

1. **Click the Pan tool in Paint Shop Pro's toolbox.**

   It's the topmost tool, the one that looks like an arrow mouse cursor.

   The tool's settings appear in Paint Shop Pro's toolbar, as shown in Figure 15-2.

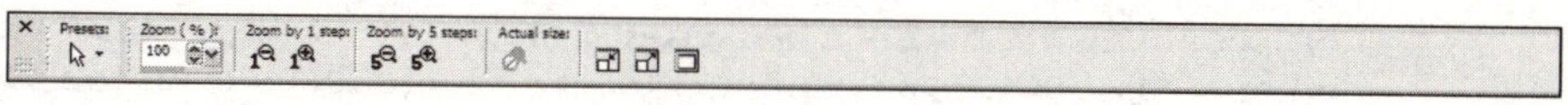

Figure 15-2: The Pan tool's settings.

2. **To zoom by a user-defined amount, type a value into the Zoom box in the Pan tool's settings, as shown in Figure 15-3; to zoom a predefined amount, click either the Zoom By 1 Step or the Zoom By 5 Steps buttons.**

   TIP

   If you're typing a value, keep in mind that this number is a percentage; values below 100 decrease the magnification, whereas values above 100 increase the magnification.

   If you click the 5+ button twice, Paint Shop Pro magnifies your button image by a factor of ten.

3. **Save your work.**

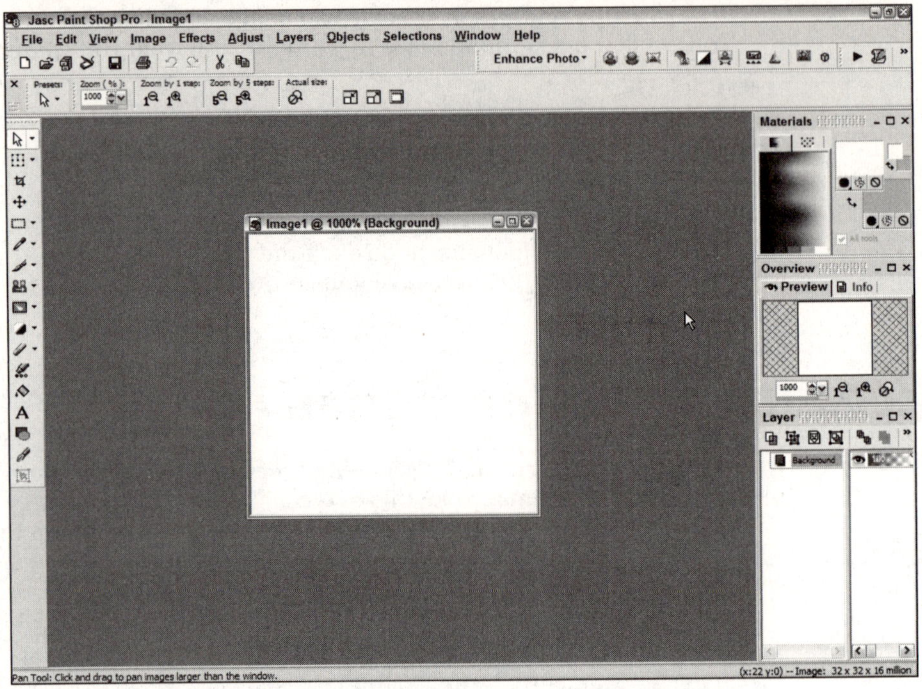

Figure 15-3: Type a value into the Zoom box in the top-left corner of the window.

Filling the Button's Background

Chances are you'll want to fill your button's blank rectangle with some color. You could stick with the white background, I suppose, but why not go for broke? Filling the button's background is as easy as 1,2,3 (plus about five other steps, but who's counting?). Here's how to fill your button's image:

1. **In the toolbox on the left of the window, select the Flood Fill tool.**

   This tool is the thirteenth one down, and it looks like a tipped paint bucket.

   The Flood Fill tool's settings appear in Paint Shop Pro's toolbar.

2. **In the Flood Fill tool's attributes, make sure that Match Mode is set to RGB Value.**

   Match Mode determines how the fill function decides which colors to fill.

3. **Set Tolerance to 0.**

Tolerance specifies how close a color has to be to the selected color (the one you click with the fill tool) to be affected by the fill. Higher tolerance values cause more colors to be filled.

4. **Set Blend Mode to Normal.**

   This setting specifies that the fill color completely replaces all affected colors, rather than blend them together in some other way.

5. **Set Opacity to 100.**

   This setting determines how transparent the fill color will be. A setting of 100 makes the fill opaque.

6. **Click inside the foreground color box in the Materials pane, as shown in Figure 15-4.**

   The Material dialog box appears.

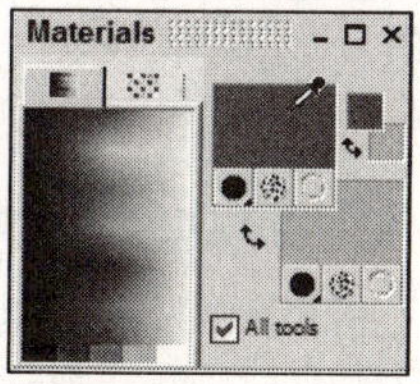

Figure 15-4: Clicking the foreground color box.

7. **Click the Color tab and then click the color you want.**

   The R, G, and B values should change to the red, green, and blue values that combine to make your chosen color.

8. **Make sure that the Texture option is not selected.**

   You don't want your fill color to have a texture pattern.

9. **Click OK.**

   The foreground color changes to the color you chose in Step 7.

10. **Place the tool over the image and click.**

    Paint Shop Pro fills the image with your chosen color.

11. **Save your work.**

TIP

If you want your button to seem to blend in to your toolbar, use the same color you chose for your toolbar's background. Of course, this tip only works if your toolbar has a solid background — that is, the toolbar hasn't been overlaid with other images, textures, or patterns.

Adding a 3-D Effect

In most cases, you want your button to look flat. This is because the browser that the Browser Construction Kit creates automatically makes the button image 3-D when the user's mouse cursor passes over it. This 3-D effect is subtle, though, so if you want, you can create cool, 3-D buttons that look 3-D all the time. Follow these steps to accomplish this task:

1. **Choose Effects⇨3D Effects⇨Buttonize.**

   The Buttonize dialog box appears.

2. **Change the Height setting to 5.**

   This setting specifies a button with a 5-pixel [LB1]top and bottom border.

   You can adjust the amount of the 3-D effect applied to your image by changing the Height and Width settings in the Buttonize dialog box. These settings control the size of the button's 3-D edge.

3. **Change the Width setting to 5.**

   This setting specifies a button with a 5-pixel left and right border.

4. **Select the Transparent edge.**

   A transparent edge looks more realistic because of the way it blends the button's colors.

5. **Select an Opacity of 75.**

   This setting specifies the amount of transparency applied to a transparent edge (see Step 4).

   Figure 15-5 shows these settings.

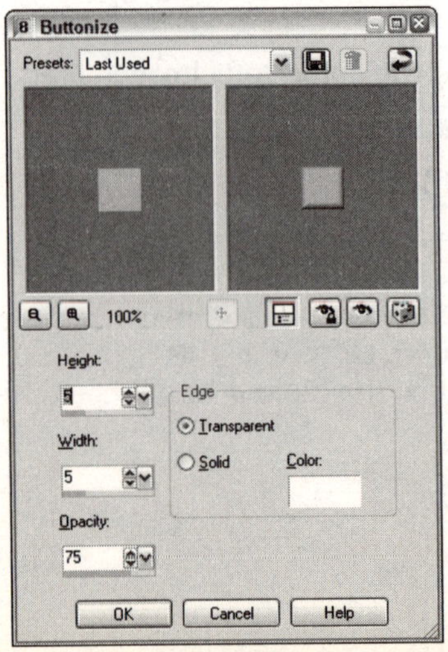

Figure 15-5: The Buttonize settings.

6. **Click OK.**

   Paint Shop Pro applies the effect, giving you the button shown in Figure 15-6.

   Because the button you created is magnified ten times, the 3-D effect doesn't seem as effective. If you press Ctrl+Alt+N, the button returns to its normal size, so you can see what it really looks like. Before moving on to the next section, though, magnify the button again.

7. **Save your work.**

Adding an Image to Your Button

A blank button, even if it does have a cool 3-D effect, doesn't help you much, because the user has no way of knowing what the button does. To give the user a clue, you need to add an icon to the button's surface. Here's how you can create a Favorites button for your toolbar:

1. **Create a new 28 x 28 image.**

   See the "Starting a New Button" section for more information on how to start a new image.

2. **Select the Transparent option.**

   You want to select the transparent option because you don't want the image to have a background color.

3. **Select the Pan tool and, in the Pan tool's settings, click the 5+ button twice.**

   The image magnifies to ten times its normal size, as shown in Figure 15-6.

Figure 15-6: The new image magnified ten times.

4. **Select the Preset Shape tool.**

   This tool is the third one from the bottom — the one that looks like an oval on top of a rectangle — in Paint Shop Pro's toolbox.

   The tool's settings appear in Paint Shop Pro's toolbar (see Figure 15-7).

Figure 15-7: The Preset Shape tool's settings.

5. **In the shape list, select the Star 2 shape, as shown in Figure 15-8.**

   The Star 2 shape appears in the tool's settings.

6. **In the Materials pane, set the foreground color to black and the fill color (the other color box on the right side of the Materials pane) to yellow.**

   If you need help setting colors, please refer to Step 6 of the "Filling the Button's Background" section.

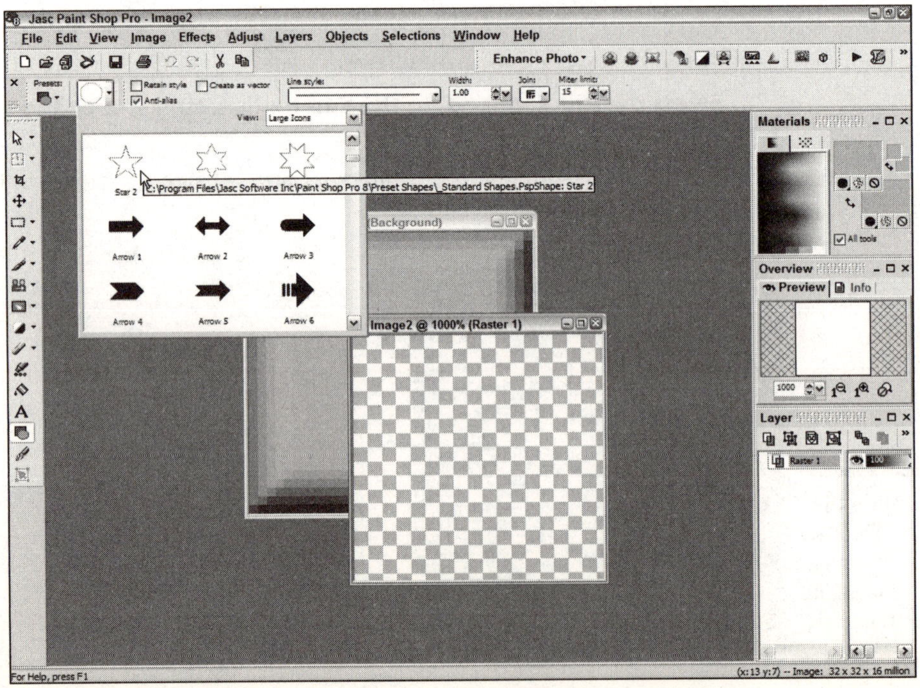

Figure 15-8: Selecting the Star 2 preset shape.

7. **Place your mouse cursor in the image's upper-left corner, hold down the left mouse button, and drag the mouse to draw a star that fills the image's rectangle, as shown in Figure 15-9.**

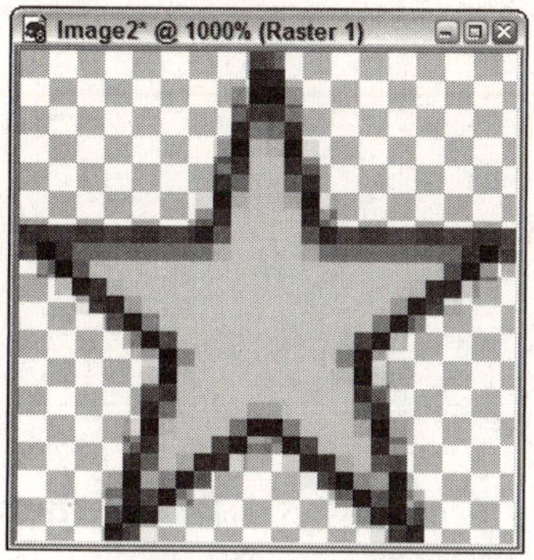

Figure 15-9: The star shape drawn in the 28 x 28 image.

8. **Choose Selections⇨Select All to select the entire 28 x 28 image.**

   You can also press Ctrl+A. Paint Shop Pro surrounds the image with an animated dashed line (see Figure 15-10), indicating that the image is selected.

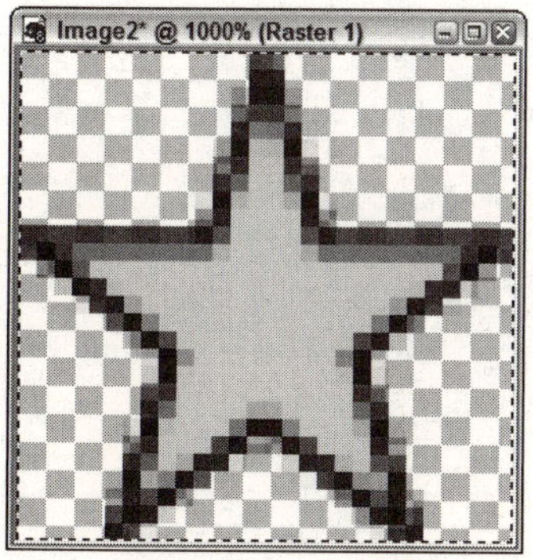

Figure 15-10: The selected 28 x 28 image.

9. **Choose Edit⇨Copy to copy the image to the Clipboard.**

   You can also press Ctrl+C.

10. **Click your 3-D button's title bar to select its window.**

11. **Paste the star into the button's window and move your mouse to position it in the center of the button.**

    You can quickly paste the image by pressing Ctrl+E. The star appears on the button, as shown in Figure 15-11.

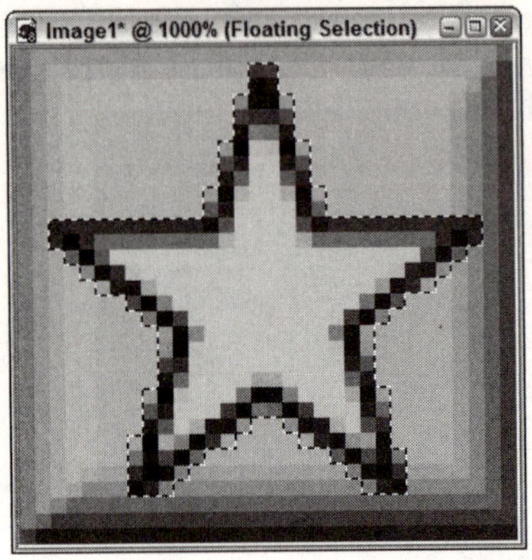

Figure 15-11: The star on the button.

12. **Deselect the star in the button (by pressing Ctrl+D) and then reduce the button to its normal size (by pressing Ctrl+Alt+N).**

    Figure 15-12 shows the button at its normal size.

Figure 15-12: The finished Favorites button.

13. **Save your work.**

Chapter 16

Producing Icons

In This Chapter

- Understanding icon editors
- Discovering the icon attributes
- Creating an icon

You can place icons in your custom browser in only two places: the window's title bar and status bar. While the icon in the status bar is optional, the main window has to have an icon. In fact, when you start a new custom browser, the default icon is already assigned to the window. The default icon looks like a globe, but you can replace it with anything you want. In this chapter, you find out how to create your own icons.

Getting an Icon Editor

Icons are different from other types of graphics. In fact, you can't even make them with Paint Shop Pro. You need a special icon editor. I use something called IconEdit32, shown in Figure 16-1. This great icon editor is a utility published in *PC Magazine,* and it's available for download from many different Web sites. Just hop onto your favorite Internet search engine and search for IconEdit32.

IconEdit32 features many of the same tools that most paint programs have, as well as commands that make creating icons easier. The program comes with a Help file that tells you everything you need to know to get the most out of the program, but you get a quick introduction in this chapter.

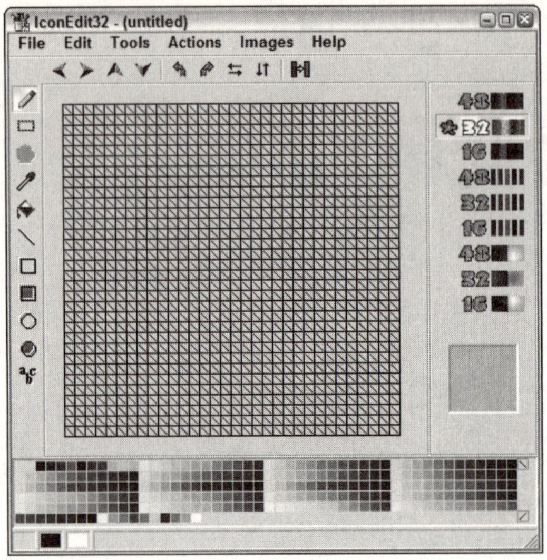

Figure 16-1: The IconEdit32 icon editor.

Understanding Icon Requirements

Icons may be different in many ways from the other graphics you use with your browsers, but they still have a set of attributes of which you must be aware. Although there are many types of icons, the ones you can add to your browser's title bar and status bar have the following requirements:

- Width of 16 pixels
- Height of 16 pixels
- 256 colors (8-bit color)

Starting a New Icon

One way icons differ from other types of graphics is that you can have more than one icon in a single icon file. When you first load IconEdit32, it'll be set up to create a 256-color, 32 x 32 icon, as you can tell by the asterisk next to that icon type on the right side of the editor's window.

You want to create a 256-color, 16 x 16 icon, so you need to click the correct icon type in the editor's window. When you do, an asterisk appears next to the icon type. The asterisk next to the 32 x 32 icon, however, doesn't go away, telling you that your icon file now contains both 32 x 32 and 16 x 16 icons. To get rid of the 32 x 32 icon, right-click its asterisk and choose the Delete 32 x 32 – 256 Color Image command from the menu that appears, as shown in Figure 16-2. The icon disappears.

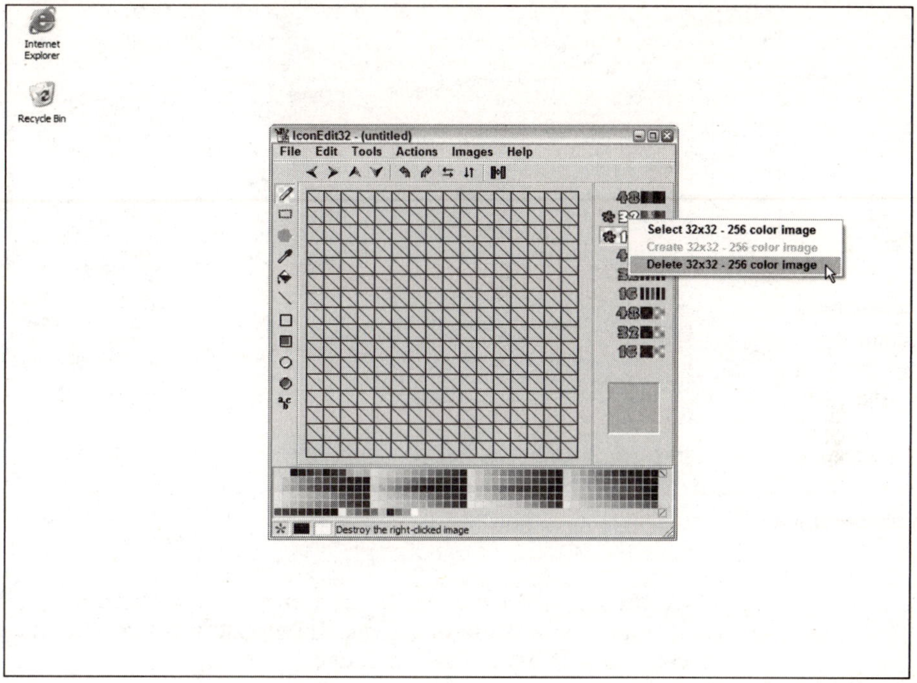

Figure 16-2: Deleting the 32 x 32 icon.

Making an Icon from Scratch

IconEdit32 contains all the tools you need to create your custom icons. Suppose, for example, that you want to make a smiley-face icon. Here's how:

1. **Start a new 16 x 16, 256-color icon.**

   (See the preceding section if you're not sure how to do so.) The icon editor displays a 16 x 16 grid in its work area, as shown in Figure 16-3.

2. **Select the Hollow Ellipse tool, which is the ninth tool down on the left side of the editor's window.**

   This tool enables you to draw the outlines of circles and ellipses.

3. **In the color boxes at the bottom of the editor's window, choose the color black.**

   The selected color appears in the foreground color indicator in the lower-left corner of the window.

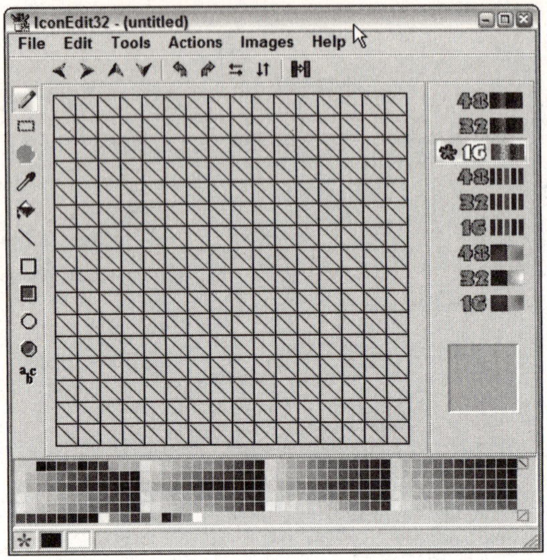

Figure 16-3: The icon editor with a 16 x 16 work-area grid.

4. **Place the mouse cursor in the center of the work-area grid, hold down the left mouse button, and drag the mouse until you've produced a circle that just fits in the work area.**

   Figure 16-4 shows the new circle in the icon grid.

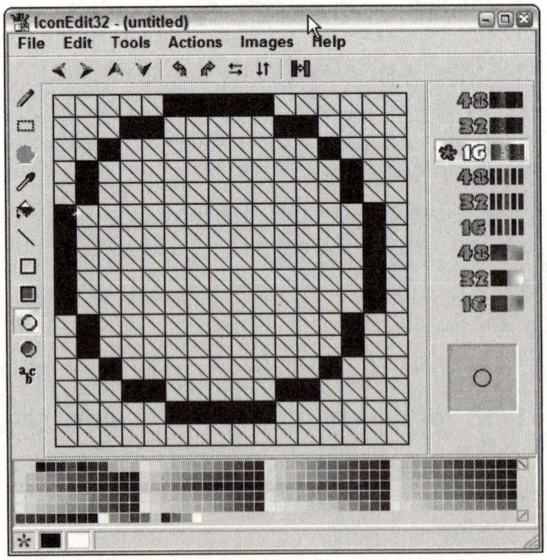

Figure 16-4: The hollow circle in the icon grid.

5. **Select the Fill tool, which is the fifth tool down (the one that looks like a tipped paint bucket) on the left side of the editor's window.**
6. **Select a shade of yellow from the color boxes at the bottom of the window.**

   The foreground color indicator turns yellow.
7. **Place the mouse cursor inside the hollow circle and click.**

   The editor fills the circle with yellow (see Figure 16-5).

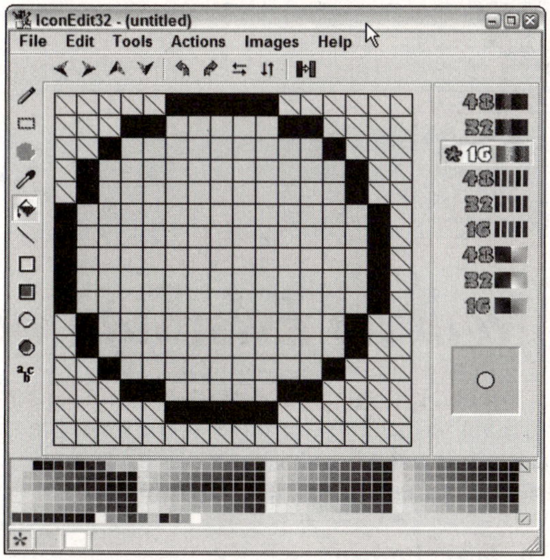

Figure 16-5: The filled circle.

8. **Select the Pen tool, which is the first tool on the left side of the editor's window.**

   You use this tool to draw in the icon's work area.
9. **Select the color green from the color selector.**
10. **Click in the appropriate grid locations to create the eyes, nose, and mouth, as shown in Figure 16-6.**

    Each time you click, the editor fills the clicked box with the color green.
11. **Choose File➪Save.**

Figure 16-6: The finished smiley-face icon.

Making an Icon from an Existing Image

Even though icons are a special graphical format, there's no reason you can't use graphics in other formats to create your icon. If, for example, you have a 16 x 16 bitmap that you want to use as an icon, IconEdit32 can do the conversion for you. Perform the following steps to see how this works:

1. **Start a new 16 x 16, 256-color icon.**

   (Refer to the section "Starting a New Icon" if you need detailed instructions.) The icon editor displays a 16 x 16 grid in its work area.

2. **Load the 16 x 16 source image (the image you want to use as an icon) into a paint program, such as Paint Shop Pro (see Figure 16-7).**

3. **Choose Selections⇨Select All to select the entire image.**

   You can also use the Ctrl+A keystroke.

4. **Choose Edit⇨Copy to copy the image to the Clipboard.**

   You can also use the Ctrl+C keystroke.

5. **Switch to IconEdit32 and choose Edit⇨Paste, or just press Ctrl+V.**

   The 16 x 16 image appears in IconEdit32's work area, as shown in Figure 16-8.

6. **In IconEdit32, choose File⇨Save to save the new icon under an appropriate name.**

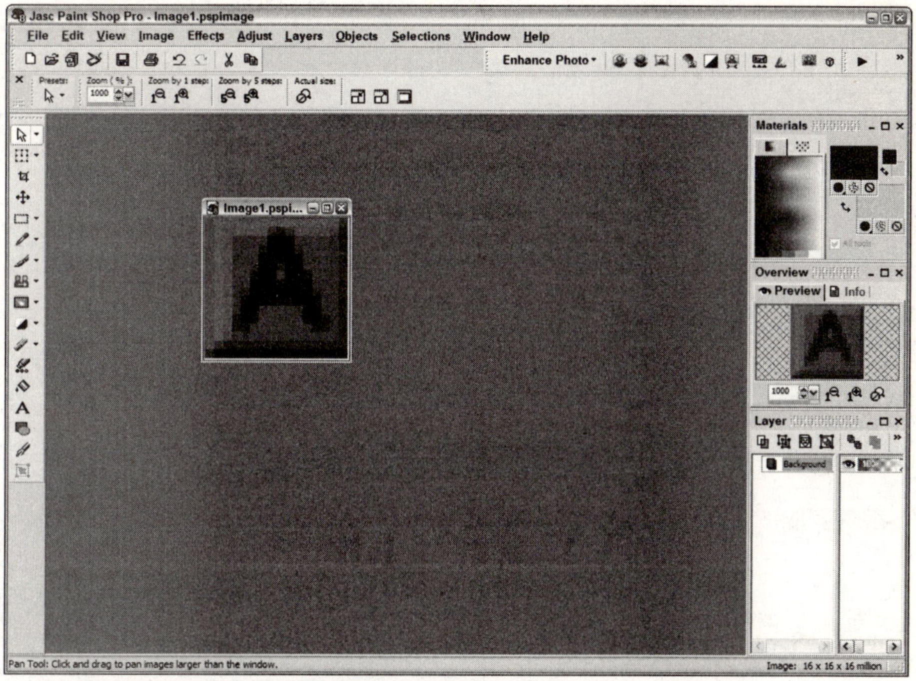

Figure 16-7: Paint Shop Pro with a 16 x 16 image loaded.

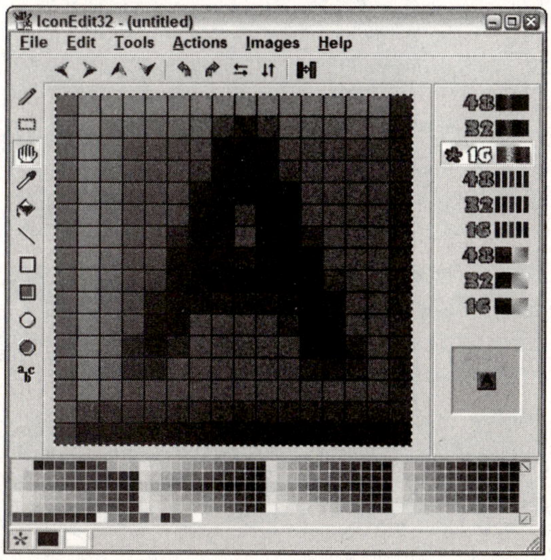

Figure 16-8: The icon editor with the pasted image in its work area.

Part IV
Controlling the Behavior of the Browser

"HONEY! OUR WEB BROWSER GOT OUT LAST NIGHT AND DUMPED THE TRASH ALL OVER MR. BELCHER'S HOME PAGE!"

In this part . . .

Your custom browser can include features you won't find in most other browsers. These features include a timer, an approved-sites list, a password manager, and a "screen spy," which takes automatic screen shots as the browser runs. Some of these special features provide a safer way for those youngun's to explore the Web. Other special features are simply handy. In this part, you also explore the script file that the browser editor generates. The browser compiler uses this script file to create the browser you designed.

Chapter 17

Controlling Access to Internet Sites

In This Chapter

- Working with the Internet alarm
- Using the approved-sites list
- Adding and deleting Web addresses to the approved-sites list

Parents who want to safeguard their kids against the dark side of the Internet rejoice! (Kids, on the other hand, commence to sulk.) The Browser Construction Kit offers a couple of ways for you to watch your kids and limit their access to certain Web sites. In this chapter, you find out how to use these safety features.

Using the Internet Alarm

For some kids, being on the Internet is a lot like playing a video game. Once they get started, they don't want to stop. Many parents limit the amount of time their offspring can sit in front of the Nintendo, and so, too, do some parents control the amount of time their kids use the Internet — except in the case of legitimate school research, of course!

One way the Browser Construction Kit keeps your kids on the straight and narrow is with the Internet alarm. Working just like the timer on your oven, you can set the Internet alarm to sound after a specific amount of time. This alarm can be audible, or it can be a message that appears, followed by the shutdown of the Browser — until you reset the timer.

To access the Internet alarm from your custom browser:

1. **Choose Tools⇨Alarms, as shown in Figure 17-1.**

   The Password box appears.

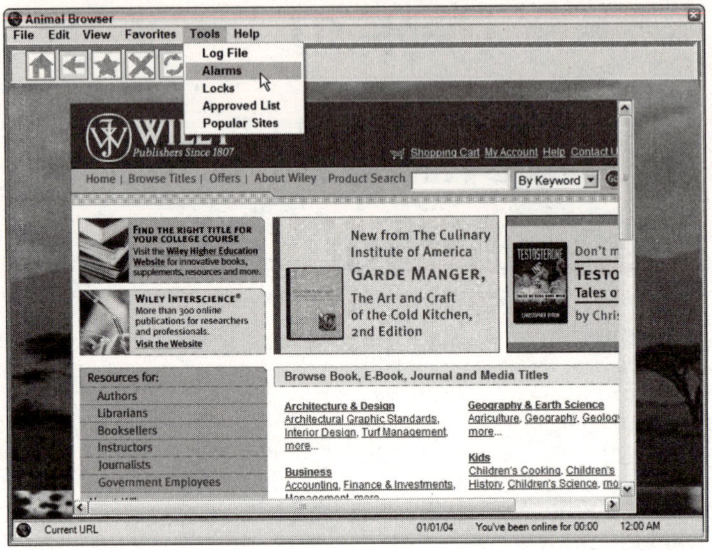

Figure 17-1: The Alarms command.

In order to access these two commands, you must add both the Tools menu and the Alarms command to your menu bar when you construct your custom browser. You cannot add or delete menus once your browser has been constructed except by using the browser editor to make changes and then recompiling the browser. (See Chapter 7 for more information on menus.)

2. **Type your password.**
3. **Click OK.**

   The Alarms dialog box, shown in Figure 17-2, appears.

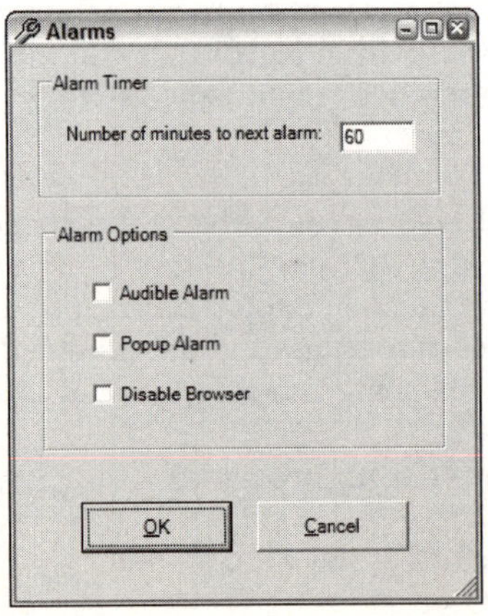

Figure 17-2: The Alarms dialog box.

4. **In the Number Of Minutes To Next Alarm box, type the number of minutes you want to elapse before the alarm is triggered.**

   If, for example, you want the alarm to go off in an hour, type 60 into the box.

5. **In the Alarm Options area, select one or both of the Audible Alarm and Popup Alarm options.**

   You have to select at least one of the Audible Alarm or Popup Alarm options. Otherwise, you have no alarm at all. The audible alarm plays a sound through your computer's audio system, whereas the popup alarm just displays a small window.

6. **If you want the browser to stop working at the end of the allotted time, select the Disable Browser option.**

   You can re-enable the browser by setting a new alarm or by turning off the alarm feature.

7. **Click OK to finalize your selections and to start the alarm timer.**

   If you change your mind, you can click Cancel instead of OK to return to the browser without setting an alarm.

If you have the Timer panel included in your browser's status bar (assuming the browser even has a status bar, which is not a requirement), the browser displays the amount of time elapsed, as shown in Figure 17-3.

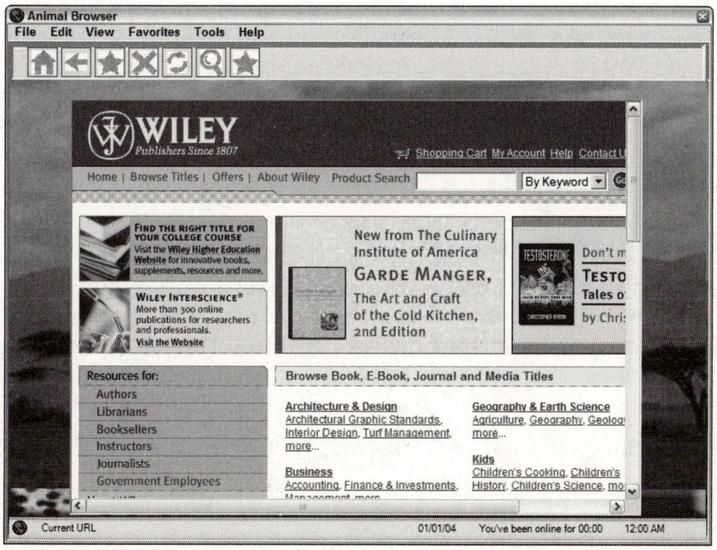

Figure 17-3: A timer in the browser's status bar.

For the status bar's countdown timer to work, you not only have to have the Timer panel included in the status bar, it must also be set as a countdown timer. You can set this timer attribute when you're designing your custom browser in the editor or by right-clicking the Timer panel and choosing a new setting from the Timer dialog box, shown in Figure 17-4. (Please see Chapter 18 for more information on timers.)

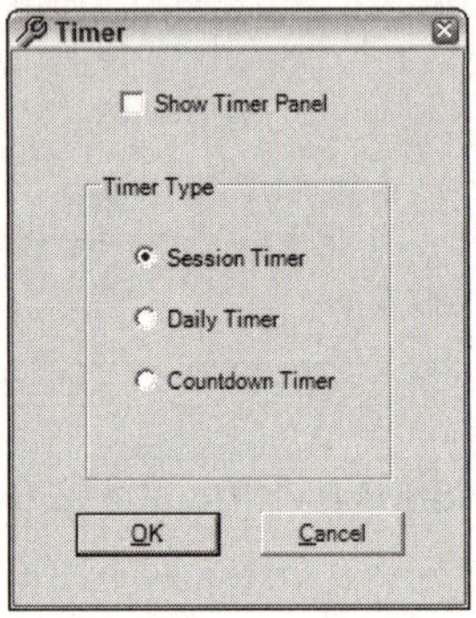

Figure 17-4: The Timer dialog box.

Setting Up an Approved-Sites List

The browser you create using the Browser Construction Kit can limit Internet access to only those sites that you've preapproved. You set this limitation with the approved-sites list. Normally, you add an approved-sites list to your browser as you're creating the browser in the browser editor. However, because you're likely to need to update the approved-sites list often, the browser itself gives you full access to the approved-sites list function.

To access the approved-sites list:

1. **Choose Tools⇨Approved Sites.**

   WARNING!

   In order to have access to the Tools menu's Approved Sites command, you must add the Tools Approved Sites commands to your menu bar when you construct your custom browser. You cannot add or delete menus once your browser has been constructed, except by using the browser editor to make changes and then recompiling the browser.

2. **When the Password box appears, type your password and click OK.**

   The Approved Sites dialog box appears, as shown in Figure 17-5.

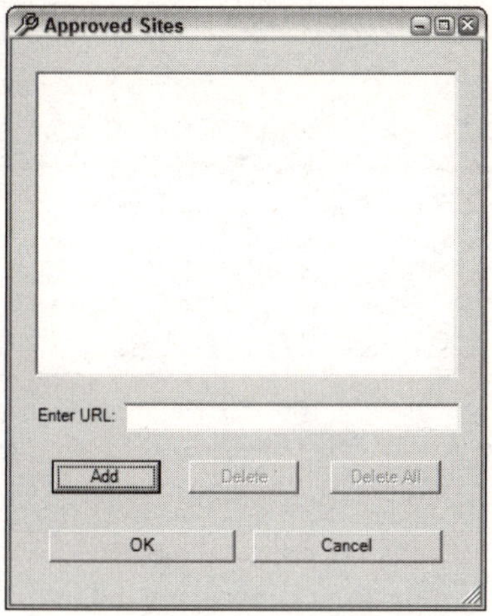

Figure 17-5: The Approved Sites dialog box.

3. **To add new entries to the approved-sites list, type the Web site's URL into the Enter URL box and then click Add.**

   The URL appears in the list above the buttons. The Web addresses in the list are the only ones that the browser can access.

4. **To remove an entry from the list, select the entry and then click Delete.**

   You can remove all the entries with a single button by clicking Delete All.

Chapter 18

Incorporating Passwords and Tracking Time Online

In This Chapter

- Setting and recovering passwords
- Changing the timer type
- Associating an alarm with a timer

Your custom browser can use one of three types of timers. You can use these timers just to keep track of how long you've been online, or you can associate the timer with the Internet alarm (see Chapter 17 for more information on alarms) and so control how long the browser stays active. All these special features are password-protected, so that only you can change their settings. In this chapter, you find out about the password and timer features.

Using the Password System

Obviously, if you're using the special custom-browser functions to keep an eye on your kids (or your parents!), you don't want anyone messing around with your settings. For this reason, you can password-protect sensitive settings such as timers and alarms.

When you first run your new browser, it uses a default password of "browser." How creative, huh? The first thing you want to do is to change the password to something else. To change your password:

1. **Choose Tools⇨Password.**

   The Password Change dialog box appears, as shown in Figure 18-1.

   WARNING! In order to have access to the Tools menu's Password command, you must add the Tools menu to your menu bar. You don't need to add the Password command. The browser does that automatically, as long as you have the Tools menu in place.

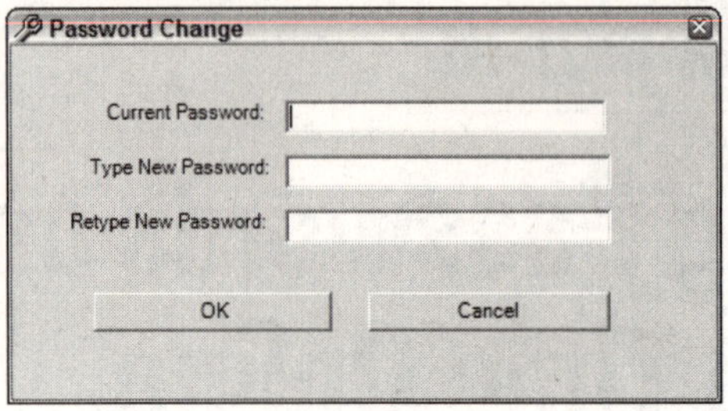

Figure 18-1: The Password Change dialog box.

2. **Type the current password into the Current Password box.**
3. **Type the new password into both the Type New Password and Retype New Password boxes.**

   Why twice? Because I think you need practice typing. Or maybe the program just wants to make sure that you didn't mistype the new password the first time. This check is important because you can't see the password as you type, just a line of asterisks. You don't want someone looking over your shoulder and discovering the password as you type, do you? (If you answered "yes" to this question, I'm guessing you have a lot to learn about computer security!)
4. **Click OK.**

   You now have a new password.

Recovering Your Password

So, what if you forget your password? Unfortunately, the only solution to this dilemma is to burn your computer (for security purposes) and buy a new one. Just kidding. There is a sneaky way to find or change your password, but you have to edit your system Registry to do it, something that you may not be too anxious to do, because editing the wrong thing could really mess up your computer.

TIP

If you're careful, though, you can search your Registry enough to recover a forgotten password. Just make sure that this information doesn't get into the wrong hands! In fact, after you read this section, you may want to obliterate these paragraphs with an indelible black marker. Just kidding again. Sort of . . . .

Here's how to recover your password from the Registry:

1. **Choose Start⇨Run, as shown in Figure 18-2.**

   The Run dialog box appears.

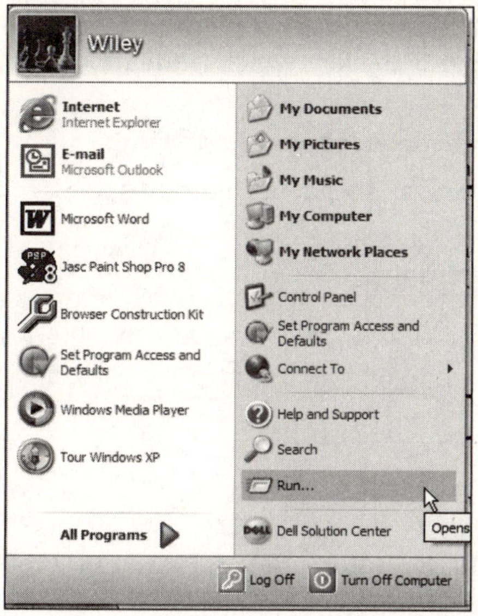

Figure 18-2: The first step in recovering your password.

2. **Type** regedit **into the Open box and click OK.**

   The Registry Editor appears on your screen, as shown in Figure 18-3.

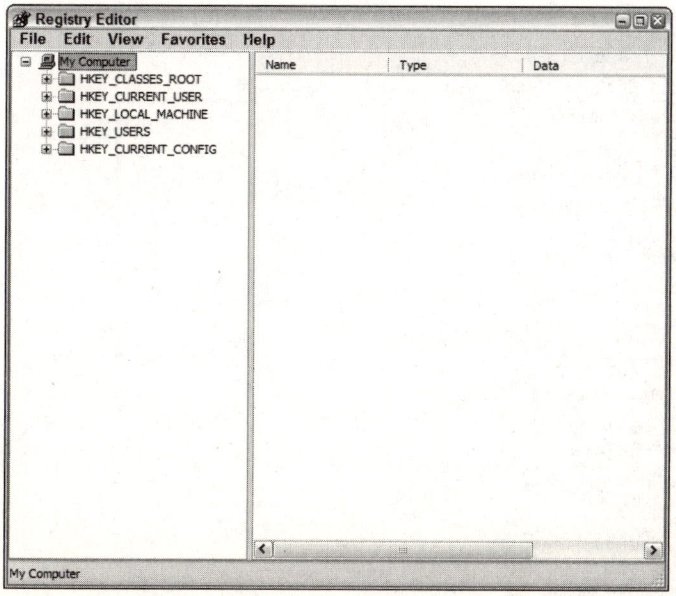

Figure 18-3: The Registry Editor.

3. **Click the My Computer key.**

   The Registry Editor highlights the key, which is the root key of the entire registry.

4. **From the Registry Editor's menu, choose Edit⇨Find.**

   The Find dialog box appears, as shown in Figure 18-4.

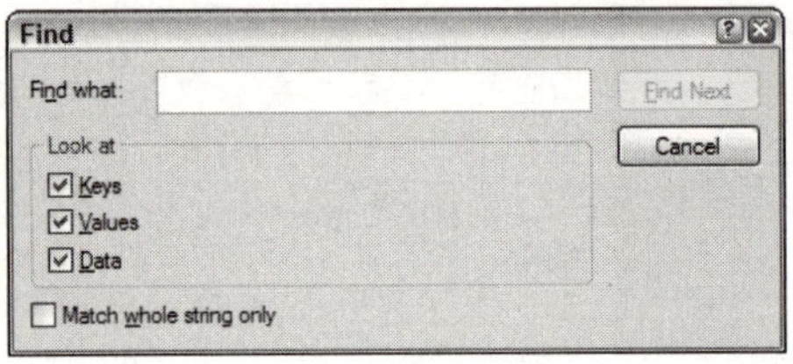

Figure 18-4: The Registry Editor's Find dialog box.

5. **Type** BCK Settings **into the Find What box, be sure that the Keys option is selected, and then click Find Next.**

   The Registry Editor finds the BCK Settings key in the registry (see Figure 18-5).

6. **If you don't see the Password key, double-click the BCK Settings key to open it.**

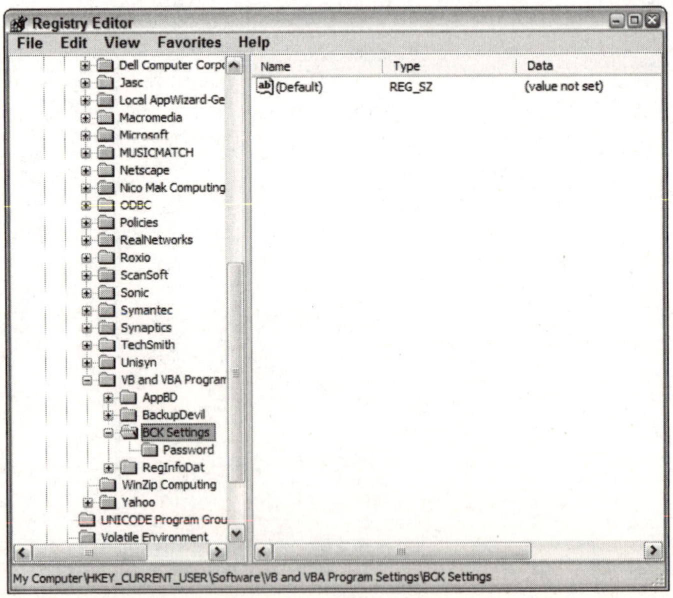

Figure 18-5: The Registry Editor after it has found the Browser Construction Kit key.

7. **Click the Password key to select it.**

   The key's value appears in the Registry Editor's right-hand pane, as shown in Figure 18-6. If you just wanted to see the password, you're all done. If you want to change it, continue with the next step.

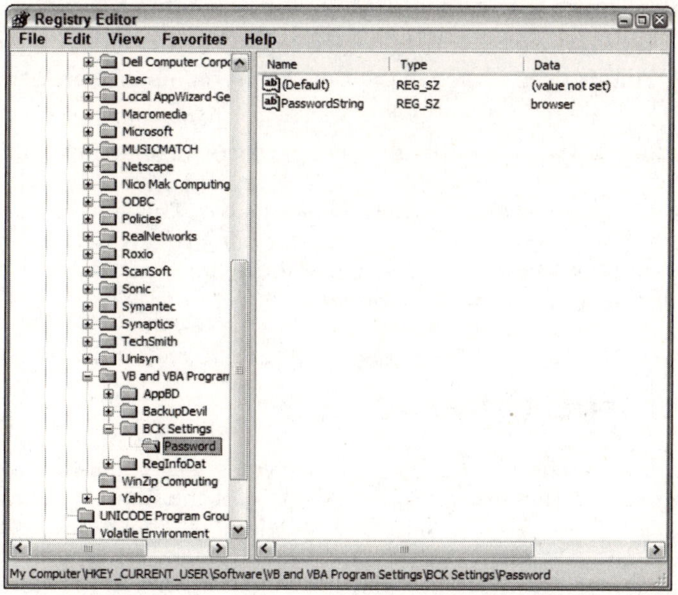

Figure 18-6: The Password key's value.

8. **Double-click the PasswordString entry.**

   The Edit String dialog box appears, as shown in Figure 18-7.

Figure 18-7: The Edit String dialog box.

9. **In the Value Name box, type the new password and click OK.**

   The Registry Editor changes the password's value.

10. **Close the Registry Editor.**

Using Timers

Your custom browser can display one of three types of timers. Here's what they are:

- **Session Timer:** Starts counting the time as soon as the browser goes online and starts over each time the browser is loaded.
- **Daily Timer:** Keeps track of the time spent online in each 24-hour period. Starts over at midnight.
- **Countdown Timer:** Counts down to zero from a specified value.

REMEMBER

The timer display lives in the browser's status bar. This means that, if you want to use the timer, you must add a status bar when you design your browser in the browser editor. You can add the timer panel to the status bar both in the editor and in the final browser.

Setting the timer options

Although you can choose the type of timer you want to use when you're designing your custom browser, you can also set the timer type from the browser itself. To do so, just right-click the timer's panel in the status bar. When you do, the Timer dialog box appears (see Figure 18-8). The Show Timer Panel option controls whether the timer appears in the status bar. The Timer Type area is where you set the type of timer you want to use. Click OK to finalize your choices or click Cancel to leave the timer settings as they were before you displayed the Timer dialog box.

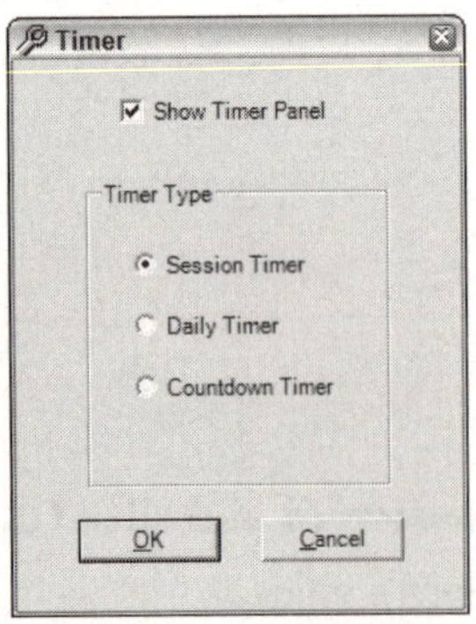

Figure 18-8: The Timer dialog box.

Associating an alarm with the countdown timer

The countdown timer can be connected to the Internet alarm feature, which can ring an audible alarm, show a popup alarm, or disable the Web browser from further use.

To access the Internet alarm from your custom browser:

1. **Choose Tools⇨Alarms.**

   The Password box appears.

2. **Type your password.**
3. **Click OK.**

   The Alarms dialog box, shown in Figure 18-9, appears. Enabling the alarm automatically associates the alarm with the countdown timer. That is, the alarm goes off when the countdown timer reaches zero. Please refer to Chapter 17 for more information about alarms.

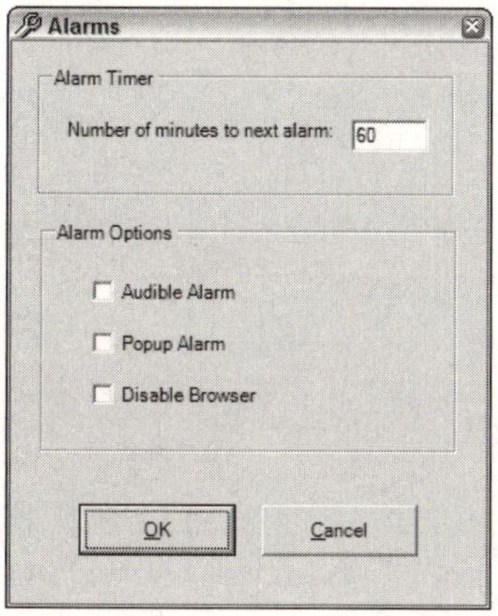

Figure 18-9: The Alarm feature works with the countdown timer.

Chapter 19

Keeping Track of Visited Sites

In This Chapter

- Starting a log file
- Viewing and deleting a log file
- Starting screen captures
- Viewing and deleting screen captures

Although the browser you create with the Browser Construction Kit features safety features like alarms and an approved-sites list, sometimes you want the browser's user to have more freedom than such safety features allow. One way to arrange for this possibility is to keep an automatic list of sites visited, as well as to take pictures of the screen at given intervals. Then you can see what the browser's user has been up to, yet the user still has complete freedom to explore the Internet. In this chapter, you explore these important "spy" features.

Generating Web Site Log Files

A *Web site log file* is a text file containing the Web sites your custom browser recently visited. You can use this file to ensure that whoever has been using the browser has not been visiting places on the Web where he or she shouldn't be.

REMEMBER

To use a Web site log file, you need to have added the Log File function when you designed your browser in the browser editor. You must also have added a menu bar with the Tools menu. Please refer to Chapter 7 for more information on menus.

Starting a log file

To start your log file, choose Tools⇨Log File. When the Password dialog box appears, type your password and click OK to display the Log File dialog box, shown in Figure 19-1. To start a log file, select the Log Visited Sites option. To stop the log file, turn off the option.

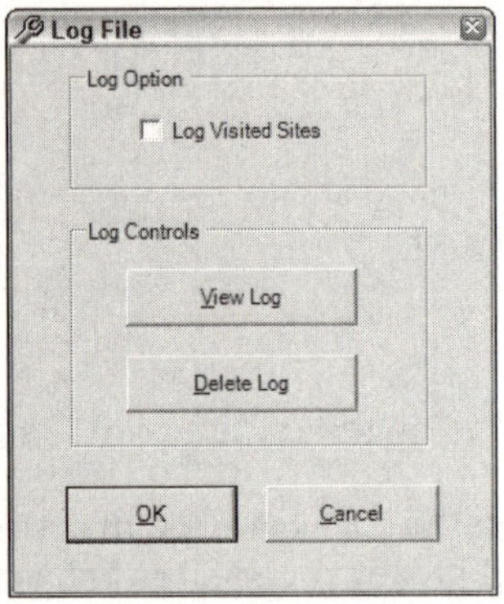

Figure 19-1: The Log File dialog box.

Viewing and deleting a log file

To view your log file, choose Tools⇨Log File. When the Password dialog box appears, type your password and click OK. The Log File dialog box appears. Click the View Log button and the browser loads the log file into Notepad for your perusal.

When you're finished viewing the log file, you can just close the Log File dialog box, which leaves the log file intact so that you can add other Web addresses. If you're completely finished with the log file, click the Delete Log button to remove the file from your computer. If you delete the log file, but keep the Log Visited Sites option selected, the browser will start a new log file.

Generating Automatic Screen Captures

The screen-capture function — which takes a screen shot once a minute — is another way to keep track of how your browser is being used. One by one, the browser stores the screen shots so that you can view them whenever it's convenient.

To use the screen-capture feature, you must have added the Screen Spy function when you designed your browser in the browser editor. You must also have added a menu bar with the Tools menu and have added the Screen Spy command to the menu. Please refer to Chapter 7 for more information.

Starting screen captures

To start your screen captures, choose Tools⇨Screen Spy. When you do, the Password dialog box appears. Type your password and click OK to display the Screen Spy dialog box (see Figure 19-2). To start screen captures, select the Capture Screens option and click OK. To stop the screen capture, turn off the option and click OK.

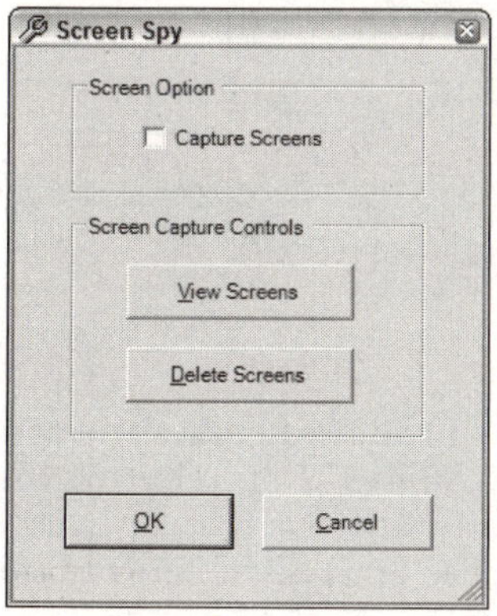

Figure 19-2: The Screen Spy dialog box.

Viewing and deleting screen captures

To view your screen captures, choose Tools⇨Screen Spy. When the Password dialog box appears, type your password and click OK. The Screen Spy dialog box appears. Click the View Screens button. When you do, the Screen Viewer window appears, as shown in Figure 19-3.

The Screen Viewer enables you to view screens manually one-by-one or using the built-in three-speed slideshow. When the Screen Viewer first appears, it loads and displays the first available screen shot. Click the Forward button to see the next screenshot. You can click the Back button to view the previous screen shot.

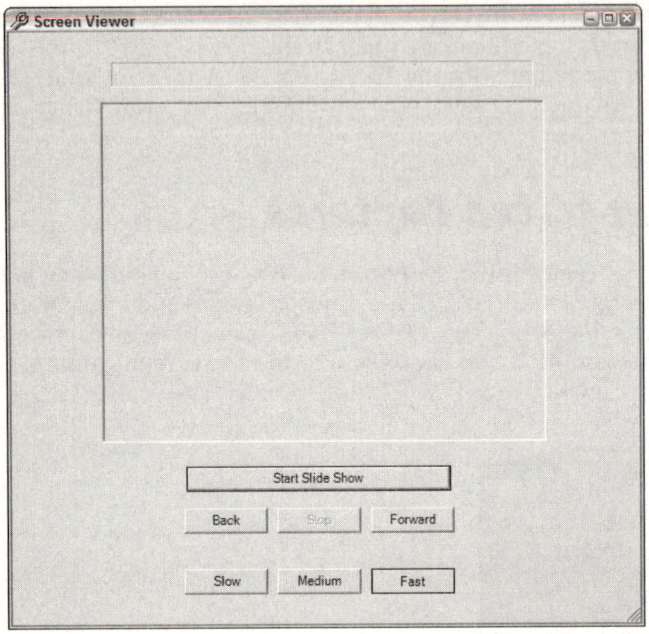

Figure 19-3: The Screen Viewer window.

To advance through the screens automatically, click the Start Slide Show button. Control the speed at which the slide show displays the screens by clicking the Slow, Medium, or Fast button. Click the Stop button to halt the slide show. You can then continue manually with the Forward and Back buttons or turn the slide show back on with the Start Slide Show button.

The larger you make the Screen Viewer window, the better the screen shots look. Click the window's Maximize button to increase the viewer to its largest size in order to view the screen shots at their best (see Figure 19-4).

When you're finished with the Screen Viewer, you can just close the window and then also close the Screen Spy dialog box. If you leave the Capture Screens option selected, the browser continues to add new screen shots to the ones that already exist. If you want to start fresh, click the Delete Screens button in the Screen Spy dialog box. The program then deletes all screens that currently exist. If the Capture Screens option is selected, the browser goes back to capturing screens.

Each screen shot's filename includes the date and time the capture was taken. This filename appears at the top of the Screen Viewer window, making it easy for you to know what was happening with the browser at any given time.

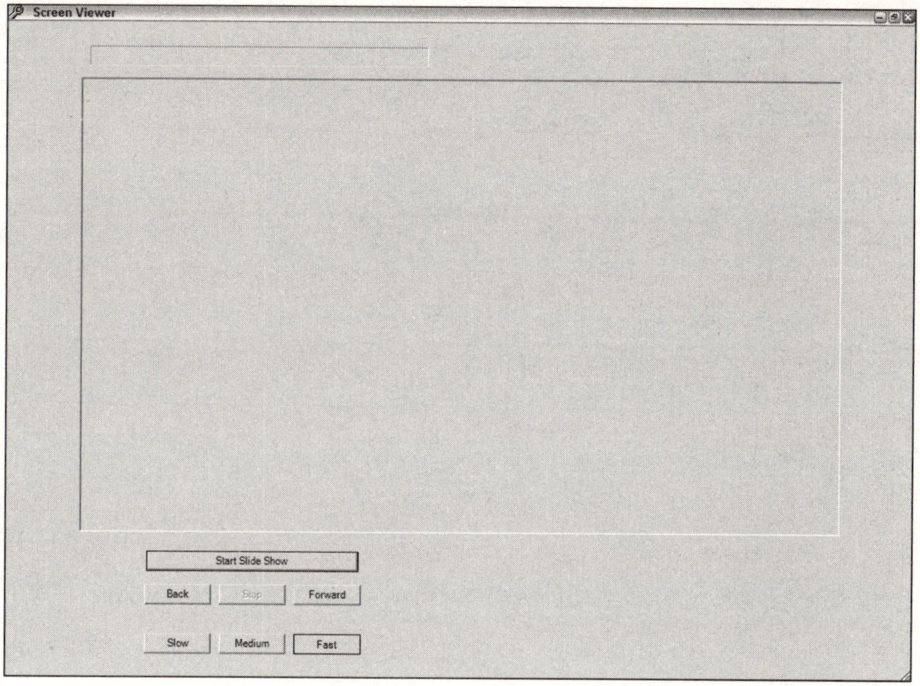

Figure 19-4: The maximized Screen Viewer window.

Chapter 20

Exploring a Browser Script File

In This Chapter

- Understanding the editor
- Discovering the seven script attribute groups
- Exploring the default script file
- Examining a complete script file
- Understanding the attributes in each script group

The Browser Construction Kit editor doesn't actually create a browser. Your browser is created by a compiler that reads a script file, creating the browser with the components and options you selected. The truth is that, although it's a convenient program, you don't even need the browser editor. You can create your browser script file by hand. I don't suggest doing this, though, because one tiny mistake could make your browser unusable. But whether you want to experiment with a browser script file or not, you may want to know more about how it works. That's what you discover in this chapter.

What the Editor Does

The Browser Construction Kit's editor is nothing more than a handy way to create a browser script file. The editor keeps track of everything you add to your custom browser, and, when you save your work, takes that information and creates the browser script file. Another advantage of the editor is that you can see the results of your settings right away, without having to first compile the browser.

The editor and the script file do share one important characteristic: the way the different browser settings are organized. As you probably know, the browser editor organizes your browser settings into seven groups (shown in Figure 20-1), each of which is accessed from the list box below the toolbox buttons. The resultant script file, too, is organized into these seven groups.

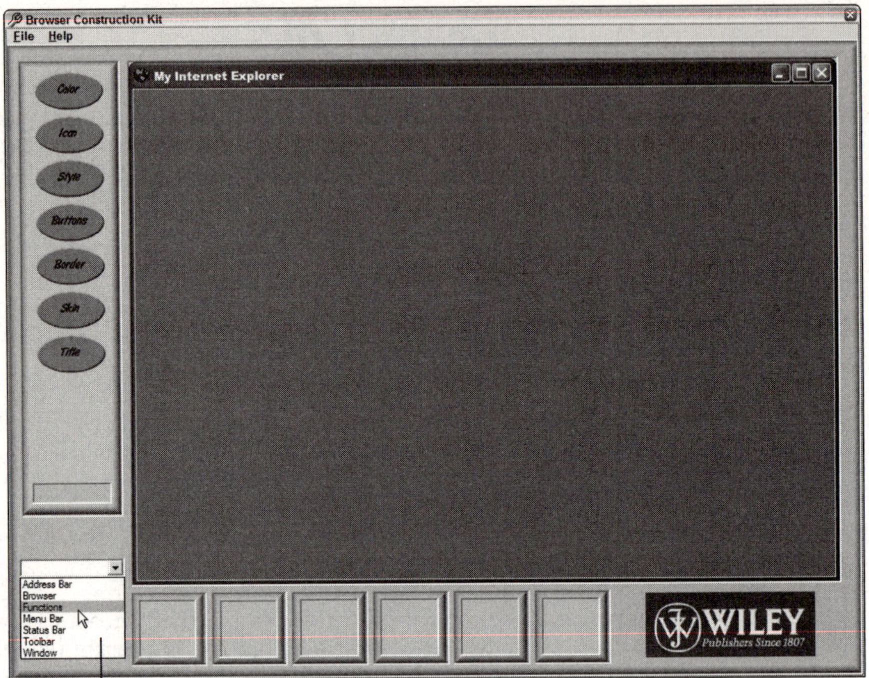

Figure 20-1: The seven attribute groups.

The seven attribute groups in the editor

The Seven Attribute Groups

Each group of settings starts with a title enclosed in square brackets. The groups are also organized into a specific order, and both the editor (when you try to reload a browser in progress) and the compiler (when you try to compile your browser) expect everything to be exactly in this order: Window Attributes, Browser Attributes, Toolbar Attributes, Status Bar Attributes, Menu Bar Attributes, Function Attributes, and Address Bar Attributes. Here's what a browser script file looks like, with the details of each section replaced with vertical ellipses:

```
[WINDOW ATTRIBUTES]
.
.
.
[BROWSER ATTRIBUTES]
.
.
.
```

```
[TOOLBAR ATTRIBUTES]
.
.
.
[STATUS BAR ATTRIBUTES]
.
.
.
[MENU BAR ATTRIBUTES]
.
.
.
[FUNCTION ATTRIBUTES]
.
.
.
[ADDRESS BAR ATTRIBUTES]
```

Attribute Settings

Each attribute group comprises specific settings, also organized into a strict order. Both the browser editor and the browser compiler expect these settings in the exact order, and any variation results in anything from a weird looking browser to a program crash.

The settings included in each section depend on which section you're looking at. The types of settings you can expect to find, however, are listed here:

- Text
- Colors
- Filenames
- Component locations
- Component sizes
- True or False switches
- Web addresses
- Style specifiers

The following sections tell you more about these different types of settings.

The Simplest Script File

Even if you were to load the Browser Construction Kit's editor and immediately save the default browser settings — without adding or changing anything — you'd still get a script file. The following listing shows this default file, which produces the browser window shown in Figure 20-2.

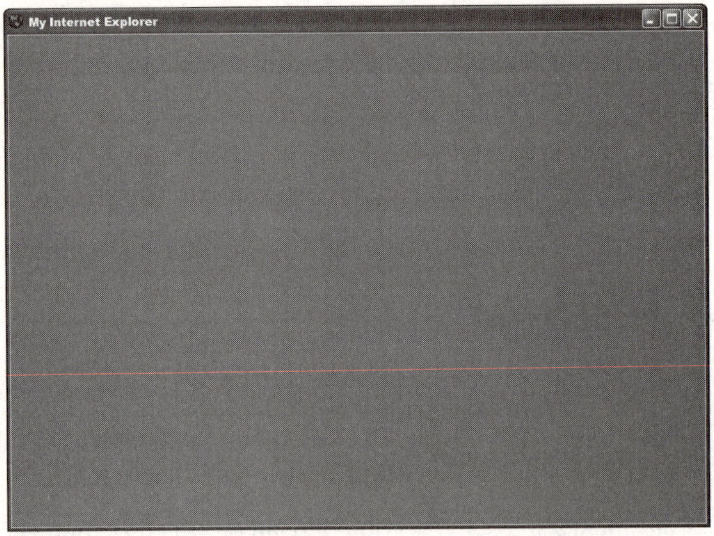

Figure 20-2: The default browser window.

```
[WINDOW ATTRIBUTES]
Title = My Internet Explorer
Color = Color [A=255, R=70, G=130, B=180]
Icon = C:\Program Files\Wiley\Browser Construction
          Kit\Graphics\Earth.ico
Style = 0
MaximizeButton = True
MinimizeButton = True
Border =
Skin =
[BROWSER ATTRIBUTES]
Browser = False
[TOOLBAR ATTRIBUTES]
Toolbar = False
[STATUS BAR ATTRIBUTES]
StatusBar = False
[Menu BAR ATTRIBUTES]
MenuBar = False
[FUNCTION ATTRIBUTES]
LogFile = False
```

```
Alarm = False
Lock = False
ApprovedList = False
ScreenSpy = False
PopularSites = False
[ADDRESS BAR ATTRIBUTES]
AddressBar = False
```

Notice in the default script file how each component of the browser, except for the main window, is set to False. That is, if you look at the BROWSER ATTRIBUTES section, you see this:

```
[BROWSER ATTRIBUTES]
Browser = False
```

These lines mean that no browser pane has been added to the browser window. For that reason, no other settings appear in the BROWSER ATTRIBUTES section. If you were to add a browser pane, the BROWSER ATTRIBUTES section would look something like this:

```
[BROWSER ATTRIBUTES]
Browser = True
Left = 75
Top = 120
Width = 640
Height = 444
BrowserBorder = False
BorderStyle = 0
StartSite = www.wiley.com
```

The same is true of the TOOLBAR ATTRIBUTES section. Because the default browser has no toolbar, its section in the script file looks like this:

```
[TOOLBAR ATTRIBUTES]
Toolbar = False
```

Look through the default script, and you'll see that all the components — browser, toolbar, status bar, menu bar, functions, and address bar — are set to False.

A Complete Script File

Suppose that you create a complete browser, including most of the available components, settings, and functions. Such a browser window might look like Figure 20-3.

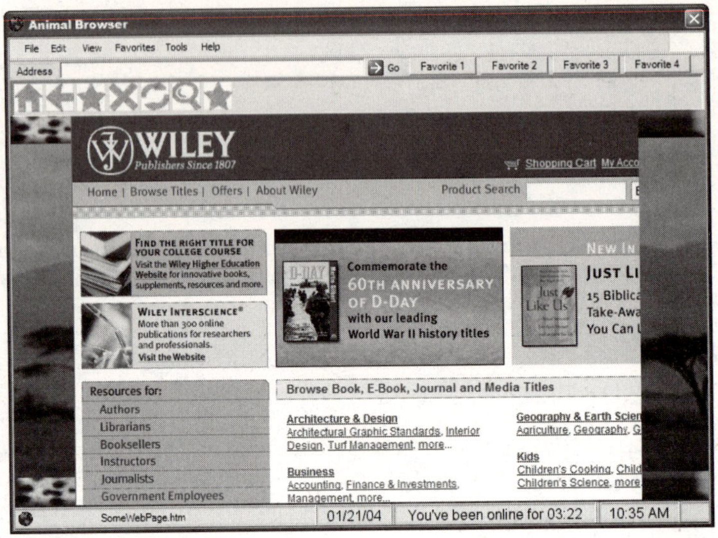

Figure 20-3: A full custom browser.

The script file for this browser holds a lot more information than the default script file did, because each browser component must include the settings needed to create the component in the custom browser's window. Here's what the script file for the browser shown in Figure 20-3 looks like:

```
[WINDOW ATTRIBUTES]
Title = Animal Browser
Color = Color [A=255, R=128, G=128, B=192]
Icon = E:\AnimalBrowser\EARTH.ICO
Style = 1
MaximizeButton = False
MinimizeButton = False
Border = E:\AnimalBrowser\Animal_Border.jpg
Skin = E:\AnimalBrowser\Animal_Background.jpg
[BROWSER ATTRIBUTES]
Browser = True
Left = 75
Top = 120
Width = 640
Height = 444
BrowserBorder = False
BorderStyle = 0
StartSite = www.wiley.com
[TOOLBAR ATTRIBUTES]
Toolbar = True
FileName = E:\AnimalBrowser\ToolbarHorz.bmp
Location = 1
NumberOfButtons = 7
Button00 = 1
FileName = E:\AnimalBrowser\Animal_Home.jpg
Button01 = 2
```

```
FileName = E:\AnimalBrowser\Animal_Back.jpg
Button02 = 3
FileName = E:\AnimalBrowser\Animal_Forward.jpg
Button03 = 4
FileName = E:\AnimalBrowser\Animal_Stop.jpg
Button04 = 5
FileName = E:\AnimalBrowser\Animal_Refresh.jpg
Button05 = 6
FileName = E:\AnimalBrowser\Animal_Search.jpg
Button06 = 7
FileName = E:\AnimalBrowser\Animal_Favorites.jpg
[STATUS BAR ATTRIBUTES]
StatusBar = True
StatusBarImageFileName = E:\AnimalBrowser\StatusBar.bmp
Location = 2
StatusBarIcon = True
StatusBarIconFileName = E:\AnimalBrowser\EARTH.ICO
StatusBarClock = True
StatusBarTimer = True
StatusBarTimerType = 1
MaxMinutesOnline = 120
StatusBarDate = True
StatusBarURL = True
[MENU BAR ATTRIBUTES]
MenuBar = True
FileMenu = True
EditMenu = True
ViewMenu = True
FavoritesMenu = True
ToolsMenu = True
HelpMenu = True
FileNewWindowCommand = True
FileOpenCommand = True
FilePropertiesCommand = True
FileCloseCommand = True
EditCutCommand = True
EditCopyCommand = True
EditPasteCommand = True
EditFindCommand = True
ViewToolbarCommand = True
ViewStatusBarCommand = True
ViewStopCommand = True
ViewGoToCommand = True
ViewRefreshCommand = True
ViewFullScreenCommand = True
FavoritesAddFavoritesCommand = True
FavoritesShowFavoritesCommand = True
ToolsLogFileCommand = True
ToolsAlarmsCommand = True
ToolsLocksCommand = True
ToolsApprovedListCommand = True
ToolsPopularSitesCommand = True
[FUNCTION ATTRIBUTES]
```

```
LogFile = True
Alarm = True
Lock = True
ApprovedList = True
ScreenSpy = True
PopularSites = True
[ADDRESS BAR ATTRIBUTES]
AddressBar = True
FileName = E:\AnimalBrowser\StatusBar.bmp
Location = 1
GoButton = True
Favorite1 = True
FavoriteURL1 = www.microsoft.com
Favorite2 = True
FavoriteURL2 = www.claytonwalnum.com
Favorite3 = True
FavoriteURL3 = www.wiley.com
Favorite4 = True
FavoriteURL4 = www.yahoo.com
```

Wow! A lot of info in that puppy, eh? As you look through it, you can probably figure out what most of the script file means, but in the following sections, you explore each section individually.

The Window Attributes Section

The WINDOW ATTRIBUTES section holds the settings for the browser's main window. For the browser you're examining, that section looks like this:

```
[WINDOW ATTRIBUTES]
Title = Animal Browser
Color = Color [A=255, R=128, G=128, B=192]
Icon = E:\AnimalBrowser\EARTH.ICO
Style = 1
MaximizeButton = False
MinimizeButton = False
Border = E:\AnimalBrowser\Animal_Border.jpg
Skin = E:\AnimalBrowser\Animal_Background.jpg
```

Figure 20-4 shows the effect of each setting. Here's what each setting means:

- **Title:** The text that appears in the window's title bar.
- **Color:** The color that fills the main window's background, given as alpha, red, green, and blue color components. The alpha value should always be 255. The red, green, and blue values combine to create the selected color.

- **Icon:** The icon that appears in the window's upper-left corner. This setting specifies the path and filename of the icon.
- **Style:** A value that specifies the window's style, where 0 = normal, 1 = normal unsizable, 2 = toolbox, 3 = toolbox unsizable, and 4 = no controls.
- **MaximizeButton:** Specifies whether the window has a Maximize button. A setting of True adds the button, whereas a setting of False removes the button.
- **MinimizeButton:** Specifies whether the window has a Minimize button. A setting of True adds the button, whereas a setting of False removes the button.
- **Border:** The border image that appears at the top and bottom of the window's client area. This setting specifies the path and filename of the border image.
- **Skin:** The background image that appears in the window's client area. This setting specifies the path and filename of the border image.

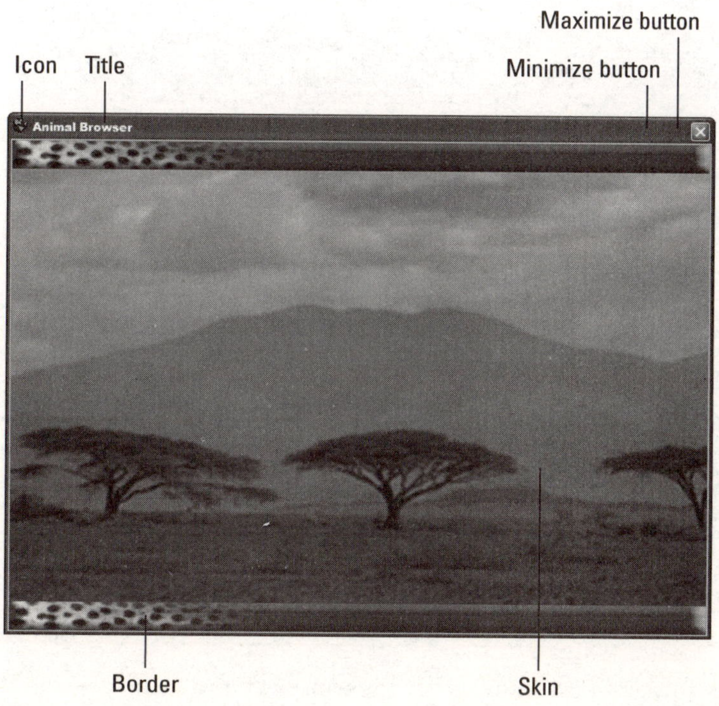

Figure 20-4: The window settings.

The Browser Attributes Section

The BROWSER ATTRIBUTES section holds the settings for the browser pane. For the browser you're examining, that section looks like this:

```
[BROWSER ATTRIBUTES]
Browser = True
Left = 75
Top = 120
Width = 640
Height = 444
BrowserBorder = False
BorderStyle = 0
StartSite = www.wiley.com
```

Figure 20-5 shows the effect of each setting, and here's what each setting means:

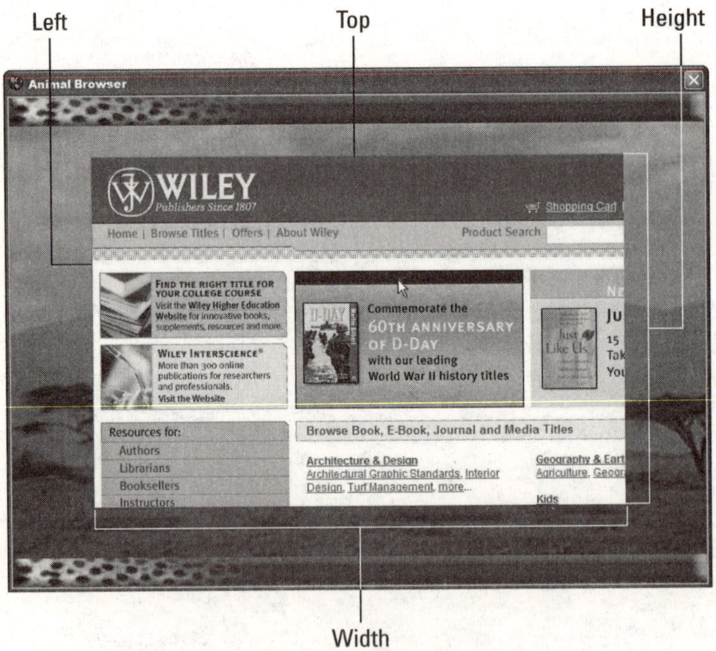

Figure 20-5: The browser pane settings.

- **Browser:** Specifies whether the window has a browser pane. A setting of True adds the browser pane, whereas a setting of False removes the browser pane.

- **Left:** The position of the browser pane's left edge.
- **Top:** The position of the browser pane's top edge.
- **Height:** The height of the browser pane.
- **Width:** The width of the browser pane.
- **BrowserBorder:** Specifies whether the browser pane has a border. A setting of True adds the border, whereas a setting of False removes the border.
- **BorderStyle:** A value that specifies the border's style, where 0 = normal, 1 = thin, 2 = 3-D, and 3 = thick 3-D.
- **StartSite:** The Web site the browser displays when the browser first opens.

The Toolbar Attributes Section

The TOOLBAR ATTRIBUTES section holds the settings for the window's toolbar. For the browser you're examining, that section looks like this:

```
[TOOLBAR ATTRIBUTES]
Toolbar = True
FileName = E:\AnimalBrowser\ToolbarHorz.bmp
Location = 1
NumberOfButtons = 7
Button00 = 1
FileName = E:\AnimalBrowser\Animal_Home.jpg
Button01 = 2
FileName = E:\AnimalBrowser\Animal_Back.jpg
Button02 = 3
FileName = E:\AnimalBrowser\Animal_Forward.jpg
Button03 = 4
FileName = E:\AnimalBrowser\Animal_Stop.jpg
Button04 = 5
FileName = E:\AnimalBrowser\Animal_Refresh.jpg
Button05 = 6
FileName = E:\AnimalBrowser\Animal_Search.jpg
Button06 = 7
FileName = E:\AnimalBrowser\Animal_Favorites.jpg
4
www.microsoft.com
www.wiley.com
www.claytonwalnum.com
WWW.GOOGLE.COM
```

Figure 20-6 shows the effect of each setting, and here's what each setting means:

- **Toolbar:** Specifies whether the window has a toolbar. A setting of True adds the toolbar, whereas a setting of False removes the toolbar.
- **FileName:** The path and filename of toolbar's background image.
- **Location:** A value that specifies the toolbar's location, where 1 = top, 2 = bottom, 3 = left, and 4 = right.
- **NumberOfButtons:** The number of buttons in the toolbar. This can be a value between 0 and 7.
- **Button*xx*:** A value that specifies the type of button, where 1 = home, 2 = back, 3 = forward, 4 = stop, 5 = refresh, 6 = search, and 7 = favorites. There will be one of these entries for each button in the toolbar. The *xx* in this description is the number of the button.
- **FileName:** The path and filename of each button's image. Each button will have one of these entries.

Following the named settings is the list of favorite URLs. The integer value is the number of URLs in the list. Following that value are the actual URLs.

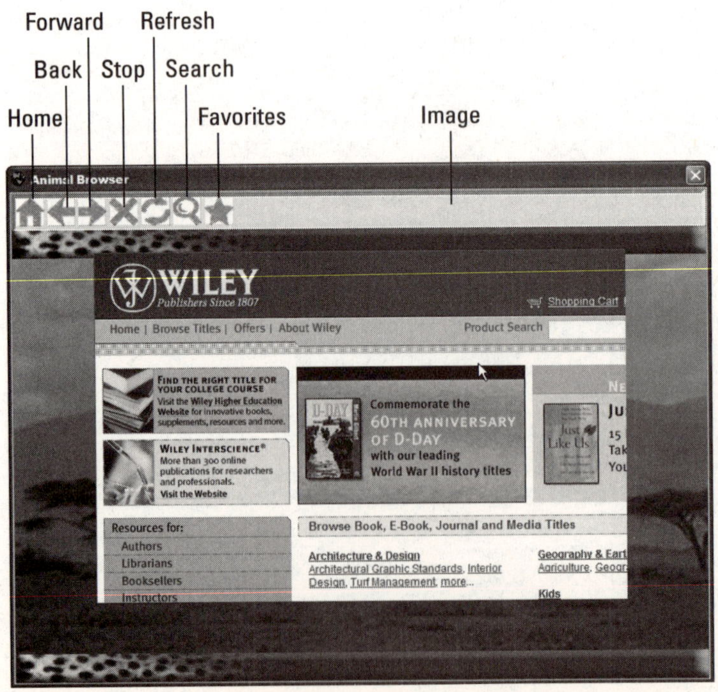

Figure 20-6: The toolbar settings.

The Status Bar Attributes Section

The STATUS BAR ATTRIBUTES section holds the settings for the window's status bar. For the browser you're examining, that section looks like this:

```
[STATUS BAR ATTRIBUTES]
StatusBar = True
StatusBarImageFileName = E:\AnimalBrowser\StatusBar.bmp
Location = 2
StatusBarIcon = True
StatusBarIconFileName = E:\AnimalBrowser\EARTH.ICO
StatusBarClock = True
StatusBarTimer = True
StatusBarTimerType = 1
MaxMinutesOnline = 120
StatusBarDate = True
StatusBarURL = True
```

Figure 20-7 shows the effect of each setting. The following list describes each setting:

- **StatusBar:** Specifies whether the window has a status bar. A setting of True adds the status bar, whereas a setting of False removes the status bar.
- **StatusBarImageFileName:** The path and filename of the status bar's background image.
- **Location:** A value that specifies the status bar's location, where 1 = top and 2 = bottom.
- **StatusBarIcon:** Specifies whether the status bar has an icon. A setting of True adds the icon, whereas a setting of False removes the icon.
- **StatusBarIconFileName:** The path and filename of status bar's icon.
- **StatusBarClock:** Specifies whether the status bar shows a clock. A setting of True adds the clock, whereas a setting of False removes the clock.
- **StatusBarTimer:** Specifies whether the status bar shows a timer. A setting of True adds the timer, whereas a setting of False removes the timer.
- **StatusBarTimerType:** A value that specifies the type of timer, where 1 = session timer, 2 = daily timer, and 3 = countdown timer.
- **MaxMinutesOnline:** A value that indicates the maximum number of minutes that the browser is allowed online each day.
- **StatusBarDate:** Specifies whether the status bar shows a date display. A setting of True adds the date, whereas a setting of False removes the date.
- **StatusBarURL:** Specifies whether the status bar shows the current URL. A setting of True adds the URL, whereas a setting of False removes the URL.

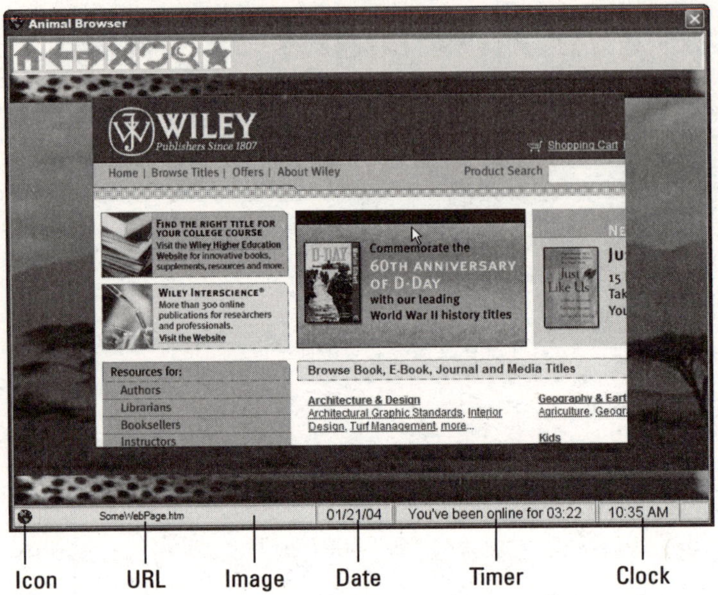

Figure 20-7: The status bar settings.

The Menu Bar Attributes Section

The MENU BAR ATTRIBUTES section holds the settings for the window's menu bar. For the browser you're examining, that section looks like this:

```
[MENU BAR ATTRIBUTES]
MenuBar = True
FileMenu = True
EditMenu = True
ViewMenu = True
FavoritesMenu = True
ToolsMenu = True
HelpMenu = True
FileNewWindowCommand = True
FileOpenCommand = True
FilePropertiesCommand = True
FileCloseCommand = True
EditCutCommand = True
EditCopyCommand = True
EditPasteCommand = True
EditFindCommand = True
ViewToolbarCommand = True
ViewStatusBarCommand = True
ViewStopCommand = True
```

```
ViewGoToCommand = True
ViewRefreshCommand = True
ViewFullScreenCommand = True
FavoritesAddFavoritesCommand = True
FavoritesShowFavoritesCommand = True
ToolsLogFileCommand = True
ToolsAlarmsCommand = True
ToolsLocksCommand = True
ToolsApprovedListCommand = True
ToolsPopularSitesCommand = True
```

Figure 20-8 shows the effect of each setting, whereas the following list describes each setting:

- **MenuBar:** Specifies whether the window has a menu bar. A setting of True adds the menu bar, whereas a setting of False removes the menu bar.
- **FileMenu:** Specifies whether the menu bar has a File menu. A setting of True adds the File menu, whereas a setting of False removes the File menu.
- **EditMenu:** Specifies whether the menu bar has an Edit menu. A setting of True adds the Edit menu, whereas a setting of False removes the Edit menu.
- **ViewMenu:** Specifies whether the menu bar has a View menu. A setting of True adds the View menu, whereas a setting of False removes the View menu.
- **FavoritesMenu:** Specifies whether the menu bar has a Favorites menu. A setting of True adds the Favorites menu, whereas a setting of False removes the Favorites menu.
- **ToolsMenu:** Specifies whether the menu bar has a Tools menu. A setting of True adds the Tools menu, whereas a setting of False removes the Tools menu.
- **HelpMenu:** Specifies whether the menu bar has a Help menu. A setting of True adds the Help menu, whereas a setting of False removes the Help menu.
- **FileNewWindowCommand:** Specifies whether the File menu has a New Window command. A setting of True adds the New Window command, whereas a setting of False removes the New Window command.
- **FileOpenCommand:** Specifies whether the File menu has an Open command. A setting of True adds the Open command, whereas a setting of False removes the Open command.
- **FilePropertiesCommand:** Specifies whether the File menu has a Properties command. A setting of True adds the Properties command, whereas a setting of False removes the Properties command.

- **FileCloseCommand:** Specifies whether the File menu has a Close command. A setting of True adds the Close command, whereas a setting of False removes the Close command.
- **EditCutCommand:** Specifies whether the Edit menu has a Cut command. A setting of True adds the Cut command, whereas a setting of False removes the Cut command.
- **EditCopyCommand:** Specifies whether the Edit menu has a Copy command. A setting of True adds the Copy command, whereas a setting of False removes the Copy command.
- **EditPasteCommand:** Specifies whether the Edit menu has a Paste command. A setting of True adds the Paste command, whereas a setting of False removes the Paste command.
- **EditFindCommand:** Specifies whether the Edit menu has a Find command. A setting of True adds the Find command, whereas a setting of False removes the Find command.
- **ViewToolbarCommand:** Specifies whether the View menu has a Toolbar command. A setting of True adds the Toolbar command, whereas a setting of False removes the Toolbar command.
- **ViewStatusBarCommand:** Specifies whether the View menu has a Status Bar command. A setting of True adds the Status Bar command, whereas a setting of False removes the Status Bar command.
- **ViewStopCommand:** Specifies whether the View menu has a Stop command. A setting of True adds the Stop command, whereas a setting of False removes the Stop command.
- **ViewGoToCommand:** Specifies whether the View menu has a Go To command. A setting of True adds the Go To command, whereas a setting of False removes the Go To command.
- **ViewRefreshCommand:** Specifies whether the View menu has a Refresh command. A setting of True adds the Refresh command, whereas a setting of False removes the Refresh command.
- **ViewFullScreenCommand:** Specifies whether the View menu has a Full Screen command. A setting of True adds the Full Screen command, whereas a setting of False removes the Full Screen command.
- **FavoritesAddFavoritesCommand:** Specifies whether the Favorites menu has an Add Favorites command. A setting of True adds the Add Favorites command, whereas a setting of False removes the Add Favorites command.
- **FavoritesShowFavoritesCommand:** Specifies whether the Favorites menu has a Show Favorites command. A setting of True adds the Show Favorites command, whereas a setting of False removes the Show Favorites command.

- **ToolsLogFileCommand:** Specifies whether the Tools menu has a Log File command. A setting of True adds the Log File command, whereas a setting of False removes the Log File command.
- **ToolsAlarmsCommand:** Specifies whether the Tools menu has an Alarms command. A setting of True adds the Alarms command, whereas a setting of False removes the Alarms command.
- **ToolsLocksCommand:** Specifies whether the Tools menu has a Locks command. A setting of True adds the Locks command, whereas a setting of False removes the Locks command.
- **ToolsApprovedListCommand:** Specifies whether the Tools menu has an Approved List command. A setting of True adds the Approved List command, whereas a setting of False removes the Approved List command.
- **ToolsPopularSitesCommand:** Specifies whether the Tools menu has a Popular Sites command. A setting of True adds the Popular Sites command, whereas a setting of False removes the Popular Sites command.

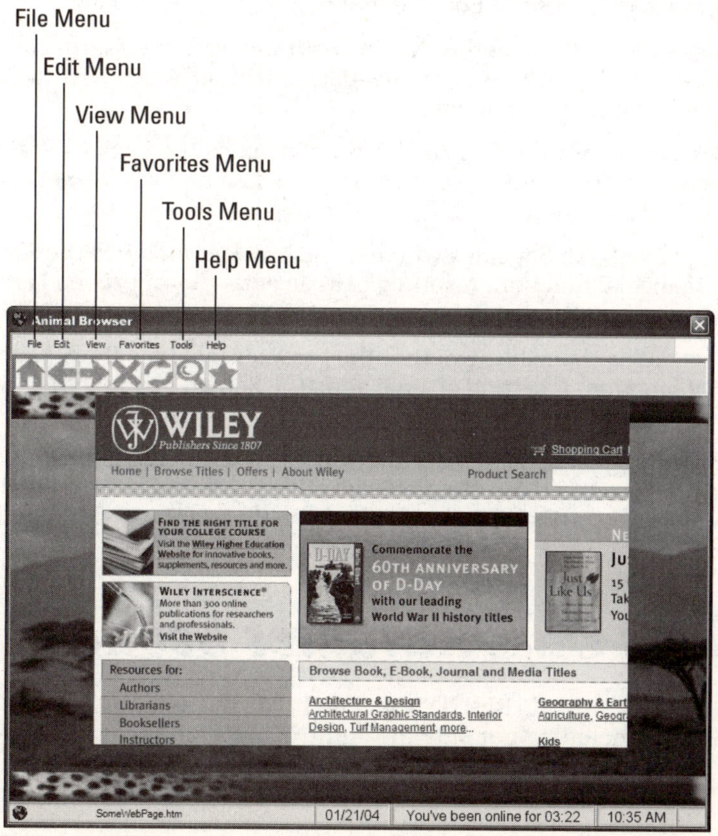

Figure 20-8: The menu bar settings.

The Function Attributes Section

The FUNCTION ATTRIBUTES section holds the settings for the window's special functions, such as alarms and locks. For the browser you're examining, which includes all the special functions, that section looks like this:

```
[FUNCTION ATTRIBUTES]
LogFile = True
Alarm = True
Lock = True
ApprovedList = True
ScreenSpy = True
PopularSites = True
```

The following list — you guessed it — describes each setting:

- **LogFile:** Specifies whether the browser includes the Log File special function. A setting of True adds the Log File function, whereas a setting of False removes the Log File function.
- **Alarm:** Specifies whether the browser includes the Alarm special function. A setting of True adds the Alarm function, whereas a setting of False removes the Alarm function.
- **Lock:** Specifies whether the browser includes the Lock special function. A setting of True adds the Lock function, whereas a setting of False removes the Lock function.
- **ApprovedList:** Specifies whether the browser includes the Approved List special function. A setting of True adds the Approved List function, whereas a setting of False removes the Approved List function.
- **ScreenSpy:** Specifies whether the browser includes the Screen Spy special function. A setting of True adds the Screen Spy function, whereas a setting of False removes the Screen Spy function.
- **PopularSites:** Specifies whether the browser includes the Popular Sites special function. A setting of True adds the Popular Sites function, whereas a setting of False removes the Popular Sites function.

The Address Bar Attributes Section

The ADDRESS BAR ATTRIBUTES section holds the settings for the window's address bar, including not only the address bar's background image, but also the type of panels it will display. For the browser you're examining, which includes all the special functions, the address bar section looks like this:

```
[ADDRESS BAR ATTRIBUTES]
AddressBar = True
FileName = E:\AnimalBrowser\StatusBar.bmp
Location = 1
GoButton = True
Favorite1 = True
FavoriteURL1 = www.microsoft.com
Favorite2 = True
FavoriteURL2 = www.claytonwalnum.com
Favorite3 = True
FavoriteURL3 = www.wiley.com
Favorite4 = True
FavoriteURL4 = www.yahoo.com
```

Figure 20-9 shows the parts of the address bar. The following list describes each setting:

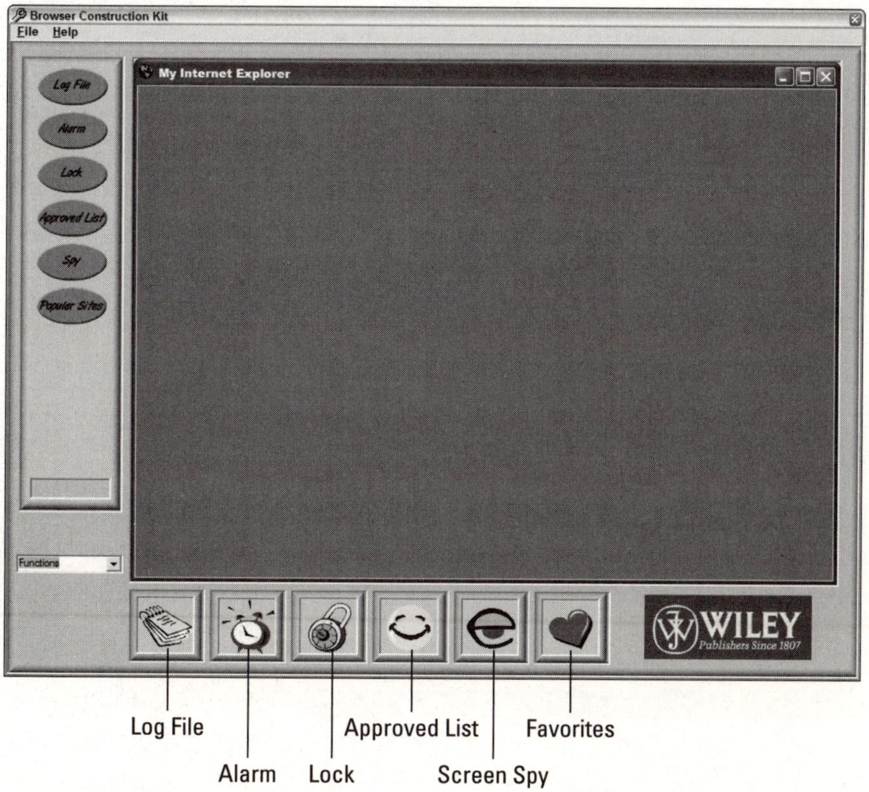

Figure 20-9: The address bar settings.

- **AddressBar:** Specifies whether the browser window has an address bar. A setting of True adds the address bar, whereas a setting of False removes the address bar.
- **FileName:** The path and filename of the address bar's background image.
- **Location:** A value that specifies the status bar's location, where 1 = top and 2 = bottom.
- **GoButton:** Specifies whether the browser's status bar includes a Go button. A setting of True adds the button, whereas a setting of False removes the button.
- **Favorite*x*:** Specifies whether the browser's status bar includes the favorite buttons. Each of the four buttons has one of these entries, where the *x* is the button's number.
- **FavoriteURL*x*:** Specifies the URL associated with favorite button *x*.

Part V

Designing Customized Web Browser Projects

The 5th Wave By Rich Tennant

"Amy surfs the Web a lot, so for protection we installed several filtering programs that allow only approved sites through. Which of those nine sites are you looking at now, Amy?"

In this part . . .

After you discover the tools and techniques for creating custom browsers, I don't just leave you stranded. In Part V, I hold your hand through the creation of a set of interesting, useful, and sometimes just fun custom browser projects. Step-by-step instructions tell you everything you need to know to not only create a custom browser, but also how to use browsers in tricky ways. Here, you build seven custom browsers in all.

Chapter 21

Developing a General-Use Web Browser

In This Chapter

- Creating a general browser window
- Adding a general menu bar
- Adding a general toolbar, status bar, and address bar
- Positioning the browser pane
- Compiling the general-use browser

In spite of all the cool things the Browser Construction Kit can do, it makes sense to start off this book's example projects with a general-use browser. By general use, I mean a browser that includes no special features and that serves as a basic tool for browsing the Internet.

Like the other chapters in this section of the book, this chapter comprises step-by-step instructions for building a specific custom Web browser. If you follow the steps in this chapter, you end up with a handy general-use Web browser.

Creating the Window

The window you create for this custom browser is what you might call plain vanilla. That is, it doesn't show off with any fancy graphics or extras. Perform the following steps to design the general-use browser's window:

1. **In the drop-down list below the toolbox, select the Window command set.**

   The Window commands appear in the toolbox.

2. **Click the Color button.**

   The Color dialog box appears, as shown in Figure 21-1.

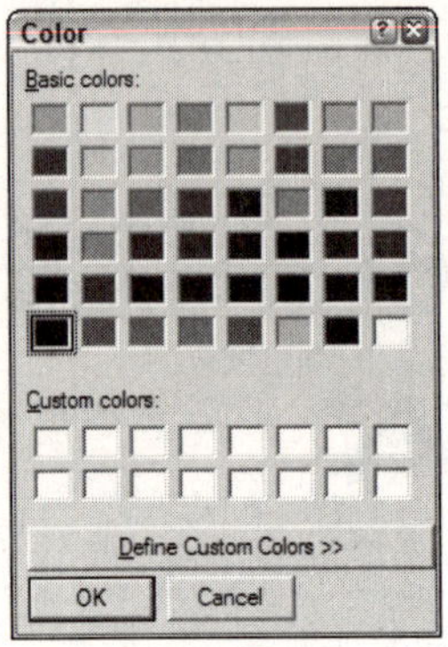

Figure 21-1: The Color dialog box.

3. **Select the color white and click OK.**

   The window's background turns white.

4. **Click the Icon button.**

   The Select Window Icon dialog box appears (see Figure 21-2).

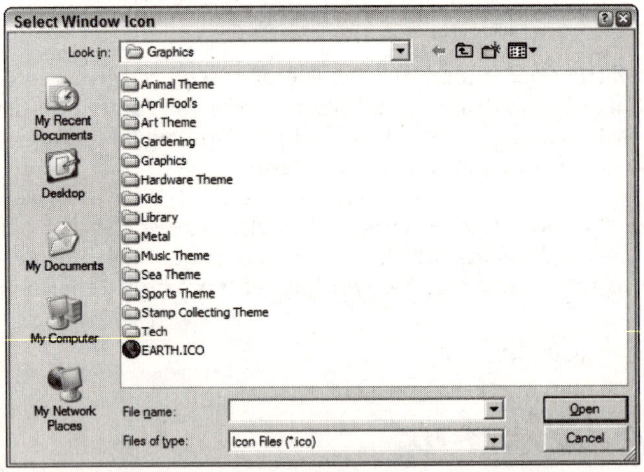

Figure 21-2: The Select Window Icon dialog box.

5. **Locate the icon you want to use and double-click the filename.**

   Alternatively, you can click the icon file once to select it and then click the dialog box's Open button.

   Your icon appears in the window's title bar.

6. **Click the Style button.**

   The Window Styles dialog box appears, as shown in Figure 21-3.

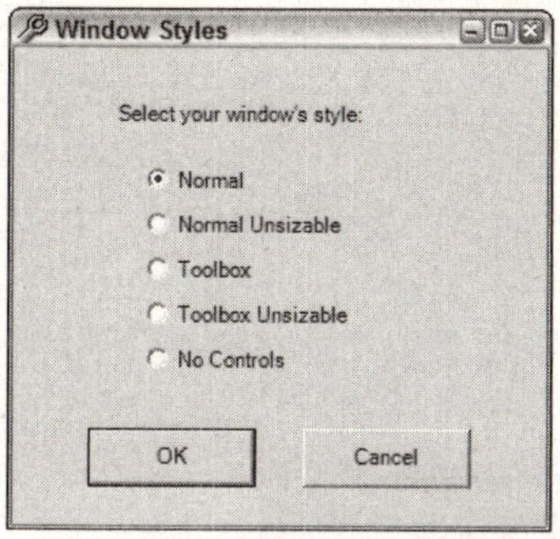

Figure 21-3: The Window Styles dialog box.

7. **Select the Normal Unsizable option and click OK.**

   The window's border style changes. (The change is so subtle that you may not even notice it.)

8. **Click the Buttons command in the toolbox.**

   The Window Buttons dialog box appears (see Figure 21-4).

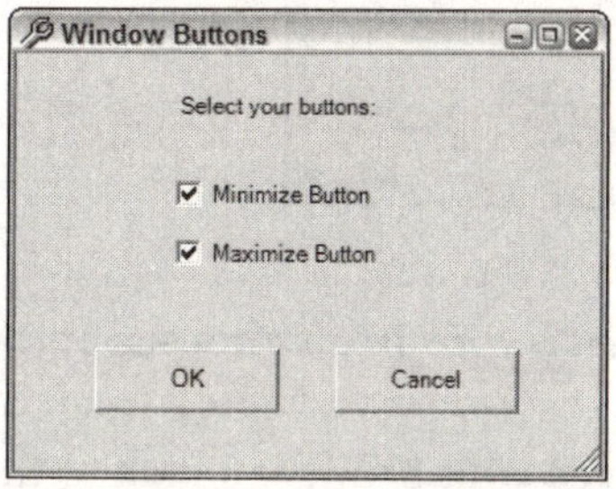

Figure 21-4: The Window Buttons dialog box.

9. **Turn off the Minimize Button and Maximize Button options so that the checks disappear and then click OK.**

   The Browser Construction Kit removes the Minimize and Maximize buttons from the window.

10. **Click the Title button.**

    The Window Title dialog box appears, as shown in Figure 21-5.

11. **Type the name you want into the text box and click OK.**

    The window's new title appears in the title bar.

12. **Choose File⇨Save As.**

    The Save Browser File dialog box appears (see Figure 21-6).

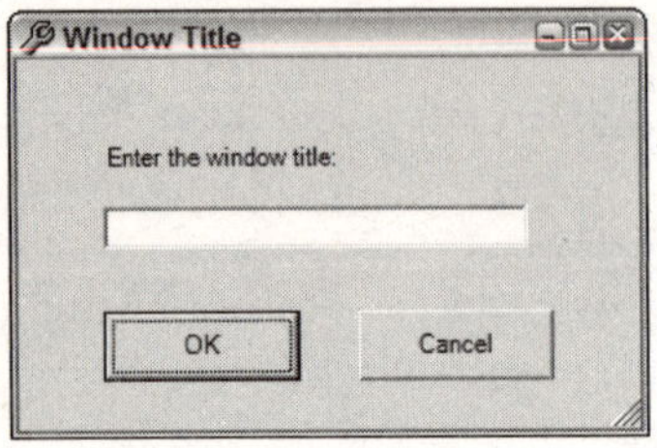

Figure 21-5: The Window Title dialog box.

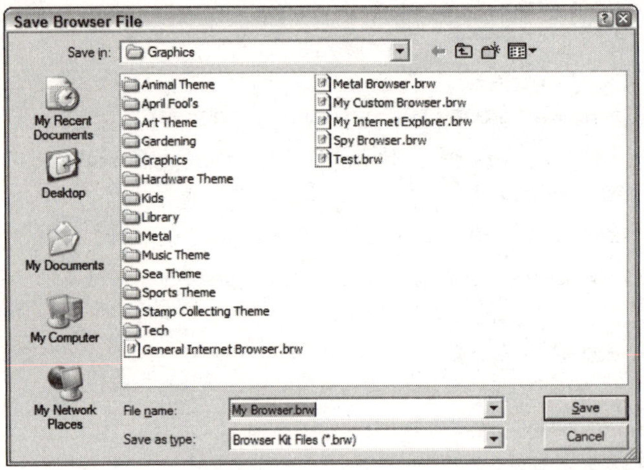

Figure 21-6: The Save Browser File dialog box.

13. **Navigate to where you want to save your browser's script file and then click Save.**

    The Browser Construction Kit saves your browser's data to the selected location, using the window's title as the filename.

Adding the Menu Bar

The menu bar for the general-use browser features a full set of menus, commands, and options. Here's how to put it together:

1. **In the drop-down menu below the toolbox, select the Menu Bar command set.**

   The Menu Bar commands appear in the toolbox.

2. **Click the Menu Bar command in the toolbox.**

   The menu bar appears in the custom browser window.

3. **Select the File button in the toolbox.**

   The File Menu dialog box appears (see Figure 21-7).

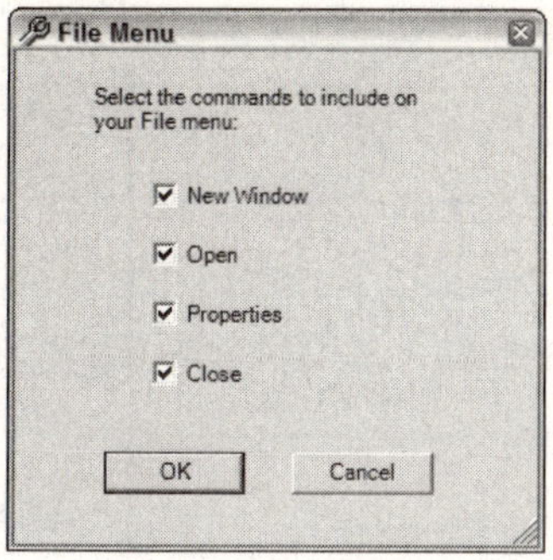

Figure 21-7: The File Menu dialog box.

4. **Select the four menu options (New Window, Open, Properties, and Close) and click the OK button.**

   The File menu appears in your custom browser window, as shown in Figure 21-8.

Figure 21-8: The custom browser window with its File menu.

5. **Use the Edit, View, Favorites, Tools, and Help commands in the toolbox to add the menus to the menu bar, the same way you added the File menu in Steps 3 and 4.**

   Your custom browser now has a complete set of menus, as shown in Figure 21-9.

6. **Choose File⇨Save As.**

   The Save Browser File dialog box appears.

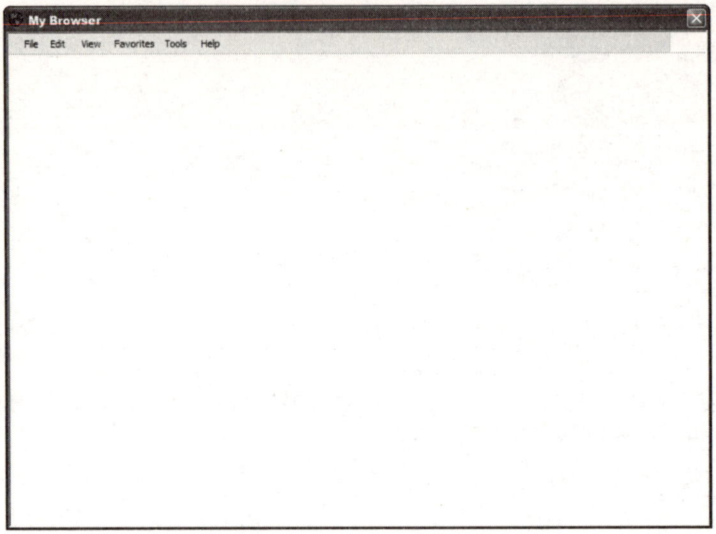

Figure 21-9: The custom browser window with its new menus.

7. **Navigate to where you want to save your browser's script file and then click Save.**

   The Browser Construction Kit saves your browser's data to the selected location, using the window's title as the filename.

Adding the Toolbar

A general-use Web browser must have all the navigation commands you need to make your way through the complex world of the Internet. For that reason, the toolbar you build here has all the toolbar features the Browser Construction Kit makes available to you. Just follow these steps to add your toolbar to the window:

1. **In the drop-down menu below the toolbox, select the Toolbar command set.**

   The Toolbar commands appear in the toolbox.

2. **Click the Toolbar button.**

   The Toolbar dialog box appears (see Figure 21-10).

3. **Select the toolbar's location and then click the Browse button.**

   The Load Toolbar Image dialog box appears, as seen in Figure 21-11.

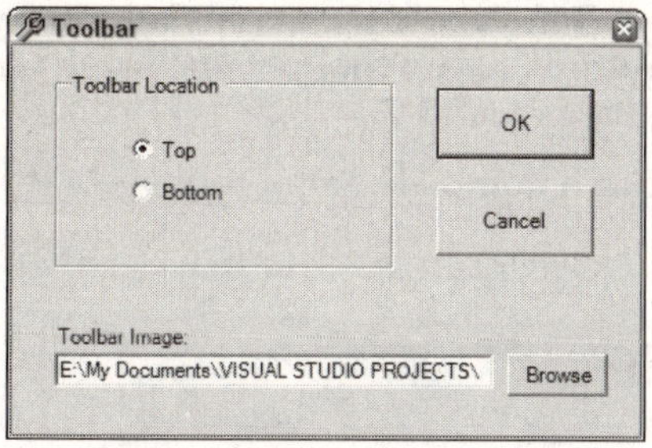

Figure 21-10: The Toolbar dialog box.

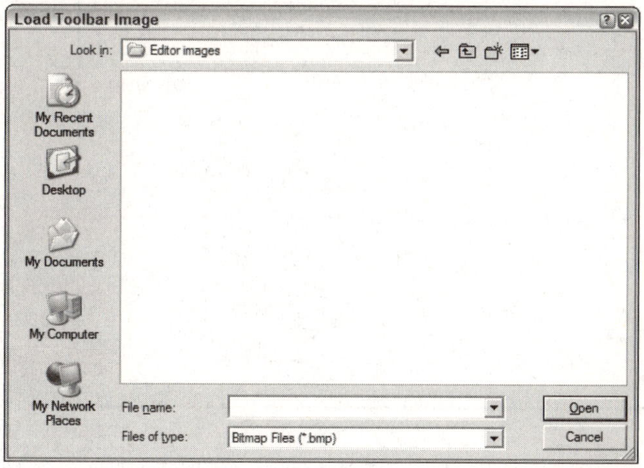

Figure 21-11: The Load Toolbar Image dialog box.

4. **Locate the image you want to use and double-click the image's filename.**

   The selected filename appears in the Toolbar dialog box's Toolbar Image text box.

5. **Click the Toolbar dialog box's OK button.**

   The toolbar appears in the custom browser window.

6. **Click the Home command in the toolbox.**

   The Load Button dialog box appears.

7. **Locate the image you want to use for the Home button and double-click the image's filename.**

   Alternatively, you can click the image file once to select it and then click the dialog box's Open button.

   The Home button appears in the custom window's toolbar.

8. **Use the Back, Forward, Stop, Refresh, Search, and Favorites commands in the toolbox to add the buttons to the toolbar, the same way you added the Home button in Steps 6 and 7.**

   Your custom browser now has a complete set of toolbar buttons, as shown in Figure 21-12.

Figure 21-12: The toolbar with a complete set of buttons.

9. **Choose File⇨Save.**

   The Browser Construction Kit saves your browser's data.

Adding the Status Bar

Although, for the most part, the general use Web browser has few special features, it does boast a status bar with a date, clock, and timer display. Here's how to build it:

1. **In the drop-down menu below the toolbox, select the Status Bar command set.**

   The Status Bar commands appear in the toolbox.

2. **Click the Status Bar button.**

   The Status Bar dialog box appears.

3. **Select the Status Bar's location and then click the Browse button.**

   The Load Status Bar Image dialog box appears.

4. **Locate the image you want to use for your status bar and double-click the image's filename.**

   The selected filename appears in the Status Bar dialog box's Status Bar Image text box.

5. **Click the Status Bar dialog box's OK button.**

   The status bar appears in the custom browser window.

6. **Click the Icon button.**

   The Load Status Bar Icon dialog box appears.

7. **Locate the icon you want to use on your status bar and double-click the image's filename.**

   Your icon appears in the status bar.

8. **Click the Clock command in the toolbox.**

   The clock panel appears in your status bar.

9. **Click the Timer command in the toolbox.**

   The Timer Type dialog box appears (see Figure 21-13).

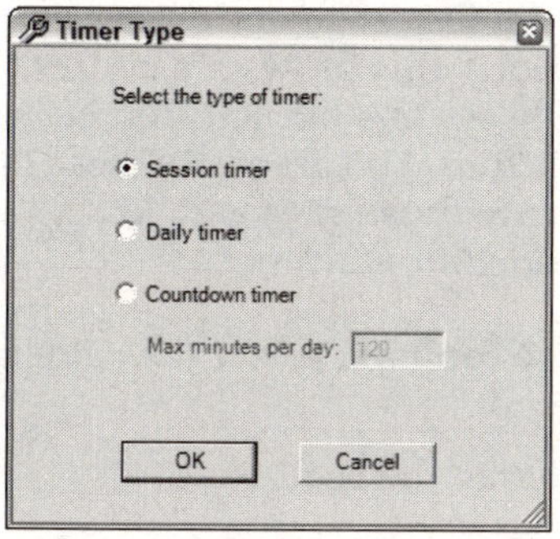

Figure 21-13: The Timer Type dialog box.

10. **Leave the timer type set to Session Timer and click OK.**

    The Timer panel appears in the status bar.

11. **Click the Date command in the toolbox.**

    The Date panel appears in your status bar.

12. **Click the Current URL command in the toolbox.**

    The Current URL panel appears in your status bar. Figure 21-14 shows the completed status bar.

13. **Choose File⇨Save.**

    The Browser Construction Kit saves your browser's data.

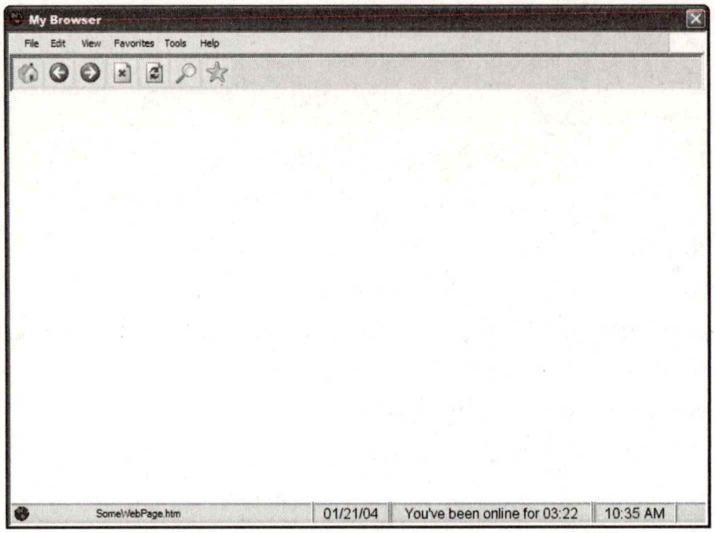

Figure 21-14: The custom-browser window with its completed status bar.

Adding the Address Bar

Like the toolbar (see the previous section), this browser's address bar sports a couple of extras that you don't usually see in a normal Web browser. These extras are what I've named Favorites buttons. You associate these buttons with favorite Web sites and then can navigate to those sites with just a single mouse click. Perform the following tasks to add your address bar:

1. **In the drop-down menu below the toolbox, select the Address Bar command set.**

   The Address Bar commands appear in the toolbox.

2. **Click the Address Bar button.**

   The Address Bar dialog box appears.

3. **Select the address bar's location and then click the Browse button.**

   The Load Address Bar Image dialog box appears.

4. **Locate the image you want to use for your address bar and double-click the image's filename.**

   The selected filename appears in the Address Bar dialog box's Address Bar Image text box.

5. **Click the Go Button command.**

   The Go button appears in your address bar.

6. **Click the Favorite 1 command.**

   The Favorite Button dialog box appears, as shown in Figure 21-15.

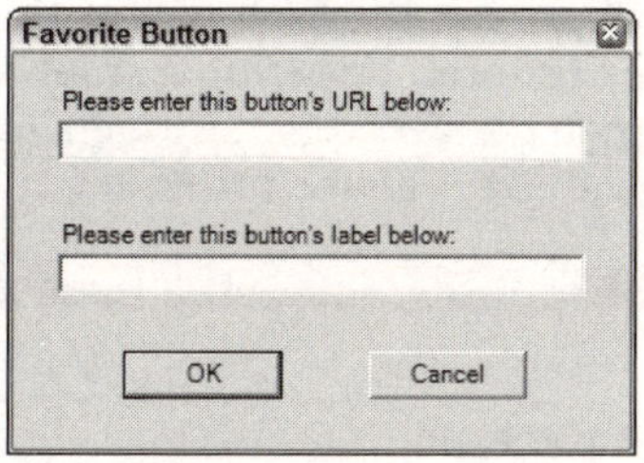

Figure 21-15: The Favorite Button dialog box.

7. **Type the URL with which you want the button associated and then click OK.**

   The Favorite 1 button appears in the address bar.

8. **Use the Favorite 2, Favorite 3, and Favorite 4 commands in the toolbox to add the remaining favorites buttons to the address bar, the same way you added the Favorite 1 button in Steps 6 and 7.**

   Your custom browser now has a complete address bar, as shown in Figure 21-16.

9. **Choose File⇨Save.**

   The Browser Construction Kit saves your browser's data.

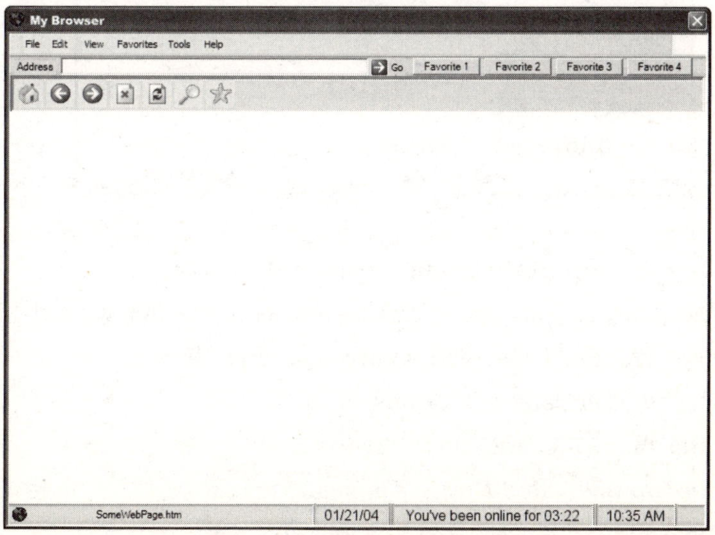

Figure 21-16: The custom-browser window with its completed address bar.

Adding the Browser Pane

You can't have a browser without a browser pane. Well, you can if you've got one of those new psychic browsers that project the Web pages directly into your brain. (I know they exist, because I ordered one from a spam e-mail I got a few weeks ago. Funny that it hasn't been delivered yet, though.) Anyway, here's how to add a browser pane to your general-use browser:

1. **In the drop-down menu below the toolbox, select the Browser command set.**

   The Browser commands appear in the toolbox.

2. **Click the Browser button.**

   The browser pane appears in your browser's window (see Figure 21-17).

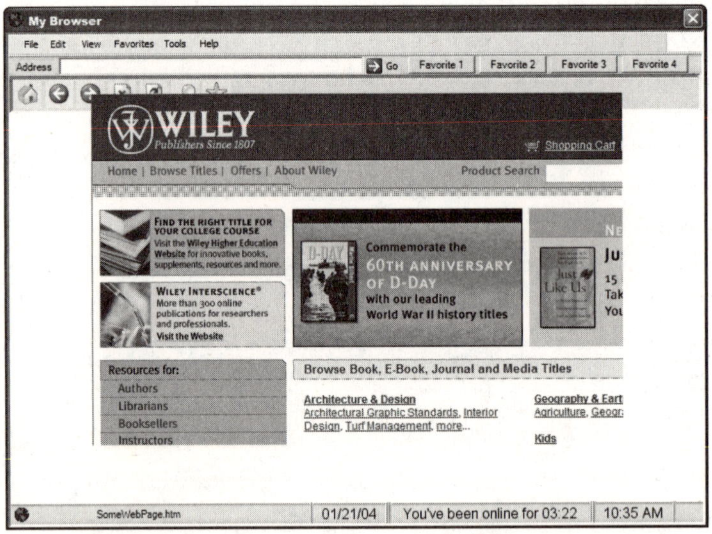

Figure 21-17: The custom-browser window with its new browser pane.

3. **Click the Top command in the toolbox.**

   The Browser Top dialog box appears, as shown in Figure 21-18.

4. **Type** 123 **into the value text box and click OK.**

   The browser pane repositions itself.

5. **Click the Left command in the toolbox.**

   The Browser Left dialog box appears.

6. **Type** 8 **into the value text box and click OK.**

   The browser pane repositions itself to the left.

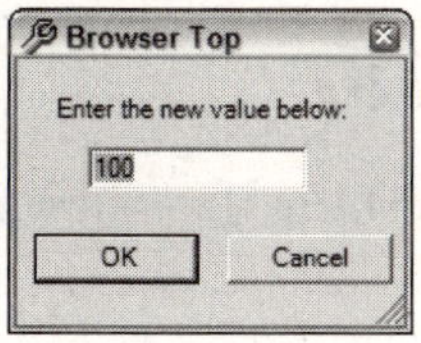

Figure 21-18: The Browser Top dialog box.

7. **Click the Width command in the toolbox.**

   The Browser Width dialog box appears.

8. **Type** 775 **into the value text box and click OK.**

   The browser pane widens.

9. **Click the Height command in the toolbox.**

   The Browser Height dialog box appears.

10. **Type** 436 **into the value text box and click OK.**

    The browser pane fills the window, as shown in Figure 21-19.

11. **Click the Start Site command.**

    The Start Site dialog box appears.

12. **Enter the URL for the Web site that you want as this browser's home page and click OK.**

    The browser pane sets its home page.

13. **Choose File⇨Save.**

    The Browser Construction Kit saves your browser's data.

Figure 21-19: The fully positioned browser pane.

Compiling the Custom Browser

One more step, and you'll be off and browsing. Perform the following tasks to compile your browser into the finished product:

1. **Choose File➪Build Browser.**

   The Build Browser dialog box appears.

2. **Navigate to where you want to save your browser's finished files and then click OK.**

   The Browser Construction Kit builds the final files for your custom browser.

To run your finished browser, double-click the Browser.exe file, located in the directory to which you built the browser.

Chapter 22

Coming Up with a Child's Web Browser

In This Chapter

- Creating a child's browser window
- Adding a menu bar
- Adding a child's toolbar, status bar, and address bar
- Positioning the browser pane
- Compiling the child's browser

I'm guessing that the most popular use of the Browser Construction Kit will be to create kid-safe browsers. Such a browser can protect children from the many not-so-nice Web sites on the Internet, and so enable parents to feel more relaxed about unleashing their children into the Web, whether for fun, for research, or just for exploring for an hour or so.

The browser you build in this chapter not only is graphically attractive to children, but also includes special features such as an approved-sites list and a browser alarm. If you want to build a kid-safe browser, then just load up your Browser Construction Kit and complete the following steps.

Creating the Window

Every browser design starts with a window. If you've been using the Browser Construction Kit at all, you already know that the Window category of commands enable you to set window attributes such as title, type, color, border, and so on. Each specific browser's design utilizes these attributes to create a window that best suits the project's theme. The following steps get you started on a child's browser. You can find the graphics you need on this book's CD-ROM or in the folder into which you installed the program.

1. **In the drop-down list below the toolbox, select the Window command set.**

   The Window commands appear in the toolbox.

2. **Click the Color button.**

   The Color dialog box appears (see Figure 22-1).

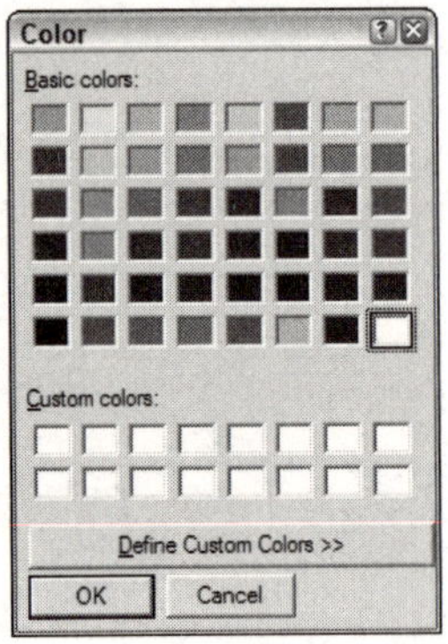

Figure 22-1: The Color dialog box.

3. **Select the light purple color and click OK.**

   The window's background turns light purple.

4. **Click the Icon button.**

   The Select Window Icon dialog box appears, as shown in Figure 22-2.

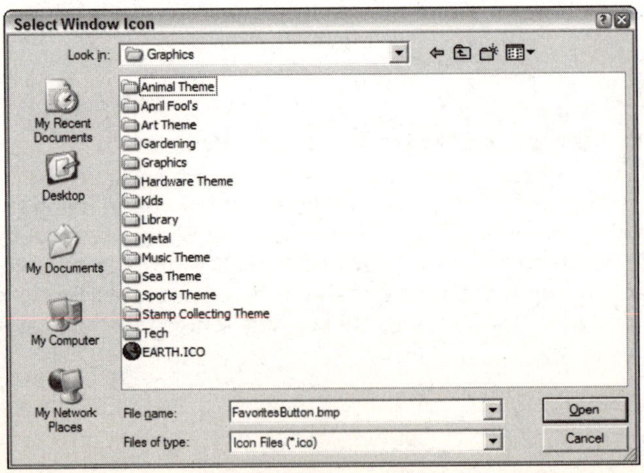

Figure 22-2: The Select Window Icon dialog box.

5. **Double-click the Kids.ico file on your Browser Construction Kit CD-ROM.**

   The kid's icon appears in the window's title bar.

6. **Click the Style button.**

   The Window Styles dialog box appears (see Figure 22-3).

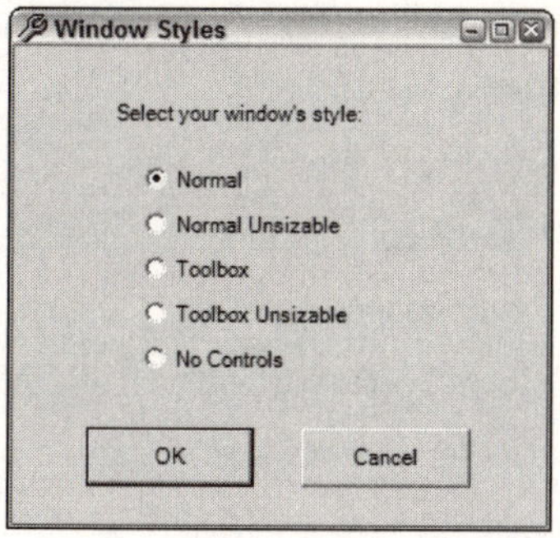

Figure 22-3: The Window Styles dialog box.

7. **Select the Normal Unsizable option and click OK.**

   The window's border style changes. (The change is subtle. You may not even notice it.)

8. **Click the Buttons command in the toolbox.**

   The Window Buttons dialog box appears, as shown in Figure 22-4.

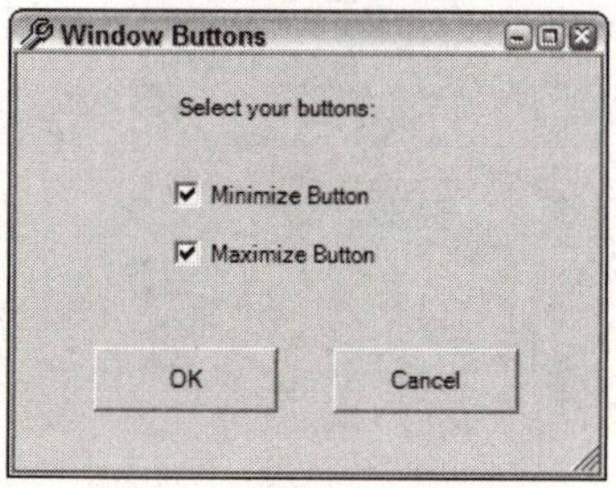

Figure 22-4: The Window Buttons dialog box.

9. **Turn off the Minimize Button and Maximize Button options and then click OK.**

   The Browser Construction Kit removes the Minimize and Maximize buttons from the window.

10. **Click the Title button.**

    The Window Title dialog box appears (see Figure 22-5).

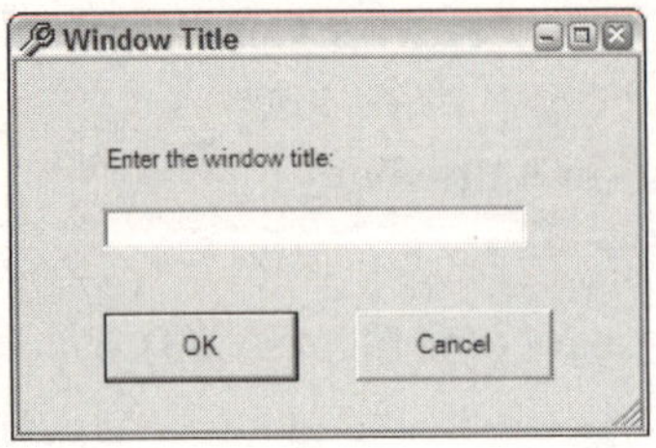

Figure 22-5: The Window Title dialog box.

11. **Type** Kids Browser **into the text box and click OK.**

    The window's new title appears in the title bar.

12. **Click the Border command in the toolbox.**

    The Select Border Image dialog box appears.

13. Double-click the KidBorder.bmp image on this book's CD-ROM.

    The borders appear in your kid-browser window (see Figure 22-6).

Figure 22-6: The kids' browser with its new border images.

14. **Choose File⇨Save As.**

    The Save Browser File dialog box appears, as shown in Figure 22-7.

15. **Navigate to where you want to save your browser's script file and then click Save.**

    The Browser Construction Kit saves your browser's data to the selected location, using the window's title as the filename.

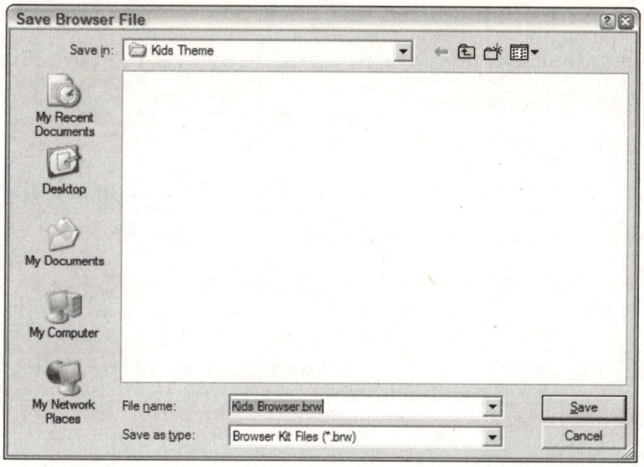

Figure 22-7: The Save Browser File dialog box.

Adding the Menu Bar

A menu bar is an important part of most applications. With a kid's browser, though, you only want to include the commands that a child is likely to need and use. Limiting the available command set helps keep the child from running into trouble. The following steps describe how to add a menu bar to the child's browser:

1. **In the drop-down list below the toolbox, select the Menu Bar command set.**

   The Menu Bar commands appear in the toolbox.

2. **Click the Menu Bar command in the toolbox.**

   The menu bar appears in the custom browser window.

3. **Select the File button in the toolbox.**

   The File Menu dialog box appears (see Figure 22-8).

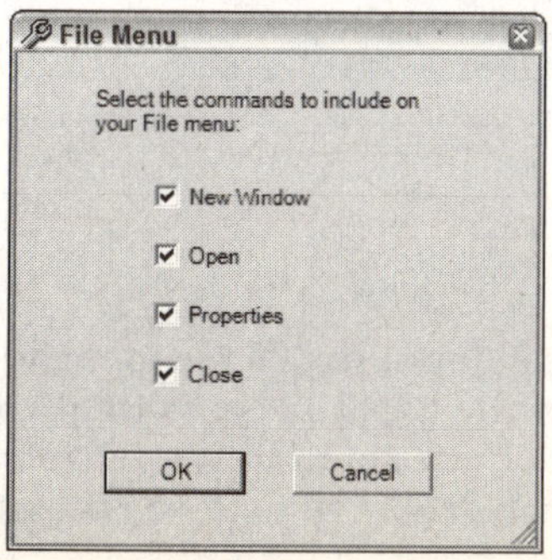

Figure 22-8: The File Menu dialog box.

4. **Select the Close menu option and click OK.**

   The File menu appears in your kid-browser window.

5. **Click the View command.**

   The View Menu dialog box appears.

6. **Select the Toolbar, Status Bar, and Full Screen options and then click OK.**

   The View menu appears in your kid-browser window.

7. **Click the Tools command in the toolbox.**

   The Tools Menu dialog box appears.

8. **Select the Alarms and Approved List options and then click OK.**

   The Tools menu appears in your kid-browser window.

9. **Click the Help command in the toolbox.**

   The Help menu appears in your kid-browser window (see Figure 22-9).

10. **Choose File⇨Save.**

    The Browser Construction Kit saves your browser's data.

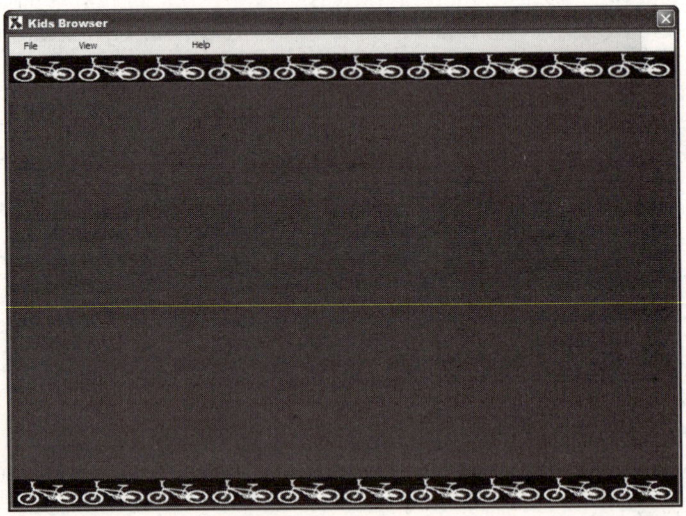

Figure 22-9: The browser and its menu bar.

Adding the Toolbar

Your menu bar may be the most important spot to place commands, but the toolbar is the most convenient place for the user to access frequently used commands. The child's browser needs a basic set of browsing commands in the toolbar so that the child can easily navigate from one Web page to another. Perform the following steps to add a toolbar to your kid browser:

1. **In the drop-down list below the toolbox, select the Toolbar command set.**

   The Toolbar commands appear in the toolbox.

2. **Click the Toolbar button.**

   The Toolbar dialog box appears, as shown in Figure 22-10.

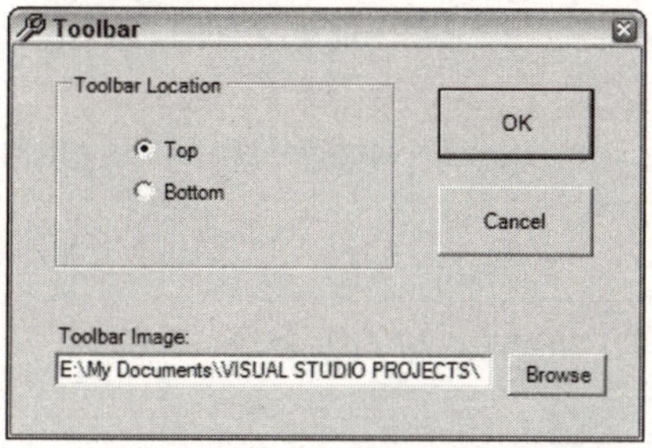

Figure 22-10: The Toolbar dialog box.

3. **Select the toolbar's Top location and then click the Browse button.**

   The Load Toolbar Image dialog box appears, as shown in Figure 22-11.

4. **Double-click the Kid_Toolbar.jpg image on this book's CD-ROM.**

   The selected filename appears in the Toolbar dialog box's Toolbar Image text box.

5. **Click OK.**

   The toolbar appears in the custom browser window.

6. **Click the Home command in the toolbox.**

   The Load Button dialog box appears.

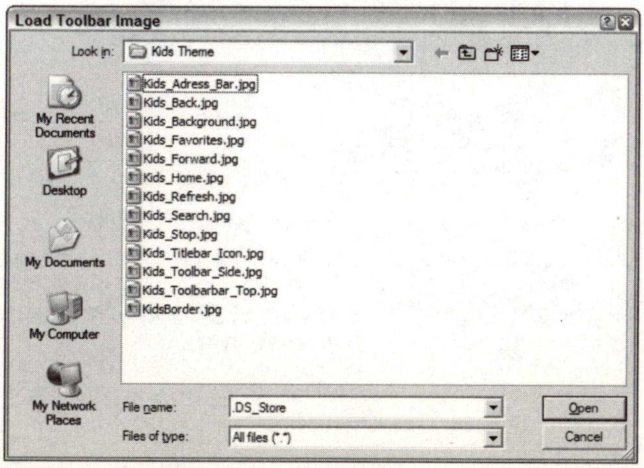

Figure 22-11: The Load Toolbar Image dialog box.

7. **Double-click the Kids_Home.jpg image's filename on this book's CD-ROM.**

   The Home button appears in the custom window's toolbar.

8. **Use the Back, Forward, and Stop commands in the toolbox to add the buttons to the toolbar, the same way you added the Home button in Steps 6 and 7.**

   The image filenames are Kids_Back.jpg, Kids_Forward.jpg, and Kids_Stop.jpg.

   Your custom kid browser now has its toolbar buttons, as shown in Figure 22-12.

9. **Choose File⇨Save.**

   The Browser Construction Kit saves your browser's data.

Figure 22-12: The toolbar and its buttons.

Adding the Address Bar

Web pages feature links that you can click to get to a specific place on the Internet, but you frequently need to get to places that don't have such convenient links. As you know, you get to such Web sites by typing their addresses into the browser's address bar. The following steps guide you through the process of adding an address bar to the kids' browser:

1. **In the drop-down list below the toolbox, select the Address Bar command set.**

   The Address Bar commands appear in the toolbox.

2. **Click the Address Bar button.**

   The Address Bar dialog box appears.

3. **Select the Address Bar's Top location and then click the Browse button.**

   The Load Address Bar Image dialog box appears.

ON THE CD

4. **Double-click the Kids_Address_Bar.jpg image's filename on this book's CD-ROM.**

   The selected filename appears in the Address Bar dialog box's Address Bar Image text box.

5. **Click OK.**

   The address bar appears in your kid-browser window.

6. **Click the Go Button command.**

   The Go button appears in your address bar.

7. **Click the Favorite 1 command.**

   The Favorite Button dialog box appears (see Figure 22-13).

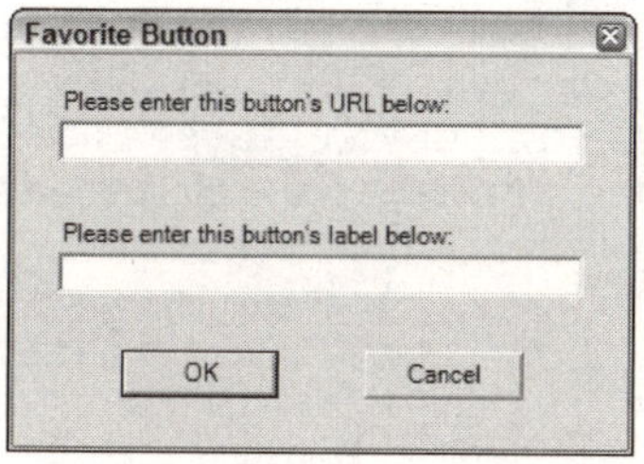

Figure 22-13: The Favorite Button dialog box.

8. **Type the URL to one of your child's favorite Web sites and then click OK.**

   The Favorite 1 button appears in the address bar.

9. **Use the Favorite 2, Favorite 3, and Favorite 4 commands in the toolbox to add the remaining favorites buttons to the address bar, the same way you added the Favorite 1 button in Steps 7 and 8.**

   Your custom browser now has a complete address bar, as shown in Figure 22-14.

10. **Choose File⇨Save.**

    The Browser Construction Kit saves your browser's data.

Figure 22-14: The kid-browser window with its completed address bar.

Adding the Browser Pane

The most important part of a Web browser is, of course, the area of the window that shows the Web pages. All the fancy controls, commands, and features in the world won't do you any good if you can't see where you're going. You wouldn't want to drive a car with an opaque windshield, would you? (If you have to think about this question, please turn in your driver's license.) In the following steps, you add the all-important browser pane to the kids' browser:

1. **In the drop-down list below the toolbox, select the Browser command set.**

   The Browser commands appear in the toolbox.

2. **Click the Browser button.**

   The browser pane appears in your browser's window.

3. **Click the Top command in the toolbox.**

   The Browser Top dialog box appears, as shown in Figure 22-15.

4. **Type** 160 **into the value text box and click OK.**

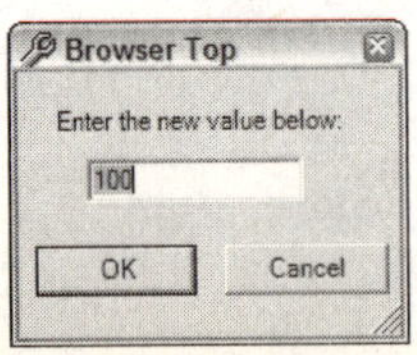

Figure 22-15: The Browser Top dialog box.

The browser pane repositions itself.

5. **Click the Left command in the toolbox.**

   The Browser Left dialog box appears.

6. **Type** 10 **into the value text box and click OK.**

   The browser pane repositions itself to the left.

7. **Click the Width command in the toolbox.**

   The Browser Width dialog box appears.

8. **Type** 776 **into the value text box and click OK.**

   The browser pane widens.

9. **Click the Height command in the toolbox.**

   The Browser Height dialog box appears.

10. **Type** 390 **into the value text box and click OK.**

    The browser pane fills the window, as shown in Figure 22-16.

11. **Click the Start Site command.**

    The Start Site dialog box appears.

12. **Type the URL for the Web site that you want as this browser's home page and click OK.**

    The browser pane sets its home page.

13. **Choose File⇨Save.**

    The Browser Construction Kit saves your browser's data.

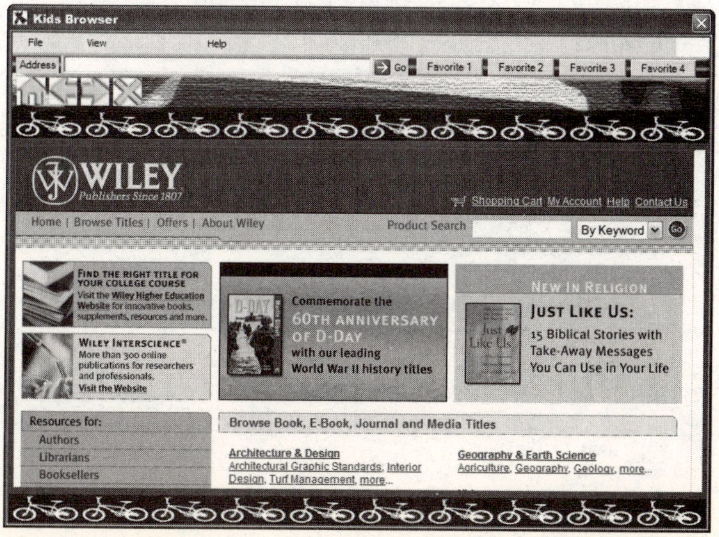

Figure 22-16: The fully positioned browser pane.

Adding Child Safety Features

Although one of the main characteristics of the kids' Web browser is its simplistic controls, the real heart of the machine is its safety features, which give you the power to protect your child from the many nasty places on the Internet. Specifically, the kids' browser features an approved-sites list that prevents your child from going anywhere on the Internet that you haven't already checked out. Here's how to add this feature:

1. **In the drop-down list below the toolbox, select the Functions command set.**

   The Functions commands appear in the toolbox.

2. **Click the Alarm button.**

   The alarm function's icon appears below the kid-browser window.

3. **Click the Approved Lists command in the toolbox.**

   The approved list function's icon appears below the kid-browser window (see Figure 22-17).

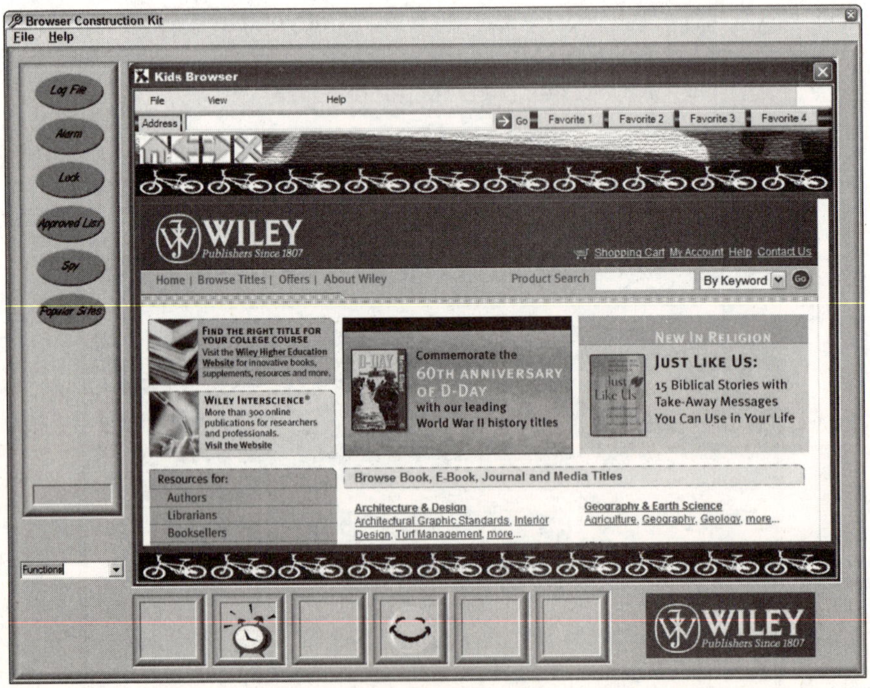

Figure 22-17: The kid-browser window with the special safety features added.

Compiling the Custom Browser

The last step in building any browser is compiling it into a program that you can actually use. It'd be pretty dumb to go through all this work and then do nothing more than look at your browser's design in the editor. At least, *I* think that'd be kind of dumb, so I assume you would, too. Here's how to compile your final kids' browser:

1. **Choose File⇨Build Browser.**

   The Build Browser dialog box appears.

2. **Navigate to where you want to save your browser's finished files and then click OK.**

   The Browser Construction Kit builds the final files for your custom browser.

To run your finished browser, double-click the Browser.exe file, located in the directory to which you built the browser.

Chapter 23

Designing a Special-Topic Browser

In This Chapter

- Creating a special-topic browser window
- Adding a special-topic menu bar
- Adding a special-topic toolbar, status bar, and address bar
- Positioning the browser pane
- Compiling the special-topic browser

Everybody has some sort of special interest. Maybe you're into cars. Or maybe it's baseball that cranks you up. Me, I dig music. Whatever makes you smile, wouldn't it be cool to have a Web browser that reflects that interest? In this chapter, you see how to use the Browser Construction Kit to create what I like to call a *special-topic browser.* In this case, the browser you create is perfect for anyone who likes gardening or plants. However, feel free to substitute other images.

ON THE CD

You can find the images used in this chapter in the Themes/Gardening folder of this book's CD-ROM or in the folder into which you installed the program.

Creating the Window

The browser's window offers an opportunity for designing an attractive layout that includes special-interest images. By special-interest images, I mean graphical items that work together to form a theme — a theme that fits with a person's interest, whether that be sports, music, electronics, or whatever. In this chapter, the theme is gardening. The following steps show how to design this special browser's window:

1. **In the drop-down list below the toolbox, select the Window command set.**

   The Window commands appear in the toolbox.

2. **Click the Icon button.**

   The Select Window Icon dialog box appears.

3. **Double-click the Garden.ico file on your Browser Construction Kit CD-ROM.**

   The garden-theme icon appears in the window's title bar, as shown in Figure 23-1.

Figure 23-1: The icon in the garden-themed browser.

4. **Click the Style button.**

   The Window Styles dialog box appears.

5. **Select the Normal Unsizable option and click OK.**

   The window's border style changes. (The change is so subtle that you may not even notice it.)

6. **Click the Buttons command in the toolbox.**

   The Window Buttons dialog box appears.

7. **Turn off the Minimize Button and Maximize Button options and then click OK.**

The Browser Construction Kit removes the Minimize and Maximize buttons from the window, as shown in Figure 23-2.

Figure 23-2: The browser window without the Minimize and Maximize buttons.

8. **Click the Title button.**

   The Window Title dialog box appears.

9. **Type Garden-Themed Browser into the text box and click OK.**

   The window's new title appears in the title bar (see Figure 23-3).

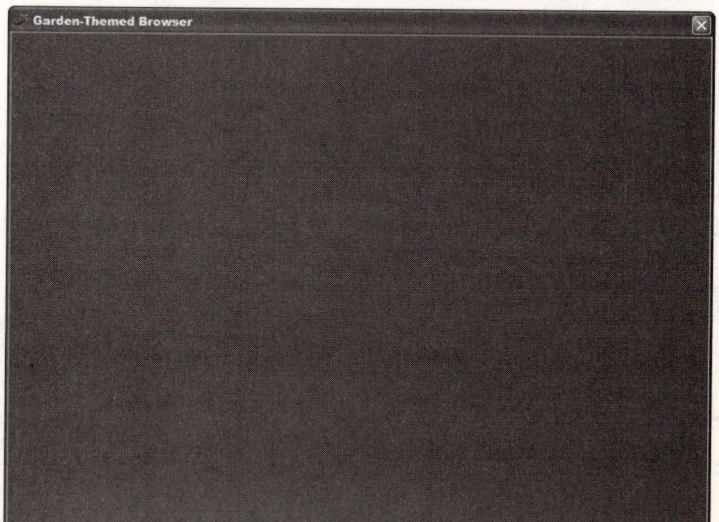

Figure 23-3: The window's new title bar.

10. **Click the Border command in the toolbox.**

    The Select Border Image dialog box appears.

11. **Double-click the Gardening_Border.jpg image filename on this book's CD-ROM.**

    The borders appear in your browser window (see Figure 23-4).

Figure 23-4: The garden browser with its new border images.

12. **Click the Skin command in the toolbox.**

    The Select Skin Image dialog box appears.

13. **Double-click the Gardening_Background.jpg image filename on this book's CD-ROM.**

    The background appears in your browser window.

14. **Choose File⇨Save As.**

    The Save Browser File dialog box appears (see Figure 23-5).

15. **Navigate to where you want to save your browser's script file and then click Save.**

    The Browser Construction Kit saves your browser's data to the selected location, using the window's title as the filename.

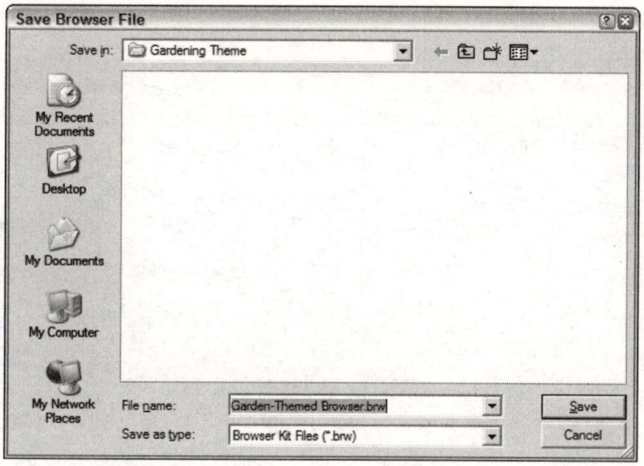

Figure 23-5: The Save Browser File dialog box.

Adding the Menu Bar

The Browser Construction Kit doesn't let you use custom graphics for you browser's menu bar, but that doesn't mean that the garden-themed browser will do without one. Here's how to add a menu bar to this themed browser's window:

1. **In the drop-down list below the toolbox, select the Menu Bar command set.**

   The Menu Bar commands appear in the toolbox (see Figure 23-6).

2. **Click the Menu Bar command in the toolbox.**

   The menu bar appears in the custom browser window.

3. **Click the File button in the toolbox.**

   The File Menu dialog box appears, as shown in Figure 23-7.

4. **Select all four menu options and then click OK.**

   The File menu appears in your custom browser window.

5. **Use the Edit, View, Favorites, Tools, and Help commands in the toolbox to add the menus to the menu bar, the same way you added the File menu in Steps 3 and 4.**

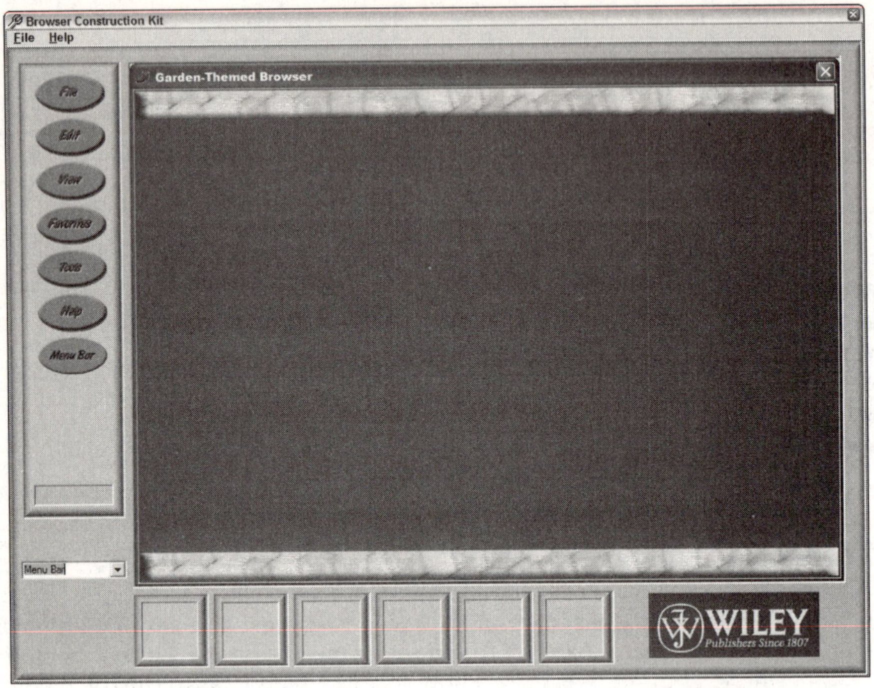

Figure 23-6: The menu bar commands in the toolbox.

Your custom browser now has a complete set of menus, as shown in Figure 23-8.

6. **Choose File➪Save.**

   The Browser Construction Kit saves your browser's data.

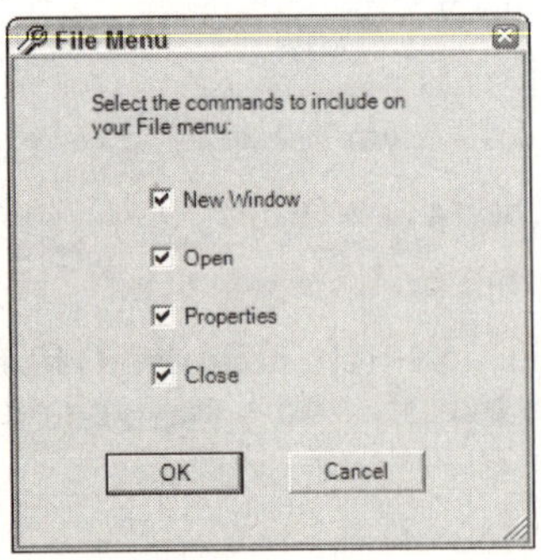

Figure 23-7: The File Menu dialog box.

Figure 23-8: The custom browser window with its new menus.

Adding the Toolbar

Just as with the main window's border and background, you can choose your own custom image as the background for the window's toolbar. This ability is, of course, another opportunity for you to create a cohesive theme of graphical elements. The follow steps guide you as you put together the garden-themed browser's toolbar.

1. **In the drop-down list below the toolbox, select the Toolbar command set.**

   The Toolbar commands appear in the toolbox, as shown in Figure 23-9.

2. **Click the Toolbar button.**

   The Toolbar dialog box appears.

3. **Select the toolbar's location and then click the Browse button.**

   The Load Toolbar Image dialog box appears.

4. **Double-click Gardening_Toolbar.jpg on this book's CD-ROM.**

   The selected filename appears in the Toolbar dialog box's Toolbar Image text box.

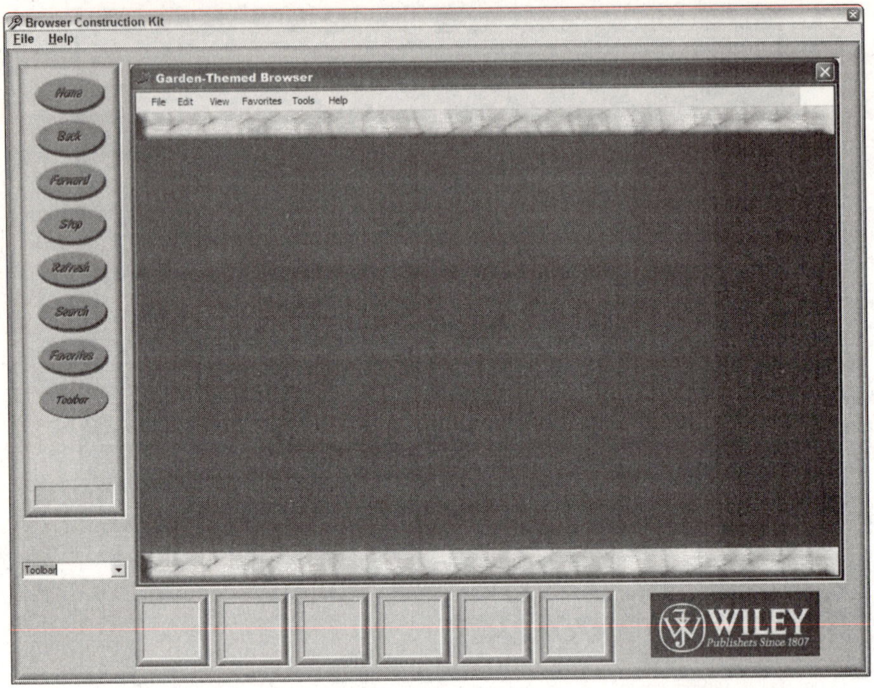

Figure 23-9: The Toolbar commands in the toolbox.

5. **Click the Toolbar dialog box's OK button.**

   The toolbar appears in the custom browser window (see Figure 23-10).

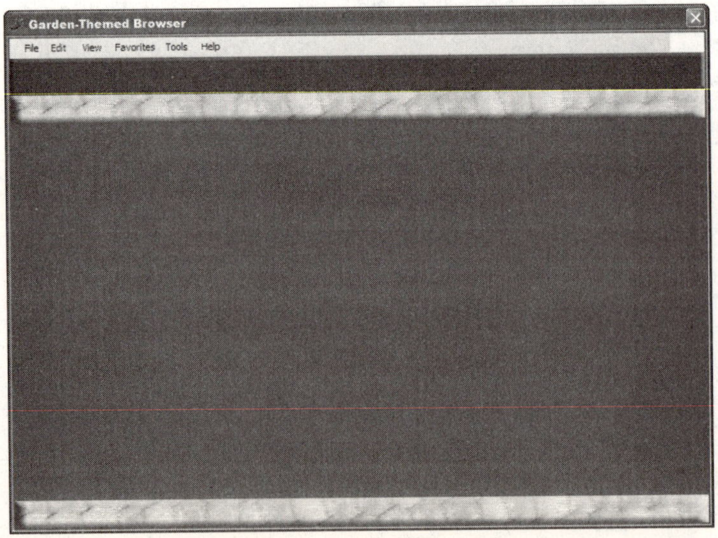

Figure 23-10: The garden-themed toolbar.

6. **Click the Home command in the toolbox.**

   The Load Button dialog box appears.

7. **Double-click the Gardening_Home.jpg button filename on this book's CD-ROM.**

   The Home button appears in the custom window's toolbar.

8. **Use the Back, Forward, Stop, Refresh, Search, and Favorites commands in the toolbox to add the buttons to the toolbar, the same way you added the Home button in Steps 6 and 7.**

   All the button files have the word "gardening" in their names (for example, Gardening_Back.jpg).

   Your custom browser now has a complete set of toolbar buttons, as shown in Figure 23-11.

9. **Choose File⇨Save.**

   The Browser Construction Kit saves your browser's data.

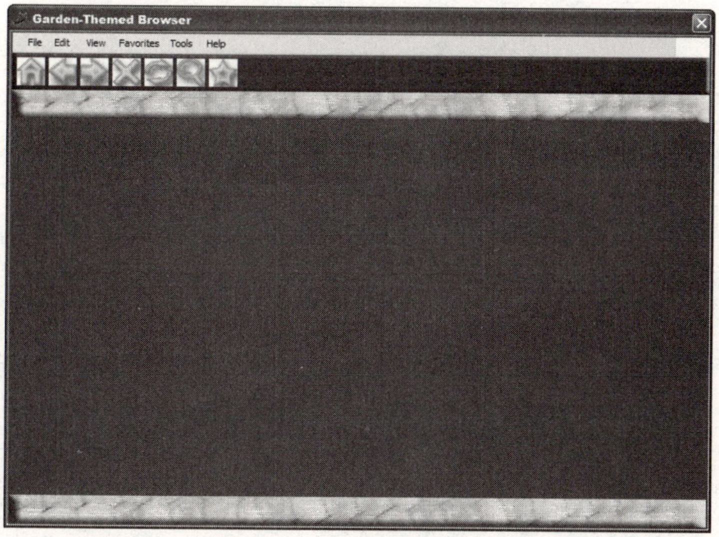

Figure 23-11: The toolbar with a complete set of buttons.

Adding the Status Bar

Your browser's status bar, too, can include images that help develop a special theme. The theme may be just a matter of complementary colors or full-fledged, photographic images. The choice is yours. In this section, you design the garden-themed browser's status bar:

1. **In the drop-down list below the toolbox, select the Status Bar command set.**

   The Status Bar commands appear in the toolbox, as shown in Figure 23-12.

2. **Click the Status Bar button.**

   The Status Bar dialog box appears.

3. **Select the Status Bar's location and then click the Browse button.**

   The Load Status Bar Image dialog box appears.

4. **Double-click the Gardening_Status_Bar.jpg image filename on this book's CD-ROM.**

   The selected filename appears in the Status Bar dialog box's Status Bar Image text box.

5. **Click the Status Bar dialog box's OK button.**

   The status bar appears in the custom browser window (see Figure 23-13).

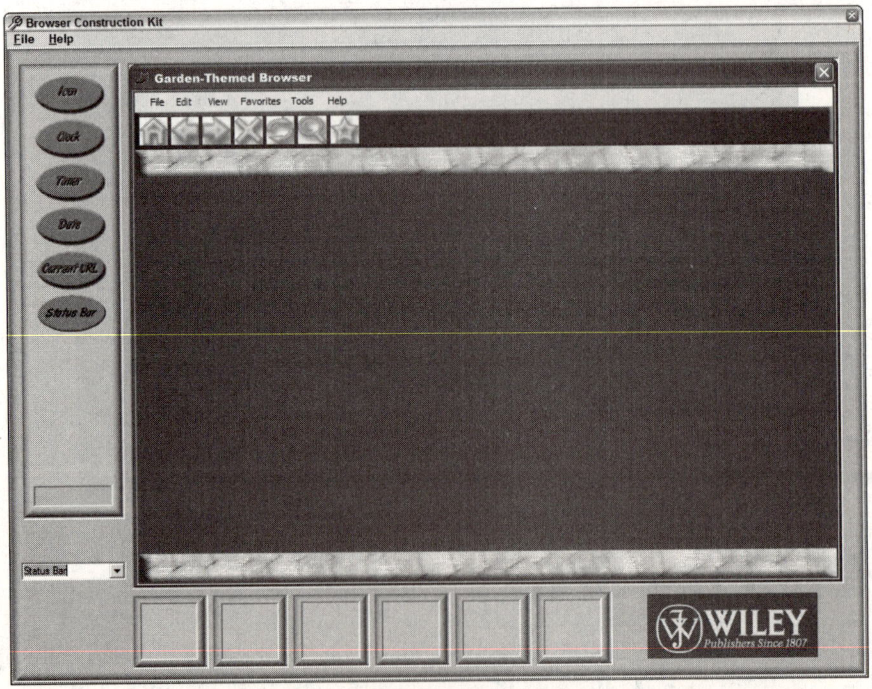

Figure 23-12: The toolbar with a complete set of buttons.

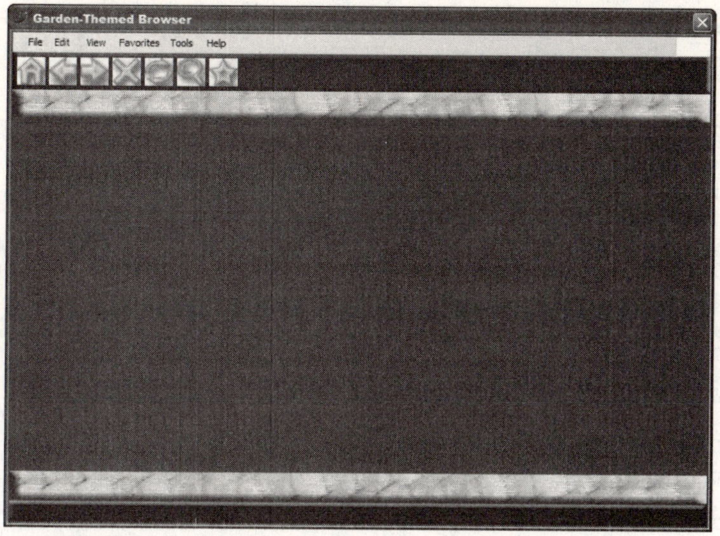

Figure 23-13: The garden-themed browser with its new status bar.

6. **Click the Icon button.**

   The Load Status Bar Icon dialog box appears.

7. **Double-click the Garden.ico image filename on this book's CD-ROM.**

   Your icon appears in the status bar.

8. **Click the Clock command in the toolbox.**

   The clock panel appears in your status bar.

9. **Click the Timer command in the toolbox.**

   The Timer Type dialog box appears.

10. **Leave the timer type set to Session Timer and click OK.**

    The Timer panel appears in the status bar.

11. **Click the Date command in the toolbox.**

    The date panel appears in your status bar.

12. **Click the Current URL command in the toolbox.**

    The current URL panel appears in your status bar. Figure 23-14 shows the completed status bar.

13. **Choose File⇨Save.**

    The Browser Construction Kit saves your browser's data.

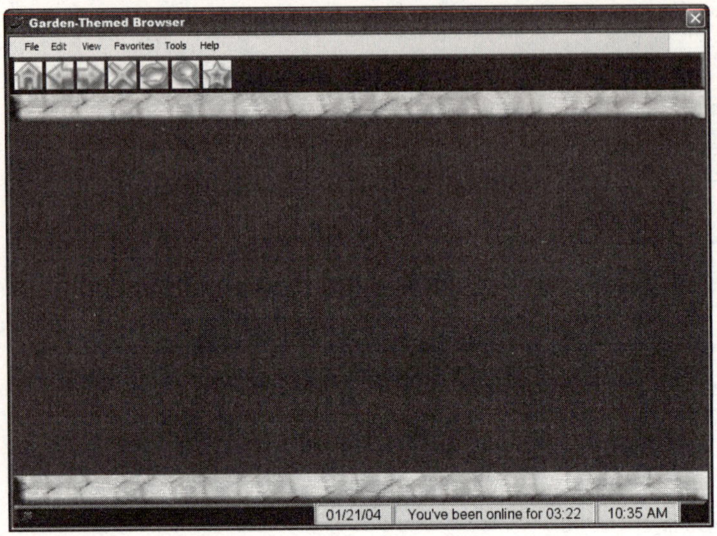

Figure 23-14: The browser window with its completed status bar.

Adding the Address Bar

Your browser's address bar is exactly the same size as the status bar, which means that you can use the same image for both, or you can design different images. Often, for the sake of the design, it's good to use the same image in both bars, and so keep the theme from becoming too cluttered. That's what you do when you add an address bar in this section. Even though the image you use is named Gardening_Address_Bar, it's exactly the same as the status bar. Perform the following steps to add the address bar to your browser:

1. **In the drop-down list below the toolbox, select the Address Bar command set.**

   The Address Bar commands appear in the toolbox (see Figure 23-15).

2. **Click the Address Bar button.**

   The Address Bar dialog box appears.

3. **Select the Address Bar's top location and then click the Browse button.**

   The Load Address Bar Image dialog box appears.

4. **Double-click the Gardening_Address_Bar.jpg image from this book's CD-ROM.**

   The selected filename appears in the Address Bar dialog box's Address Bar Image text box.

5. **Click the Address Bar dialog box's OK button.**

   The new address bar appears in the window (see Figure 23-16).

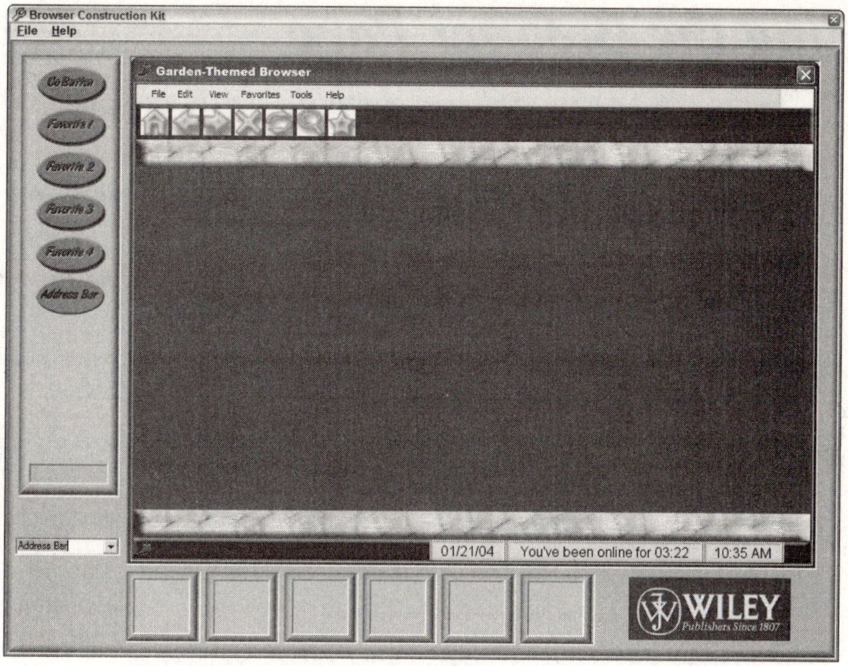

Figure 23-15: The address bar commands in the toolbox.

6. **Click the Go Button command.**

   The Go button appears in your address bar.

7. **Choose File⇨Save.**

   The Browser Construction Kit saves your browser's data.

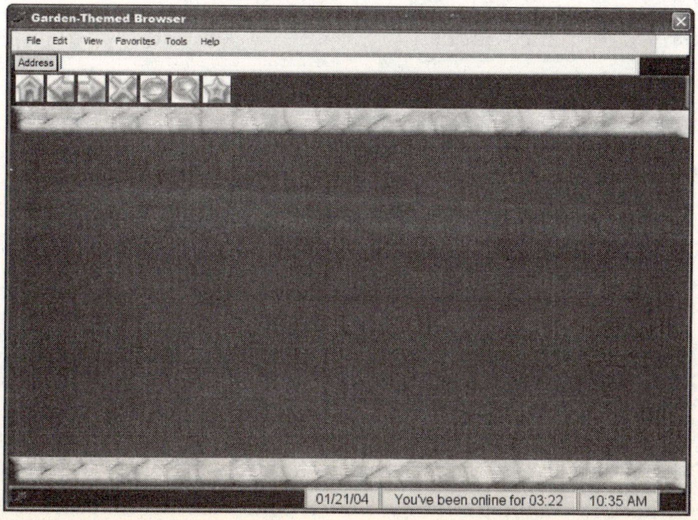

Figure 23-16: The browser window with its new address bar.

Adding the Browser Pane

Because the browser pane must display the current Web page, you can't do much to match it to your theme. You can, however, add one of a few different predefined borders, as well as position the browser pane such that different parts of the window's borders and background show. However you choose to add your browser pane, here's the basic procedure:

1. **In the drop-down list below the toolbox, select the Browser command set.**

   The Browser commands appear in the toolbox.

2. **Click the Browser button.**

   The browser pane appears in your browser's window.

3. **Click the Top command in the toolbox.**

   The Browser Top dialog box appears.

4. **Type** 160 **into the value text box and click OK.**

   The browser pane repositions itself.

5. **Click the Left command in the toolbox.**

   The Browser Left dialog box appears.

6. **Type** 10 **into the value text box and click OK.**

   The browser pane repositions itself to the left.

7. **Click the Width command in the toolbox.**

   The Browser Width dialog box appears.

8. **Type** 776 **into the value text box and click OK.**

   The browser pane widens.

9. **Click the Height command in the toolbox.**

   The Browser Height dialog box appears.

10. **Type** 390 **into the value text box and click OK.**

    The browser pane fills the window, as shown in Figure 23-17.

11. **Click the Start Site command.**

    The Start Site dialog box appears.

12. **Type the URL for the Web site that you want as this browser's home page and click OK.**

    The browser pane sets its home page.

13. **Choose File⇨Save.**

    The Browser Construction Kit saves your browser's data.

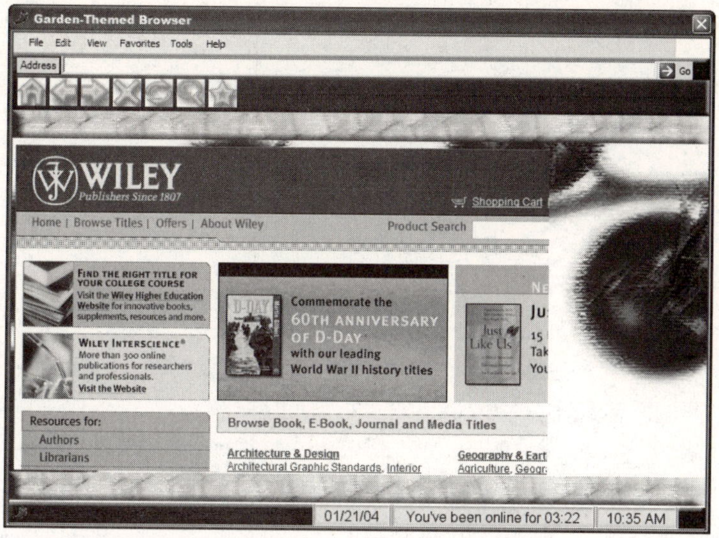

Figure 23-17: The fully positioned browser pane.

Compiling the Custom Browser

Ready to get your garden-themed browser up and running? All you have to do now is compile the data files into the final product. Here's how:

1. **Choose File⇨Build Browser.**

   The Build Browser dialog box appears.

2. **Navigate to where you want to save your browser's finished files and then click OK.**

   The Browser Construction Kit builds the final files for your custom browser.

To run your finished browser, double-click the Browser.exe file, located in the directory to which you built the browser.

Chapter 24

Developing a Dedicated-Site Browser

In This Chapter

- Creating a dedicated-site browser window
- Adding a dedicated-site toolbar, status bar, and menu bar
- Positioning the browser pane
- Compiling the dedicated-site browser

A dedicated-site browser displays only a single Web site. That is, the user is not allowed to browse to any other site on the Internet, although he or she can browse to different pages in the allowed Web site. When might you want to use such a limited browser? Maybe you have a small bookstore, and you've got information, such as an inventory list, about your store online. A dedicated-site browser provides your customers with access to your Web site, without the customers being able to use the browser for anything except viewing your site. In this chapter, you find out how to build the dedicated-site Web browser.

ON THE CD

You can find the graphics for this project in the Themes/Dedicated folder of this book's CD-ROM or in the folder to which you installed the Browser Construction Kit.

Creating the Window

As always, the first thing you do to start a new browser design is to set up the browser's window. In this case, there's not anything special about the window, as it uses a fairly standard look and set of commands. Here's how to create the browser's window:

1. **In the drop-down list below the toolbox, select the Window command set.**

   The Window commands appear in the toolbox.

2. **Click the Color button.**

   The Color dialog box appears.

3. **Select the white color and click OK.**

   The window's background turns white.

4. **Click the Icon button.**

   The Select Window Icon dialog box appears (see Figure 24-1).

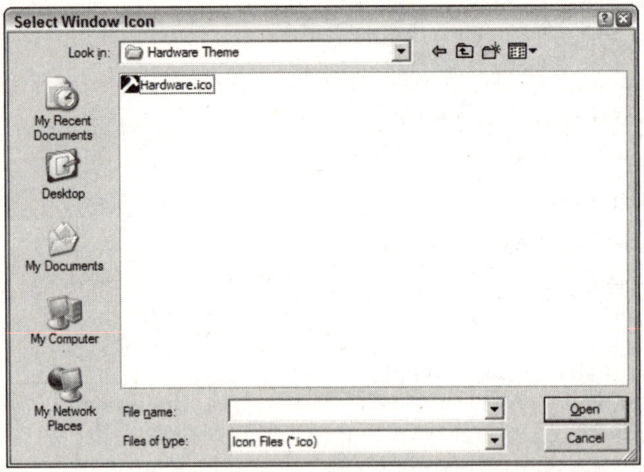

Figure 24-1: The Select Window Icon dialog box.

5. **Double-click the filename of the icon you want to use.**

   The icon appears in the window's title bar.

6. **Click the Style button.**

   The Window Styles dialog box appears, as shown in Figure 24-2.

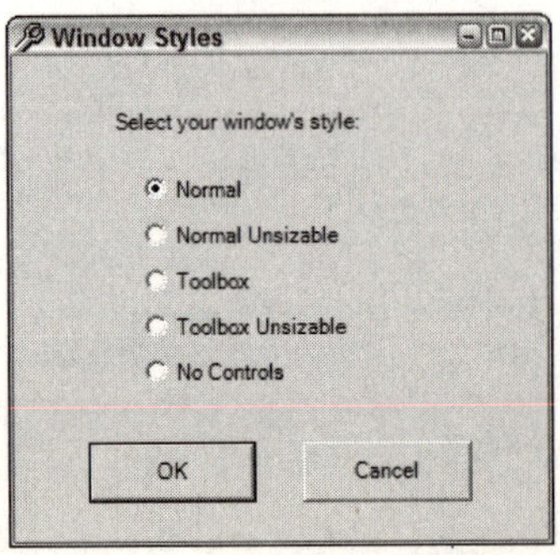

Figure 24-2: The Window Styles dialog box.

7. **Select the Normal option (it'll probably already be selected by default) and click OK.**

   If you had a different style selected, the window's border style changes.

8. **Click the Buttons command in the toolbox.**

   The Window Buttons dialog box appears.

9. **Make sure that the Minimize Button and Maximize Button options are selected and then click OK.**

   The Minimize and Maximize buttons will be included in the window.

10. **Click the Title button.**

    The Window Title dialog box appears.

11. **Type the browser name you want into the text box and click OK.**

    The window's new title appears in the title bar (see Figure 24-3).

Figure 24-3: The window's new title bar.

12. **Choose File⇨Save As.**

    The Save Browser File dialog box appears.

13. **Navigate to where you want to save your browser's script file and then click Save.**

    The Browser Construction Kit saves your browser's data to the selected location, using the window's title as the filename.

Adding the Menu Bar

This particular browser features a full menu bar, replete with all the commands available for browsers created with the Browser Construction Kit. Perform the following steps to add the menu bar:

1. **In the drop-down list below the toolbox, select the Menu Bar command set.**

   The Menu Bar commands appear in the toolbox.

2. **Click the Menu Bar command in the toolbox.**

   The menu bar appears in the custom browser window.

3. **Select the File button in the toolbox.**

   The File Menu dialog box appears (see Figure 24-4).

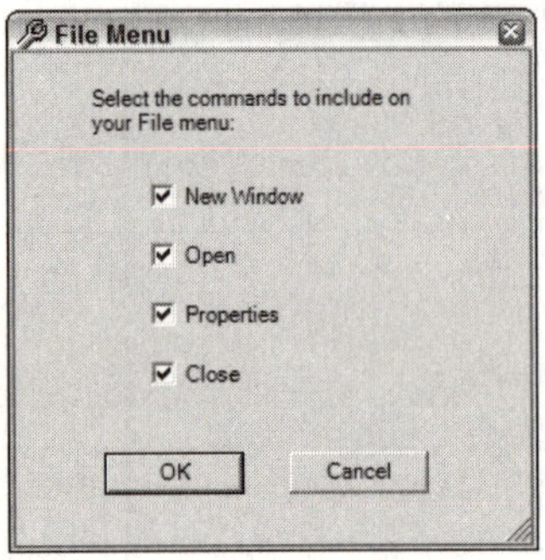

Figure 24-4: The File Menu dialog box.

4. **Select all four menu options and click OK.**

   The File menu appears in your custom browser window.

5. **Use the Edit, View, and Help commands in the toolbox to add these menus and their menu items to the menu bar, just as you did with the File menu in Steps 3 and 4.**

   The Edit, View, and Help menus appear in your custom browser's window.

6. **Add a Tools menu to the browser, but select only the Approved List option (see Figure 24-5).**

7. **Choose File⇨Save.**

   The Browser Construction Kit saves your browser's data.

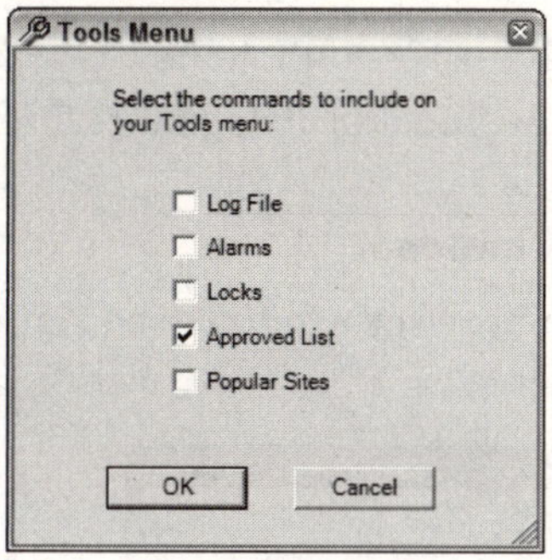

Figure 24-5: Adding the Tools menu.

Adding the Toolbar

The toolbar for your dedicated-site browser contains a full set of navigation buttons. You can use whatever background image you want for the toolbar, or just stick with the default image used in these steps. Follow these steps to add your toolbar:

1. **In the drop-down list below the toolbox, select the Toolbar command set.**

   The Toolbar commands appear in the toolbox.

2. **Click the Toolbar button.**

   The Toolbar dialog box appears (see Figure 24-6).

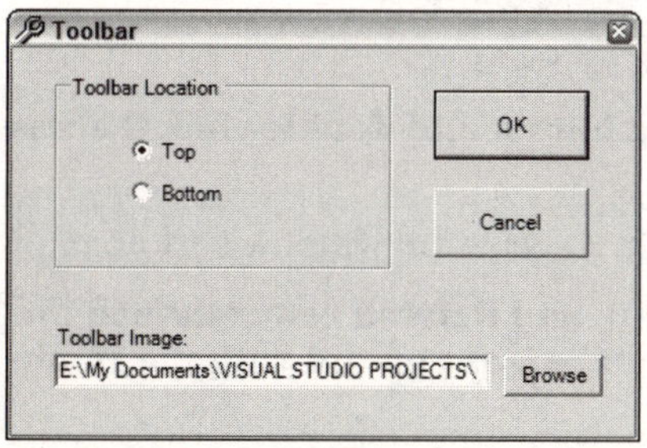

Figure 24-6: The Toolbar dialog box.

3. **Select the toolbar's Top location and then click the Browse button.**

   The Load Toolbar Image dialog box appears.

4. **Locate the Toolbar.jpg file and double-click the image's filename.**

   The selected filename appears in the Toolbar dialog box's Toolbar Image text box.

5. **Click the Toolbar dialog box's OK button.**

   The toolbar appears in the custom browser window (see Figure 24-7).

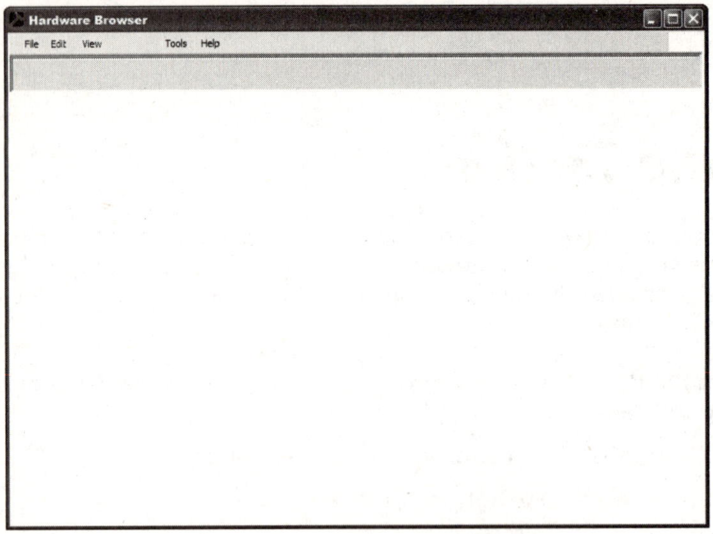

Figure 24-7: The custom browser window with its new toolbar.

6. **Click the Home command in the toolbox.**

   The Load Button dialog box appears.

7. **Locate the HomeButton.jpg button and double-click the image's filename.**

   The Home button appears in the custom window's toolbar.

8. **Use the Back, Forward, Stop, and Refresh commands in the toolbox to add the buttons to the toolbar, as you did with the Home button in Steps 6 and 7.**

   Your custom browser now has its set of toolbar buttons, as shown in Figure 24-8.

9. **Choose File⇨Save.**

   The Browser Construction Kit saves your browser's data.

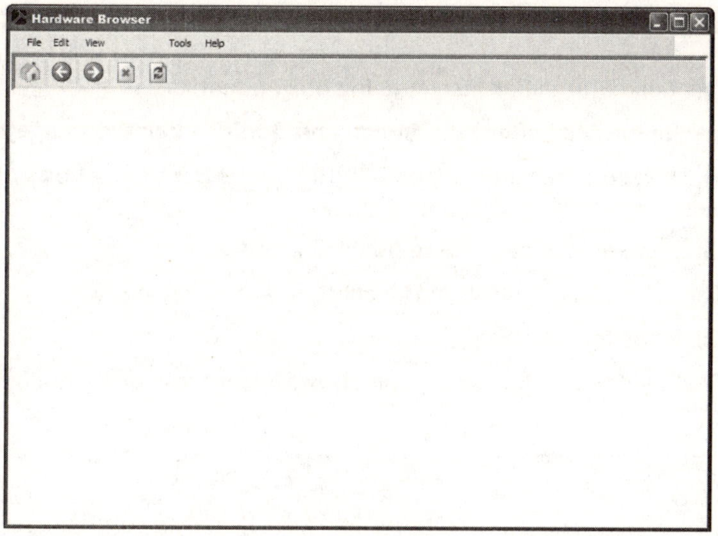

Figure 24-8: The toolbar with a complete set of buttons.

Adding the Status Bar

As with this browser's toolbar, the status bar can hold a custom graphic of your own design, or you can just go with the default choice given in these steps. In any case, when you're done, the status bar displays all the features available for status bars in the Browser Construction Kit. Here's how to get the task done:

1. **In the drop-down list below the toolbox, select the Status Bar command set.**

   The Status Bar commands appear in the toolbox.

2. **Click the Status Bar button.**

   The Status Bar dialog box appears (see Figure 24-9).

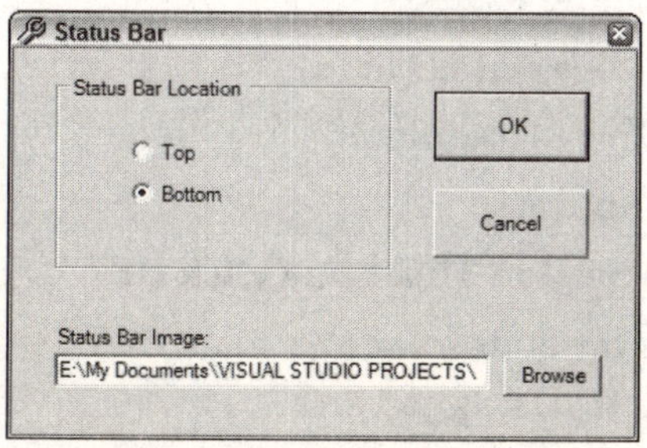

Figure 24-9: The Status Bar dialog box.

3. **Select the Status Bar's Bottom location and then click the Browse button.**

   The Load Status Bar Image dialog box appears.

4. **Locate the StatusBar.bmp image and double-click the image's filename.**

   The selected filename appears in the Status Bar dialog box's Status Bar Image text box.

5. **Click the Status Bar dialog box's OK button.**

   The status bar appears in the custom browser window.

6. **Click the Icon button.**

   The Load Status Bar Icon dialog box appears, as shown in Figure 24-10.

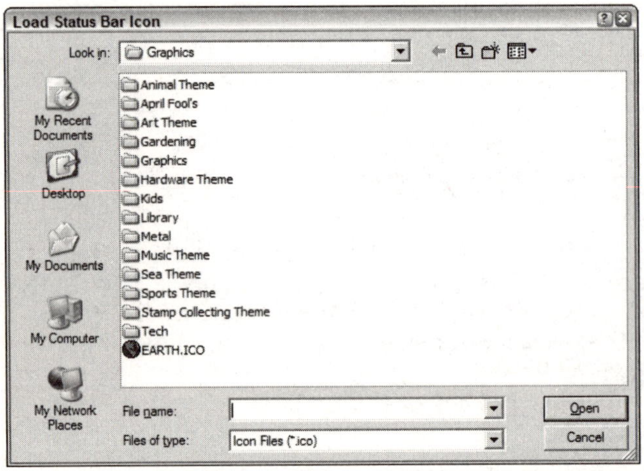

Figure 24-10: The Load Status Bar Icon dialog box.

7. **Locate the icon you want to use and double-click the image's filename.**

   Your icon appears in the status bar.

8. **Click the Clock command in the toolbox.**

   The clock panel appears in your status bar.

9. **Click the Timer command in the toolbox.**

   The Timer Type dialog box appears.

10. **Leave the timer type set to Session Timer and click OK.**

    The Timer panel appears in the status bar.

11. **Click the Date command in the toolbox.**

    The date panel appears in your status bar.

12. **Click the Current URL command in the toolbox.**

    The current URL panel appears in your status bar. Figure 24-11 shows the completed status bar.

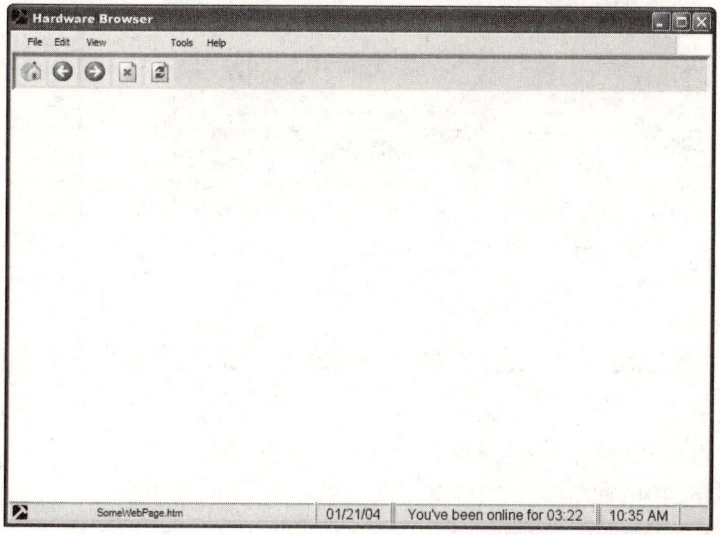

Figure 24-11: The browser window with its completed status bar.

13. **Choose File➪Save.**

    The Browser Construction Kit saves your browser's data.

Adding the Browser Pane

Yep, you've got to have a browser pane — unless you have such a great imagination that you can pretend that you're browsing the Internet! (Last time I tried that, I ended up at a Web site that gave me nightmares for a week.) Here's how to add the browser pane to your dedicated-site browser:

1. **In the drop-down list below the toolbox, select the Browser command set.**

    The Browser commands appear in the toolbox.

2. **Click the Browser button.**

    The browser pane appears in your browser's window (see Figure 24-12).

3. **Click the Top command in the toolbox.**

    The Browser Top dialog box appears.

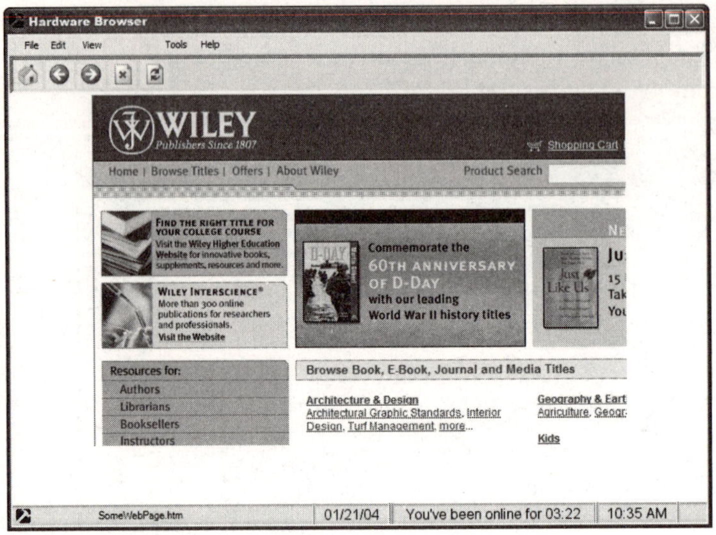

Figure 24-12: The browser pane when it first appears.

4. **Type** 100 **into the value text box and click OK.**

   The browser pane repositions itself.

5. **Click the Left command in the toolbox.**

   The Browser Left dialog box appears.

6. **Type** 10 **into the value text box and click OK.**

   The browser pane repositions itself to the left.

7. **Click the Width command in the toolbox.**

   The Browser Width dialog box appears.

8. **Type** 776 **into the value text box and click OK.**

   The browser pane widens.

9. **Click the Height command in the toolbox.**

   The Browser Height dialog box appears.

10. **Type** 460 **into the value text box and click OK.**

    The browser pane fills the window, as shown in Figure 24-13.

11. **Click the Start Site command.**

    The Start Site dialog box appears (see Figure 24-14).

12. **Enter the URL for the Web site that you want as this browser's home page and click OK.**

    The browser pane sets its home page.

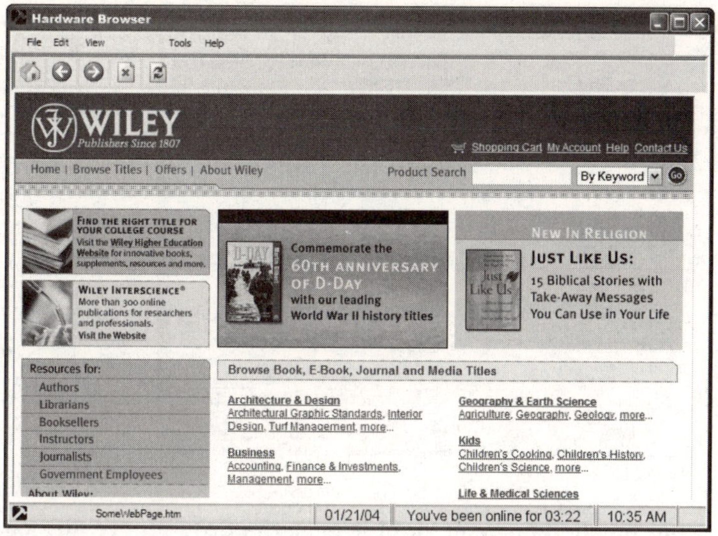

Figure 24-13: The fully positioned browser pane.

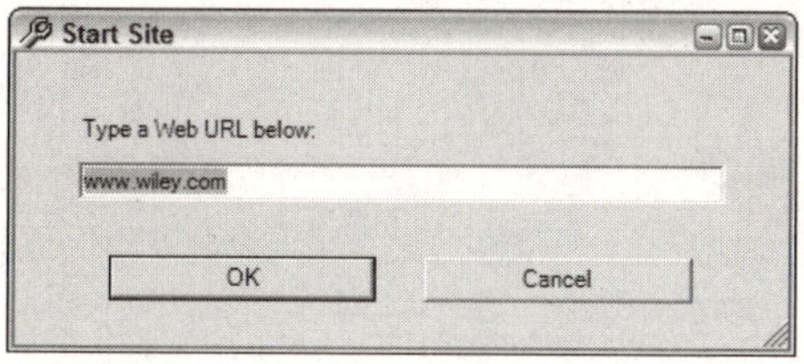

Figure 24-14: The Start Site dialog box.

13. **Choose File⇨Save.**

    The Browser Construction Kit saves your browser's data.

Compiling the Custom Browser

Time to get that browser up and running. I'm guessing you've probably already compiled a browser or two, but in case you haven't — or in case your memory is shot — here's what to do:

1. **Choose File⇨Build Browser.**

   The Build Browser dialog box appears (see Figure 24-15).

2. **Navigate to where you want to save your browser's finished files and then click Save.**

   The Browser Construction Kit builds the final files for your custom browser.

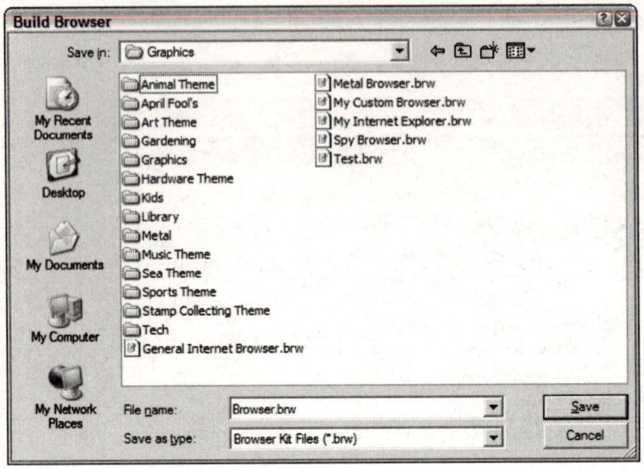

Figure 24-15: The Build Browser dialog box.

To run your finished browser, double-click the Browser.exe file, located in the directory to which you built the browser.

Chapter 25

Creating a Spy Browser

In This Chapter

- Designing the spy browser window
- Adding the menu bar, toolbar, status bar, and address bar
- Incorporating spy features
- Compiling the spy browser

Those kids! They always seem to find so many ways to get into trouble, don't they? The last thing you need to worry about is what they're doing on the Internet. This is where a spy browser comes in. Using the Browser Construction Kit, you can create a browser that not only tracks the sites your kids access, but also takes periodic screen shots. Now you can see exactly what the tikes are up to. You'll be amazed at how well kids behave when they know that inappropriate behavior will be caught on film. In this chapter, you build a browser that helps keep your kids' Internet experience on the straight and narrow, while still allowing free access to all that the Internet has to offer.

ON THE CD

You can find the images for this project in the Themes/Spy folder of this book's CD-ROM or in the folder into which you installed the Browser Construction Kit.

Creating the Window

The spy browser looks pretty normal to the untrained eye. Actually, because all the spy functions operate in the background, the spy browser even looks normal to the trained eye. The point is that there's nothing special about its window, as you will see as you perform the following tasks:

1. **In the drop-down list below the toolbox, select the Window command set.**

   The Window commands appear in the toolbox.

2. **Click the Color button.**

   The Color dialog box appears.

3. **Select the light gray color and click OK.**

   The window's background turns light gray.

4. **Click the Icon button.**

   The Select Window Icon dialog box appears (see Figure 25-1).

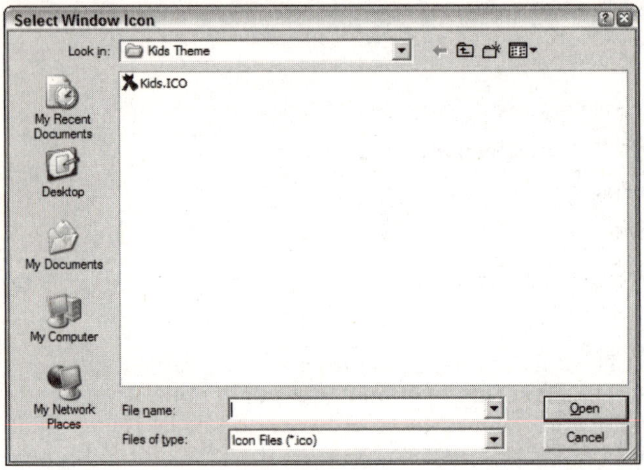

Figure 25-1: The Select Window Icon dialog box.

5. **Double-click the filename of the icon you want to use.**

   The icon appears in the window's title bar.

6. **Click the Style button.**

   The Window Styles dialog box appears, as shown in Figure 25-2.

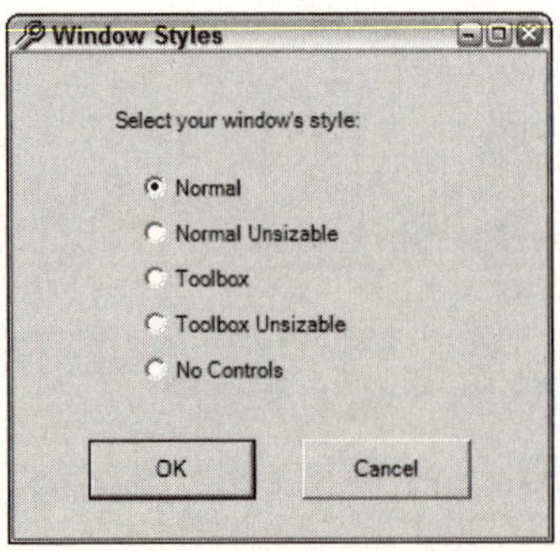

Figure 25-2: The Window Styles dialog box.

7. **Select the Normal option (if it's not already selected) and then click OK.**

   If you had a different style selected, the window's border style changes.

8. **Click the Buttons command in the toolbox.**

   The Window Buttons dialog box appears.

9. **Make sure that the Minimize Button and Maximize Button options are selected and then click OK.**

   The Minimize and Maximize buttons stay in the browser window.

10. **Click the Title button.**

    The Window Title dialog box appears.

11. **Type the browser name you want into the text box and click OK.**

    The window's new title appears in the title bar.

12. **Choose File⇨Save As.**

    The Save Browser File dialog box appears, as shown in Figure 25-3.

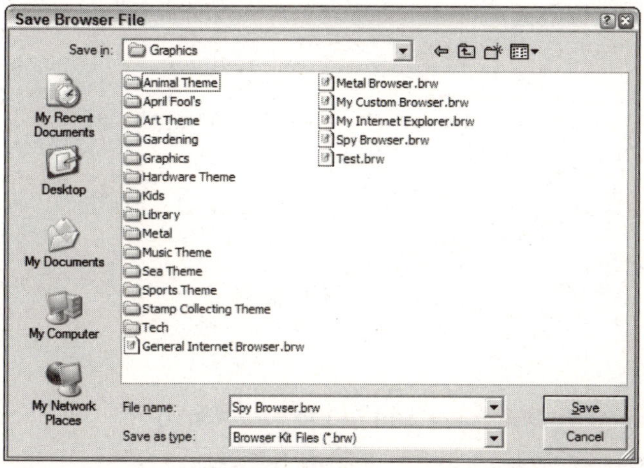

Figure 25-3: The Save Browser File dialog box.

13. **In the Save In drop-down list, navigate to where you want to save your browser's script file and then click Save.**

    The Browser Construction Kit saves your browser's data to the selected location, using the window's title as the filename.

Adding the Menu Bar

The spy browser features a complete set of menus and commands. After all, you're not trying to limit what someone can do with the browser; you just want to keep an eye on them while they do it. (Insert evil chuckle here.) So, perform the following steps to add a full-featured menu bar to the browser:

1. **In the drop-down list below the toolbox, select the Menu Bar command set.**

   The Menu Bar commands appear in the toolbox (see Figure 25-4).

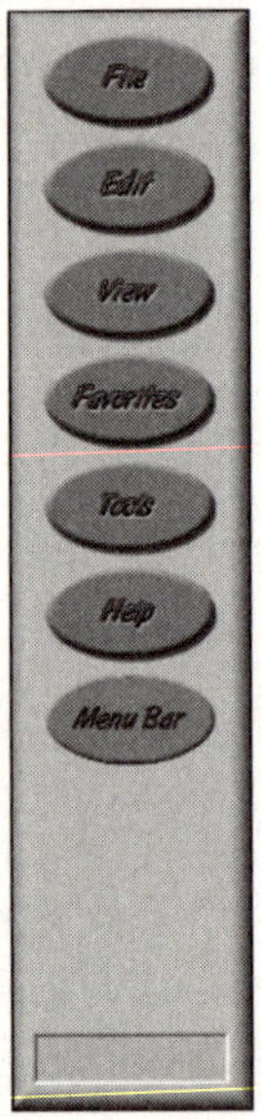

Figure 25-4: The Menu Bar commands in the toolbar.

2. **Click the Menu Bar command in the toolbox.**

   The menu bar appears in the custom browser window.

3. **Click the File button in the toolbox.**

   The File Menu dialog box appears (see Figure 25-5).

4. **Select all four menu options and then click OK.**

   The File menu appears in your custom browser window.

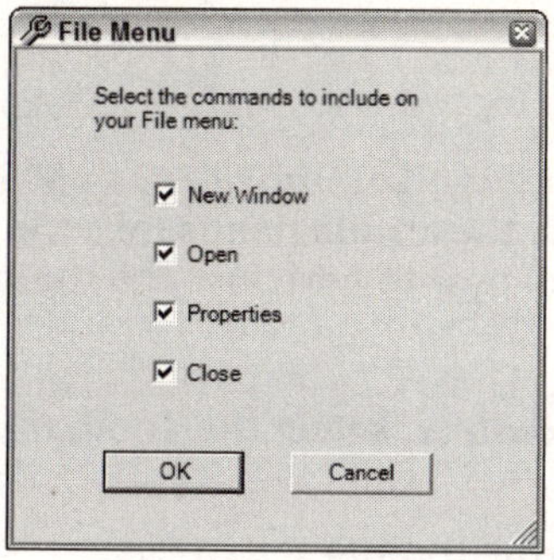

Figure 25-5: The File Menu dialog box.

5. **Use the Edit, View, Favorites, Tools, and Help commands in the toolbox to add these menus and all of their menu items to the menu bar, just as you did with the File menu in Steps 3 and 4.**

   The complete set of menus appears in your custom browser's window, as shown in Figure 25-6.

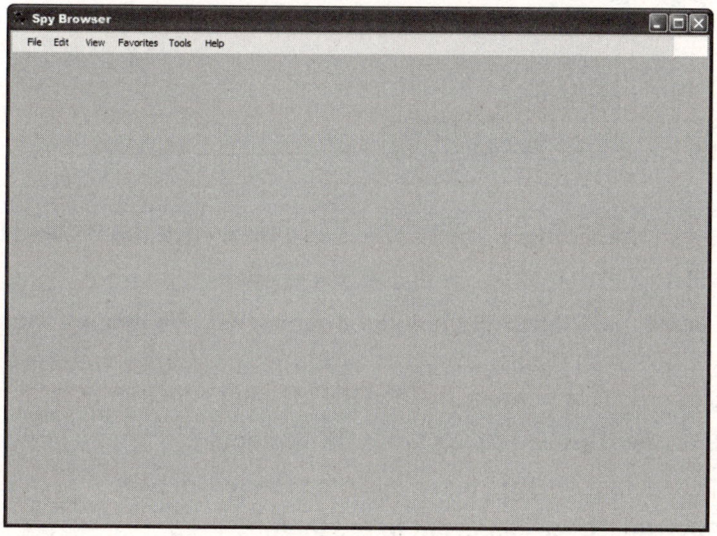

Figure 25-6: Your browser window with its complete set of menus.

6. **Choose File➪Save.**

   The Browser Construction Kit saves your browser's data.

Adding the Toolbar

The spy-browser toolbar, like every other toolbar, provides quick access to frequently used commands. In this case, these commands take the form of the browser's navigation buttons. Here's how to add both the toolbar and its buttons:

1. **In the drop-down list below the toolbox, select the Toolbar command set.**

   The Toolbar commands appear in the toolbox.

2. **Click the Toolbar button.**

   The Toolbar dialog box appears (see Figure 25-7).

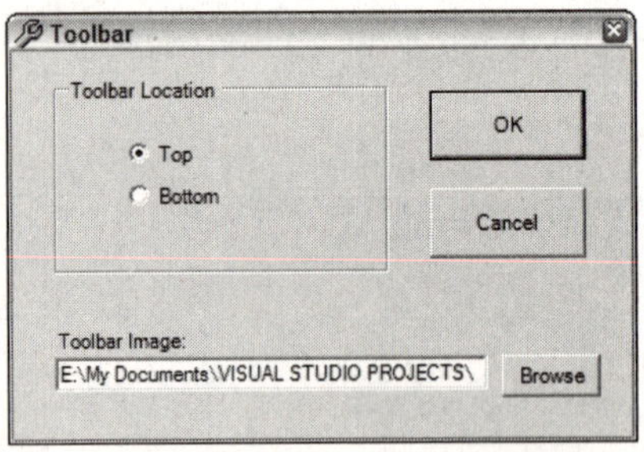

Figure 25-7: The Toolbar dialog box.

3. **Select the toolbar's Top location and then click the Browse button.**

   The Load Toolbar Image dialog box appears.

4. **Locate the Toolbar.jpg file and double-click the image's filename.**

   The selected filename appears in the Toolbar dialog box's Toolbar Image text box. This image is the one the browser's toolbar uses.

5. **Click the Toolbar dialog box's OK button.**

   The toolbar appears in the custom browser window.

6. **Click the Home command in the toolbox.**

   The Load Button Image dialog box appears (see Figure 25-8).

7. **Locate the HomeButton.jpg button and double-click the image's filename.**

   The Home button appears in the custom window's toolbar.

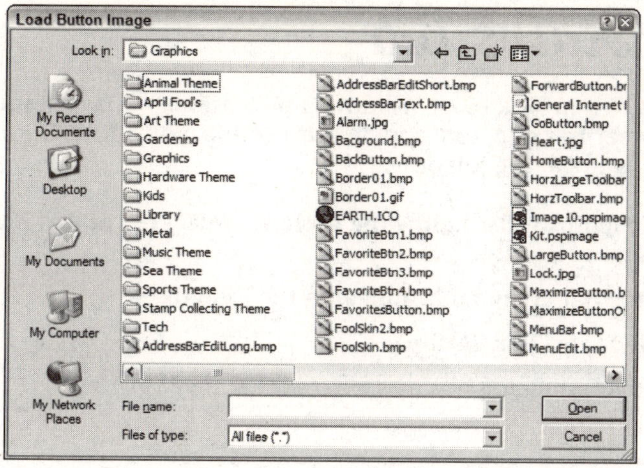

Figure 25-8: The Load Button Image dialog box.

8. **Add the Back, Forward, Stop, Refresh, Search, and Favorites buttons, just as you did the Home button in Steps 6 and 7.**

   Your custom browser now has a complete set of toolbar buttons, as shown in Figure 25-9.

9. **Choose File⇨Save.**

   The Browser Construction Kit saves your browser's data.

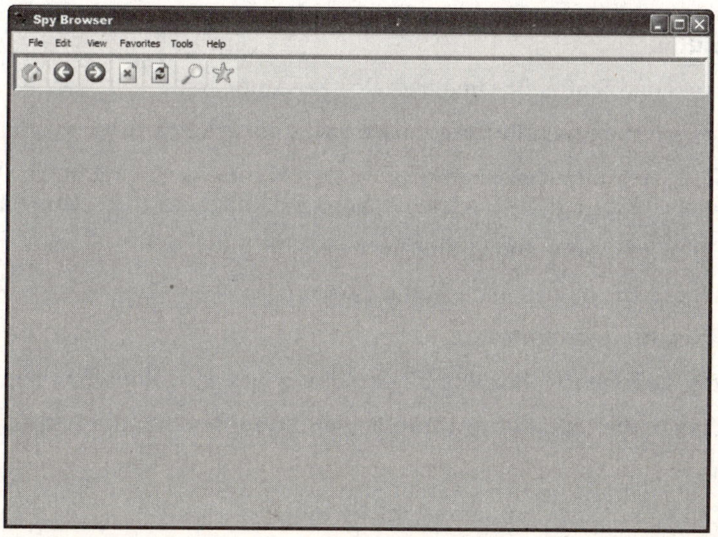

Figure 25-9: The toolbar with a complete set of buttons.

Adding the Status Bar

Most browsers — in fact, most Windows applications — have status bars. The spy browser has one, too, and, in this section, you add it. Perform the following steps to get the job done:

1. **In the drop-down list below the toolbox, select the Status Bar command set.**

   The Status Bar commands appear in the toolbox.

2. **Click the Status Bar button.**

   The Status Bar dialog box appears (see Figure 25-10).

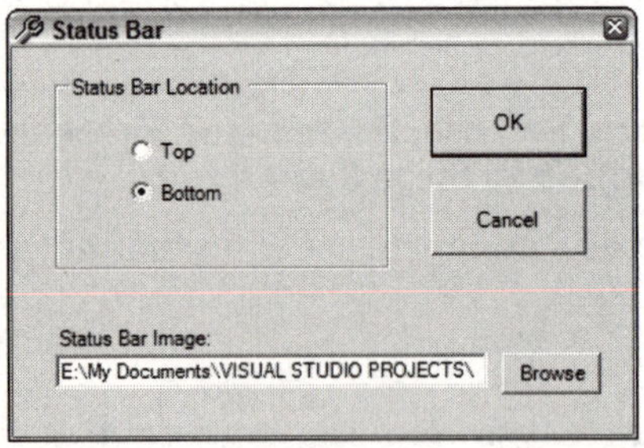

Figure 25-10: The Status Bar dialog box.

3. **Select the Status Bar's Bottom location and then click the Browse button.**

   The Load Status Bar Image dialog box appears.

4. **Locate the StatusBar.jpg image and double-click the image's filename.**

   The selected filename appears in the Status Bar dialog box's Status Bar Image text box. This is the background image for the status bar.

5. **Click the Status Bar dialog box's OK button.**

   The status bar appears in the custom browser window.

6. **Click the Icon button.**

   The Load Status Bar Icon dialog box appears, as shown in Figure 25-11.

7. **Locate the icon you want to use and double-click the image's filename.**

   Your icon appears in the status bar.

8. **Click the Clock command in the toolbox.**

   The clock panel appears in your status bar.

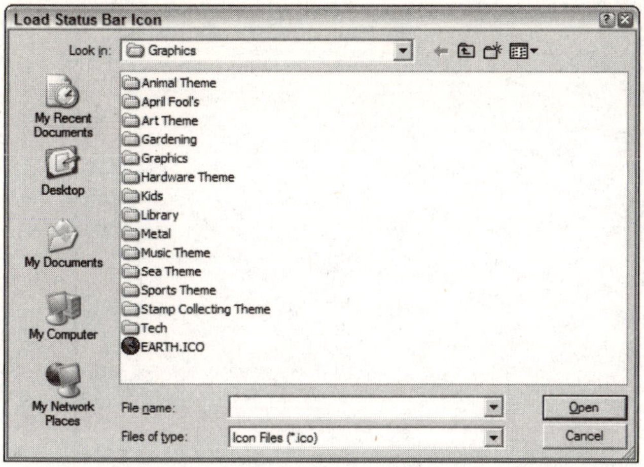

Figure 25-11: The Load Status Bar Icon dialog box.

9. **Click the Timer command in the toolbox.**

   The Timer Type dialog box appears (see Figure 25-12).

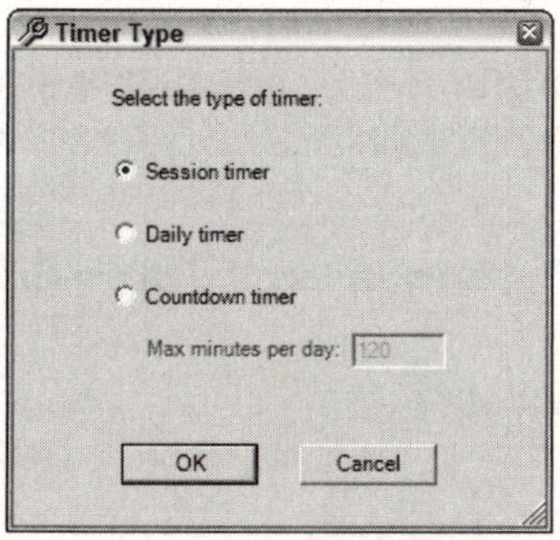

Figure 25-12: The Timer Type dialog box.

10. **Leave the timer type set to Session Timer and click OK.**

    The Timer panel appears in the status bar.

11. **Click the Date command in the toolbox.**

    The date panel appears in your status bar.

12. **Click the Current URL command in the toolbox.**

    The current URL panel appears in your status bar. Figure 25-13 shows the completed status bar.

13. **Choose File⇨Save.**

    The Browser Construction Kit saves your browser's data.

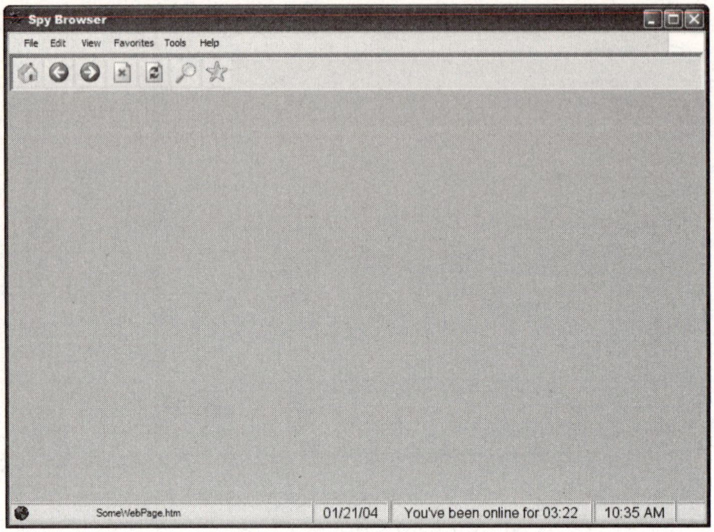

Figure 25-13: The browser window with its completed status bar.

Adding the Browser Pane

Time to add the browser pane to the spy browser. You won't find anything unusual here, just a place to display the Web pages your browser user views. Here's how to add the browser pane:

1. **In the drop-down list below the toolbox, select the Browser command set.**

   The Browser commands appear in the toolbox.

2. **Click the Browser button.**

   The browser pane appears in your browser's window (see Figure 25-14). Currently, because the browser pane in so small, it can display only a portion of a Web page. By enlarging the pane (as you do soon), more of the Web page becomes visible.

3. **Click the Top command in the toolbox.**

   The Browser Top dialog box appears (see Figure 25-15).

4. **Type** 125 **into the value text box and click OK.**

   The browser pane repositions itself.

5. **Click the Left command in the toolbox.**

   The Browser Left dialog box appears.

6. **Type** 10 **into the value text box and click OK.**

   The browser pane repositions itself to the left.

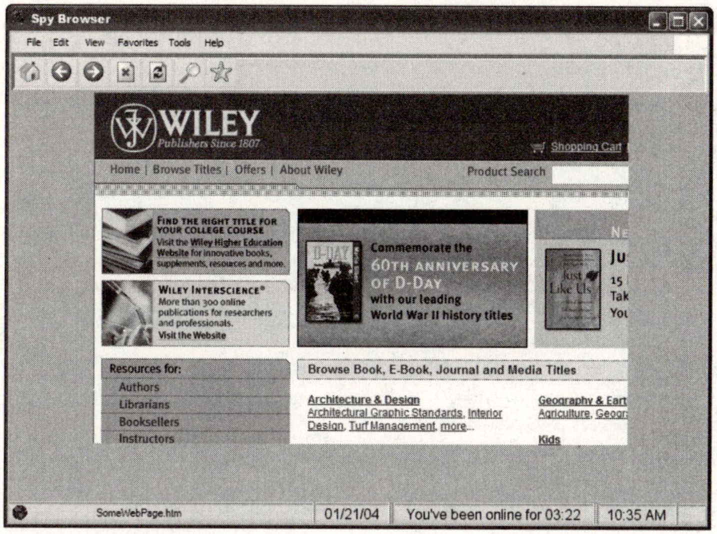

Figure 25-14: The browser pane when it first appears.

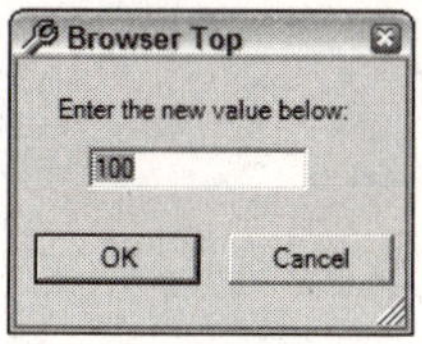

Figure 25-15: The Browser Top dialog box.

7. **Click the Width command in the toolbox.**

   The Browser Width dialog box appears.

8. **Type** 776 **into the value text box and click OK.**

   The browser pane widens.

9. **Click the Height command in the toolbox.**

   The Browser Height dialog box appears.

10. **Type** 430 **into the value text box and click OK.**

    The browser pane fills the window, as shown in Figure 25-16.

11. **Click the Start Site command.**

    The Start Site dialog box appears (see Figure 25-17).

12. **Type the URL for the Web site that you want as this browser's home page and click OK.**

    The browser pane sets its home page.

13. **Choose File➪Save.**

    The Browser Construction Kit saves your browser's data.

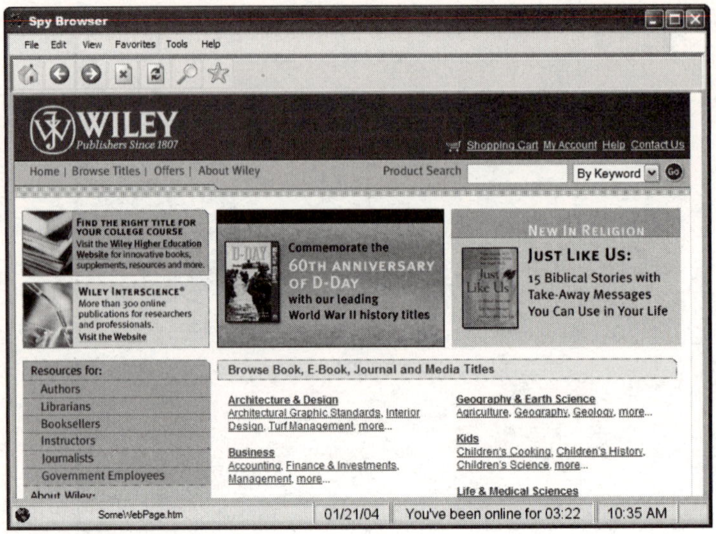

Figure 25-16: The fully positioned browser pane.

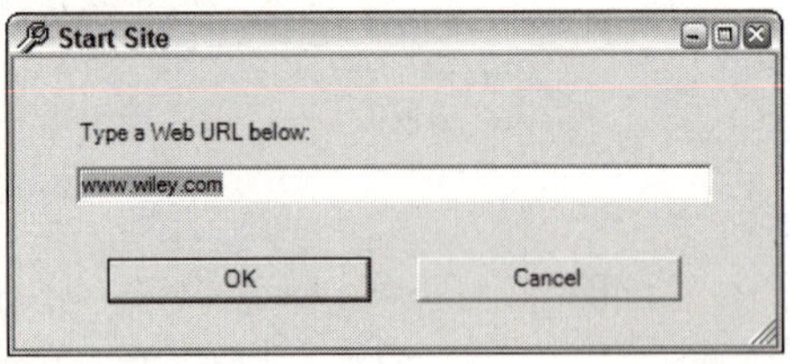

Figure 25-17: The Start Site dialog box.

Adding the Address Bar

The address bar enables the browser's user to type the URLs of Web sites he wants to visit. Without the address bar, the user would be able to visit only Web sites associated with links displayed in the browser pane. Perform the following steps to add an address bar to the spy browser:

1. **In the drop-down list below the toolbox, select the Address Bar command set.**

   The Address Bar commands appear in the toolbox.

2. **Click the Address Bar button.**

   The Address Bar dialog box appears (see Figure 25-18).

3. **Select the Address Bar's Top location and then click the Browse button.**

   The Load Address Bar Image dialog box appears.

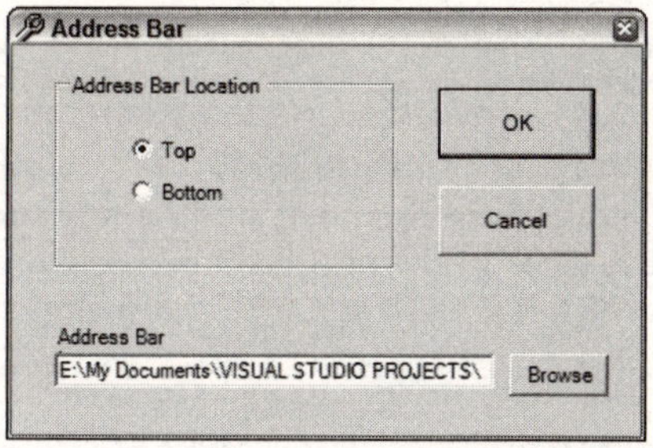

Figure 25-18: The Address Bar dialog box.

ON THE CD

4. **Locate the AddressBar.jpg image on this book's CD-ROM and double-click the image's filename.**

   The selected filename appears in the Address Bar dialog box's Address Bar Image text box. This is the image that the browser will use as the address bar's background.

5. **Click the dialog box's OK button.**

   The address bar appears in your Spy browser window.

6. **Click the Go Button command.**

   The Go button appears in your address bar.

7. **Click the Favorite 1 command.**

   The Favorite Button dialog box appears (see Figure 25-19).

8. **Type the URL to one of your favorite Web sites and then click OK.**

   The Favorite 1 button appears in the address bar.

9. **Use the Favorite 2, Favorite 3, and Favorite 4 commands in the toolbox to add the remaining favorites buttons to the address bar, the same way you added the Favorite 1 button in Steps 7 and 8.**

   Your custom browser now has a complete address bar.

10. **Choose File⇨Save.**

    The Browser Construction Kit saves your browser's data.

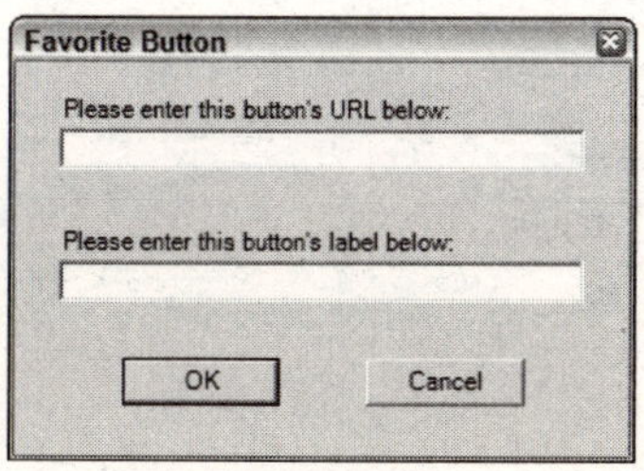

Figure 25-19: The Favorite Button dialog box.

Adding the Spy Features

Here's where you add the stuff that makes the spy browser . . . well, a spy browser. After you've added the features in this section, the spy browser keeps a list of all Web sites visited. It also takes periodic screen shots so that you can easily see how the browser has been used. The following steps add the spy features to the browser:

1. **In the drop-down list below the toolbox, select the Functions command set.**

   The Functions commands appear in the toolbox.

2. **Click the Log File button.**

   The log file's function's icon appears below the browser's window.

3. **Click the Spy command in the toolbox.**

   The screen spy function's icon appears below the browser's window (Figure 25-20).

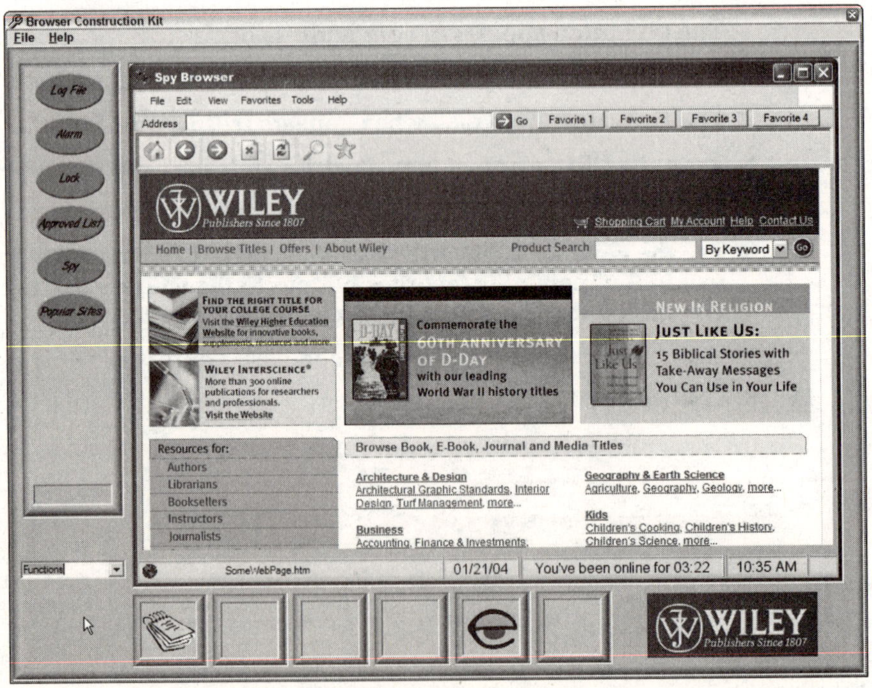

Figure 25-20: The Spy features in the functions.

Compiling the Spy Browser

Get ready to unleash your spy browser out into the world. After completing the following steps, you'll have a working browser whose special features encourage users to use the Internet according to your rules:

1. **Choose File⇨Build Browser.**

   The Build Browser dialog box appears.

2. **Use the drop-down list to navigate to where you want to save your browser's finished files, and then click OK.**

   The Browser Construction Kit builds the final files for your custom browser.

To run your finished browser, double-click the Browser.exe file, located in the directory to which you built the browser in Step 2.

Chapter 26

Designing a Library Browser

In This Chapter

- Creating a library browser window
- Adding a toolbar, status bar, address bar, and menu bar
- Positioning the browser pane
- Compiling the library browser

Public libraries these days typically provide Internet access to their patrons. Although free-speech issues generally prevent libraries from filtering Web content, a library has a perfect right to keep a log of Web usage. Moreover, nothing says that a library's Web browser can't be designed with graphical elements that fit the browser's purpose, namely books and research. In this chapter, you create a library browser that incorporates these ideas.

Creating the Window

The window for the library-themed browser features special graphics that bring to mind a library-like environment, including a background and special icon. Perform the following steps to create your browser's window:

1. **In the drop-down list below the toolbox, select the Window command set.**

   The Window commands appear in the toolbox.

2. **Click the Color button.**

   The Color dialog box appears.

3. **Select the color white and click OK.**

   The window's background turns white.

4. **Click the Icon button.**

   The Select Window Icon dialog box appears, as shown in Figure 26-1.

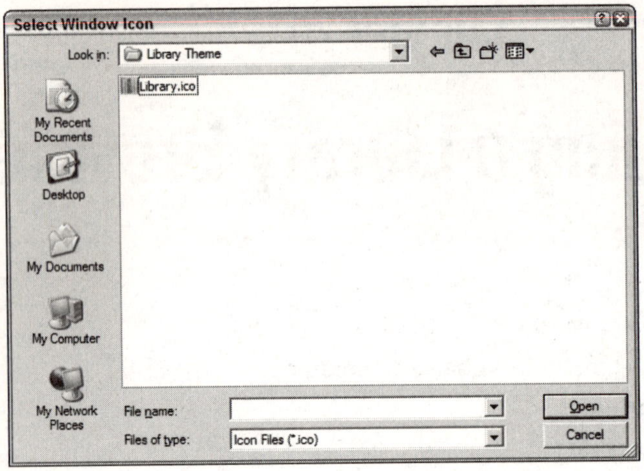

Figure 26-1: The Select Window Icon dialog box.

5. **Open the Library.ico file from this book's CD-ROM.**

   Your icon appears in the window's title bar.

6. **Click the Style button.**

   The Window Styles dialog box appears.

7. **Make sure that the Normal option is selected and click OK.**
8. **Click the Buttons command in the toolbox.**

   The Window Buttons dialog box appears, as shown in Figure 26-2.

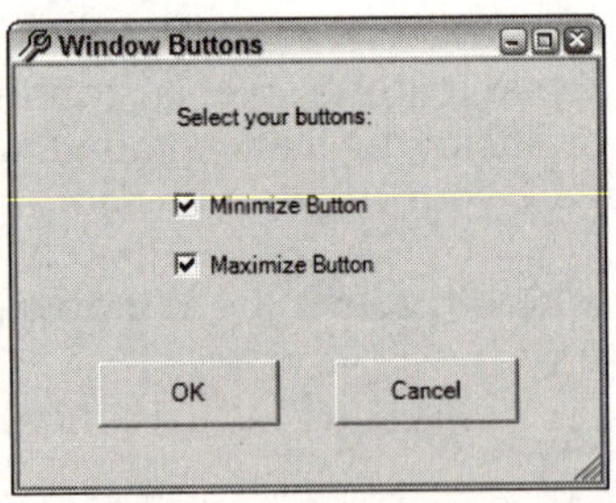

Figure 26-2: The Window Buttons dialog box.

9. **Make sure that the Minimize Button and Maximize Button options are selected and then click OK.**
10. **Click the Title button.**

    The Window Title dialog box appears, as shown in Figure 26-3.

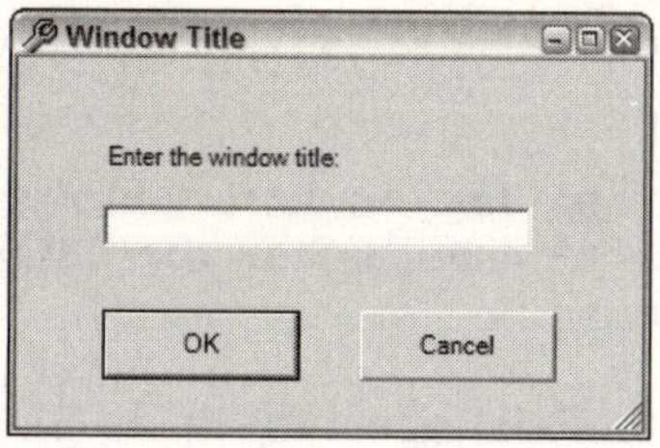

Figure 26-3: The Window Title dialog box.

11. **Type the name** Library Browser **and click OK.**

    The window's new title appears in the title bar.

12. **Click the Skin button.**

    The Select Skin Image dialog box appears.

13. **Open the Library_Background.jpg image (see Figure 26-4).**

    The window's new background appears.

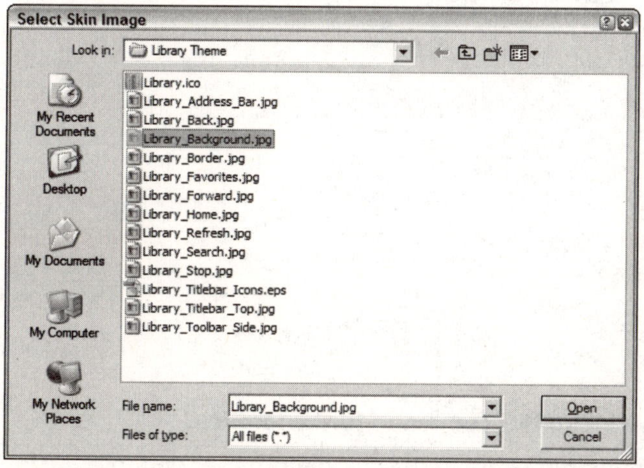

Figure 26-4: The Select Skin Image dialog box.

14. **Choose File⇨Save As.**

    The Save Browser File dialog box appears.

15. **Navigate to where you want to save your browser's script file and then click Save.**

    The Browser Construction Kit saves your browser's data to the selected location, using the window's title as the filename.

Adding the Menu Bar

There's nothing special about the menu bar for your library browser, but it does feature every available menu and command. Follow these steps to add the menu bar to the browser:

1. **In the drop-down list below the toolbox, select the Menu Bar command set (see Figure 26-5).**

   The Menu Bar commands appear in the toolbox.

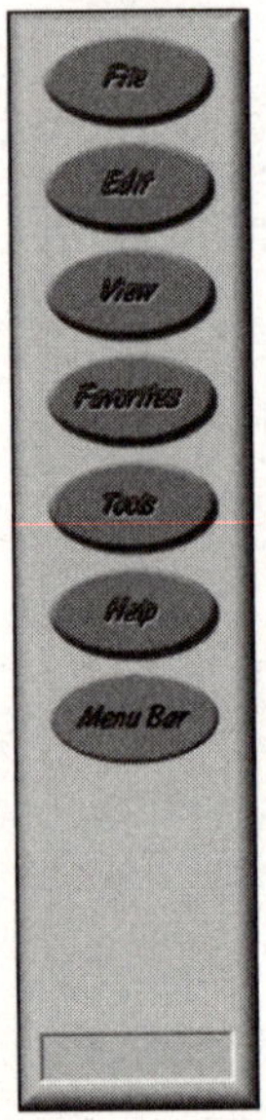

Figure 26-5: The Menu Bar commands in the toolbox.

2. **Click the Menu Bar command in the toolbox.**

   The menu bar appears in the custom browser window.

3. **Select the File button in the toolbox.**

   The File Menu dialog box appears.

4. **Select the four menu options (New Window, Open, Properties, and Close) and click OK.**

   The File menu appears in your custom browser window.

5. **Use the Edit, View, Favorites, Tools, and Help commands in the toolbox to add the menus to the menu bar, the same way you added the File menu in Steps 3 and 4.**

   Your custom browser now has a complete set of menus, as shown in Figure 26-6.

6. **Choose File⇨Save.**

   The Browser Construction Kit saves your browser's data.

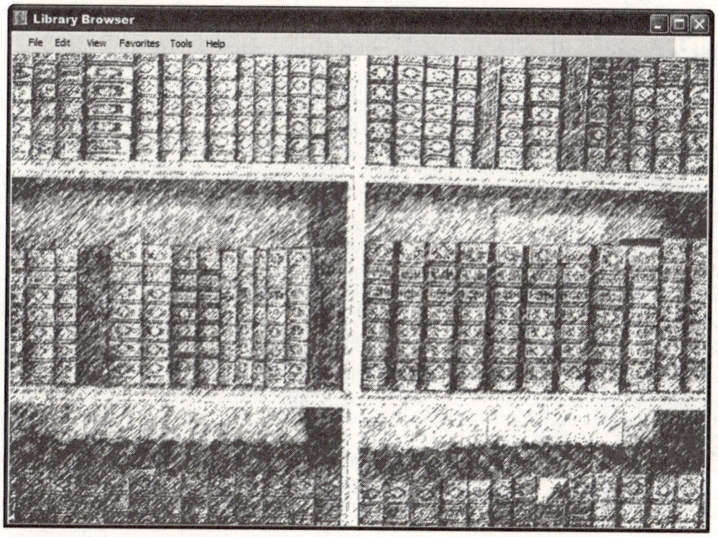

Figure 26-6: The custom browser window with its new menus.

Adding the Toolbar

This browser's toolbar features not only a special image, but also special buttons for each of the navigation buttons. The following steps install your toolbar:

1. **In the drop-down list below the toolbox, select the Toolbar command set.**

   The Toolbar commands appear in the toolbox.

2. **Click the Toolbar button.**

   The Toolbar dialog box appears (see Figure 26-7).

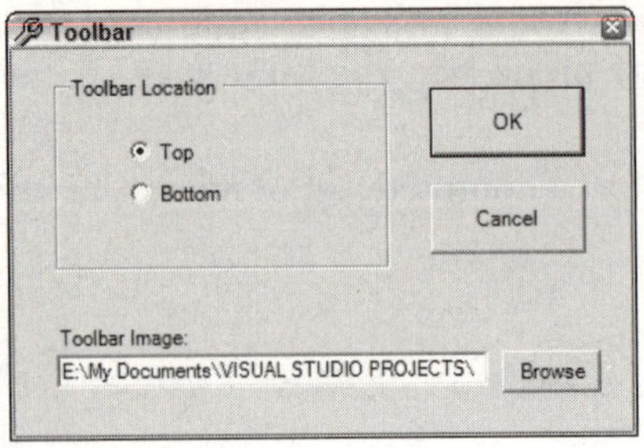

Figure 26-7: The Toolbar dialog box.

3. **Select the toolbar's location and then click Browse.**

   The Load Toolbar Image dialog box appears.

4. **Open the Library_Toolbar.jpg image.**

   The selected filename appears in the Toolbar dialog box's Toolbar Image text box.

5. **Click the Toolbar dialog box's OK button.**

   The toolbar appears in the custom browser window, as shown in Figure 26-8.

6. **Click the Home command in the toolbox.**

   The Load Button Image dialog box appears.

7. **Open the Library_Home.jpg image (see Figure 26-9).**

   The Home button appears in the custom window's toolbar.

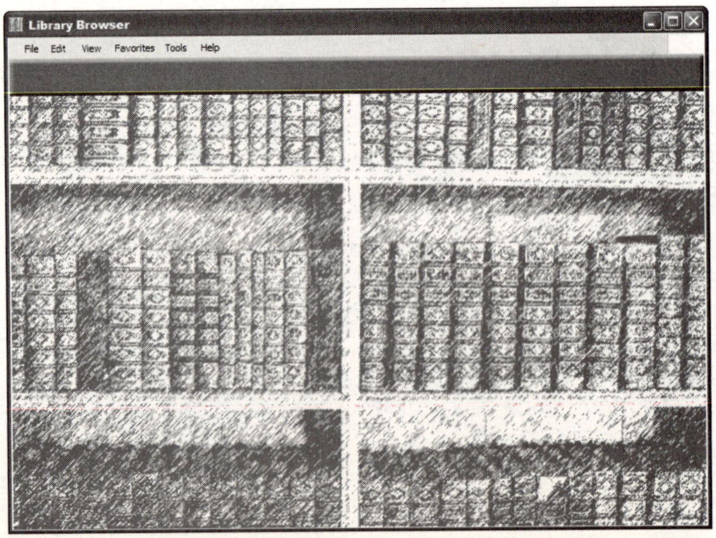

Figure 26-8: The toolbar in your browser's window.

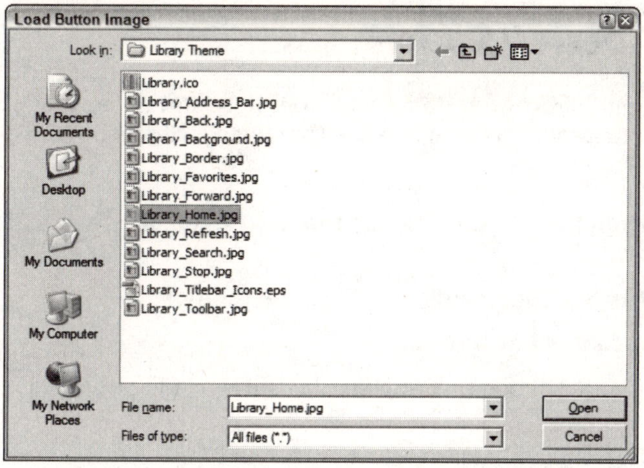

Figure 26-9: Choosing the Home button.

8. **Use the Back, Forward, Stop, Refresh, Search, and Favorites commands in the toolbox to add the buttons to the toolbar, the same way you added the Home button in Steps 6 and 7.**

   The image filenames are Library_Back.jpg, Library_Forward.jpg, Library_Stop.jpg, Library_Refresh.jpg, Library_Search.jpg, and Library_Favorites.jpg.

   Your custom browser now has a complete set of toolbar buttons, as shown in Figure 26-10.

9. **Choose File⇨Save.**

   The Browser Construction Kit saves your browser's data.

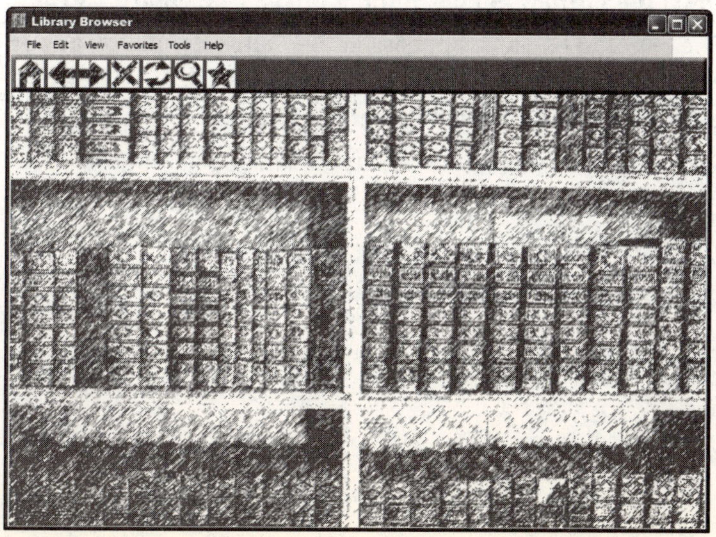

Figure 26-10: The toolbar with a complete set of buttons.

Adding the Status Bar

The library-themed browser contains a complete status bar that shows all the available panels, as well as a custom image. Here's how to add the status bar:

1. **In the drop-down list below the toolbox, select the Status Bar command set.**

   The Status Bar commands appear in the toolbox.

2. **Click the Status Bar button.**

   The Status Bar dialog box appears, as shown in Figure 26-11.

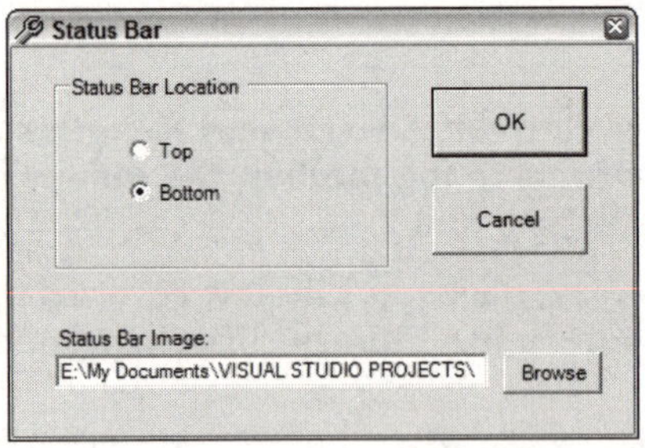

Figure 26-11: The Status Bar dialog box.

3. **Select the Status Bar's Bottom location and then click the Browse button.**

   The Load Status Bar Image dialog box appears.

4. **Open the Library_Status_Bar.jpg image (see Figure 26-12).**

   The selected filename appears in the Status Bar dialog box's Status Bar Image text box.

5. **Click the Status Bar dialog box's OK button.**

   The status bar appears in the custom browser window.

6. **Click the Icon button.**

   The Load Status Bar Icon dialog box appears.

7. **Open the Library.ico file.**

   Your icon appears in the status bar.

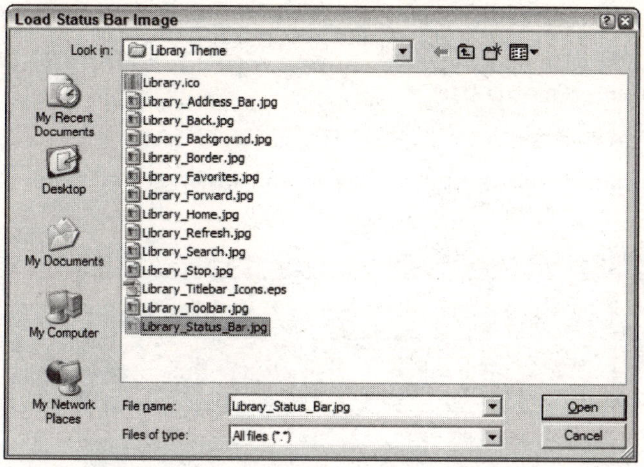

Figure 26-12: Selecting the status bar's image.

8. **Click the Clock command in the toolbox.**

   The clock panel appears in your status bar.

9. **Click the Timer command in the toolbox.**

   The Timer Type dialog box appears (see Figure 26-13).

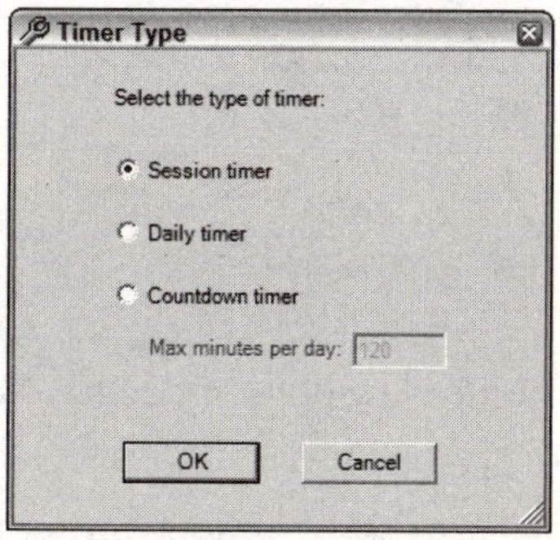

Figure 26-13: The Timer Type dialog box.

10. **Leave the timer type set to Session Timer and click OK.**

    The Timer panel appears in the status bar.

11. **Click the Date command in the toolbox.**

    The date panel appears in your status bar.

12. **Click the Current URL command in the toolbox.**

    The current URL panel appears in your status bar. Figure 26-14 shows the completed status bar.

13. **Choose File⇨Save.**

    The Browser Construction Kit saves your browser's data.

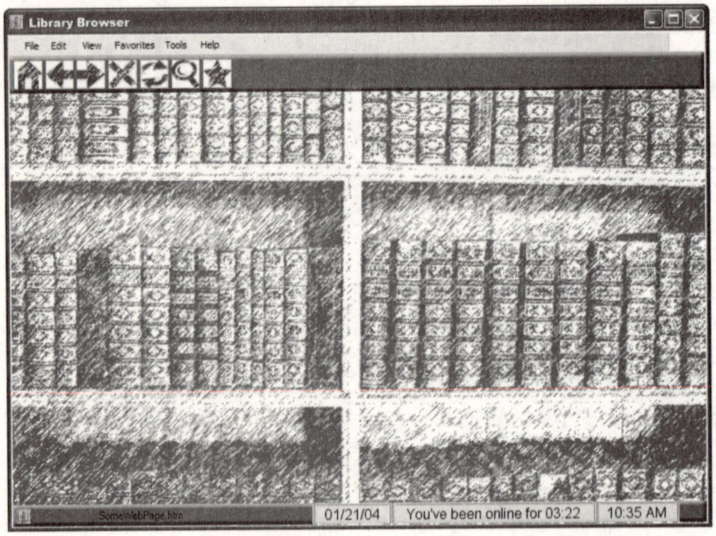

Figure 26-14: The custom-browser window with its completed status bar.

Adding the Address Bar

Your new browser's address bar uses the same image that you used for the status bar. Of course, the address bar holds very different controls, as you see as you complete the following steps:

1. **In the drop-down list below the toolbox, select the Address Bar command set.**

   The Address Bar commands appear in the toolbox.

2. **Click the Address Bar button.**

   The Address Bar dialog box appears (see Figure 26-15).

3. **Select the Address Bar's Top location and then click Browse.**

   The Load Address Bar Image dialog box appears.

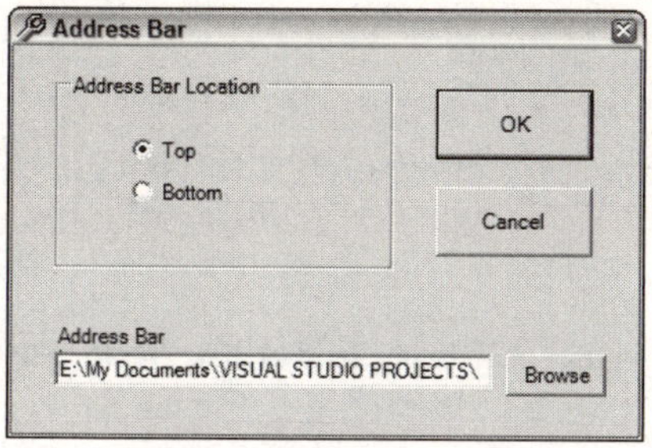

Figure 26-15: The Address Bar dialog box.

4. **Open the Library_Address_Bar.jpg image.**

   The selected filename appears in the Address Bar dialog box's Address Bar Image text box.

5. **Click OK.**

   The address bar appears in your browser's window.

6. **Click the Go Button command.**

   The Go button appears in your address bar. Your custom browser now has a complete address bar, as shown in Figure 26-16.

7. **Choose File⇨Save.**

   The Browser Construction Kit saves your browser's data.

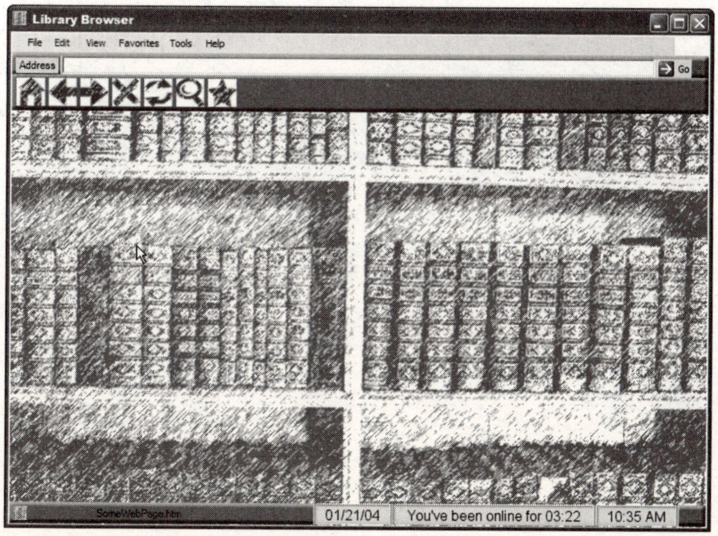

Figure 26-16: The custom-browser window with its completed address bar.

Adding the Browser Pane

Time to add the all-important browser pane, which is the part of the custom browser that displays the current Web page. Perform the following steps to complete this task:

1. **In the drop-down list below the toolbox, select the Browser command set.**

   The Browser commands appear in the toolbox.

2. **Click the Browser button.**

   The browser pane appears in your browser's window (see Figure 26-17).

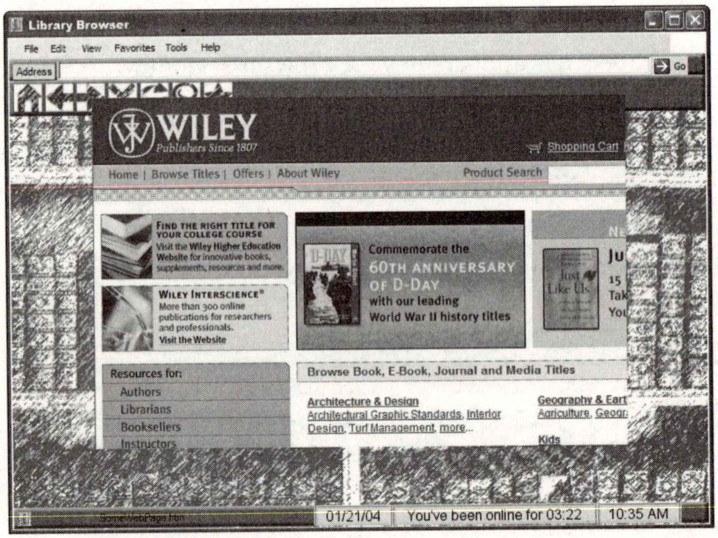

Figure 26-17: The custom-browser window with its new browser pane.

3. **Click the Top command in the toolbox.**

   The Browser Top dialog box appears, as shown in Figure 26-18.

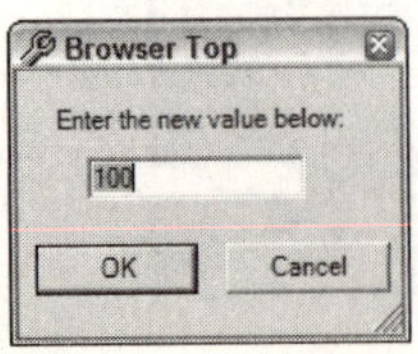

Figure 26-18: The Browser Top dialog box.

4. **Type** 123 **into the value text box and click OK.**

   The browser pane repositions itself.

5. **Click the Height command in the toolbox.**

   The Browser Height dialog box appears.

6. **Type** 436 **into the value text box and click OK.**

   The browser pane fits the window.

7. **Click the Start Site command.**

   The Start Site dialog box appears.

8. **Type the URL for the Web site that you want as this browser's home page and click OK.**

   The browser pane sets its home page.

9. **Choose File⇨Save.**

   The Browser Construction Kit saves your browser's data.

Compiling the Custom Browser

The last step in creating your library-themed browser is to compile your settings into the actual application that you can run and use to surf the Web. These steps get the job done:

1. **Choose File⇨Build Browser.**

   The Build Browser dialog box appears.

2. **Navigate to where you want to save your browser's finished files and then click OK.**

   The Browser Construction Kit builds the final files for your custom browser.

To run your finished browser, double-click the Browser.exe file, located in the directory to which you built the browser.

Chapter 27

Getting a Laugh with an April Fool's Browser

In This Chapter

- Creating the April Fool's window
- Adding your toolbar, status bar, address bar, and menu bar
- Positioning the browser pane
- Compiling the April Fool's browser

Making a custom browser with the Browser Construction Kit is so easy that you can afford to waste a little time doing crazy stuff. For example, how about creating a browser whose buttons don't do the expected thing, as well as a window that's so confusing, your victim may never figure it out? That's the idea behind the April Fool's browser, which you put together in this chapter.

Creating the Window

The main window for the April Fool's browser is unsizable and contains a special background graphic that looks like a browser window, but really isn't. (Chuckle.) Perform the following steps to build this project's window:

1. **In the drop-down list below the toolbox, select the Window command set.**

   The Window commands appear in the toolbox.

2. **Click the Icon button.**

   The Select Window Icon dialog box appears.

3. **Open the Earth.ico file from this book's CD-ROM.**

   Your icon appears in the window's title bar.

4. **Click the Style button.**

   The Window Styles dialog box appears.

5. **Select the Normal Unsizable option (see Figure 27-1) and click OK.**

   The Browser Construction Kit changes the window style.

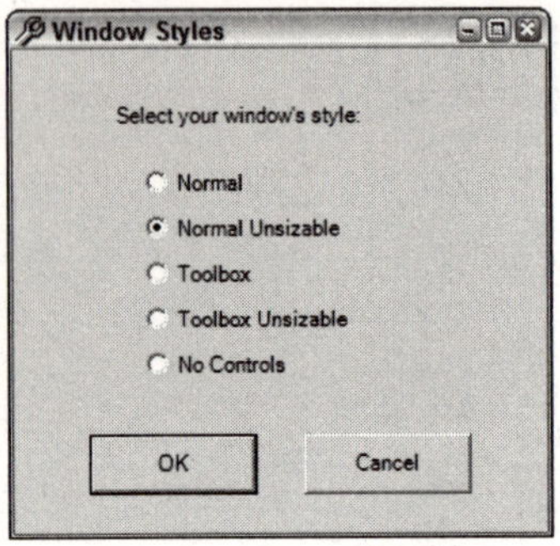

Figure 27-1: Creating an unsizable window.

6. **Click the Buttons command in the toolbox.**

   The Window Buttons dialog box appears.

7. **Turn off the Minimize and Maximize buttons (see Figure 27-2) and then click OK.**

   The Browser Construction Kit removes the buttons from the window.

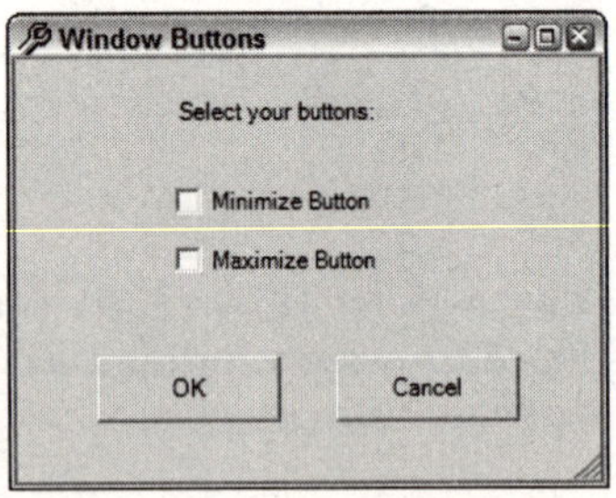

Figure 27-2: Turning off the window's buttons.

8. **Click the Title button.**

   The Window Title dialog box appears.

9. **Type the name** Internet Browser **and click OK.**

   The window's new title appears in the title bar.

10. **Click the Skin button.**

    The Select Skin Image dialog box appears, as shown in Figure 27-3.

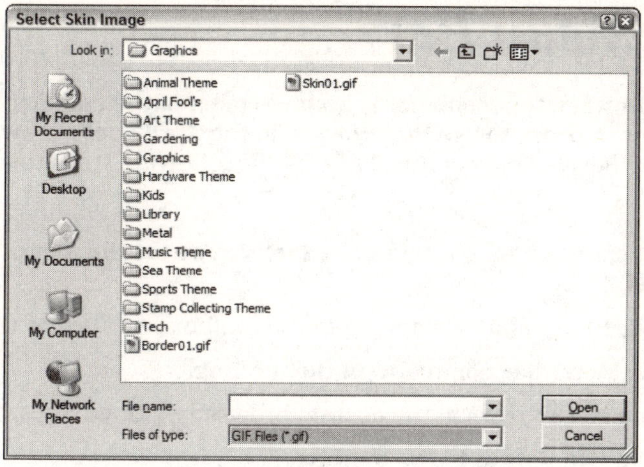

Figure 27-3: The Select Skin Image dialog box.

ON THE CD

11. **Open the FoolSkin.jpg image.**

    The window's new background appears (see Figure 27-4).

12. **Save your file.**

    The Browser Construction Kit saves your browser's data to the selected location, using the window's title as the filename.

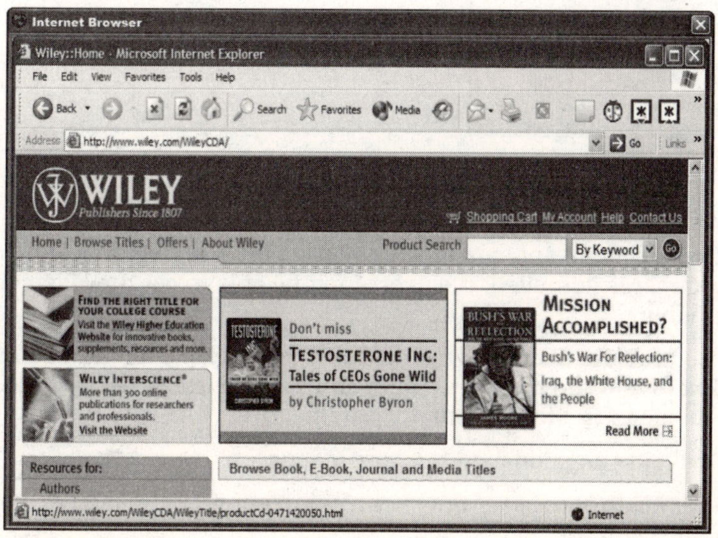

Figure 27-4: The window with its April Fool's skin.

Adding the Menu Bar

In a normal browser, the menu bar is home to most of the commands that the user needs in order to use the browser. In the April Fool's browser, the menus remain perplexingly empty. Perform the following steps to add the menu bar.

1. **In the drop-down menu below the toolbox, select the Menu Bar command set.**

   The Menu Bar commands appear in the toolbox.

2. **Click the Menu Bar command in the toolbox.**

   The menu bar appears in the custom browser window.

3. **Select the File button in the toolbox.**

   The File Menu dialog box appears, as shown in Figure 27-5.

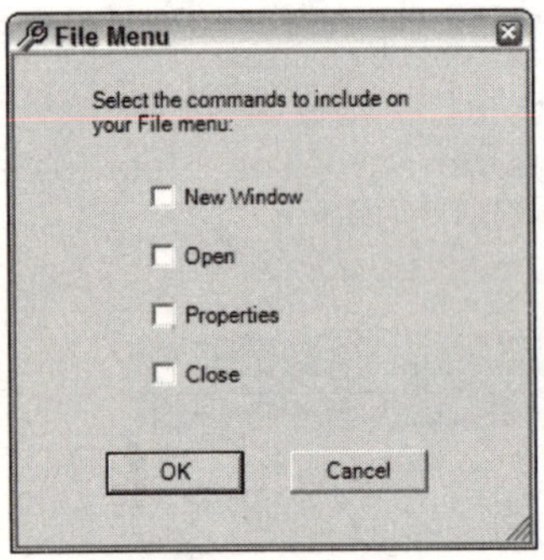

Figure 27-5: Setting up the File menu with no commands.

4. **Don't select any of the commands; simply click OK.**

   The File menu appears in your custom browser window, but, after the browser is compiled, the user won't be able to get the File menu to do anything.

5. **Use the Edit, View, Favorites, Tools, and Help commands in the toolbox to add the menus to the menu bar, the same way you added the File menu in Steps 3 and 4.**

   Don't add any commands to the menus.

   Your custom browser now has a complete set of menus, as shown in Figure 27-6.

6. **Save your data.**

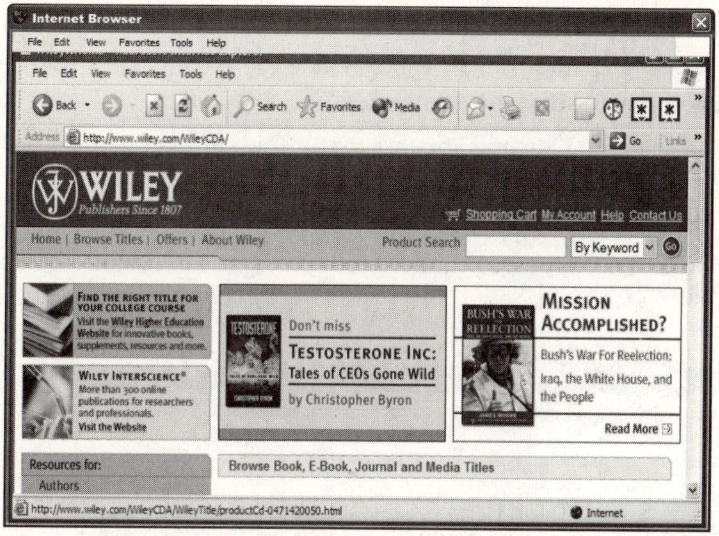

Figure 27-6: The April Fool's browser window with its new menus.

Adding the Toolbar

The toolbar is home to the commands needed to control the browsing experience. These controls include the Home, Back, and Refresh buttons, among others. In the April Fool's browser, however, the toolbar buttons don't work the way the user expects. The following steps get your toolbar installed and ready to go:

1. **In the drop-down menu below the toolbox, select the Toolbar command set.**

   The Toolbar commands appear in the toolbox.

2. **Click the Toolbar button.**

   The Toolbar dialog box appears, as shown in Figure 27-7.

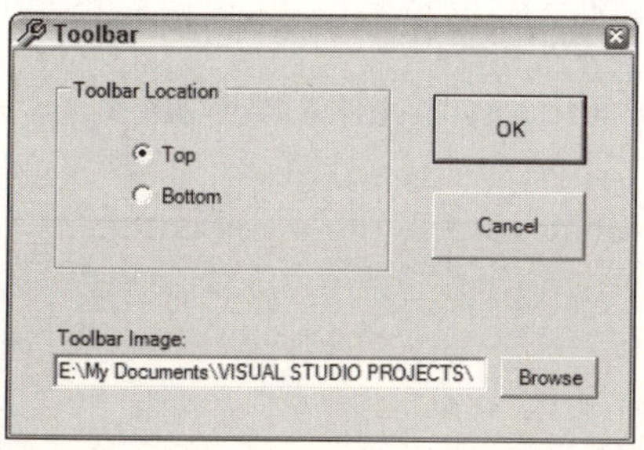

Figure 27-7: The Toolbar dialog box.

3. **Select the toolbar's Top location and then click Browse.**

   The Load Toolbar Image dialog box appears.

4. **Open the Toolbar.jpg image.**

   The selected filename appears in the Toolbar dialog box's Toolbar Image text box.

5. **Click the Toolbar dialog box's OK button.**

   The toolbar appears in the custom browser window, as shown in Figure 27-8.

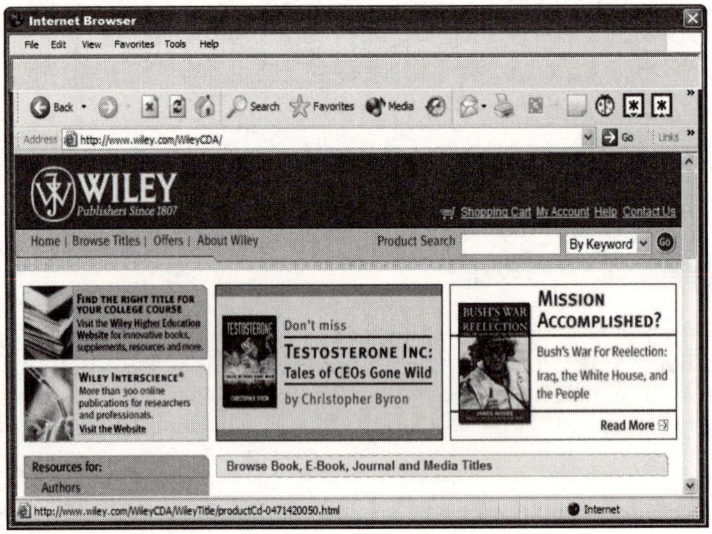

Figure 27-8: The toolbar at the top of your April Fool's browser.

6. **Click the Favorites command in the toolbox.**

   The Load Button dialog box appears.

7. **Open the HomeButton image (see Figure 27-9).**

   The Home button image appears in the custom window's toolbar, but it's associated with the Favorites command.

8. **In the Favorites dialog box, add any favorite Web sites you want associated with the button.**

   The Browser Construction Kit stores the URLs you enter.

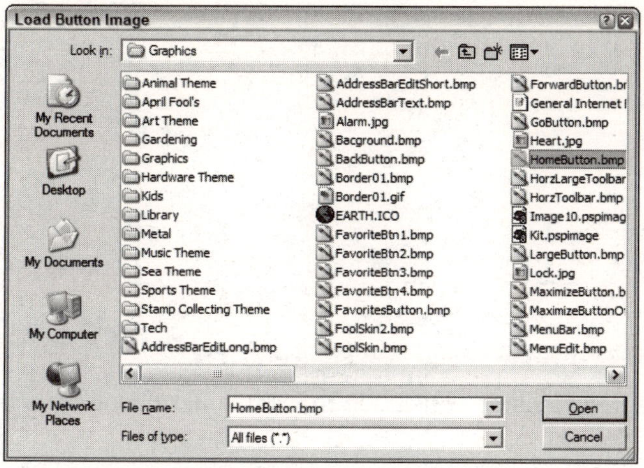

Figure 27-9: Choosing the Home button image for the Favorites menu.

9. **Use the Home, Back, Forward, Stop, Refresh, and Search commands in the toolbox to add the buttons to the toolbar, the same way you added the Home button in Steps 7 and 8.**

   Make sure you use the wrong image for each button.

   Your custom browser now has a complete set of toolbar buttons.

10. **Save your browser's data.**

Adding the Status Bar

There's nothing special about the April Fool's browser's status bar. Here's how to add it to your window:

1. **In the drop-down list below the toolbox, select the Status Bar command set.**

   The Status Bar commands appear in the toolbox.

2. **Click the Status Bar button.**

   The Status Bar dialog box appears, as shown in Figure 27-10.

3. **Select the Status Bar's Bottom location and then click Browse.**

   The Load Status Bar Image dialog box appears.

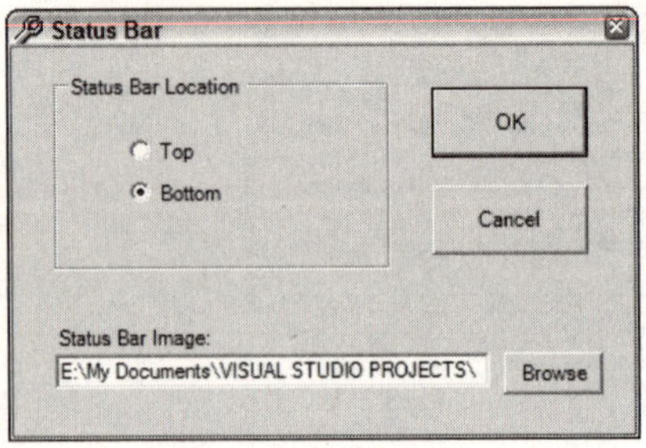

Figure 27-10: The Status Bar dialog box.

ON THE CD

4. Open the StatusBar image (see Figure 27-11).

The selected filename appears in the Status Bar dialog box's Status Bar Image text box.

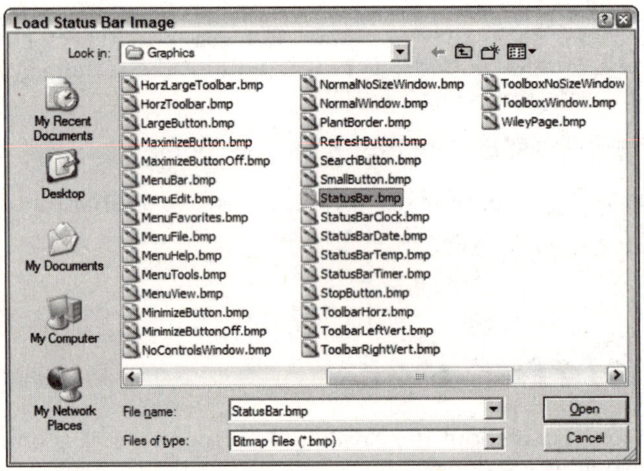

Figure 27-11: Selecting the status bar's image.

5. Click the Status Bar dialog box's OK button.

The status bar appears in the custom browser window.

6. Click the Icon button.

The Load Status Bar Icon dialog box appears.

7. Open the Earth.ico file.

Your icon appears in the status bar.

8. Click the Clock command in the toolbox.

The clock panel appears in your status bar.

9. **Click the Timer command in the toolbox.**

   The Timer Type dialog box appears.

10. **Leave the timer type set to Session Timer and click OK.**

    The Timer panel appears in the status bar.

11. **Click the Date command in the toolbox.**

    The date panel appears in your status bar.

12. **Click the Current URL command in the toolbox.**

    The current URL panel appears in your status bar. Figure 27-12 shows the completed status bar at the bottom of the window.

13. **Save your browser's data.**

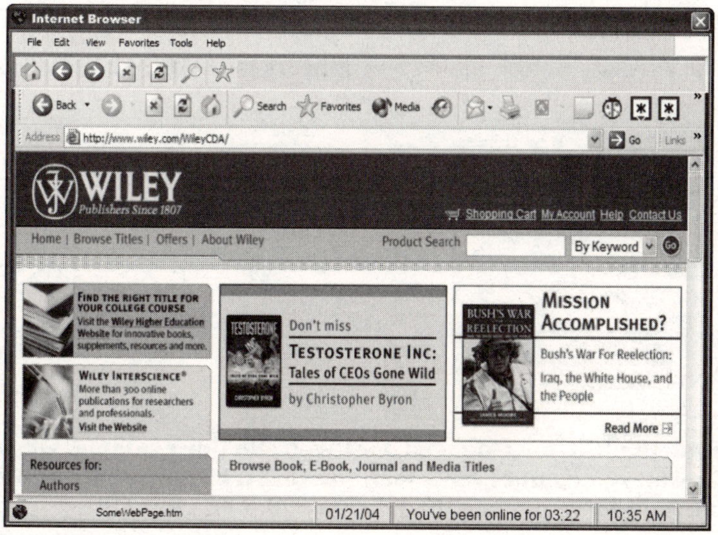

Figure 27-12: The April Fool's window with its completed status bar.

Adding the Address Bar

A browser's address bar enables the user to navigate to any Web address. This is also true of the April Fool's browser. However, feel free to set the favorites buttons on the address bar to the wildest Web sites you can come up with. Here's how:

1. **In the drop-down list below the toolbox, select the Address Bar command set.**

   The Address Bar commands appear in the toolbox.

2. **Click the Address Bar button.**

   The Address Bar dialog box appears.

3. **Select the Address Bar's Top location and then click Browse.**

   The Load Address Bar Image dialog box appears.

4. **Open the AddressBar.jpg image.**

   The selected filename appears in the Address Bar dialog box's Address Bar Image text box.

5. **Click OK.**

   The address bar appears in your browser's window.

6. **Click the Go Button command.**

   The Go button appears in your address bar.

7. **Click the Favorite 1 command.**

   The Favorite Button dialog box appears (see Figure 27-13).

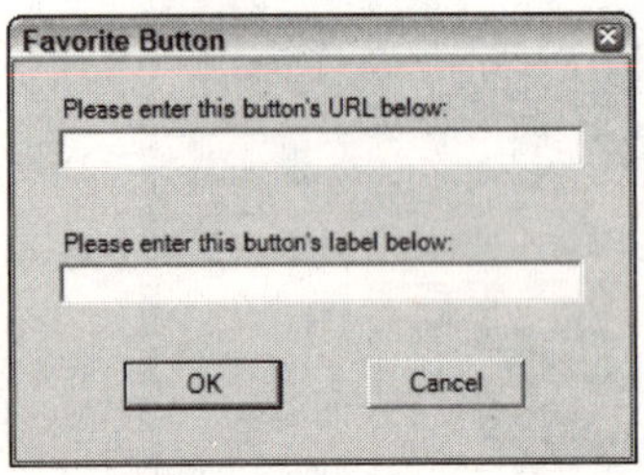

Figure 27-13: The Favorite Button dialog box.

8. **Type the URL for a non-existent Web site (for example, www.doesntexist.com) or for a Web site that'll be surprising to the person you're playing the joke on and then click OK.**

   The Favorite 1 button appears in the address bar.

9. **Add the Favorite 2, Favorite 3, and Favorite 4 buttons in the same way that you did in Steps 7 and 8.**

   Your custom browser now has a complete address bar, as shown in Figure 27-14.

10. **Save your browser's data.**

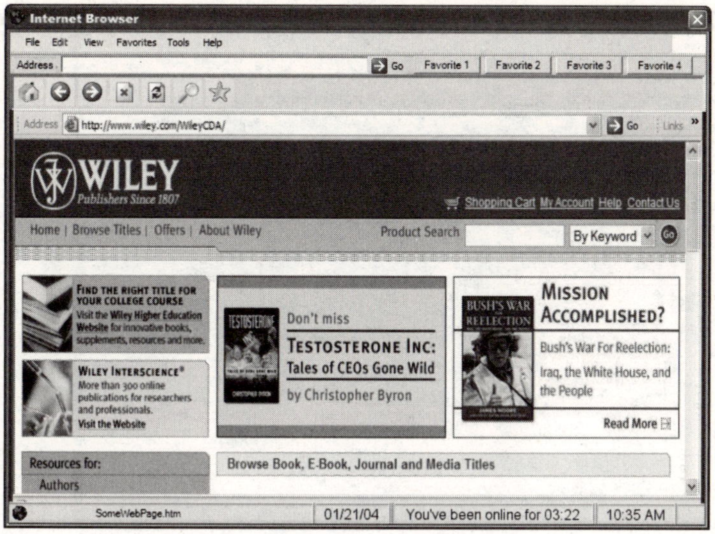

Figure 27-14: The April Fool's window with its completed address bar.

Adding the Browser Pane

There's no way you can do strange things with the browser pane, but you still have to put one in — otherwise, you don't have a browser! By adjusting the size of the browser pane just right, however, you ensure that enough of the window's background image remains visible, which makes the window look as if it's got a browser inside a browser. That'll confuse just about anybody! Perform these steps to add the browser pane:

1. **In the drop-down list below the toolbox, select the Browser command set.**

   The Browser commands appear in the toolbox.

2. **Click the Browser button.**

   The browser pane appears in your browser's window (see Figure 27-15).

3. **Click the Top command in the toolbox.**

   The Browser Top dialog box appears.

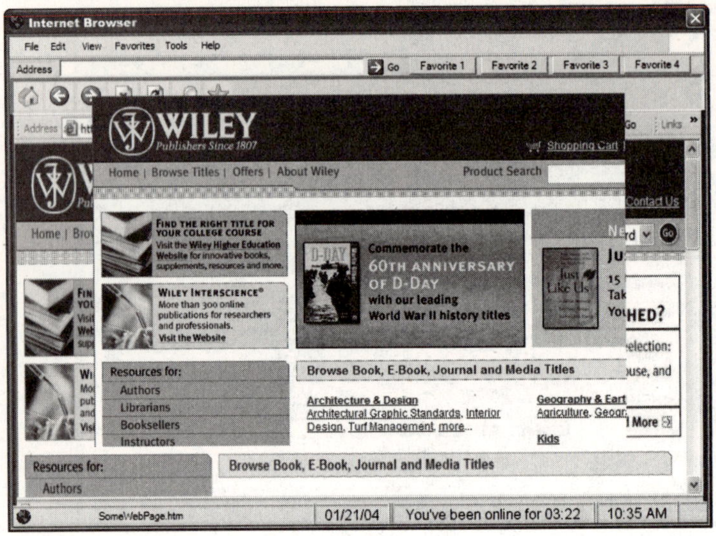

Figure 27-15: The custom-browser window with its new browser pane.

4. **Type** 156 **into the value text box, as shown in Figure 27-16, and click OK.**

   The browser pane repositions itself.

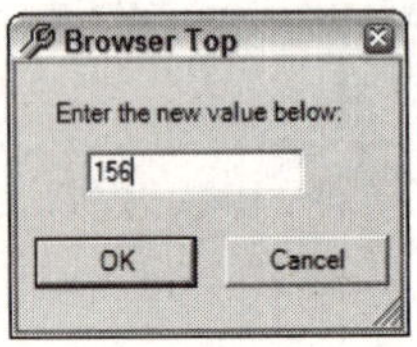

Figure 27-16: The Browser Top dialog box.

5. **Click the Height command in the toolbox.**

   The Browser Height dialog box appears.

6. **Type** 368 **into the value text box and click OK.**

   The browser pane fits itself in the window.

7. **Click the Start Site command.**

   The Start Site dialog box appears.

8. **Type the URL for the Web site that you want as this browser's home page and click OK.**

   The browser pane sets its home page.

9. **Save your browser's data.**

Compiling the Custom Browser

Soon the fun begins. All you have to do is compile the browser and then put it on a computer for your victims to use. Here's how to get the browser compiled:

1. **Choose File⇨Build Browser.**

   The Build Browser dialog box appears.

2. **Navigate to where you want to save your browser's finished files and then click OK.**

   The Browser Construction Kit builds the final files for your custom browser.

To run your finished browser, double-click the Browser.exe file, located in the directory to which you built the browser.

Chapter 28

Constructing a Sheet-Metal Browser

In This Chapter

- Creating a sheet-metal browser window
- Adding a sheet-metal toolbar, status bar, address bar, and menu bar
- Positioning the browser pane
- Compiling the sheet-metal browser

If you don't want to add any special features to your browser, why not create one that just looks plain cool? In this chapter, I show you how to create a Web browser that looks like it's been constructed from metal components, all screwed and riveted together. The design brings a whole new look to Web-browsing tools.

Creating the Window

The first thing you need to do is to create a window. The following steps show you how.

1. **In the drop-down list below the toolbox, select the Window command set.**

   The Window commands appear in the toolbox.

2. **Click the Color button.**

   The Color dialog box appears (see Figure 28-1).

3. **Select light gray and click OK.**

   The window's background turns gray.

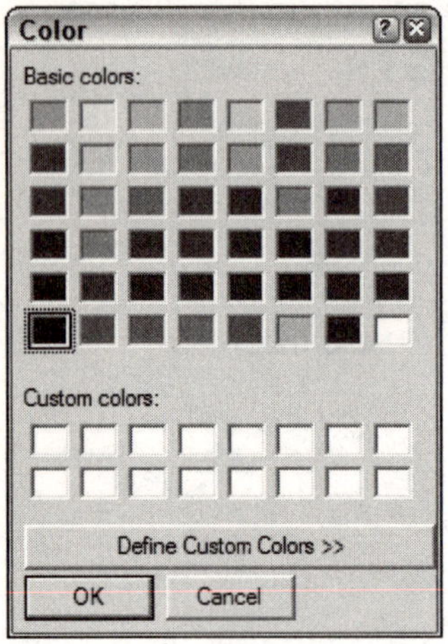

Figure 28-1: The Color dialog box.

4. **Click the Icon button.**

   The Select Window Icon dialog box appears (see Figure 28-2).

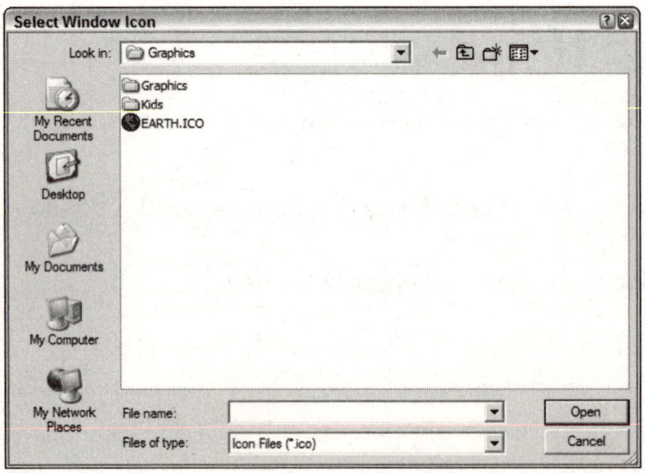

Figure 28-2: The Select Window Icon dialog box.

5. **Locate the Metal.ico file from this book's CD-ROM and double-click its filename.**

   Your icon appears in the window's title bar.

6. **Click the Style button.**

   The Window Styles dialog box appears (see Figure 28-3).

7. **Make sure that the Normal option is selected and click OK.**

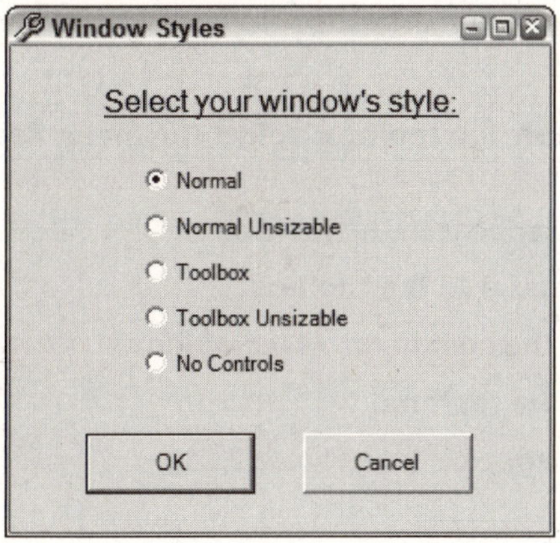

Figure 28-3: The Window Styles dialog box.

8. **Click the Buttons command in the toolbox.**

   The Window Buttons dialog box appears.

9. **Make sure that the Minimize Button and Maximize Button options are selected and then click OK.**

10. **Click the Title button.**

    The Window Title dialog box appears.

11. **Type the name** Metal Browser **and click OK.**

    The window's new title appears in the title bar.

12. **Click the Skin button.**

    The Select Skin Image dialog box appears.

13. **Double-click the MetalSkin.bmp image filename.**

    The window's new background appears.

14. **Choose File⇨Save As.**

    The Save Browser File dialog box appears.

15. **Navigate to where you want to save your browser's script file and then click Save.**

    The Browser Construction Kit saves your browser's data to the selected location, using the window's title as the filename.

Adding the Menu Bar

You can also make the menu bar your very own. To add a menu bar, follow these steps:

1. **In the drop-down list below the toolbox, select the Menu Bar command set.**

   The Menu Bar commands appear in the toolbox.

2. **Click the Menu Bar command in the toolbox.**

   The menu bar appears in the custom browser window.

3. **Select the File button in the toolbox.**

   The File Menu dialog box appears (see Figure 28-4).

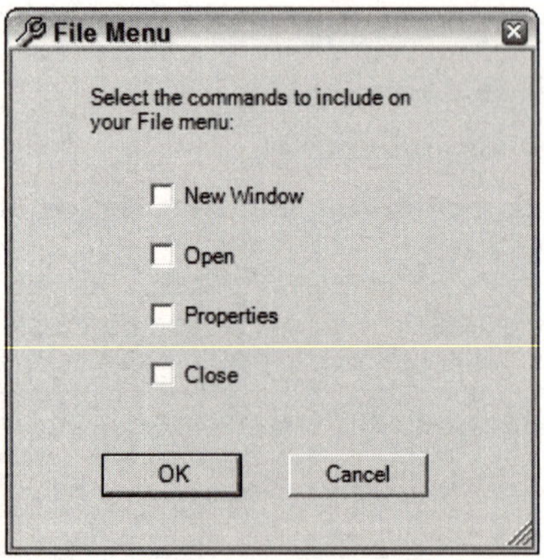

Figure 28-4: The File Menu dialog box.

4. **Select all four menu options and click OK.**

   The File menu appears in your custom browser window.

5. **Use the Edit, View, Favorites, Tools, and Help commands in the toolbox to add the menus to the menu bar, the same way you added the File menu.**

Your custom browser now has a complete set of menus.

6. **Choose File⇨Save.**

   The Browser Construction Kit saves your browser's data.

Adding the Toolbar

The following steps show you how to add your customized toolbar:

1. **In the drop-down list below the toolbox, select the Toolbar command set.**

   The Toolbar commands appear in the toolbox.

2. **Click the Toolbar button.**

   The Toolbar dialog box appears (see Figure 28-5).

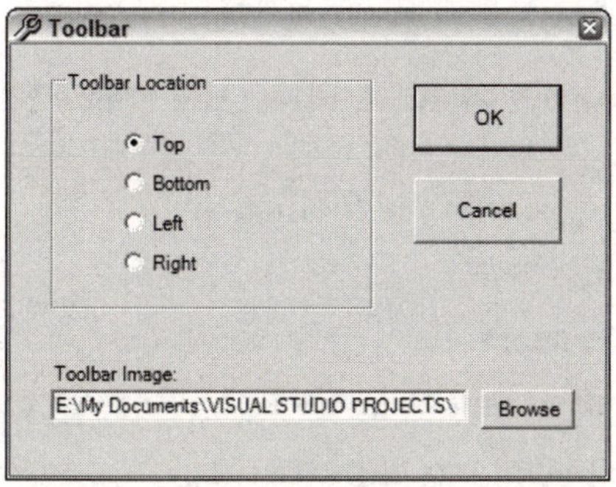

Figure 28-5: The Toolbar dialog box.

3. **Select the toolbar's location and then click the Browse button.**

   The Load Toolbar Image dialog box appears.

4. **Locate the MetalToolbar.bmp image and double-click the image's filename.**

   The selected filename appears in the Toolbar dialog box's Toolbar Image text box.

5. **Click the Toolbar dialog box's OK button.**

   The toolbar appears in the custom browser window.

6. **Click the Home command in the toolbox.**

   The Load Button dialog box appears.

7. **Double-click the MetalHomeBtn.bmp image's filename.**

   The Home button appears in the custom window's toolbar.

8. **Use the Back, Forward, Stop, Refresh, Search, and Favorites commands in the toolbox to add the buttons to the toolbar, the same way you added the Home button.**

   The image filenames are MetalBackBtn.bmp, MetalForwardBtn.bmp, MetalStopBtn.bmp, MetalRefreshBtn.bmp, MetalSearchBtn.bmp, and MetalFavoritesBtn.bmp.

   Your custom browser now has a complete set of toolbar buttons.

9. **Choose File⇨Save.**

   The Browser Construction Kit saves your browser's data.

Adding the Status Bar

To add your sheet-metal status bar, follow these steps:

1. **In the drop-down list below the toolbox, select the Status Bar command set.**

   The Status Bar commands appear in the toolbox.

2. **Click the Status Bar button.**

   The Status Bar dialog box appears.

3. **Select the Status Bar's location and then click the Browse button.**

   The Load Status Bar Image dialog box appears.

4. **Double-click the MetalStatusBar.bmp image's filename.**

   The selected filename appears in the Status Bar dialog box's Status Bar Image text box.

5. **Click the Status Bar dialog box's OK button.**

   The status bar appears in the custom browser window.

6. **Click the Icon button.**

   The Load Status Bar Icon dialog box appears.

7. **Double-click the Metal.ico image's filename.**

   Your icon appears in the status bar.

8. **Click the Clock command in the toolbox.**

   The Clock panel appears in your status bar.

9. **Click the Timer command in the toolbox.**

   The Timer Type dialog box appears (see Figure 28-6).

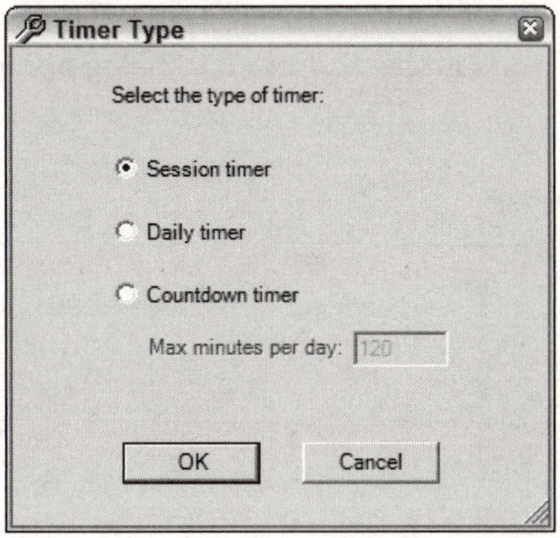

Figure 28-6: The Timer Type dialog box.

10. **Leave the timer type set to Session Timer and click OK.**

    The Timer panel appears in the status bar.

11. **Click the Date command in the toolbox.**

    The Date panel appears in your status bar.

12. **Click the Current URL command in the toolbox.**

    The current URL panel appears in your status bar.

13. **Choose File⇨Save.**

    The Browser Construction Kit saves your browser's data.

Adding the Address Bar

What's a browser without an address bar? In this series of steps, you find out how to include one.

1. **In the drop-down list below the toolbox, select the Address Bar command set.**

   The Address Bar commands appear in the toolbox.

2. **Click the Address Bar button.**

   The Address Bar dialog box appears (see Figure 28-7).

3. **Select the address bar's Top location and then click the Browse button.**

   The Load Address Bar Image dialog box appears.

4. **Double-click the MetalAddressBar.bmp image's filename.**

   The selected filename appears in the Address Bar dialog box's Address Bar Image text box.

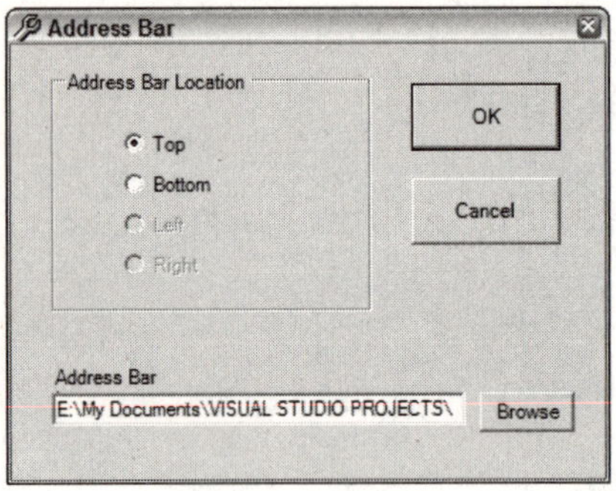

Figure 28-7: The Address Bar dialog box.

5. **Click OK.**

   The address bar appears in your browser's window.

6. **Click the Go Button command.**

   The Go button appears in your address bar.

7. **Click the Icon button.**

   The Load Status Bar Icon dialog box appears.

8. **Click the Favorite 1 command.**

   The Favorite Button dialog box appears (see Figure 28-8).

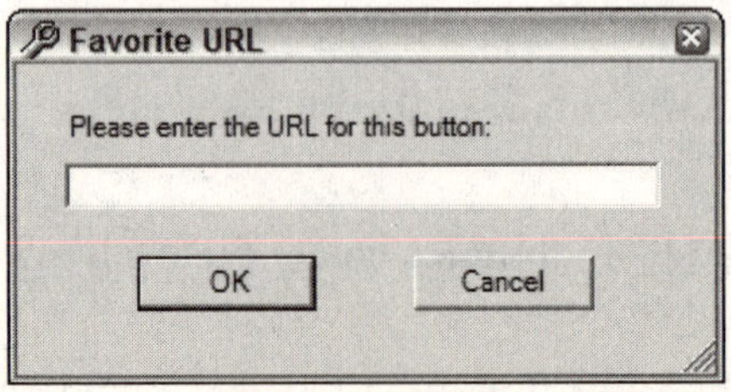

Figure 28-8: The Favorite Button dialog box.

9. **Type the URL with which you want the button associated and then click OK.**

   The Favorite 1 button appears in the address bar.

10. **Use the Favorite 2, Favorite 3, and Favorite 4 commands in the toolbox to add the remaining favorites buttons to the address bar, the same way you added the Favorite 1 button.**

    Your custom browser now has a complete address bar.

11. **Choose File⇨Save.**

    The Browser Construction Kit saves your browser's data.

Adding the Browser Pane

The following steps guide you through creating and positioning your browser pane.

1. **In the drop-down list below the toolbox, select the Browser command set.**

   The Browser commands appear in the toolbox.

2. **Click the Browser button.**

   The browser pane appears in your browser's window.

3. **Click the Top command in the toolbox.**

   The Browser Top dialog box appears, as shown in Figure 28-9.

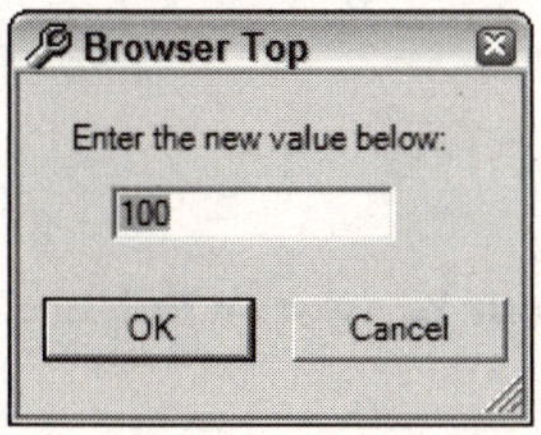

Figure 28-9: The Browser Top dialog box.

4. **Type** 123 **into the value text box and click OK.**

   The browser pane repositions itself.

5. **Click the Left command in the toolbox.**

   The Browser Left dialog box appears.

6. **Type** 8 **into the value text box and click OK.**

   The browser pane repositions itself to the left.

7. **Click the Width command in the toolbox.**

   The Browser Width dialog box appears.

8. **Type** 778 **into the value text box and click OK.**

   The browser pane widens.

9. **Click the Height command in the toolbox.**

   The Browser Height dialog box appears.

10. **Type** 436 **into the value text box and click OK.**

    The browser pane fills the window.

11. **Click the Start Site command.**

    The Start Site dialog box appears.

12. **Type the URL for the Web site that you want as this browser's home page and click OK.**

    The browser pane sets its home page.

13. **Choose File⇨Save.**

    The Browser Construction Kit saves your browser's data.

Compiling the Custom Browser

Now it's time to make all your hard work pay off. These steps show you how to compile your custom browser.

1. **Choose File⇨Build Browser.**

   The Build Browser dialog box appears.

2. **Navigate to where you want to save your browser's finished files and then click OK.**

   The Browser Construction Kit builds the final files for your custom browser.

To run your finished browser, double-click the Browser.exe file, located in the directory to which you built the browser.

Part VI
The Part of Tens

"Honey—remember that pool party last summer where you showed everyone how to do the limbo in just a sombrero and a dish towel? Well, look at what the MSN Daily Video Download is."

In this part . . .

To wrap things up and send you on your way, this part offers another set of browser ideas, complete with the graphics you need to create them. As in Part V of the book, step-by-step instructions guide you through the projects, but this time the instructions are much more concise, since you should pretty much be a pro by the time you dig into this stuff. Finally, also in this part, you discover some powerful tools to help you create browsers. You also get pointed in the direction of some excellent informational resources for everyone interested in programming Internet Explorer.

Chapter 29

Ten More Browser Ideas

In This Chapter

- Building extra browsers with graphical themes
- Putting together more traditional browsers
- Creating a quick-and-dirty browser

As if you don't have enough browsers from this book, now I'm going to give you ten more. (Hey, I want to make sure you get your money's worth! Also, once I got started with the Browser Construction Kit, I just couldn't tear myself away. It's fun, dude!)

REMEMBER

Anyway, most of the following browsers are similar except that they use themed graphics. To build a specific browser, find the project's settings (for example, if you want to build the animal-themed browser, get the details from the following section "The Animal Theme") and then use the Browser Construction Kit's editor to assemble the browser. If you don't remember how to do something, refer back to the appropriate section of the book.

The Animal Theme

ON THE CD

The first of the ten new browser themes is an animal theme with an African look (see Figure 29-1). You can find all of the graphics in the Themes/Animal directory of this book's CD-ROM or in the subdirectory where you installed the Browser Construction Kit. Use the following settings in the browser editor to create the browser:

Window Settings:

- Icon: Animal.ico
- Style: Normal Unsizable

- Buttons: No Minimize or Maximize button
- Border: Animal_Border.jpg
- Skin: Animal_Background.jpg
- Title: Animal Browser (or whatever you want)

Address Bar Settings:

- Location: Top
- Background: Animal_Address_Bar.jpg
- Go Button: Yes

Menu Bar Settings:

- Menus: All menus and commands

Toolbar Settings:

- Location: Top
- Background: Animal_Toolbar_Top.jpg
- Buttons: All buttons, using the Animal_Home.jpg, Animal_Back.jpg, Animal_Forward.jpg, Animal_Stop.jpg, Animal_Refresh.jpg, Animal_Search.jpg, and Animal_Favorites.jpg images

Status Bar Settings:

- Location: Bottom
- Background: Animal_Status_Bar.jpg
- Icon: Animal.ico
- Panels: Clock, Date, and Current URL

Browser Settings:

- Top: 154
- Left: 50
- Width: 696
- Height: 376
- Start Site: Anything you want

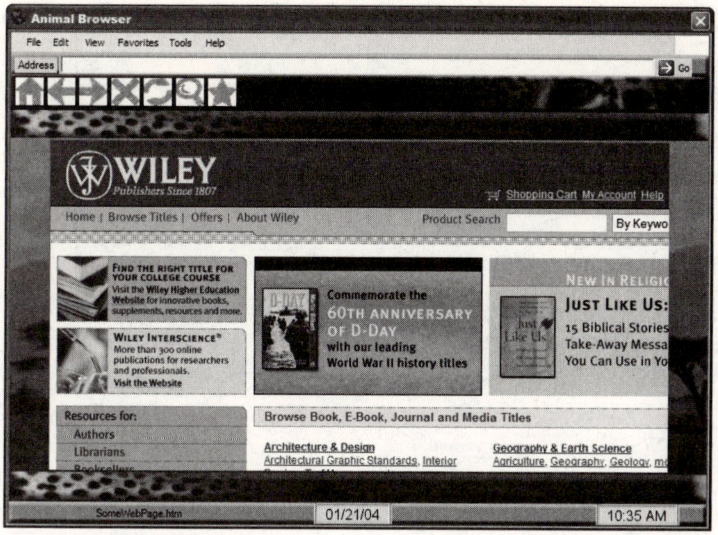

Figure 29-1: An animal theme.

The Art Theme

Are you an artist? Looking for a browser that fits your artistic interests? The second of this chapter's ten new browsers features an art theme (see Figure 29-2). You can find all the graphics in the Themes/Art directory of this book's CD-ROM or in the subdirectory where you installed the Browser Construction Kit. Use the following settings in the browser editor to create the browser:

Window Settings:

- Icon: Art.ico
- Style: Normal Unsizable
- Buttons: No Minimize or Maximize button
- Border: Art_Border.jpg
- Skin: Art_Background.jpg
- Title: Art Browser (or whatever you want)

Address Bar Settings:

- Location: Top
- Background: Art_Address_Bar.jpg
- Go Button: Yes

Figure 29-2: An arts theme.

Menu Bar Settings:

- Menus: All menus and commands

Toolbar Settings:

- Location: Top
- Background: Art_Toolbar_Top.jpg
- Buttons: All buttons, using the Art _Home.jpg, Art _Back.jpg, Art_Forward.jpg, Art_Stop.jpg, Art_Refresh.jpg, Art_Search.jpg, and Art_Favorites.jpg images

Status Bar Settings:

- Location: Bottom
- Background: Art_Status_Bar.jpg
- Icon: Art.ico
- Panels: Clock, Date, and Current URL

Browser Settings:

- Top: 154
- Left: 50

- Width: 696
- Height: 376
- Start Site: Anything you want

The Music Theme

If you're a musician, or just an avid music lover, you'll dig this chapter's third new browser theme, which is a music theme (see Figure 29-3). Look for the graphics in the Themes/Music directory of this book's CD-ROM or in the subdirectory where you installed the Browser Construction Kit. Use the following settings in the browser editor to create the browser:

Window Settings:

- Icon: Music.ico
- Style: Normal Unsizable
- Buttons: No Minimize or Maximize button
- Border: Music _Border.jpg
- Skin: Music _Background.jpg
- Title: Music Browser (or whatever you want)

Address Bar Settings:

- Location: Top
- Background: Music_Address_Bar.jpg
- Go Button: Yes

Menu Bar Settings:

- Menus: All menus and commands

Toolbar Settings:

- Location: Top
- Background: Music_Toolbar_Top.jpg
- Buttons: All buttons, using the Music_Home.jpg, Music_Back.jpg, Music_Forward.jpg, Music_Stop.jpg, Music_Refresh.jpg, Music_Search.jpg, and Music_Favorites.jpg images

Status Bar Settings:

- Location: Bottom
- Background: Music_Status_Bar.jpg
- Icon: Music.ico
- Panels: Clock, Date, and Current URL

Browser Settings:

- Top: 154
- Left: 10
- Width: 640
- Height: 376
- Start Site: Anything you want

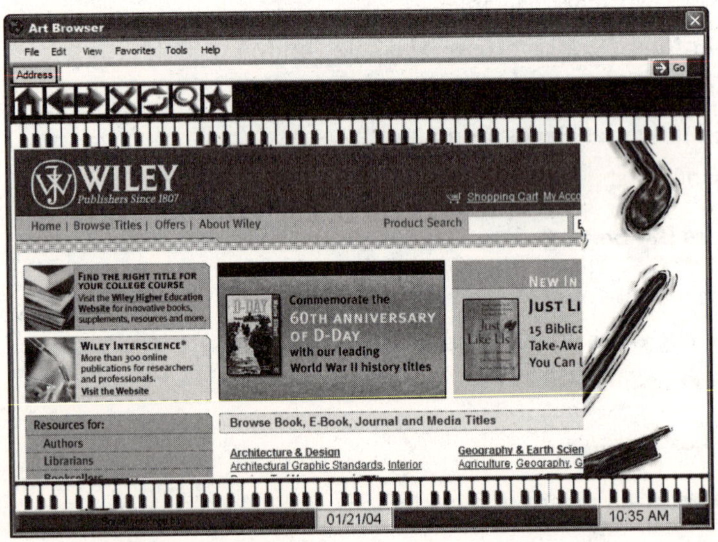

Figure 29-3: A music theme.

The Sea Theme

The oceans hold some of the most beautiful sites on the planet. So why not a browser with a sea theme? That's exactly what this chapter's fourth new browser theme is (see Figure 29-4). All the graphics are in the Themes\Sea directory of this book's CD-ROM or in the subdirectory where you installed the Browser Construction Kit. Here are the settings to create the browser:

Window Settings:

- Icon: Sea.ico
- Style: Normal Unsizable
- Buttons: No Minimize or Maximize button
- Border: Sea_Border.jpg
- Skin: Sea_Background.jpg
- Title: Sea Browser (or whatever you want)

Address Bar Settings:

- Location: Top
- Background: Sea_Address_Bar.jpg
- Go Button: Yes

Menu Bar Settings:

- Menus: All menus and commands

Toolbar Settings:

- Location: Top
- Background: Sea_Toolbar_Top.jpg
- Buttons: All buttons, using the Sea_Home.jpg, Sea_Back.jpg, Sea_Forward.jpg, Sea_Stop.jpg, Sea_Refresh.jpg, Sea_Search.jpg, and Sea_Favorites.jpg images

Status Bar Settings:

- Location: Bottom
- Background: Sea_Status_Bar.jpg
- Icon: Sea.ico
- Panels: Clock, Date, and Current URL

Browser Settings:

- Top: 154
- Left: 50

- Width: 696
- Height: 376
- Start Site: Anything you want

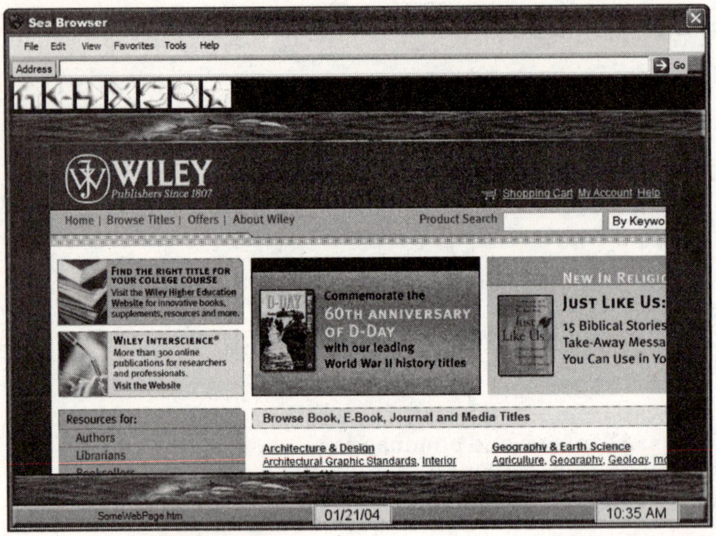

Figure 29-4: A sea theme.

The Sports Theme

Sports fans will line up around the block (okay, I'm exaggerating a teensy bit) to use this chapter's fifth new browser theme, which is, of course, sports (see Figure 29-5). All the graphics are in the Themes\Sports directory of this book's CD-ROM or in the subdirectory where you installed the Browser Construction Kit. Here are the settings to create the browser:

Window Settings:

- Icon: Sports.ico
- Style: Normal Unsizable
- Buttons: No Minimize or Maximize button
- Border: Sports_Border.jpg
- Skin: Sports_Background.jpg
- Title: Sports Browser (or whatever you want)

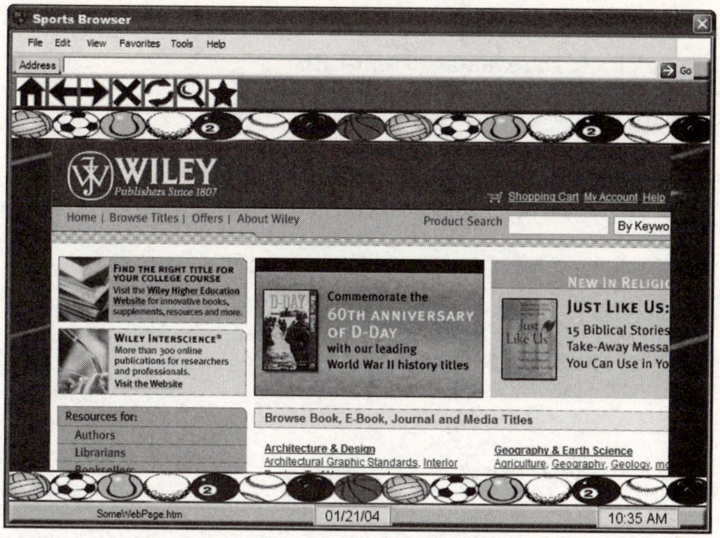

Figure 29-5: A sports theme.

Address Bar Settings:

- Location: Top
- Background: Sports_Address_Bar.jpg
- Go Button: Yes

Menu Bar Settings:

- Menus: All menus and commands

Toolbar Settings:

- Location: Top
- Background: Sports_Toolbar_Top.jpg
- Buttons: All buttons, using the Sports_Home.jpg, Sports_Back.jpg, Sports_Forward.jpg, Sports_Stop.jpg, Sports_Refresh.jpg, Sports_Search.jpg, and Sports_Favorites.jpg images

Status Bar Settings:

- Location: Bottom
- Background: Sports_Status_Bar.jpg

- Icon: Sports.ico
- Panels: Clock, Date, and Current URL

Browser Settings:

- Top: 154
- Left: 50
- Width: 696
- Height: 376
- Start Site: Anything you want

The Stamps Theme

Stamp collecting may not be as exciting as playing football, but stamps can sure make a good-looking browser theme. Guess what? This chapter's sixth new browser theme is stamps (see Figure 29-6). Look for the graphics in the Themes\Stamps directory of this book's CD-ROM or in the subdirectory where you installed the Browser Construction Kit. Here are the settings:

Window Settings:

- Icon: Stamps.ico
- Style: Normal Unsizable
- Buttons: No Minimize or Maximize button
- Border: Stamps_Border.jpg
- Skin: Stamps_Background.jpg
- Title: Stamps Browser (or whatever you want)

Address Bar Settings:

- Location: Top
- Background: Stamps_Address_Bar.jpg
- Go Button: Yes

Menu Bar Settings:

- Menus: All menus and commands

Toolbar Settings:

- Location: Top
- Background: Stamps_Toolbar_Top.jpg
- Buttons: All buttons, using the Stamps_Home.jpg, Stamps_Back.jpg, Stamps_Forward.jpg, Stamps_Stop.jpg, Stamps_Refresh.jpg, Stamps_Search.jpg, and Stamps_Favorites.jpg images

Status Bar Settings:

- Location: Bottom
- Background: Stamps_Status_Bar.jpg
- Icon: Stamps.ico
- Panels: Clock, Date, and Current URL

Browser Settings:

- Top: 120
- Left: 80
- Width: 640
- Height: 444
- Start Site: Anything you want

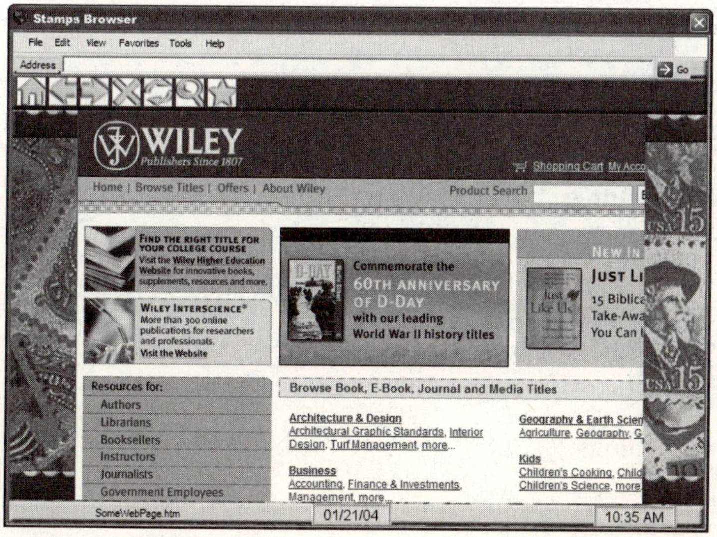

Figure 29-6: A stamps theme.

The Browse-Only Browser

Did you ever play that game in the car where you just keep driving, nowhere in particular, just taking new roads to see where you end up? You can do the same thing with the Browse-Only browser, which has no controls at all, except for whatever links appear in the browser panel (see Figure 29-7). All the graphics for this project live in the Themes\Browse-Only directory of this book's CD-ROM or in the subdirectory where you installed the Browser Construction Kit. Here are the settings to create the browser:

Window Settings:

- Icon: Browse_Only.ico
- Style: Normal
- Buttons: Both Minimize and Maximize buttons
- Border: None
- Skin: None
- Title: Browse-Only Browser (or whatever you want)

Address Bar Settings:

- No address bar

Menu Bar Settings:

- Menus: File menu with only the Close command

Toolbar Settings:

- No toolbar

Status Bar Settings:

- Location: Bottom
- Background: Browse_Only_Status_Bar.jpg
- Icon: Browse_Only.ico
- Panels: Clock, Date, and Current URL

Browser Settings:

- Top: 60
- Left: 10

- Width: 776
- Height: 500
- Start Site: Anything you want

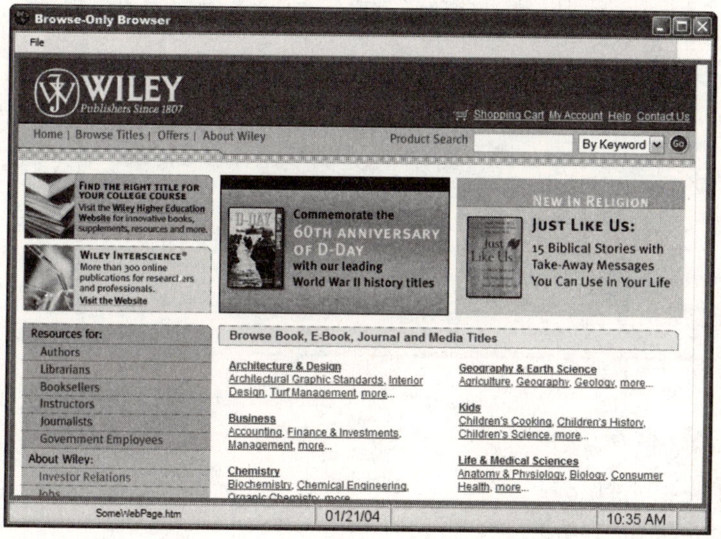

Figure 29-7: The browse-only browser.

The Traditional Theme

What's that you say? Who needs all these silly themes? Just give you a simple browser that'll get the job done? Your wish is my command! This chapter's next browser project (notice I avoided the word "theme") sticks with a traditional Windows look (see Figure 29-8). All the graphics for this project are in the Themes\Traditional directory of this book's CD-ROM or in the subdirectory where you installed the Browser Construction Kit. Use the following settings to create the browser:

Window Settings:

- Icon: Earth.ico
- Style: Normal
- Buttons: Both Minimize and Maximize buttons
- Border: None
- Skin: None
- Title: Traditional Browser (or whatever you want)

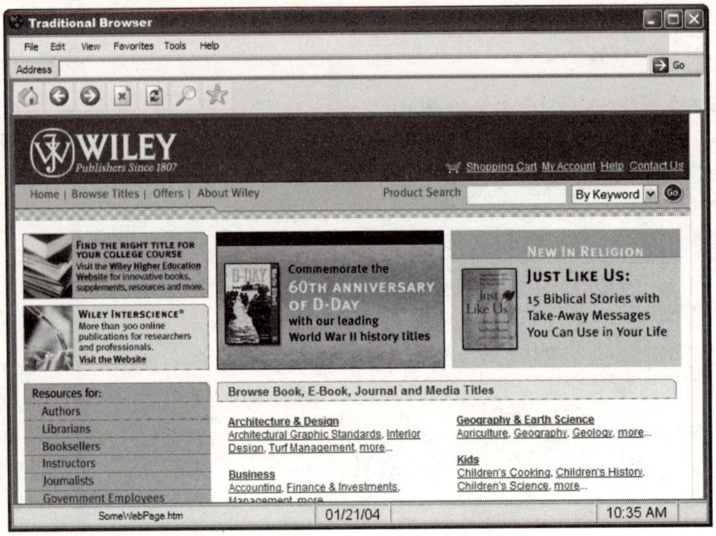

Figure 29-8: A traditional browser.

Address Bar Settings:

- Location: Top
- Background: AddressBar.jpg
- Go Button: Yes

Menu Bar Settings:

- Menus: All menus and commands

Toolbar Settings:

- Location: Top
- Background: Toolbar.jpg
- Buttons: All buttons, using the HomeButton.jpg, BackButton.jpg, ForwardButton.jpg, StopButton.jpg, RefreshButton.jpg, SearchButton.jpg, and FavoritesButton.jpg images

Status Bar Settings:

- Location: Bottom
- Background: StatusBar.jpg
- Icon: Earth.ico
- Panels: Clock, Date, and Current URL

Browser Settings:

- Top: 124
- Left: 10
- Width: 776
- Height: 440
- Start Site: Anything you want

The Minimal Browser

ON THE CD

Sometimes you get overwhelmed with all the stuff they cram into software these days. Whatever happened to the KISS (Keep It Simple, Stupid) principle of design? If you're a fan of KISS (the design theory, not the rock group), you'll love this quick-and-dirty browser design (see Figure 29-9). All the graphics for this project are in the Themes/Minimal directory of this book's CD-ROM or in the subdirectory where you installed the Browser Construction Kit. Use the following settings to create the browser:

Window Settings:

- Icon: Earth.ico
- Style: Normal
- Buttons: Both Minimize and Maximize buttons
- Border: None
- Skin: None
- Title: Minimal Browser (or whatever you want)

Address Bar Settings:

- Location: Top
- Background: AddressBar.jpg
- Go Button: Yes

Menu Bar Settings:

- None

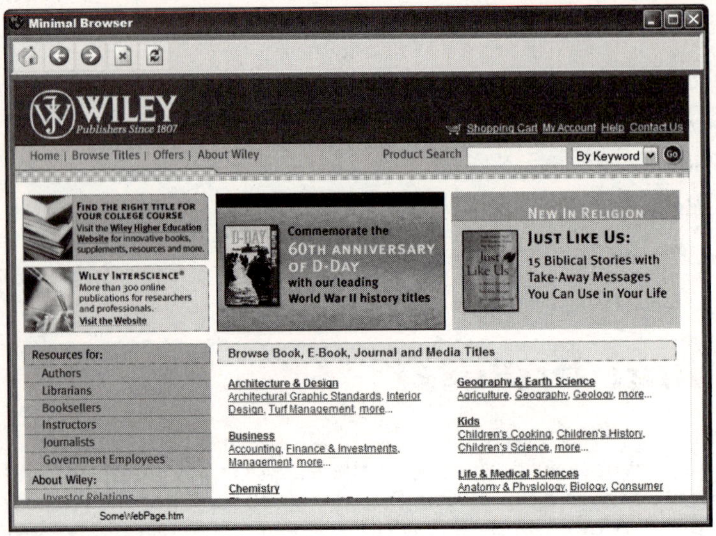

Figure 29-9: A minimal browser.

Toolbar Settings:

- Location: Top
- Background: Toolbar.jpg
- Buttons: Home, Back, Forward, Stop, and Refresh buttons, using the HomeButton.jpg, BackButton.jpg, ForwardButton.jpg, StopButton.jpg, and RefreshButton.jpg images

Status Bar Settings:

- Location: Bottom
- Background: StatusBar.jpg
- Panels: Current URL

Browser Settings:

- Top: 80
- Left: 10
- Width: 776
- Height: 480
- Start Site: Anything you want

The Dream Browser

What's the dream browser? The perfect browser for you, of course. Unfortunately, I can't possibly know what you'd include in your dream browser, so you'll have to fill in the settings for this tenth and final browser yourself. No whining. I've told you everything you need to know to use the Browser Construction Kit. Anyway, because this is almost the end of the book, don't you think it's about time that I turned the Browser Construction Kit over to you? Yeah, I thought so.

Chapter 30

Ten Tools and Resources for Web Browser Builders

In This Chapter

- Exploring graphical tools
- Discovering programming tools
- Finding programming instructions
- Updating your computer for security

This book includes everything you need to get started with Internet Explorer customization. However, you can always expand your horizons — and your custom browsers — with new tools and techniques. Such tools include graphics editors and programming languages. In this chapter, you discover ten ways you can add to your custom browser arsenal of software and documentation.

Microsoft Paint

Although this book comes with a trial version of Paint Shop Pro, to keep using that software, you're going to have to shell out some dough. The truth is, though, that you don't need such a fancy software package to create browser graphics. Sure, all those extra features provide a computer-full of graphical power, but if you just want to get the job done, quick and easy, you already have all the software you need installed with Windows. Specifically, I'm referring to Microsoft Paint, which features all the basic tools for creating images. You can find Paint in your Programs menu, inside the Accessories folder.

Clicking Paint's entry in your Start menu brings up its main window. Paint features a small toolbox with tools that can do everything from select parts of a drawing to draw shapes, erase areas, fill shapes with color, and even add text. Paint also has a few special features — such as Flip, Stretch, and Skew — that manipulate your images in handy ways.

ImageForge

If you want more graphics power than that offered by Paint, but don't want to mortgage your house for it, you may want to give ImageForge a try. The basic version of this handy graphics editing package is free (yes, free!), but the company also has a Pro version that you can buy at a reasonable price ($28.95) if you want extra features.

To try ImageForge, you must first download it. Point your browser to `www.cursorarts.com/ca_imffw.html`, which is the Cursor Arts (the publisher) Web page from which you can download the free version. After installing the software, you'll have a Cursor Arts entry in your Programs menu. Click the ImageForge command in the menu to run the program.

Adobe Photoshop

If you want to go way off the deep end and get one of the best paint programs available, you could do a whole lot worse than Adobe Photoshop. The full version of this fabulous package goes for $650! Luckily, you can download a trial version from Adobe's Web site. Just point your browser (your custom browser, of course) to `www.adobe.com/products/tryadobe/main.jsp#product=39`. The trial version runs for a month, after which you must purchase the full package to keep using it.

Photoshop does just about anything possible for a paint program to do. Once you have this puppy on your machine, you'll be set for life (well, a couple of years, anyway, which is a lifetime in terms of computer technology). Plan to spend a whole lot of time learning its intricacies, though. Photoshop is one serious piece of software.

Microsoft Visual Basic .NET

ON THE CD

I wrote the Browser Construction Kit — both the editor and the creator — using Visual Basic .NET. Moreover, the complete source code for the programs is included on this book's CD. In case you haven't figured out where I'm going with this, it means that you can modify the program to suit your needs. To do so, however, you need a copy of Visual Basic .NET.

Visual Basic .NET is one of the languages included with Visual Studio .NET. As such, you can buy a version of Visual Studio .NET with just Visual Basic, or you can buy other languages as well, including Visual C++ .NET and Visual C# .NET.

Visual Basic .NET For Dummies

Visual Basic .NET won't do you much good unless you know how to program with it. Luckily, a *For Dummies* book can get you started quickly. This book, aptly titled *Visual Basic .NET For Dummies* by Wallace Wang, covers everything from the core language to creating a user interface, programming menus, and even object-oriented programming. The contents of this book can take you a long way toward understanding the source code for the Browser Construction Kit.

MSDN

Another great place to get programming information with regards to anything related to Visual Studio .NET is Microsoft's own developer network, usually referred to as the MSDN. The core programming library for Visual Studio .NET — a portion of the MSDN — comes with Visual Studio, and you can purchase a subscription to have the library and all its updates mailed to you four times a year. However, Microsoft makes the entire library, as well as tons of other material, available free online. Just point your browser to `msdn.microsoft.com`.

Internet Explorer Programming Support Center

In addition to MSDN, Microsoft has a large support area online dedicated specifically to Internet Explorer programming. You can find it at `support.microsoft.com/default.aspx?pr=iep`. This Web site provides programming information, but also utilities for managing your IE programming projects, as well as updates for the IE libraries, and more. They even have WebCasts that provide a kind of virtual classroom for learning more about IE programming issues.

IEAK

If you'd just as soon avoid programming, then continue using the Browser Construction Kit as it is. Or you can also try downloading Microsoft's Internet Explorer Administration Kit (more commonly know as the IEAK) at `www.microsoft.com/windows/ieak/default.mspx`. This handy program doesn't let you rebuild IE from scratch, but it does let you customize many of IE's features. This application is great for people who want to create a *branded* version of IE — that is, a version of IE that includes a customized setup program, your own digital certificate, custom logos, a home page, links, and so on.

Your Favorite Internet Search Engine

The Internet is so immense that you can find the answer to just about any question, including questions about Internet explorer programming. Just head over to your favorite search site (Google? Yahoo? MSN?), type your search criteria (for example, "Internet Explorer programming"), and you're off. You'll probably get thousands of hits.

Microsoft Windows Update

You may not think of Windows Update as being a resource for IE programming, but the fact is that many of the fixes that keep your Web browsing safe come from this Web site. You may have Windows configured to automatically download critical updates, but if you don't, you should check this Web site often to be sure your system has the latest security features. The URL is `windowsupdate.microsoft.com`. Why don't you jump over there right now?

If you have Windows XP and want to turn on the automatic update feature, follow these steps:

1. **Choose Start⇨Control Panel.**

   The Control Panel appears on your screen. (How the Control Panel looks varies depending on your system settings and the software you have installed on your system.)

2. **Click Performance and Maintenance.**

   If you don't see the Performance and Maintenance category, click the Switch To Category View command on the left side of the window.

The Performance and Maintenance window appears.

3. **Click the System command near the bottom of the window.**

   The System Properties dialog box appears.

4. **Select the Automatic Updates tab.**

   The Automatic Updates page appears.

5. **Select the Keep My Computer Up To Date option and choose one of the update settings.**

   I suggest the Download The Updates Automatically And Notify Me When They Are Ready To Be Installed setting.

6. **Click OK to finalize your choices.**

Appendix

What's on the CD-ROM

This appendix provides you with information on the contents of the CD that accompanies this book. For the latest and greatest information, please refer to the ReadMe file located at the root of the CD. Here is what you'll find on the CD:

- System requirements
- Using the CD with Windows
- Troubleshooting

System Requirements

Make sure that your computer meets the minimum system requirements shown in the following list. If your computer doesn't match up to most of these requirements, you may have problems using the software and files on the CD. For the latest and greatest information, please refer to the ReadMe file located at the root of the CD-ROM.

- A PC with a Pentium III or faster processor
- Microsoft Windows XP or Windows 2000
- At least 160MB of total RAM installed on your computer; for best performance, I recommend at least 256MB
- A CD-ROM drive
- A sound card for PCs
- A monitor capable of displaying at least 256 colors or grayscale

If you need more information on the basics, check out these books published by Wiley Publishing, Inc.: *PCs For Dummies,* by Dan Gookin; and *Windows 2000 Professional For Dummies* and *Windows XP For Dummies,* both by Andy Rathbone.

Using the CD

To install the items from the CD to your hard drive, follow these steps:

1. **Insert the CD into your computer's CD-ROM drive.**

   The license agreement appears.

   Note to Windows users: The interface won't launch if you have `autorun` disabled. In that case, choose Start⇨Run. In the dialog box that appears, type **D:\start.exe**. (Replace D with the proper letter if your CD-ROM drive uses a different letter. If you don't know the letter, see how your CD-ROM drive is listed under My Computer.) Click OK.

2. **Read through the license agreement and then click the Accept button if you want to use the CD.**

   After you click Accept, the License Agreement window won't appear again.

   The CD interface appears. The interface allows you to install the programs and run the demos with just a click of a button (or two).

What You'll Find on the CD

The following sections are arranged by category and provide a summary of the software and other goodies you'll find on the CD. If you need help with installing the items provided on the CD, refer back to the installation instructions in the preceding section.

TECHNICAL STUFF

Trial, demo, or *evaluation* versions of software are usually limited either by time or functionality (such as not letting you save a project after you create it).

Author-created material

For Windows. The Browser Construction Kit is located in the Author directory on the CD and works with Windows 98/NT/Me/2000/XP and later computers. These files include the complete program, along with its Visual Basic .NET source code and a number of graphical themes for use with the software.

Paint Shop Pro

Evaluation version.

For Windows. Paint Shop Pro is a full-featured Paint program. This evaluation version gives you 30 days to use the software, after which you can choose to purchase the full version from Jasc Software's Web site.

For more information and updates of Paint Shop Pro, visit the Jasc Software Web site at `www.jasc.com`.

Troubleshooting

I tried my best to compile programs that work on most computers with the minimum system requirements. Alas, your computer may differ, and some programs may not work properly for some reason.

The two likeliest problems are that you don't have enough memory (RAM) for the programs you want to use, or you have other programs running that are affecting the installation or running of a program. If you get an error message such as `Not enough memory` or `Setup cannot continue`, try one or more of the following suggestions and then try using the software again:

- **Turn off any antivirus software running on your computer.** Installation programs sometimes mimic virus activity and may make your computer incorrectly believe that it's being infected by a virus.
- **Close all running programs.** The more programs you have running, the less memory is available to other programs. Installation programs typically update files and programs; so if you keep other programs running, installation may not work properly.
- **Have your local computer store add more RAM to your computer.** This step is, admittedly, drastic and somewhat expensive. However, adding more memory can really help the speed of your computer and allow more programs to run at the same time.

If you still have trouble with the CD, please call the Customer Care phone number: 800-762-2974. Outside the United States, call 1-317-572-3994. You can also contact Customer Service by visiting our Web site at `www.wiley.com/techsupport`. Wiley Publishing Inc. will provide technical support only for installation and other general quality control items; for technical support on the applications themselves, consult the program's vendor or author.

To place additional orders or to request information about other Wiley products, please call (877) 762-2974.

Index

Numerics

• A •

• B •

• C •

• H •

• I •

• M •

• N •

• O •

• P •

• R •

• T •

• Z •